Communication Behavior in Organizations

Communication Behavior in Organizations

Aubrey C. Sanford

Department of Management
University of Southern Mississippi

Gary T. Hunt

Department of Speech Communication
California State University, Los Angeles

Hyler J. Bracey

President, Development Consultants, Inc.

CHARLES E. MERRILL PUBLISHING COMPANY
A Bell & Howell Company
Columbus, Ohio

Published by
Charles E. Merrill Publishing Company
A Bell & Howell Company
Columbus, Ohio 43216

This book was set in Times Roman.
The production editor was Linda Gambaiani.
The cover was designed by Will Chenoweth.

ISBN: 0-675-08601-9

Library of Congress Catalog Card Number: 75-40542

3 4 5 6 7 8 9 — 84 83 82 81 80 79

Printed in the United States of America

To   Lesa and Shawn
            Jonathan and Michael
            Belinda, Jep, Brian, and Scott

Preface

It was our purpose in writing this book to provide students with a background which will hopefully enable them to participate successfully as members of organizations. Our focus has been on the human communication behavior which occurs within organizations, or *organizational communication*. In recent years students from communication, psychology, sociology, management, journalism, and marketing have begun to study organizational communication. Certainly the subject is multidisciplinary in that the theoretical and research contributions come from many fields.

This book, then, was written as an introductory text for those courses dealing with organizations which have communication as their primary or secondary emphasis, whether they are taught in the speech, communication, journalism, management, or other departments.

The three authors represent three different academic backgrounds. One is a professor of management who works closely with industries as a consultant. Another is a teacher of organizational communication in a department of speech communication who also serves as a consultant to numerous organizations. The third is president of a consulting firm which specializes in organizational development and change. We trust that this difference in orientation adds a "good mix" of the practical and theoretical to this book. Our aim has been to examine what we consider to be the *major* concepts which influence organizational communication. We attempt to interpret those concepts in a readable manner for the student.

A unique contribution of this book is the model of organizational communication presented in chapter two. The model provides the introduction to the rest of the chapters in the book. In developing the model, we have included those variables important in organizational communication and have presented our thinking about how the variables are interrelated. Part One is the foundation for the rest of the book. In addition to the model, Part One contains a chapter on the role of communication in helping to achieve organizational effectiveness. Part Two examines those background factors likely to influence organizational communication, such as managerial assumptions and economic conditions. In Part Three important internal organizational elements (the individual, organizational structure, technology, leadership, and group relations) are investigated as they influence organizational communication. We feel that it is important for the student to understand such things as organizational structure, the individual, and technology *before* studying the organizational communication system in depth. In Part Four, we consider the formal system of organizational communication (which we have labeled as the "formal subsystem" as a subunit of the total organizational communication system), the climate for organizational communication, and the important individual interpersonal skills in organizational communication. Part Five suggests some ways in which organizational communication might be improved. Among the methods covered are communication training and organizational development.

We consider the behavioral incidents which follow each part to be a major feature of this book. The incidents have been developed to help the student understand and integrate the material presented in the part. The incidents are short, lifelike situations, many similar to our own consulting experiences, which center on one or more of the variables treated in the part. Each incident is followed by questions which provide the guidelines for analysis of the information contained in the incident. We think the incidents will help "pull together" the content material in the text.

By blending the theoretical with the practical we have tried to provide the reader with an interesting and useful look at organizational communication. We are confident that by learning more about how organizations "behave" and "communicate," students will increase their personal effectiveness as workers, community leaders, church members, and family members. Because in all of these roles, organizational communication plays a vital part.

It would be impossible to acknowledge all of the people who contributed to this book, but there are some who must be mentioned. The people at Charles Merrill, especially Tom Hutchinson, had the courage to throw this unlikely trio together. We hope that the product warrants their early support. Also, Linda Gambaiani, our production editor, has been patient and cheerful and has taught us much about book publishing. Our students at Cal State, Los Angeles, Ohio State, and Southern Mississippi have certainly influenced our thinking and have served as a sounding board for our ideas. Roslyn Hunt contributed a number of incidents, read and typed much of the final manuscript, and offered her usual perceptive comments. She also did much to keep one of the authors down to earth. Finally, the kids, to whom this book is dedicated, provided the necessary distraction while this project was being completed.

A.C.S.

G.T.H.

H.J.B.

Contents

List of Figures and Tables

Figure

Table

PART ONE

ORGANIZATIONAL COMMUNICATION

Chapter One

Introduction to Organizational Communication

Each individual in our society relates with every other individual by means of *communication*. It is through communication that we reach the lives of those around us, and the way others reach us. From our first cry at birth, we have been a communicating organism transmitting our thoughts, attitudes, and ideas. As we grew and developed as persons with unique qualities and characteristics, we learned increasingly sophisticated skills which enabled us to transmit our feelings very precisely.

A Definition of Communication

Because communication is a somewhat complicated process, not all scholars agree to one generalizable definition. However, for our purposes, we shall define communication as the *process by which humans transmit and receive information*. There are five significant aspects of this definition:

Process. The process aspect of communication suggests that it is *ongoing* and *dynamic*. Communication is taking place all around us constantly. We cannot "stop" communication to examine it. Even when two people "refuse" to interact, their very refusal sends messages that hostility or anger may exist between them. A variety of external stimuli can enter the communication relationship between two people influencing the accuracy of the information transmission between them.

Not only is the "now" of communication important, but also the "past" and "future" as well.

Humans. In this book we are concerned with the people aspect of communication behavior. People learn about, adapt to, and manage their environment through communication. Communication allows us to reduce the natural uncertainty in our existence by helping us learn to control our surroundings. It provides the vehicle which enables us to gain from other people's knowledge and experience and thus prevents us from making their mistakes.

Transmit. The "sending" aspect of communication suggests that we attempt to transmit some bit of information to someone else. We have something to say and we try to say it so that someone else will understand it. Normally we do this by structuring an idea in our mind and then trying to articulate it. However, "talking" represents only a small percentage of the total sending aspects of our communicating behavior. We also communicate by the way we walk, the way we sound, the way we look, and by hundreds of other things that we do. Message transmission involves both the *intentional* sending, our conscious attempt to project an idea to someone, and the *unintentional* sending, the nondeliberate transmission of information.

Receive. If someone transmits information, for communication to take place, there must be someone to receive it. People receive information not only by means of their ears, but also with their eyes, mouth, nose, and touch as well. In our daily routine, we are continually receiving intentional and unintentional messages from many sources all around us. The aroma of a freshly cut lawn on a spring morning or the view of sunrise on an ocean beach certainly communicates information to those fortunate enough to be near.

Message. The idea or information which gets communicated is sometimes referred to as the message. There are two kinds of messages. Those which are voiced, or written down, are referred to as *verbal.* Those which are neither voiced nor written down are called *nonverbal.* Thousands of potential pieces of information are transmitted in even the shortest exchange between two people, but those potential stimuli only become information after they are processed by someone.

The definition of communication behavior provided above did not mention the concept of feedback, but it is very important in the communication process.

Feedback. For communication to fully involve both participants, it is necessary for the sender to judge the effect of his or her message upon the receiver. This allows him or her to adapt the message to the needs of his or her listener. *Feedback is the response which a receiver provides to a bit of information which she or he has received* and may be provided both verbally and nonverbally. For example, if after hearing a very sad story, we have tears in our eyes, we are providing feedback to the storyteller. Feedback provides the closing "loop" which links the sender to the receiver and keeps communication dynamic.

This book will be concerned with that particular communication behavior which occurs in organizations. It has been suggested that we know little about this type of communication (Roberts and O'Reilly 1974b). The literature which deals with organizations only considers communication peripherally while communication scholars rarely mention the organization. Few have attempted to integrate both organizational theory and communication theory (Roberts and O'Reilly 1974b; Farace and MacDonald 1974), yet communication remains as one of the most important processes occurring in the organization.

Our purpose will be to try to bring together the most important elements from the study of both organizations and communication. We shall do this to provide some understanding for the reader as to how communication operates in the organization. Since most of us will be members of organizations throughout our lives, the authors trust that this knowledge of organizational communication will help the reader become an effective organizational participant.

In this chapter we shall examine some models of both communication and organizational behavior. Later, we will attempt to integrate the models as we turn our attention specifically to the functions of communication in the organization.

Models of the Communication Process

Since communication involves so many important behavioral components, scholars who study the process have proposed a variety of models, or diagrams, which help to explain how it works (Shannon and Weaver 1949; Westley and McLean 1957; Berlo 1960). These models help us understand the interrelationship among the components of the communication process. Probably the most widely accepted model was developed by Berlo (fig. 1-1). Berlo has laid out what he considers to be the important components of communication (*S*ource, *M*essage, *C*hannel, and *R*eceiver) and suggests that each component has various dimensions which govern the effectiveness of interaction within a particular exchange. For example, the sender possesses some degree of communication skill and level of knowledge, holds a variety of attitudes, and operates within a particular cultural

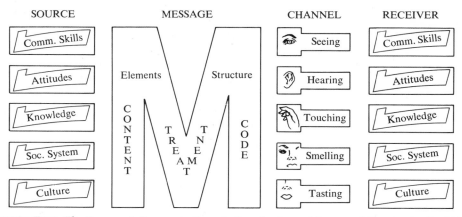

SOURCE: From *The Process of Communication, An Introduction to Theory and Practice* by David K. Berlo, p. 72. Copyright © 1960 by Holt, Rinehart and Winston, Inc. Reprinted by permission of Holt, Rinehart and Winston.

Figure 1-1   Berlo Communication Model

framework. All of these dimensions will have an effect on the sender's ability to transmit information. Similarly, the dimensions listed under Message, Channel, and Receiver will also determine the effectiveness of information transmission.

A model which focuses upon the environment, or atmosphere, in which communication takes place was developed by Lesikar (1968). (See fig. 1-2.) The Lesikar model deals primarily with what is going on within the receiver's mental set. As you will note, there are numerous potentially meaningful signs and symbols, or possible informational inputs, within the communication environment of each individual. Indeed, there are so many of these that it would be impossible for our sensory receptors (eyes, ears, and so on) to perceive all of them. Instead, we can process only a small portion of them. Within the communication environment of a specific exchange, Person 1 may perceive symbols A, B, and C while Person 2 may perceive symbols X, Y, and Z. In what may appear to be the "same" communication exchange, people rarely receive exactly the same information. We shall come back to this point later when we draw some generalizations about the communication process.

The models described so far each focus on different aspects of communication behavior. We now offer a third model (fig. 1-3) which will simplify and integrate, hopefully, some of the features of the Berlo and Lesikar models. We have attempted to diagram some of the aspects of communication presented in our definition of the process on page 3. The basic transmission of information from the sender to receiver has been included but there are a number of other important variables which may influence this transmission. First of all, as mentioned in our consideration of the Berlo model, the sender and the receiver each possess some level of communication, or interpersonal skills.* Second, the environment, or climate, which involves the *feelings of the participants about the particular communication exchange* would be expected to influence transmission. Finally, some type of purpose,

---

*The terms *communication skills* and *interpersonal skills* will be used interchangeably throughout the book. At this point, we are primarily referring to speaking and listening skills. A full discussion of interpersonal skills will be the topic for chapter fourteen.

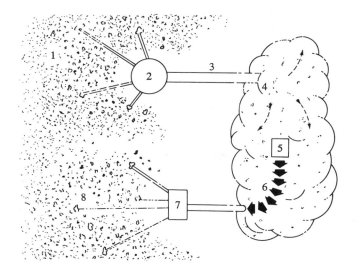

Explanation:

1. This area represents our communication environment. It is all the signs and symbols that exist in the real world that surrounds us.

2. Our sensory receptors pick up some (far from all) of the signs and symbols.

3. Those signs and symbols which are picked up go through our nervous systems and into our mental filters.

4. Our mental filters give the signs and symbols meaning. The meanings received add to the content of the filters.

5. Sometimes the meanings we form trigger communication responses.

6. We form these responses through our mental filters.

7. We send our responses as symbols through speaking, writing, etc.

8. These symbols become part of the communication environments of others. Here they may be picked up by the sensory receptors of others, and another cycle begins.

SOURCE: R. V. Lesikar, *Business Communication Theory and Practice* (Homewood, Ill.: Irwin, 1968), p. 26. Used by permission.

Figure 1-2   Lesikar Communication Model

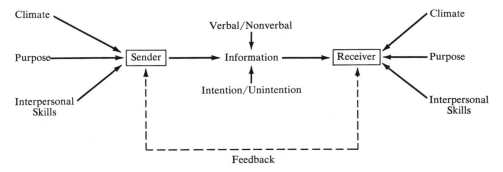

Figure 1-3   Simplified Communication Model

or objective, is normally associated with a communication exchange. In this context, purpose refers to *the reasons why it is necessary for the participants to communicate.*

Building upon the three models presented, it may be helpful to make some general observations about communication behavior before turning our attention to that communication occurring within organizations.

1. Communication is extremely complex because there are numerous places in the model where misunderstanding and confusion might occur. Communication may fail because one (or more) of the participants in an exchange possesses insufficient interpersonal skills to get the point across. Another reason for failure might be the existence of a climate which is not *conducive* to communication. Or, communication may break down because there is confusion about the purpose of a particular exchange. It is likely that some degree of misunderstanding will enter every exchange due to this complexity.

2. The sender may help himself or herself in achieving successful transmission by building some degree of *redundancy* into his or her message-sending activities. Redundancy refers to the *conscious attempt by the sender to use a variety of methods, treatments, and channels to transmit his or her information.* It is fairly typical for an individual to miss an idea the first time she or he hears it. But, given the opportunity to be exposed to the same idea a second and third time, understanding will likely occur. Redundancy helps reduce misunderstanding.

3. The human being has a limited channel capacity for processing informational inputs. It would be impossible for us to process all of the information in even the most simple communication exchange between just two people. When "too much" is going on around us, we sometimes withdraw or "tune out." Each of us has a different capacity for processing information.

4. Information, in and of itself, has no inherent meaning. Potential messages become meaningful only when someone assigns meaning to them. People assign meaning based on the climate and the purpose associated with a communication exchange. Meanings are also assigned based on the receiver's background, perceptions, attitudinal set, and his or her relationship with the sender. In the organization, many of the elements considered in the next chapter and later in the book also influence the meanings assigned by a receiver to an informational input. Within this framework it can be said that the important message in a communication exchange is *not* the one which the sender sends but rather the one the receiver receives.

The above discussion introduced some of the important ideas and principles involved in the communication process. These concepts will be important throughout the rest of the book. We now turn our attention to an examination of the nature of organizations.

The Nature of Organizations

Throughout our lives, we function as members of organizations. We are born into an existing organization, the family. We are taught moral and ethical conduct through an organization, the church. We acquire cognitive skills and knowledge in an organization, the school. And, we go through adulthood earning our living in an organization. We satisfy many of our social, physical, and emotional needs through our membership in organizations.

Definitions of Organizations

Scholars have offered a variety of definitions to describe organizations. To Etzioni (1965, p. 650) organizations are "social units that have specific purposes.

They are planned, deliberately structured, constantly and self-consciously reviewing their performance and structuring themselves accordingly." Building on Etzioni's concept, we can see that organizations have some degree of *structure*. This structure is composed of the organization's attempt to *codify rules for operations and to prescribe formalized relationships among individuals, work units, and departments.*

Blau and Scott (1962, p. 6) suggest that organizations require "coordination of activities of many persons that have a deliberately established purpose." The coordination concept is important in many definitions of organizations. Even when only two people attempt to coordinate their behavior for a common purpose, they are operating as an organization. For example, two children who design a system to solicit subscriptions to the evening newspaper on their street have formed an organization.

Perrow (1965) has argued that organizations are systems which have a variety of interrelated parts. He explained:

> Organizations are viewed as systems which utilize energy (given up by humans and nonhuman devices) in a patterned directed effort to alter the condition of the basic materials in a predetermined manner. (p. 913)

This systems view suggests that organizations operate as single units which "do something" to raw materials. More will be said about organizations as systems below.

Barnard (1938) was one of the first theorists to conclude that communication was a crucial element in organizations:

> An organization comes into being when there are persons (1) able to communicate with each other, (2) who are willing to contribute action, (3) to accomplish a common purpose . . . the elements of an organization therefore are (1) communication, (2) willingness to serve, and (3) common purpose. The elements are necessary and sufficient conditions initially and they are found in all organizations. (p. 82)

A Synthesis

Each writer cited above has chosen to emphasize different elements in his definition of organizations. We now offer a definition of organizations which, we believe, brings together many of the ideas which have already been introduced separately.

An organization is a social system of structured individual roles and tasks which require coordination and communication to accomplish a specific purpose.

Let us examine each part of this definition to learn more about organizations.

Social System. Organizations are social systems which can be characterized as possessing: (1) the need for raw materials and informational inputs as to what to do with those materials, (2) a mechanism which enables them to transform raw materials into some kind of product, or *output,* (3) the human abilities to accomplish the transformation, and (4) the ability to operate within the constraints of an environment. A systems approach to organizations assumes that each part of the system is linked to each other part so that a change in one part of the system will affect all other parts.* For example, we can see that a college is a social system as it takes inputs of high-school students (raw materials) and educates (transformation) them into college graduates (products) four years later. Similarly, the aircraft factory takes raw materials (tin, glass, steel) and human talent to process finished airplanes. Both systems must obtain their raw materials within an *environment* which is composed of *all relevant cultural, economic, social, and historical factors likely to influence the organization.*

Structured Roles and Tasks.   Within organizations there is a need for some degree of structure which enables them to codify rules and formalize hierarchical relationships among subunits and individuals. There is a tendency in an organization to write down job descriptions, operating procedures, schematic charts, and so on to document these hierarchical relationships. The codes and rules become the standard operating procedure of the organization. In writing these down, the organization hopes to control its own destiny by efficiently reaching its goal. The codifying of these roles and tasks assumes that they are meant to be performed, regardless of the *person* occupying the position assigned the particular task. Positions are structured by the organization based on the objective to be accomplished.

Coordination.   The separate roles and tasks of the organization do not operate in a vacuum apart from each other, however. Instead, each task must be done in concert with each other for the organization to reach goal attainment. Coordination is necessary among individuals, work groups, departments, and divisions. Normally in organizations, one of the responsibilities of supervision is coordination. For coordination to be achieved each work group must be aware of the activities of other related work groups to minimize duplication.

Communication.   Communication is the vehicle through which coordination is accomplished. Simple work-related conversation between two workers in a single department helps achieve some degree of coordination. Coordination and communication are so similar in effect that it is difficult to conceive of one without the other. The transfer of information within the organization enables the system to transform raw materials into outputs. Before tin, glass, and steel can be processed into an airplane, the information, or "know-how," must be disseminated throughout the organization.

Specific Purpose.   The *mission* of the organization is what it does, or its *task.* The extent to which the organization's mission is accomplished establishes whether the organization is successful. Sometimes the goals of the organization are not in harmony with some of the goals of the individual members. But a satisfactory level of commitment must come from members who do the work of the organization. When some overlap between individual and organizational goals is present, the likelihood of organizational effectiveness is increased.

In this book, we regard organizations as collections of people. Size is not really important. A group of people in a single family may well meet our definition of an

---

*For a thorough treatment of the role of systems theory in organizations, see K.E. Boulding, "General Systems Theory," *General Systems,* 1956 Yearbook of the Society for the Advancement of General Systems Theory, and D. Katz and R.L. Kahn, *The Social Psychology of Organizations* (New York: McGraw Hill, 1966), chapter 3.

organization. Certainly a family is a social system which attempts to process inputs, such as finances, into outputs, such as growth and development. Roles and tasks are well structured in that most families have task requirements for the mother, the father, and the children. The accomplishment of these tasks requires communication and coordination. But, as the small family unit is an organization, so is the behemoth like General Motors. Given this background, we are now prepared to examine an important prerequisite to organization—communication.

The Nature of Communication in the Organization

We shall now consider how communication functions in the organization. This treatment is intended to introduce the reader to the model of organizational communication which will be presented in chapter two. We hope that the reader will consider the first three chapters (Part One) as a unit since they have been developed to provide the background for the rest of the book. Here we are explaining *why* communication is important in the organization, and in the next chapter we will demonstrate *how* communication operates in the organization. In chapter three we shall examine the role which communication plays in contributing to effective organizations.

We may demonstrate why communication is vital to the organization by examining some functions it performs. As we have suggested, the very existence of the organization depends upon the coordination of activities through communication. For the organization to remain organic, or alive, this coordination must occur and is probably the most important single function the process accomplishes. But communication fulfills other functions as well.

Functions of Organizational Communication

We assume that communication does certain tasks, or functions, for an organization. Each function makes a unique contribution to the organization and results only through human communication.*

Integration. Coordination and integration are very closely related, but some important differences are apparent. In dealing with coordination we were concerned with the need for awareness of the activities of organizational members (groups, departments, divisions, and so on) on the part of other members. Integration is more than this in that it involves taking the *ideas, products, and contributions of others, generated elsewhere, and utilizing them in one's own task*. Integration suggests that all individuals in the organization operate within a framework of mutual dependency. This point will be clarified if we return to our definition of organizations on page 3. We implied that all behavior in the organization is related to other behavior. Each isolated task must be integrated into the global effort for the organization to be effective. For example, in the case of salespeople marketing a particular product out in the field, the sales efforts must be integrated into the production processes of the home office. The sales effort and the production effort are mutually dependent. Information transfer between both departments, as well as between other

---

*See R. Farace and D. McDonald, "New Directions in Organizational Communication," *Personnel Psychology* (1974), pp. 1-11, for a creative treatment of the functions which communication accomplishes in the organization.

related departments, is a prerequisite for effective organizational operations. Some levels of integration *and* coordination are present in all successful organizations.

Maintenance.   Like all living organisms, the organization must maintain itself within an environment of limited resources. Informational inputs are processed to allow the system to adapt to changing conditions. These changing conditions must be observed early and information about them must be transmitted to the primary decision makers in the organization so that adjustments in operating procedures can be made. If the organization does not have some mechanism to do this, it cannot survive. This point is well illustrated by an example taken from the American economy in the early seventies. Because of the worldwide shortage of oil and oil products, Americans reexamined their dependency on the large luxury automobile which consumed much fuel. Instead, auto customers demanded small cars. For major automobile manufacturing organizations to stay in business, they had to detect these changes in people's attitudes within the environment. Generally, they were successful and slowed down the production of large cars in favor of small cars.

Orientation.   Within any organization, there is a need to disseminate work-related information to the members of the organization, or *orient* them. Without some degree of knowledge about the job, the individual cannot perform the task. Often, full-scale orientation programs are structured into the operating procedures of the organization. At other times, orientation is accomplished through work manuals or job descriptions. The need for orientation is continual within the organization since preparations must always be made to accomplish new tasks.

Member Growth.   As suggested earlier, to the extent to which our own individual goals overlap with our organization's, we will be committed to the success of the organization. The individual may be able to grow and develop as a person through his or her association with the organization. However, this occurs only when information about opportunities for growth are transmitted to him or her. As the individual is made aware of the opportunities, seeing how the opportunities enable him or her to reach a personal goal, he or she may be motivated to take advantage of them. The transmission of information about promotion, tenure, training, educational advancement, travel, and the like becomes an important use of the organizational communication system.

Decision Making.   Organizations are continually required to make decisions to resolve apparent conflict. Alternative courses of action provide a source of ambiguity for the organization. To reduce the ambiguity, a particular action is selected and the organization attempts to implement it. Good decisions are made when good information is transmitted to decision makers. Inadequate information produces poor decision making.

With the functions considered above, we have attempted to suggest why communication is vital to the organization. The rest of this book will be devoted to an examination of each of the important components of the organizational communication process.

Preview

Part One of this book provides background for the importance and operation of organizational communication. As suggested earlier, we hope that Part One will be treated as a unit. In reading the rest of the book, it may be helpful to keep in mind that the first three chapters contain introductory material. Chapters four through ten treat background variables which influence organizational communication. Chapters eleven through fourteen detail the communication system in organizations, while suggestions for improvement in that system are covered in chapters fifteen through seventeen.

REVIEW AND DISCUSSION

1. It was suggested in the chapter that communication is a dynamic process. Do you perceive any difference between the *process* of communication and the *effects* of communication?

2. Think of an organization of which you have been a member. Try to remember some examples of intentional communication and unintentional communication which took place in that organization.

3. What do you see as similarities among the Berlo, Lesikar, and Simplified communication models presented in this chapter? What are the important differences? Find other models in the literature for even further comparison.

4. Provide some examples as to why communication breaks down in organizations. What can be done to facilitate organizational communication?

5. Trace the components of our definition of organization through an organization with which you are familiar. Does the definition apply? What do you see as the most important aspect of the definition?

6. What tasks does communication accomplish in the organization? Which of these would be considered essential?

Chapter Two

A Model of Organizational Communication

While systematic study of the field of organizational communication is relatively new, research and theory have already produced some knowledge in the area. As is the case in most relatively new fields of study, much of what has been learned has not been woven into an overall pattern or general theory. Knowledge exists as bits and pieces, similar to the pieces of a jigsaw puzzle before it is put together. While this knowledge is helpful in understanding particular elements of organizational communication, it is often difficult to relate it to particular problems in practical situations.

A systematic way of thinking (a model or conceptual framework) is needed about organizational communication. A model would be useful for two important, related reasons. First, a model would be helpful in making sense of organizational communication, because it would provide a framework for organizing knowledge. Thus, a model would provide a set of "pigeonholes" or categories into which knowledge about organizational communication could be filed. Second, and just as important, a model would be useful as a tool to help managers understand and analyze communication problems in organizations. So, a model would promote both understanding and analytical problem solving.

We believe that the most useful approach to the study of organizations is the systems approach. Primarily as a result of general systems theory, organizations today are recognized as manmade systems which interact with other systems and with their total environment. Johnson and his colleagues put it this way: "The organization is an open, sociotechnical system composed of a number of subsystems and in continuing interaction with its environmental suprasystem" (1973, p. 23).

Essentially the systems approach to the study of organizations means two things. One is that the organization itself is a system — "a set of interrelated elements" (Ackoff 1971, p. 661). That is, organizations are complex wholes made up of many different parts that fit together in some way and affect each in some way. The second idea is that organizations are "open systems." This means simply that organizations do not exist in isolation; they are a part of some larger environmental "system" that affects them and is, in turn, affected by them.

We use a systems approach in this book. We consider organizations to be composed of several internal elements, such as structure, people, goals, and so on, which interact to form the "whole" organization. We also consider the interaction between the organization and its environment. The external environment exerts forces which shape the organization. The organization, in turn, produces some consequences, i.e. produces products, provides people some level of satisfaction, which feed back on and affect the environment. Keeping these ideas in mind will help make this book more meaningful.

This chapter presents an outline of the systems model that is explained in detail in the remainder of this book. Thus, this chapter previews the remainder of the book and provides an overview of the organization and content of the book.

Figure 2-1 is a diagram of the model of organizational communication. As can be seen, the model has the following four major parts:

1. external environmental influences,
2. internal organizational elements,
3. the organizational communication system, and
4. organizational effectiveness.

Cause and effect relationships between the major parts of the model run from left to right (in the direction of the arrows) and ultimate consequences feed back on all of the parts of the model. Thus, external environmental factors affect internal environmental factors; in turn, the resulting internal environment results in a particular system of organizational communication. The consequent system of organizational communication influences organizational effectiveness. Finally, organizational effectiveness produces consequences which feed back on the various parts of the model. This then is the "bare bones" of the model.

The approach to explaining this model may, at first, seem somewhat illogical. The most obvious approach is to begin at the left and explain the most basic part of the model, external environmental factors, and then proceed to the second part of the model. Our experience in the classroom indicates that a slight modification of this obvious approach is helpful. Therefore, the approach used is to begin at the right-hand side of the model and develop the criteria of organizational effectiveness first and then go back to the most basic part of the model and move forward in a logical manner.

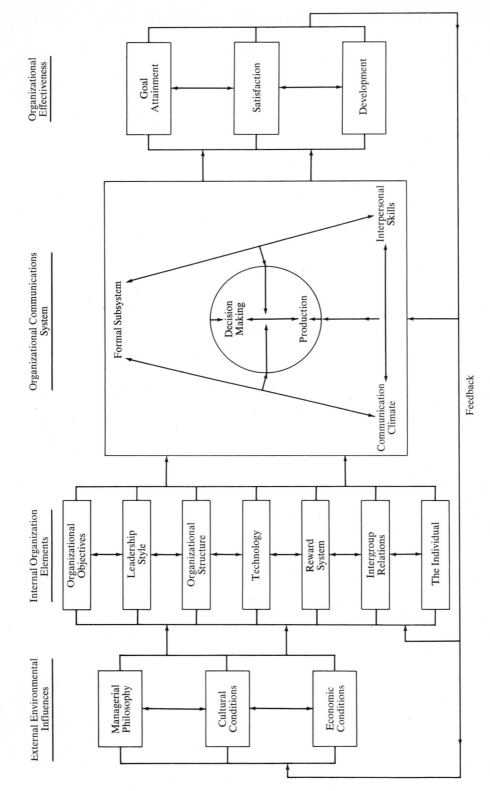

Figure 2-1   Model of Organizational Communication

Organizational Effectiveness

The effectiveness of any society's organizations is a major determinant of the quality of life available to the people who make up the society. Most people depend on organizations not only to supply them the goods and services that they need and want but also to provide the source of their livelihood. Thus, the effectiveness with which organizations operate has a direct effect on most people and an indirect effect on all people.

But by what criteria are organizations judged effective or ineffective? The usual answer is that organizations are effective to the degree that they achieve their objectives with minimum use of resources. We have no basic disagreement with this concept, however, we do believe that it is more meaningful to say that organizations are effective to the degree that they achieve their objectives, satisfy the needs of their members, and grow in their ability to continue to do both of these things. Thus, as figure 2-1 shows, organizational effectiveness is measured by (1) goal attainment, (2) satisfaction, and (3) development.*

Goal Attainment

Organizations are created and operated to satisfy the needs of society through achieving their own goals — goals of producing goods and services. Thus, goal

*We have been strongly influenced in our thinking concerning organizational effectiveness by Gibson, *Organizations,* 1973. This discussion draws heavily on that source.

attainment depends on the ability of the organization to produce the goods and services society expects it to produce. Organizations that consistently fail to achieve their goals certainly are ineffective and will die. The most common measures of goal attainment include profit, sales, market share, students graduated, patients released, documents processed, clients served, and the like (Gibson 1973).

Consider the automobile industry. General Motors, Ford, Chrysler, and American Motors all continue to exist. They have succeeded in attaining their goals, at least to the degree that they remain in existence. In contrast, Studebaker failed to attain its goals and "died" in the 1950s. Thus, the degree to which organizations attain their goals is a measure of their effectiveness.

Satisfaction

The second criterion of organizational effectiveness is the degree to which members of the organization experience satisfaction from their membership and their contribution to the attainment of organizational goals. Organizations exist to serve the needs of society in general, but all organizations exist to serve the needs of specific groups of people — owners, customers, suppliers, and employees. In a relatively free society, any organization that consistently fails to satisfy any one of these groups of people will fail and die. Strictly speaking, employee satisfaction is a major determinant of the degree to which organizations achieve their goals. However, employee satisfaction has such important long-run effects on goal achievement that we believe it should be considered one of the standards of effectiveness, especially in the short run. Measures which reflect satisfaction are attitudes, productivity, turnover, absenteeism, tardiness, grievances, and so on (Gibson 1973).

Development

The third criterion of organizational effectiveness is development. Development refers to changes in the organization's ability to achieve its goals through serving the interests of society. More specifically, development refers to changes in the organization's problem-solving ability and to changes in its ability to respond to external and internal change and ultimately to its ability to survive. That is, development is a measure of the organization's ability to continue to achieve its goals and to satisfy its employees.

Survival is the ultimate criterion of organizational effectiveness. An organization can be quite effective in attaining its goals and satisfying its employees in the short run at the expense of being able to do so in the future. So development adds a time dimension to organizational effectiveness.

There are no precise, concrete measures of development. Attempts directed toward development usually center around education and training, and the real effects of such types of actions are difficult to measure. Most often development is measured in relative terms by questionnaire assessment of such things as (1) the way conflict is handled, (2) how planning takes place, (3) the methods used to make decisions, (4) degree of goal orientation, and (5) communication climate. Measurements of these variables are then compared with measurements in other organizations or previous measurements in the same organization to identify any differences or changes. Based on normative theory, judgments about development are then made.

In summary, the model proposed here assumes that organizational effectiveness includes the three dimensions of goal attainment, satisfaction, and development.

Determinants of Organizational Effectiveness

Organizational effectiveness (measured by the three criteria above) is influenced by several factors, one of which is the organizational communication system. This system is, however, the result of internal organizational variables that are themselves significantly influenced by external environmental factors.

External Environmental Influences

It has been said that to understand anything one must understand its surroundings. Organizations do not exist in isolation; like people, they interact with their environment. More specifically, organizations are significantly influenced by the environment that surrounds them; they, in turn, influence their environment.

As figure 2-1 indicates, three sets of factors — managerial philosophy and assumptions, cultural conditions, and economic conditions — external to the organization have important effects on the organization. It is with the nature of these environmental factors and how they help shape the internal character of the organization that this part of the model is concerned.

Managerial Philosophy and Assumptions

While it is difficult to separate managerial philosophy and assumptions from internal elements of the organization, it undoubtedly has a major impact on the makeup of the organization and ultimately on its effectiveness. Managerial philosophy and assumptions are considered an external environmental factor for two reasons. First, managerial philosophy and assumptions are only more specific forms of the general sociocultural values that surround the organization. Second, managerial philosophy and assumptions are basic variables that shape the character of the more specific internal elements of the organization. That is, the source of managerial philosophy and assumptions is the environment, and managerial philosophy is a basic influence on actions that determine how the organization operates.

Consider, for example, the differences in the way different classes are conducted. Some involve more lecture or more discussion or more homework than others. Certainly, part of these differences arise because different instructors have different ideas about students and the best way to help people learn.

As we use it, managerial philosophy and assumptions refer to basic values and beliefs about the nature of people, organizations, and managing. Philosophies differ and different philosophies result in different organizational objectives, organization structures, leadership styles, technologies used, and reward systems.

Cultural Influences

Cultural influences affect many of the internal factors in organization. Culture refers to a way of life, including such things as knowledge, beliefs, values, customs, practices, and socially prescribed roles. It is one of the predominant sets of determinants of the basic nature of individual behavior. Cultures vary, and the particular culture surrounding any organization has definite effects on the internal makeup of the organization. And, to some degree, culture determines what technologies are available for use in the organization, what rewards are used, what leadership styles are acceptable, what specific objectives are sought, and, through prescribing roles, the way different groups in the organization interact.

Economic Influences

A third factor that influences the internal makeup of the organization is economic conditions. Economic influences refer primarily to the availability and/or scarcity of resources and to competitive conditions in the market for the organization's goods or services. These environmental conditions have significant effects on individual behavior, the leadership style used, the rewards offered members for performance, the technology used, the way jobs and the entire organization are structured, and most important, the nature of the specific objectives the organization strives to achieve.

Interrelation of External Influences

The external environmental influences on organizations are not independent; they are interrelated. Managerial philosophy is greatly influenced by both cultural and economic conditions. Culture also influences what economic values and conditions tend to surround the organization. These three distinct, yet related, sets of factors interact to determine the internal makeup of the organization.

Internal Organizational Elements

The internal nature and characteristics of the organization are determined primarily by the three external environmental factors discussed above. In turn, the internal characteristics have significant influences on the organizational communication system and its effectiveness. Different managerial assumptions, cultures, and economic conditions are likely to result in organizations being developed and operated differently. This part of the model identifies the most important elements of the organization that affect the communication system.

Organizational Objectives

All organizations have more or less specific objectives which they try to achieve. These objectives are the specific, immediate reasons that organizations exist. These same organizational objectives are a product of the organization's environment, and they influence organizational communication.

It should be apparent that the specific objectives that any organization seeks to achieve are greatly influenced by the organization's environment. Cultural and economic conditions tend to determine what opportunities for objectives are available to the organization. Within the broad limits imposed by cultural and economic conditions, managerial philosophy and assumptions operate to determine the particular objectives that the organization will seek to achieve.

The objectives of the organization have a significant effect on the nature of the communication system, especially the formal design and climate elements. Certainly, the objectives being striven for determine what specific decisions need to be made, when, and by whom. Since the formal communication subsystem is intended to supply decision makers with appropriate information, it follows that the organizational objectives are major determinants of the design of the formal communication subsystem. Objectives also affect the climate that prevails. The degree to which objectives are known, understood, and accepted by organizational members has important influences on people's attitudes and motivations toward actually using the formal subsystem and communicating. Knowledge of and acceptance of objectives promotes positive communication attitudes, while lack of knowledge, understanding, and/or acceptance tend to promote negative attitudes.

The Nature of the Individual

A second important internal characteristic of the organization is individual behavior. The behavior individuals exhibit in organizations is significantly influenced by their past experience and by other internal organizational characteristics.

Obviously, this factor influences the general level of interpersonal skills in the communication system. In addition, individuals are basically selfish in that their behavior is directed toward satisfaction of their own internal needs. As a consequence, individuals have an almost unlimited need for information about the things that affect them. Thus, the design of the formal subsystem is determined in part by the needs of the individuals involved as well as by the needs of the organization. Moreover, the climate that prevails is also partly a result of the way individuals go about getting their needs (communication and otherwise) satisfied.

Organizational Structure

The formal structure of authority and activity is the third factor that influences the nature of the organizational communication system. Cultural attitudes toward the appropriate and legitimate use of authority and the acceptability and desirability of various types of activity impose broad limits within which managerial philosophy operates to structure the organization. Lines of authority and authority relationships make up a large part of the design of the formal communication subsystem. In other ways, the nature of the organizational structure has significant effects on job content and therefore on individuals' attitudes and the communication climate that exists.

Technology and Job Design

Still another internal factor (not unrelated to those above) affecting the communication system is technology and job design. Different cultural conditions tend to determine what technologies are available for use, and differing economic conditions and managerial philosophies determine what technology is used and how specific jobs are structured. The type of technology used to achieve organizational objectives affects the design of the formal communication subsystem in much the same way as does the nature of organizational objectives. That is, the way things are done determines who needs to communicate what, to whom, and when. Technology also influences communication climate. The type of technology used by the organization is a major determinant of the way jobs are designed and of the nature of the job that any individual performs. Research, today, indicates that the content of jobs is a major factor in motivation, including attitudes toward communication.

Leadership Style

Leadership style, as used here, refers to the general style of leadership that is characteristic of the organization. Individuals, not organizations, exercise leadership styles, but in most organizations, one particular leadership style seems to be the most prevalent and characteristic style. This style is referred to as the leadership style of the organization. Leadership styles are roles and such types of organizational roles tend to be determined by sociocultural values and managerial philosophy and assumptions. Different cultures and philosophies produce different leadership styles.

The leadership style of the organization influences both the design of the formal system and the climate that prevails. Leadership style is a major factor affecting who makes what decisions and *how* such decisions are made. Thus, it influences the design of the formal communication subsystem. Leadership style also influences the *use* that is made of information, and it has significant effects on people's willingness to communicate.

Reward System

Similar to the above elements of the organization, the nature of the reward system used by the organization also varies according to cultural and economic conditions and the philosophy of management. Certainly, the type of reward system used affects the type of information needed to reward people; so reward systems influence the design of the formal subsystem of communication. Certainly, the reward system affects the communication climate; people's attitudes toward communicating are highly likely to be influenced by their perceptions of the effect that such communication has on their rewards.

Intergroup Relations

The last element of the organization is intergroup relations. As with all of the preceding six elements of the organization, the nature of intergroup relations in the organization tends to be a function of the environment and the interaction of the other six internal organizational elements.

The nature of the relations which prevail between various subgroups in the organization also affects both the design of the formal subsystem and the climate that exists. The formal subsystem may be designed to take advantage of or to compensate for the relations that exist between particular groups. Certainly, intergroup relations affect the willingness of members of the groups to communicate.

One point needs to be made about the effects of each of the above factors on interpersonal skills. With the exception of the individual which has obvious effects on the level of interpersonal skill, none of the factors influence individuals' skills directly; but all of them have indirect influences to the extent to which they encourage or discourage development and improvement of skills.

Interrelationship of Internal Environment Factors

While the above discussion assumes that the seven internal organizational factors are not related (or at least it did not point out specific interrelations), this is certainly not the case. Each of the factors tends to affect and be affected by the other six factors. For example, in practice the factors of organizational structure, leadership, technology, and reward systems are usually quite closely related. Such interrelations will be discussed later.

In summary, a system made up of seven sets of factors within the organization results from environmental influences and produces an organizational communication system that operates with some degree of effectiveness and that has important influences on overall organizational effectiveness. What effects do these factors have on organizational communication?

The Organizational Communication System

The organizational communication system is a result of the seven internal elements identified in the preceding section, and its effectiveness is a major determinant of overall organizational effectiveness. All organizational communication systems are made up of three major parts or elements—the formally designed subsystem, people's attitudes (climate) toward using the system, and people's interpersonal communication abilities. These three elements interact to determine the effectiveness of organizational communication. In turn, the effectiveness of communication in the organization influences two important processes—decision making and production—that affect overall organizational effectiveness.

Elements of Organizational Communication

One way to look at systems of organizational communication is to divide them into the major parts or elements which determine their effectiveness. The effectiveness of any organizational communication system is determined primarily by the design of the formal subsystem itself, people's attitudes toward communication (climate), and people's abilities to communicate.

Design of the Formal Subsystem. All organizations have formal systems of communication to serve their information needs. Simply stated, the formal communication subsystem refers to *who* is supposed to send *what* information to *whom;* who is supposed to receive that information from whom; and when such information is to be sent or received. This formal subsystem may or may not be written or official, but it is the way things are "supposed" to be done.

The beginning and basis of all formal subsystems is the organizational structure. The chain of command and all authority relationships make up a major part of the formal communication subsystem. In addition to these vertical channels, most organizations also need and have numerous lateral channels to provide information needed for people to do their jobs. The formal communication subsystem is made up of all of the communication links consciously developed and maintained by the organization to serve its needs.

Communication Climate. Communication climate refers to the overall atmosphere in which communication takes place and to people's attitudes toward communicating. Climate is generally a result of the level of trust, support, and respect that exists between people in the organization. Favorable attitudes toward communication are normally found where there is a high level of trust and respect and relatively little fear. In such cases, communication is generally open, honest, and candid. Lack of respect for people's opinions and feelings and lack of trust and support and the consequent fear result in negative attitudes and a closed communication climate. Thus, the dimensions of climate are openness and honesty.

Interpersonal Skills. The third component of an organizational communication system is the communication skills of the people in the system. Ultimately, *all* communication takes place between people and depends upon the skills of the people communicating. By skills we mean people's abilities to express themselves, to respond to others, and to actively listen for understanding. Thus, the communication skills of the people in the organization are a major element of the organizational communication system.

Communication System Effectiveness

The effectiveness of any organizational communication system depends on the quality of each of the three elements or subsystems, and their interaction. Certainly, the adequacy of the design of the formal subsystem influences the effectiveness of organizational communication. To the degree that the subsystem is well designed (designed to provide people the information that they need when they need it), the greater is its potential for effective communication. Well-designed subsystems promote, but do not insure, effective communication, because the climate and skill level of people are unknown factors. However, poorly designed subsystems tend to preclude effective communication.

The communication climate also influences the effectiveness of organizational communication. Basically, climate influences people's motivations and attitudes toward communicating. People's predispositions to communicate are then determined by their attitudes. Favorable climates result in positive attitudes, and unfavorable climates result in negative attitudes.

Ultimately, the quality of all organizational communication is dependent on people's personal communication skills. The communication that occurs in organizations normally takes place among people. Thus, the quality of organizational communication can be no better than the general levels of people's communication skills. No matter how well designed the formal subsystem or what people's attitudes, the effectiveness of organizational communication is limited by the ability of people to transfer information and understanding. These three elements of organizational communication are not necessarily independent; they each tend to affect the other two. People's attitudes are affected by the nature of the formal subsystem, and the formal subsystem usually tries to compensate for negative attitudes and lack of ability. In turn, both attitudes and the formal subsystem either encourage or discourage improvement in people's communication skills.

An analogy helps make the elements of organizational communication and their influence on effectiveness easier to understand. Consider the situation concerning automobile safety. Certainly the design of automobiles, people's attitudes toward driving, and driving ability are important factors affecting auto safety. Well-designed cars are likely to cause less accidents, but well-designed cars can be misused. Auto safety also depends on the way people *want* to drive cars. The safest automobiles that could be built could be driven dangerously. Finally, no matter how safe cars are and how safely people want to drive them, they can actually drive only as safely as their level of driving ability allows. Thus, auto safety, like organizational communication, depends on the three factors of system design, climate, and skill.

How Communication Affects Organizational Effectiveness

Effective organizational communication is not an end in itself; it is one of the means to the end of organizational effectiveness. Basically, communication serves the following two purposes in all organizations: (1) it provides information for decision making, and (2) it makes possible the attitudes and motivations for the decision-making and producing processes (Davis 1972).

Decision Making. Organizational communication affects organizational effectiveness through the decision-making process. Decision making is an important process which influences organizational effectiveness. It pervades all organizational activity, and it has a direct impact on such things as what goals will be sought. Thus, the quality of decision making is a significant determinant of the degree to which goals are attained, people are satisfied, and development takes place.

The quality of decision making in organizations is influenced by many things, but one of the most important is the quality and quantity of information available. Among other things, good decision making requires that adequate and timely information be available to managers making decisions. Information is provided by the communication system, and, therefore, the effectiveness of organizational communication determines the quality and quantity of information available for decision makers.

Producing.   Not only do decisions have to be made, but people also have to produce for organizations to be effective. There is increasing evidence today that many of the problems associated with producing are more closely related to attitudes and motivation than to any other cause. In short, people must be motivated to produce if organizations are to be effective. Motivating people to produce is a matter of integrating organizational goals and individual goals. This integration takes place through *communication.* Thus, communication effectiveness influences the producing process and, consequently, organizational effectiveness.

In addition to these two purposes of organizational communication, we would emphasize a related third purpose implied above—that of integration of all processes affecting organizational effectiveness. It is through communication that the decision-making and producing processes are related (and that all other organizational processes are related for that matter).

To some degree this model is both a model of communication in organizations and of the "role" of communication in organizations. We see organizational communication as *one* of the most important systems affecting organizational effectiveness. In another light, we also see organizational communication as the system through which the subsystems of decision making and producing are integrated. In summary, the effectiveness of organizational communication is determined by the design of the formal communication subsystem, the climate in which the system operates, and people's abilities to communicate. The degree to which communication is effective influences the decision-making and producing processes and the integration of these two processes.

REVIEW AND DISCUSSION

1. What is meant by the systems approach to organization? How is the systems approach different from other approaches?

2. Explain what organizational effectiveness is and how it is affected by communication.

3. Describe the three elements of organizational communication.

4. Describe the internal elements of the organization.

5. What is meant by background factors in the model?

6. Pick an organization with which you are familiar and try to describe it using the model in the chapter as a framework.

Chapter Three

Organizational Communication Effectiveness

The effectiveness with which a society's organizations operate is of vital concern to everyone. Modern societies are highly complex and interdependent. Most people are members of many different organizations. Moreover, most people are to a large degree dependent on organizations to provide them with the things that they *need* to survive and the things that they *want* to enjoy life. In fact, in many societies most people are dependent on organizations for their livelihood. Thus, the effectiveness with which organizations perform is a major determinant of the quality of life available to the people who make up society, and the quality of communication contributes to this effectiveness.

Most people agree that societies' organizations need to be effective, but there is less understanding and agreement concerning what organizational effectiveness really is. To some people, organizational effectiveness means that the organization achieves its objectives; to others, it means that the organization is a good place to work; and to still others, it means that the organization is able to survive over a long period of time. As we see it, the general concept of organizational effectiveness includes two things: (1) the degree to which objectives are achieved, and (2) the efficiency with which objectives are achieved. Perhaps the classic statement of this view of effectiveness was made by Chester Barnard (1938). He stated that an organization is effective to the degree that it achieves its objectives and efficient to the degree that it does so with a minimum of resources and undesirable consequences. Thus we agree with Gibson and his colleagues, who state that ". . . organizational effectiveness is the extent to which an organization achieves its objectives within the constraints of limited resources" (1973, p. 20).

We intend to explain the concept of organizational effectiveness and indicate the role of communication in effectiveness. Since our overall purpose is the development of an understanding of the impact of communication on organizational effectiveness, we should establish a common frame of reference for the concept of effectiveness. To do this we will, first, make explicit some of our assumptions about organizations; second, explore some of the more important theories relevant to the subject; and third, present a model of effectiveness. The rest of this book will be devoted to examining the role which quality communication fulfills in aiding organizations to achieve effectiveness.

Basic Assumptions About Organizations

All models or theories are built on a philosophical foundation and the concept of organizational effectiveness is no different. The philosophical foundation of organizational effectiveness includes basic values and beliefs about the nature and purpose of organizations themselves. To understand and fully appreciate what is said about organizational effectiveness we need to be aware of the values and beliefs which underlie the discussion. The most important assumptions about organizations which determine our beliefs about organizational effectiveness deal with what organizations are, why they exist, and what they do. Each of these will be considered below. The assumptions to be discussed will build upon the definition of organizations offered in chapter one.

What Organizations Are

"An organization is a structured process in which persons interact for objectives" (Hicks 1972, p. 23). This view of an organization contains several important elements. First of all, organizations are always made up of people. Second, the people in organizations interact; that is, the people in organizations are related to each other in some fashion. Third, the interactions of the people are ordered by some structure that can be described. Fourth, the structured interactions are designed to achieve the *personal* objectives of the people interacting. In short, people join and/or participate in organizations in order to achieve their own personal objectives. Finally, the interactions which result in the achievement of personal objectives also influence the achievement of superordinate organizational objectives that may or may not be identical to the personal objectives of any member of the organization. This somewhat simple view of organization leads to a second important assumption.

Why Organizations Exist

The ultimate purpose of an organization is to serve individuals. Organizations come into existence and remain in existence only because they help individuals achieve objectives that they could not otherwise achieve by themselves and/or because they make the achievement of personal objectives easier. Organizations are the tools of people; in the final analysis they are the means for achievement of personal objectives rather than ends in themselves.

These assumptions do not imply that organizations do not have objectives or that organizations exist to serve the interests of only one group of people whose objectives are similar. It is through the achievement of superordinate organizational objectives that the achievement of personal objectives is made possible. While the achievement of individual objectives is the purpose of organizations, there are many different groups of individuals whose objectives must be served. Successful organizations must serve the needs of the people who comprise the organization (owners, managers, and employees) and the needs of customers, suppliers, and society in general. The important point is that organizations exist to serve individuals rather than the individuals existing to serve organizations.

Organizations Are Integrative Social Processes

The above assumptions point out that organizations are social systems made up of people interacting according to some more or less defined pattern or structure. The existence of such structured interaction results in status and role relationships which affect the behavior of individuals in the organization. Thus, the behavior exhibited by individuals in organizations is socially as well as psychologically determined.

In addition to being social systems, organizations are also integrative (and, hopefully, synergistic) in nature. Organizations combine physical resources, technology, and human resources to produce output. More specifically, organizations apply human effort and ability to physical resources through technology to produce outputs. Hopefully, this combination of resources produces outputs that are greater than the sum of the three inputs. Only social systems such as organizations (because of the nature of human ability) are capable of producing outputs in excess of the simple sum of the inputs.

In summary, organizations exist to serve society through serving the needs of various groups of individuals, and they do this through a process which combines physical and human resources with technology to achieve superordinate organizational objectives. These assumptions about organizations are the base of organizational effectiveness.

The Theory of Organizational Effectiveness

While there is little theory whose chief objective is the identification and explanation of concrete criteria of organizational effectiveness, both economic theory and systems theory help provide a framework for identifying such criteria. The most important elements of economic theory and systems theory may help to shed some light on the concept of organizational effectiveness. We start with economic theory because it is the oldest and because it deals specifically with what is the most basic criteria—survival. From economic theory the discussion moves to systems theory.

Economic Theory and Effectiveness

Economics was probably the first science to deal in any systematic manner with organizational effectiveness. It should be pointed out that early economic theory dealt mainly with profit-seeking organizations rather than all organizations in general; however, most of the concepts apply to nonprofit seeking organizations with little modification.

Classical economic theory dealt primarily with explaining organizational effectiveness rather than with the development of criteria of effectiveness. In the classical system, effectiveness was measured by profitability, and profitability, in turn, was the chief determinant of whether or not the firm survived. So economic theory advanced survival of the organization as the major criterion of effectiveness, and survival is still the ultimate criterion of organizational effectiveness. For that reason, we present a brief discussion of the basic concepts from the classical economic theory that are relevant to this point.

Economic Man. Classical economics explained the behavior of people with the economic man concept, which assumed that people were motivated solely by money and that all of their characteristics were economic. Moreover, it was also believed that the economic man concept was representative of all people. Adam Smith's classic statement (1937, p. 14) that "it is not from the benevolence of the butcher, brewer, or baker that we expect our dinner, but from their own regard to their own self-interest" vividly illustrates the idea of the economic man. It was believed that people (and organizations) tried to maximize their economic rewards and satisfaction and that they responded primarily to wages and costs.

Harmony of Interests. The second fundamental belief of classical economics was that a harmony of interests existed between individuals or organizations and society as a whole (Oser 1963). The idea was that if individuals and organizations were allowed to own property and to pursue their own best interests (profit) free from governmental regulation, competition would develop and regulate the actions of people and organizations so that the best interests of society were served. In short, each individual and organization seeking its own objectives serves the best interests of society.

Competition.   With people being motivated by economic causes and having personal and organizational freedom, competition would develop to regulate behavior so that it was in the best interests of society (Oser 1963). Competition regulated behavior through the operation of the laws of demand and supply.

The economic concept *demand* refers to the amount of a good or service that people will buy at a particular price. Demand was believed to be determined by peoples' wants and tastes and by their economic means. The law of demand states that, for most goods and services, the higher the price, the less people will buy; or conversely, the lower the price, the more people will buy. Thus, the amount of a good or service people buy is usually inversely related to the price of the good or service.

The economic concept *supply* refers to the amount of a good or service that people and organizations will make available at a particular price. Supply was thought to be influenced primarily by the costs of production. The law of supply indicated that producers would normally supply more of a good or service the higher the price received. Thus, supplies of goods and services were related to price in a positive manner.

Competition operates through the interaction of demand and supply in the following way. If more of a good or service is demanded than is supplied, prices and profits will increase. This happened because consumers would "bid" up the prices of the item in short supply. Conversely, if more of a good or service is supplied than is demanded, producers will "bid" down the price and profits will decrease. Thus, consumers competing for goods and services and producers competing for profit will regulate individual and organizational behavior so that society gets the amount of goods and services that it wants at the price it is willing to pay.

Profit Maximization.   Since they were motivated by money, individuals and organizations were believed to try to maximize their profits. Because of competition profit maximization for all firms occurred when producers supplied exactly the amount of goods and services that people would buy at the price they were willing to pay.

Profit and Survival.   In a system where people and organizations were free to choose what they would do and where profit was the incentive for production, organizations that failed to make a profit or that made less than "minimum" profits would die. In such a system profit is a necessity for survival. Thus profit determines survival and profit is determined by how well society is served.

Survival and Effectiveness.   While classical economic theory dealt mainly with profit-seeking organizations, the same logic applies to nonprofit organizations. Organizations that serve society and the various specific groups—employees, owners, customers, and suppliers—associated with them are the ones that survive in the long run. For example, colleges which continue to draw students, raise money, and maintain faculty will survive and would, therefore, be considered effective. The college which fails to attract students and cannot raise money will be forced to close its doors. So it seems reasonable to conclude that survival is the ultimate measure of organizational effectiveness.

Systems Theory and Effectiveness

Modern systems theory builds upon classical economic theory to provide a more detailed explanation of organizational effectiveness. In this section the concepts of systems theory that are most relevant to organizational effectiveness are discussed.

The Concept of System. "A system in the simplest sense of the word, is a 'set of objects together with the relationships between the objects and between their attributes' " (Seiler et al. 1967, p. 4). Thus a system is some entity made up of a series of parts where each of the parts interacts with and affects each of the other parts and the whole.

A second important idea in systems theory is the concept of feedback. The idea is that all systems are part of some larger system. System entities of the type mentioned above produce some consequences (have some outcomes) which feed back on the system entity. More specifically feedback is the primary source of the system's interaction with its environment and it is the element that makes the system dynamic and able to learn from its experiences (Gibson 1973).

Systems and Organizations. As a system, organizations can be looked at, as indicated in figure 3-1, as input-process-output cycles. The organization takes resources,

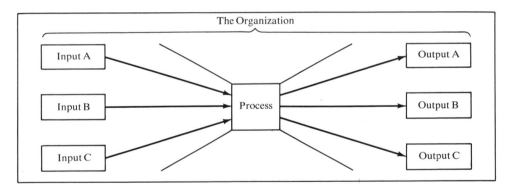

Figure 3-1   Organizations as Input-Process-Output Cycles

processes these resources, and produces some outputs. In turn, these outputs feed back through the environment to affect the organization itself. Examples of this input-process-output cycle are all around us—for example, universities process resources to help people learn and develop new knowledge.

Seiler (1967) identifies four classes of organization inputs—human, social, technological, and organizational. Human inputs consist of the skills, knowledge, attitudes, values, motives, and ways of behaving that the immediate members (employees) of the organization bring to it. Social inputs include mainly the prescribed roles, statuses, and values that develop and that affect both the processes and outputs of the organization. Organizational inputs include the choices, such as the reward system, the leadership style, and the way jobs are structured, that the organization makes about how it will use resources to produce outputs. Technological inputs refer to the way work is done in the organization. These four inputs are combined to produce some outputs.

Seiler further identifies the outputs of organizations as productivity, satisfaction, and development. Productivity refers to the ratio of inputs to outputs and therefore to producing outputs with minimum use of resources. Satisfaction refers to fulfilling the needs of employees. Development refers to the organization's ability to continue to live in harmony with its environment.

We can see that Seiler's concept of organizational effectiveness is similar to that which we advanced in the summary statement of the model of organizational communication in the previous chapter. In fact, the entire model in chapter two contains a number of similarities to the Seiler model.

Systems View of Effectiveness.   The systems concept of organizational effectiveness emphasizes two things: (1) the survival of the organization depends on its ability to adapt to its environment and (2) the total cycle of input-process-output must be the focus of managerial attention (Gibson 1973).

The systems view of effectiveness implies that organizations have to live in both the short run and the long run. An organization can "die" in the short run while preparing for the long run. So too, an organization can die by living entirely in the short run and neglecting long-run adaptation. So the systems view of effectiveness focuses on maintaining the proper balance between short-run and long-run survival.

Model of Organizational Effectiveness

While both economic and systems theory provide concepts which help to understand organizational effectiveness, what the potential and practicing manager needs is a model that is consistent with established theory and also meaningful in the real world of organizations. We believe that the model described below fits both of these criteria.*

Criteria of Effectiveness

Essentially this is an integration of the economic and systems criteria with a time dimension added (Gibson 1973). As figure 3-2 indicates, survival is the ultimate criterion of organizational effectiveness. In a democratic private enterprise society only those organizations which satisfy the interests of employees, customers, suppliers, and society as a whole on a continuing basis will survive. Those that do not will either die or by "due process" be "killed" or controlled.

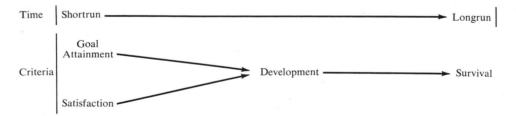

SOURCE: Adapted from J.L. Gibson, J. M. Ivancevich, J.H. Donnelly, *Organizations Structure, Processes, Behavior* (Dallas: Business Publications, 1973). Used by permission.

Figure 3-2   Model of Organizational Effectiveness

---

*We point out again that our thinking about organizational effectiveness has been heavily influenced by Gibson, *Organizations,* 1973. The discussion which follows draws heavily on this source.

Long-run survival depends primarily on shorter term efforts to adapt to the environment or to develop. In this sense development refers to the changes in the organization's ability to solve problems of adaptation and ultimately to the organization's ability to continue to achieve its goals and provide satisfaction to its members. Goal attainment and satisfaction are short-run measures of organizational effectiveness. These are the things that can be observed on a daily or yearly basis to determine how effectively the organization is operating.

There is no simple list of criteria of organizational effectiveness. Different criteria with different time frames must be used to arrive at a subjective estimate of the effectiveness of any organization at a given point in time. The degree of goal attainment and employee satisfaction provide indications of short-run effectiveness which can be combined with measures of development that indicate intermediate term effectiveness to come to some conclusions about the organization's ability to survive in the long run.

Studies of Effectiveness

While systematic studies of organizational effectiveness are not plentiful, there have been some attempts to empirically study organizational effectiveness. For the most part, these studies support the model of effectiveness presented above. One study (Geogopoulos 1957) found that effectiveness was directly related to productivity and flexibility and inversely related to tension. Productivity and flexibility were defined similarly to goal attainment and development respectively in our model and tension corresponded to satisfaction. A second study (Mott 1972) found productivity, adaptability, and flexibility related to effectiveness. Friedlander and Pickle (1968) determined that the three measures of profitability, satisfaction, and perceived social value were significantly interrelated. Certainly these studies do not "prove" our model but they do tend to support its logic with hard evidence.

Measuring Organizational Effectiveness

Since survival is the ultimate criterion of effectiveness it is easy to measure organizational effectiveness in hindsight. It is merely a matter of looking back to see if and/or for how long the organization survived. Such measurement is of only limited value, however, since managers and others concerned with organizational effectiveness need effectiveness measures that provide some guidance through prediction.

The methods of measuring organizational effectiveness are practically useful but are far from perfect. Generally speaking, the farther into the future the criterion being measured falls, the less satisfactory it is. The discussion of the measurement of organizational effectiveness begins with short-run measures and proceeds forward in time.

Short-term Measures of Effectiveness.   While the measures are not precise, both the degree of goal attainment and employee satisfaction are capable of being measured on at least practically useful levels. Several alternatives exist for measuring goal attainment. Some of the more commonly used measures are profit, costs, customers served, and the like. Regardless of the specific measures of goal attainment, the currently popular technique of Management by Objectives (MBO) is probably the most systematic way of measuring short-run goal attainment. In its most elemental form, MBO is a process where specific measurable organizational objectives are set on a continuing basis and progress toward the achievement of the objectives is systematically measured on a periodic basis.*

Various measures of satisfaction also exist. Among them are measures of employee turnover, absenteeism, tardiness, grievances, and data on attitudes. The best measure of true satisfaction is probably a combination of the various tangible effects of satisfaction (such as turnover) coupled with well-conducted periodic attitude surveys. Attitudinal data can be collected by in-depth unstructured interviews, projective tests, and by objective pencil and paper questionnaires. By far the most widely used are objective pencil and paper questionnaires.† Results of such questionnaires can be compared with previous measurements and other organizations and can be used with tangible measures to arrive at a fairly accurate indication of the level of satisfaction being produced.

Intermediate Measures of Development. Because they deal more with the future than with the present, measures of development, if anything, are less precise than the measures of goal attainment and satisfaction. However, useful measures of development do exist. The most commonly used measures of organizational development are pencil and paper questionnaire surveys dealing not so much with employee attitudes, but with ideas and opinions about such things as how problems are solved, how information is shared, how conflict is handled, how decisions are made, the degree of candidness and openness in interpersonal communication, and so on.‡ Measures of employees' opinions about these things can be compared to previous measurements to determine what changes have taken place and to measurement in other organizations and normative theory to determine the relative level of development of the organization. A second measure of development that is sometimes used is public image. The idea is to measure indirectly how well the organization is serving society by measuring such things as community and customer relations, and the like.

Measures of Survival. Realistically, there is no way to measure survival itself except in retrospect. Practically speaking, survival depends on both short-term and intermediate-term effectiveness, so combining these two types of effectiveness measures provides a useful predictor of the organization's ability to adapt and survive in the long run.

Communication and Effectiveness

It is a basic assumption in this book that organizational communication is a primary determinant of organizational effectiveness. Organizations combine resources (human, physical, and technological) to produce outputs. This combination process

---

*See George S. Odiorne, *Management by Objectives* (New York: Pitman, 1965); John W. Humble, ed., *Management by Objectives in Action* (London: McGraw-Hill Book Co., 1970); W. J. Reddin, *Effective Management by Objectives* (New York: McGraw-Hill, 1970); and Aubrey Sanford, *Human Relations: Theory and Practice* (Columbus, Ohio: Charles E. Merrill, 1973), pp. 322-80, for more detailed explanations of the MBO process.

†Objective attitude survey questionnaires are available from several sources. One widely used instrument is the *SRA Employee Inventory* (Chicago: Science Research Associates).

‡A widely used instrument for this purpose is *CRUSK* developed by and available from the Center for Research and Utilization of Scientific Knowledge, Institute for Social Research, The University of Michigan, Ann Arbor.

requires decision making and the application of human effort. In short, organization requires that people interact, communicate, and cooperate. People in the organization must maintain some level of communication. While effective communication does not insure organizational effectiveness, ineffective communication precludes effective organization. Communication is the vehicle through which cooperation and coordination are possible, as suggested in the definition of organizations in chapter one.

Summary

Organizations are effective to the degree that they achieve their goals, provide satisfaction for their members, and grow and develop in their ability to continue to do both of these things. The ultimate measure of effectiveness—survival—depends on these three things.

Our view of organizational effectiveness is based on certain assumptions. Organizations are structured processes where people interact to achieve objectives and organizations exist to help individuals achieve their objectives and satisfy their needs. Also, organizations are social processes which integrate material and human resources through technology.

The theory of organizational effectiveness is based mainly on economic and systems theory. Economic theory proposes that survival is the ultimate criterion of effectiveness. Systems theory elaborates on that view to point out that organizations are themselves systems which are part of larger systems and that survival depends on the degree to which all interested parties are served and therefore to the degree that the organization is able to live in harmony with its environment. Studies of organizational effectiveness generally tend to support these ideas. Measures of organizational effectiveness are less than precise but are useful to assess the relative degree of effectiveness.

REVIEW AND DISCUSSION

1. Explain the three basic assumptions about organizations.

2. Explain the concept of organizational effectiveness implicit in classical economic theory.

3. Explain the systems approach to organizational effectiveness.

4. Describe the model of organizational effectiveness presented in the chapter.

5. Explain how organizational effectiveness and communication are related.

6. Using the model of effectiveness presented in the chapter, explain why some organizations with which you are familiar "live" or have "died."

PART ONE: Organizational Communication

Incidents

The Family Reunion

The Lawrence family of Texas is large and spread all over the state. Members are engaged in numerous activities such as farming, manufacturing, and oil exploration. Each year the whole family meets for a reunion at a different state park. A member is elected to the job of planning the reunion for the next year. Last year Leonard Lawrence, thirty-five, personnel manager of the Lone Star Bank in Dallas, was selected. Normally, about 400 members of the family show up and each contributes $20 to a special account to be used for the next year's reunion. In the account this year is $8,400. The family gathering is held over the Labor Day weekend and it is the responsibility of the planner to arrange for the food and entertainment.

Leonard wanted the widest possible participation and involvement in this year's reunion. After listening to suggestions from a number of family members, he had arranged for this year's outing to be held at the Smith State Park near Waco. Since the park is located near the center of the state and was well recommended, it seemed like an ideal location.

In the past different members have avoided some family reunions because they did not feel that they were consulted in the planning. To insure that everyone felt included this year, Leonard, during his business travels, made an effort to talk with every faction of the Lawrence family about the upcoming reunion. During these meetings, he asked what the member liked and disliked about previous reunions and what they would like to see this year. From these discussions Leonard obtained much information about the attitudes of family members. To insure that everyone learned about what was taking place at each phase of the reunion planning, he initiated a newsletter which he mailed to every member of the family regularly. The newsletter contained information about the park, maps, ideas for entertainment and so forth. He got permission from family members to stage an early election of next year's reunion chairman through the newsletter and Jill Lawrence, a Houston high school teacher, was elected. Leonard was very concerned about making Jill feel a part of the planning so he consulted her at each phase. He wanted to be sure that she had a good start in planning next year's reunion.

As Labor Day drew closer, Leonard sent special reunion invitations to each family member. He also mailed out a list of possible activities which he had arranged from the earlier discussions with members. He had been careful to plan activities for all age groups. In the past, a number of the older family members had wanted to attend the reunion but had been unable to do so because they did not have transportation. To help this year, Leonard had arranged for others to pick up elderly members and bring them. He had reserved rooms in the park lodge for those members requesting them and had established a shuttle bus service to get members from the lodge to reunion activities.

For the children, Leonard, upon the suggestion of one of the younger members of the family, had set aside a "reservation" where all the Lawrence children could camp out and cook their own meals. He hired a college student to supervise.

On the first day of the reunion all of Leonard's efforts seemed to pay off. Nearly 550 Lawrence family members registered at the gathering.

"This is the best darned reunion I have ever been to, Lenny," said one of the older Lawrences. "I have been coming to these things for forty years and I have never seen a better one."

By all those in attendance, this year's Lawrence family reunion was judged successful.

Guidelines for Analysis

1. Why do you think that this year's reunion was so successful?

2. Using the model of organizational communication presented early in this part, analyze the communication within the Lawrence family. Was high-quality "organizational" communication achieved? Why?

3. In your own words, characterize Leonard's leadership style. Do you think his leadership contributed to the success of the reunion?

4. What criteria might be established to judge the effectiveness of a family organization? Are these criteria realistic in terms of your own family?

5. What steps did Leonard take in investing in the future development of the Lawrence family reunion? What is your reaction to these steps?

6. If the definition of Leonard's task was "the planning of the Lawrence family reunion," would you agree that the task influenced the communication within the family? Why?

7. What formal techniques of communication did Leonard implement to help with the reunion? Do you think that these techniques helped organizational communication? Why?

8. Simply, describe your perception of the climate within the family organization before Leonard assumed the leadership role. How about after he stepped down as leader? What differences are apparent?

The Prospectus

Becky Hale, twenty-six, holds the B.S. from Midwestern State University in marketing and since graduation she has been employed as a sales representative for Hunter Manufacturing Company, makers of home recreation centers such as swimming pools, game rooms, and patios. Most of Becky's contacts are with contractors and construction supply firms. She markets Hunter's design concepts and support services to these groups, who in turn deal directly with the customer, the homeowner. Becky likes her job and she enjoys the salary-plus-incentive system she works under. Her supervisor at Hunter is Ann Meyer, sales manager, who had Becky's job before she was promoted. Ann has worked at Hunter since she completed her M.B.A. at Marion University eight years ago. Both Ann and Becky are ambitious and basically "promotion minded" (in that they are normally submitting ideas to top management about possible new markets for Hunter products).

In her spare time, Becky plays tennis to stay physically fit. During the spring, summer and fall, she tries to play every day. But during the last year or so, she has been having some trouble getting on a tennis court. It seems that everyone in town is playing tennis. Sometimes Becky and her partner will go out as early as 7 A.M. and there will still be four or five players waiting to get on a public court. She has also noticed that many families are playing tennis. Some people seem to wait up to two or three hours to get on a public court. Recently Becky called up the Northside Tennis Club to ask about membership. She was told that membership for a single person in the club cost $350 per year. In addition, she would have to pay $10 an hour to play on the club's indoor courts or $5 an hour on the outdoor courts. Membership for a family cost even more. Becky decided not to join the tennis club but it did give her an idea.

"If some families would be willing to pay $1,000 just to play tennis at a private club, I wonder how much they would pay for their own private court at their homes," Becky asked Ann during one of their regular meetings. "Before, a tennis court was thought of as a luxury of the rich. But I bet with our company's skill, we could design a low-cost, scaled-down model which many people could afford. Listen Ann, you only have to be standing in line at 7 A.M. on a weekday waiting for a court to realize how popular tennis is."

Ann gave Becky the "go ahead" to do more research on the topic. Later, Becky came back with data which suggested that 20 percent of the homes in their area sat on at least an acre, the minimum property requirement, and were zoned to allow a court to be constructed. She also uncovered some statistics to suggest that the number of people playing tennis has increased nearly 400 percent in the last two years. After getting some preliminary cost estimates, she found that a tennis court with chain-link fence could be built for around $3,500, well within the price range of many people, and not much when she considered that many people were paying $1,000 just to belong to a tennis club.

Ann was beginning to share Becky's enthusiasm about the project. She called her boss, the Hunter vice-president for marketing, to ask for the procedure for the sales department to suggest a new market. As Ann sounded out her boss on the plan, she thought that she was getting encouragement.

"You write all this up. Send a copy to me, to the vice-president of production, one to market research, and one to the controller. We'll get back to you when we have a decision," Ann's boss told her.

Becky and Ann spent the next five weeks developing a detailed prospectus of their ideas. The document was well supported and was nearly 100 pages when it was finally complete. The prospectus called for a line of mass-produced tennis courts selling for around $3,500 marketed directly to the customer out of the Hunter Sales Office.

As Ann signed the final copies and delivered them herself to the appropriate offices, she was confident that she and Becky had identified a new and potentially highly profitable market for Hunter. "Maybe they will put us in charge of the new swimming pool division," Becky said to Ann as they finished deliveries.

Weeks passed with no word on their prospectus. One night Becky had dinner with a member of the marketing research department at Hunter. In casual conversation, Becky's dinner companion mentioned that his department had done some work with her and Ann's proposal and the results were very positive. "Our department liked your figures and we did two surveys and both indicated that there might be a market for your product. We submitted a favorable report nearly four weeks ago with the recommendation to 'go ahead' on a limited basis," said the researcher. "We understood that the brass was going to consider the idea weeks ago."

Becky was disconcerted by this information. The first thing the next morning, she was in Ann's office to report on her dinner conversation the previous evening.

"What do you think we ought to do?" Becky asked Ann.

Guidelines for Analysis

1. What do you think Ann and Becky ought to do next? Why?

2. From only the information we have contained in the situation above, characterize the communication in the Hunter Manufacturing Company.

3. Using the models of communication presented in this part as a basis, draw your own model of the communication between Becky and her boss, Ann; between Ann and her boss, the vice-president of marketing.

4. List five possible reasons which might account for the current situation in the sales department at Hunter. Which reason do you feel is most justified by the facts, as they are presented in the background above? Why?

5. If you were Becky, what would be going through your mind if you were again ready to suggest a new market for Hunter? Why?

6. Do you think that Becky was justified in submitting the prospectus? Was the handling of the prospectus appropriate for the situation? What changes may have been made?

7. In terms of the functions of organizational communication covered in this part (i.e. integration, coordination), what functions do you see organizational communication providing at Hunter?

8. What techniques might you suggest to improve communication within Hunter? How might these techniques be used?

The Class Gift

The senior class of Highland High, a suburban school in the west, is approaching graduation. A tradition at Highland is for the senior class to present the school with some kind of gift. The gift would serve as a remembrance to the school of the class. Normally, the primary job of the executive committee of the class (the class president, vice-president, secretary, and treasurer) is to organize the efforts of the class in providing the class gift. Gene Felman, the senior class president, has been unable to rally support behind his ideas. All year long, Gene has been pushing a drive for added books for the school library, which he considers to be chronically undersupplied. He has been collecting books himself all year and he thinks the $4,500 the senior class normally raises should go into the fund drive for new books.

Although classmates and teachers have commended Gene's activities on behalf of the library, his plan to make the book drive the senior class gift does not have wide support among class members. In the vote to determine the gift, held two months ago, the book drive finished in a four-way tie with three other proposals. The school Letterman's Club has proposed a senior gift of a system of lighting for the school's baseball field. The Letterman's Club seems to have the support of the varsity cheerleaders and the Pep Club. Larry Layton, president of the Highland Marching Scotchmen, the Highland school band, suggested that the senior class gift be new band uniforms and choir robes. This idea has some support because the uniforms and the current robes are nearly twenty years old. The final idea for the class gift came from the Future Teachers of America Club who felt that the money in the senior fund should be donated to the local Boys' and Girls' Clubs which were each attempting to broaden their programs among disadvantaged and minority children in Highland. Most students in the class felt that each suggestion had merit and that accounted for the four-way "dead heat" during the voting. In cases of ties, the school constitution states that the class executive committee will decide how the money will be spent. But Gene has not been able to get any of the other members of the committee to go along with his ideas about the book drive for the library.

In recent weeks, the situation has worsened. Supporters of each of the four suggestions for class gifts have begun collecting money from people in the community for their respective class gift ideas. Gene has been told that each group has been claiming that they are collecting for the "official" class gift. A number of local merchants have called the school principal to complain about being contacted by four groups soliciting money. None of the groups had been authorized by the class executive committee or the school administration to collect money. A great deal of confusion has spread over the class as to exactly what is going to happen. Gene is torn between his feeling that the class must get this situation resolved, regardless of the outcome, and his support for his own proposal. But he is confused as to what should be done. The problem has come out in a number of classes. In one English IV class, the teacher almost had to break up a fist fight between a member of the varsity base-ball team and a member of the band when each of them read essays they had written supporting their ideas for a class gift. Normally apathetic students, who rarely take any interest in class politics, have chosen sides. The class gift has been the major topic of discussion in the cafeteria and on school buses every day. The school faculty and administration appeared to have taken a "hands off" attitude about the issue, apparently leaving it to the class to decide.

Two recent meetings of the class executive committee have had to be cancelled when they turned into shouting matches among groups supporting each of the four proposals.

"I think Gene Felman should resign as class president because he is so tied to one proposal," yelled one of the Lettermen at the last meeting. A number of students seemed to agree with him.

It appears that none of the warring groups understand the motivations and reasons of the other groups. Inaccurate rumors and distorted information are rampant in the class. Groups have not taken the opportunity to sit down with each other to explain their respective positions. Members of the school newspaper staff have editorially supported the gift to the local Boys' and Girls' Clubs and have not given space to other groups to write about their suggestions.

Since it is already May and graduation is less than six weeks away, the situation has become tense. Two very unpleasant results are likely to occur unless this matter is resolved. First, many of the fun activities of graduation (class trip, graduation ceremonies, class party, and so on) are being threatened by the controversy. Second, if no decision is made the money already raised by the class will revert back into the general fund of the school and there will be no class gift at all.

Guidelines for Analysis

1. In your own words describe what you consider to be the state of organizational communication within the senior class of Highland High.

2. Using the definitions of organizations presented early in this part, what are some of the things wrong with this organization?

3. List five things which might be done to improve operations within the class. Tell how each of the ideas from your list would help the situation.

4. Should Gene Felman resign from his position of leadership within the class? What is to be gained if he stays? What would happen if he were to resign?

5. Can you select a methodology which might allow members of the class to evaluate the four proposals suggested for the class gift? Would this help to resolve the problems within the class?

6. What steps might be taken to restore communication among class members? Do you think that this conflict over the gift will likely spread to other class activities? Why?

7. If you were called in as an expert in organizational communication, what would you do to help the class? Provide a rationale for each of your ideas.

8. Characterize, in your own words, the climate within the class. Why did this type of climate result?

Modern Methods

The McGeorge Electronic Company has a patent to produce a tiny component which is used in the manufacturing of transistor radios and televisions. The firm employs 1,200 workers in two plants located in Springdale, a city of 35,000 in the Pacific Northwest. Owen Simms founded McGeorge nearly twenty-five years ago and has watched the firm grow rapidly. He was personally responsible for hiring many of the current employees. Through the years the firm has maintained a "hometown family" atmosphere. But the grueling fourteen-hour workdays that Owen has been keeping have begun to have their effect on him. His physician recently advised him to step down as chief executive officer (CEO) of McGeorge and remain only as chairman of the board.

Kevin Simms, Owen's thirty-two-year-old son, has been working for his father for ten years after he received his electrical engineering degree from Northwest State University. For the past six years, Kevin has been working on his M.B.A. at night. He recently received the degree. Fresh out of college, Kevin started as a shipping clerk and eventually worked his way up through various management levels to his present position as vice-president of production, one of the five members of "upper management" who work with Owen. Kevin is bright, aggressive, and did a commendable job at each position as he rose through the ranks. He has widespread support among the management team to replace his father as CEO.

But Owen has some doubts about his son as CEO. In their many opportunities to talk about the future of McGeorge, over the years, they have very different ideas about how the organization should function. Owen would like to keep all of his longtime employees on until their retirement. He likes it when they drop in his office to chat about their jobs and families. He has often been invited to the weddings and graduations of the children of his employees. He takes great pride in the knowledge that his workers are the best paid in Springdale and that almost all say they like their jobs at McGeorge. Kevin has taken a different approach to the employees. He has told his father that McGeorge needs highly skilled technicians from technical and trade schools in other towns. Over the years, he has hired nearly forty-five professional engineers from universities. Many of these have risen to middle management positions and are supervising the older employees, which the elder Simms hired years before.

Father and son have different ideas about marketing and growth. Owen is fairly content with the profit McGeorge has made making electronic components.

"We live comfortably, we do our part to help our community, we have made a profit every year since you were born," Owen has often told his son.

Kevin, on the other hand, has devoted some of his department's budget to research and development and has three new products ready for manufacturing If one of the products hits, he is confident that the total assets of McGeorge could double in three years. But the new products would require a bank loan, much training for employees, re-tooling some of the manufacturing stations, and, perhaps, the construction of a new plant. Since McGeorge has never borrowed money, Owen has been hesitant to approve Kevin's plans, even though they have the complete support of the other members of the management team.

"You've got good ideas here, no question about it," Owen told Kevin, "but we're just a small organization. One of the things that bothers me most is that you want to build the new plant in Seattle. What would all the folks think here in Springdale? They would say that McGeorge is deserting them after all these years."

However, about six months ago, Owen finally gave a limited "go ahead" to the three products Kevin proposed. Although Owen has high trust in his son's judgment, he is hesitant about turning over the daily management of McGeorge to him. Many of Owen's old "cronies" have stopped in recently to ask him about their fate if Kevin takes over. Their concern bothers Owen greatly. He feels a deep loyalty to his employees and he wants to see them protected.

"Dad, the twentieth century is here. We must expand our thinking beyond the city limits of Springdale. We have a good product, the possibilities of new markets, and sound management," Kevin said to his father after he raised his concern at the last meeting of the management team. "Don't worry. Things will be run effectively."

Guidelines for Analysis

1. To your way of thinking, under the leadership of Owen, was McGeorge an effective organization? Do you think that it would be effective under Kevin? Why?

2. Characterize the organizational communication which probably existed under Owen. How do you think organizational communication would change under Kevin? Why?

3. Review the criteria of effectiveness presented in this part. In terms of the criteria, rate the effectiveness of McGeorge under Owen. Rate McGeorge, using the same criteria, a year after Kevin has taken over. What changes are likely to occur?

4. Think of your own working "style." In which McGeorge would you prefer to work (Owen's or Kevin's)? Why?

5. Do you think the style which Owen manifests in the situation above is still present in today's organizations? Why?

6. In your opinion, who should establish the criteria by which an organization should be judged? Are different groups (stockholders, workers, the general public) likely to judge organizations by different standards? Does it make sense to talk about the "right" standards?

7. Using the situation above as a springboard, what are some other criteria by which we might judge organizational effectiveness? Provide a rationale for each of your criteria.

8. How important is communication in helping achieve organizational effectiveness? Can organizations be effective without communication? Why?

PART TWO

ENVIRONMENTAL BACKGROUND FACTORS

Chapter Four

Cultural and Economic Influences

Organizations of any type are *open systems*. That is, they exist within an environment; they are significantly affected by this environment; and they, in turn, affect the environment of which they are a part. The specific external environment is different for various types of organizations in various locations.

"The external environment is made up of those influences which are beyond the boundary of the organization, but which interact with it" (Tosi and Hamner 1974, p. 5). For our purposes, the relevant external environment consists of those aspects of culture and economics which significantly affect the internal elements of the organization and organizational communication. These are certainly not all of the external environmental influences that affect organizations; but they are the more important ones. The discussion is limited to these two environmental influences.

Culture and Organizations

Organizations develop and exist as a part of a larger social system commonly referred to as society. One of the more important aspects of any society is its culture. Thus, culture has important influences on organizations. If we are to truly understand organizational communication and behavior, we need to begin with an understanding of culture and how culture affects the organization.

The Concept of Culture

Culture has no universal definition. "The term has been variously defined as a society's attitudes, beliefs, and values; as all those features characteristic of a society's stage of advancement; and as all of a society's social, political, educational, legal and economic characteristics" (Hellriegel and Slocum 1974, p. 17). While all of these definitions are "correct," we need a more explicit conception of the term *culture*.

What Culture Really Is.   Culture is an all-inclusive term used to refer to the life-style of some identifiable group of people. It changes slowly and is transmitted from one generation to the next. In its simplest form, it refers to a "way of life" and to all of the components of that way of life. So, culture is not something that only some people have. Cultures differ, and some are more highly developed than are others; but all people and all environments have a "way of life" and, thus, a culture.

Elements of Culture.   Since culture refers to a way of life and to all of the components of that way of life, an exhaustive listing of all of the elements of culture is an impossible task, but the more important elements can be identified and described. The more important elements of culture that affect organizations are values, knowledge, and standards of conduct (Thompson and Van Houten 1970).

Values—One of the major components of any culture is its values. As we are using the term, *values* refer to general beliefs, ideas, opinions, attitudes, and so on about what is right or wrong and what is good or bad. The specific values of any culture are almost endless, but some values have greater effect on organizations than others. Farmer and Richman (1965) state that the following values in any culture have significant impact on organizations in that culture:

1. attitudes toward authority
2. attitudes toward wealth and material things
3. attitudes toward change and risk taking
4. attitudes toward freedom and independence
5. attitudes toward achievement and work
6. attitudes toward social status and the prestige of particular types of occupations
7. attitudes toward education in general and various types of education in particular
8. attitudes toward property and ownership

The specific form that these attitudes take have more or less obvious effects on organizations. We will comment more on this later.

Knowledge—A second major component of any culture is its knowledge. As an element of culture, knowledge refers to the level of development of the general state of knowledge and to the level of development of its application. It includes such things as:

1. the literacy level
2. the types of knowledge that exist
3. the level of scientific knowledge generally available

4. the prevalence of particular types of technical and scientific knowledge
5. the tools and machines available for use

As with the element of values, the specific forms of knowledge that exist have tremendous implications for organizations in that culture.

Standards of behavior—The third major element of all cultures is the standards and codes of acceptable and unacceptable behaviors. All societies and cultures develop patterns of behavior, known as roles, that individuals are expected to behave within or "live up to." These roles serve as the standards of behavior. The system of roles developed in any culture is elaborate and complex. Usually, no composite universal roles exist. Rather roles develop on a multitude of bases at varying levels. For example, roles usually develop on the basis of sex, age, occupation, marital status, social status, and so on.

These elements — values, knowledge, and standards of behavior — are the major cultural elements of the environment. They exist in some form in the particular environment that surrounds any organization.

Culture and the Environment

One of the definitions of culture presented earlier included as a part of culture the political, educational, legal, and economic characteristics of society. While this is valid, it is more useful to consider these elements as social institutions shaped by culture rather than fundamental elements of culture. These institutions are certainly a part of culture as we have defined it, but the particular form that these institutions take is highly dependent on the basic cultural elements of values, knowledge, and standards of behavior. Thus, the relationship can be shown as in figure 4-1. Culture shapes social institutions which determine the way of life in the society and the consequences of this way of life feed back on and affect cultural changes.

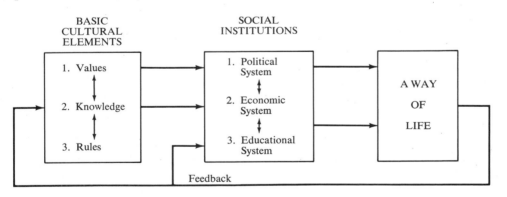

Figure 4-1   Model of Culture

Political System.   "The political system can be considered a subsystem of the cultural system" (Hellriegel and Slocum 1974, p. 28). Based on its values, knowledge, and standards of behavior, society establishes political systems to serve and regulate itself. The particular type of political system established is chiefly dependent on the particular form that the basic cultural variables take. From history and political science, most of us are familiar with the more common types of political systems — democracy, monarchy, and dictatorship.

Certainly the political system that exists has definite influences on organizations within the environment. In fact, much of the influence that culture has on organizations is indirectly exerted through the existing political system and government. An example is the current values associated with consumerism in our society. Many of the effects of these values on organizations are occurring through governmental legislation and regulation of business organizations. A very similar situation exists with respect to the ecology movement and with government regulation of air and water pollution. The culture that surrounds any organization has important, direct influences on the organization, but it also shapes political institutions which have tremendous effects on the organization. Or said another way, what happens "outside" the organization (environment) affects its internal process such as organizational communication.

Economic System. The economic system is also a cultural subsystem built upon the three basic cultural variables. In addition, the economic system is closely related to and in many respects an extension of the political system. Basically, the political system is the most immediate determinant of the type of economic system that is allowed to operate, and in systems such as that of the United States, it has a major influence on the nature of the economic conditions that exist at any given time. Because economic influences have such a major influence on internal organizational elements, they are discussed separately later in the chapter.

Educational System. The educational system is the third major subsystem included in our discussion of the cultural system; it is important because it is one of the primary means through which culture is transferred from one generation to the next generation. Probably even more than the economic system, the education system is a direct product of and reflects the three basic cultural elements of values, knowledge, and standards of behavior.

The educational system and the products it produces — technology and human skills — have immediate and direct influences on organizations and on communication behavior by organizational members. This system primarily determines the types of technology available to organizations and the availability of the skills needed by the organization.

As yet we have mainly been concerned with describing and explaining culture as a general element that exists in the environment of all organizations. We now turn our attention specifically to identifying the internal organizational elements most affected by culture.

Cultural Effects on Organizations

Culture, to a large degree, determines the general role that organizations will play in society and how they can operate in playing that role. That is, through its direct effects and through its indirect effects, culture determines the standards of behavior for organizations.

In this section, the internal organizational elements most affected by culture are identified. No attempt is made at explaining whether the effects occur directly on the organization or whether they occur through the political, economic, or educational system; the result is the same. The most important variables in our model of organizational communication affected by culture are the individual, managerial philosophy and assumptions, goals, technology, and structure.

Goals. Perhaps the first point of interface between the organization and its environment is organizational goals. It is primarily through the goals which they seek to achieve that organizations relate to their environment. More importantly, however, is the fact that culture largely determines what goals organizations can realistically seek. It is through communication that information about goals is transmitted to organizational members.

All organizations depend on society as their reason for being. Specifically, they depend on some customer group(s) as a market for their product or service. Thus, culture tends to limit the goals or objectives organizations can seek and the ways that they go about seeking their goals and objectives.

The Individual. At this point it should come as little or no surprise that culture is probably the primary, basic determinant of the individual. True, behavior is psychologically determined, but much behavior, as we shall see later in chapters six and ten, is learned behavior aimed at satisfying learned needs. Both needs and perceived goals are culturally influenced.

In a somewhat more practical vein, culture has certain specific influences on behavior. It tends to determine what individuals like and dislike; it tends to determine individual interaction, or communication patterns, i.e., who interacts with whom and what the nature of that interaction is. Take the example of students and professors. Acceptable standards of behavior are that individuals in these roles can interact in certain circumstances and not others and that the interactions that do take place be of a certain nature. Professors and students are expected to interact in their educational roles, but not necessarily in their social roles. Even the messages between the two groups are supposed to be formal, distant, and not intimate. We might conclude that certain cultural dimensions determine communication behavior.

Managerial Philosophy and Assumptions.   The element in the organizational communication model that is most closely associated with culture is managerial philosophy and assumptions. To a large degree managerial philosophy and assumptions are only a specialized part of a philosophy of life. If we look closely at the three major elements of culture, especially as they exist in the individual, they constitute an overall philosophy of life. Managerial philosophy stems directly from overall life philosophy and culture. Managerial philosophy and assumptions will be explored in detail later.

Technology.   The technology or, more specifically, the level of technology that is available to any organization with specific goals depends largely on the cultural elements of values and knowledge. Simply stated, values determine the emphasis placed on particular types of knowledge, research, and education in a society and those things in turn determine the level of technological development. Thus, culture tends to limit the technological alternatives available to organizations. Because of its importance as an internal organizational element, technology is discussed in detail in chapter eight.

  In a related manner culture determines the skills that are available to organizations to fill their jobs. While particular technological alternatives may be available to organizations, the necessary range of skills to implement particular technologies may or may not be available to organizations because of other cultural educational values and conditions. So, in the final analysis, culture influences both technological choices and the alternatives associated with the design of jobs within particular technological alternatives.

Organizational Structure.   If culture influences technology, it must also influence organizational structure because the two elements are closely related. To some degree, technology determines structure. In addition, such cultural variables as attitudes toward authority and the prestige associated with particular types of work and occupations influence how work is divided and how activities are related through the use of authority. On a practical level, these cultural attitudes tend to determine what organizations can and cannot reasonably require and expect people to do.

Leadership.   Last, but by no means least, culture affects the overall style of leadership in the organization. Again, attitudes concerning the legitimate use of authority and attitudes toward freedom and independence have a significant impact on the styles of leadership that are realistic alternatives for the organization. In behavioral terms, only styles, at least in the short run, which match culturally determined standards of behavior stand any real chance of being effective. Organizational leadership styles will be covered more thoroughly in chapter nine.

In later chapters, where appropriate, the influence of culture on the organization and on specific internal elements of the organizations is discussed further. We will end the discussion of culture by saying that organizations are in large part products of their environment, and culture is one of the major elements in that environment. We look now at one of the major cultural forces — economic system and economic conditions — that affects all organizations.

Economics and Organizations

All organizations, no matter whether they actively seek profit or exist for other reasons, use resources to try to achieve goals and satisfy people's needs. Because of this fact all operate within an economic system and are subject to the influence of whatever economic conditions happen to prevail. The second part of the chapter will provide a basic overview of the most important economic influences affecting organizations.

The Concept of Economics

The study of economics has been referred to in numerous ways. Thomas Carlyle (Oser 1963) called it the "dismal science." In contrast, Samuelson (1973) described it as "the queen of the social sciences." It is probably both of these things and many more besides.

What Economics Is. Most modern definitions of economics seem to focus on the allocation of a limited amount of resources in an attempt to satisfy an unlimited number of wants. The Nobel prize winner, Samuelson (1973, p. 3), provides the following definition:

> Economics is the study of how men and society end up in choosing, with or without the help of money, to employ *scarce* productive resources that could have alternative uses, to produce various commodities and distribute them for consumption, now or in the future, among various people and groups in society.

In a similar fashion McConnell (1975, p. 25), defines economics as *"the social science concerned with the problem of using or administering scarce resources (the means of producing) so as to attain the greatest or maximum fulfillment of society's unlimited wants (the goal of producing).* Thus, we see economics as the study of the allocation and distribution of limited resources to satisfy unlimited individual and social needs.

Economic Systems. Every society has to have some means of answering the following two basic economic questions: What goods and services will be produced and in what quantities? Who will get what amounts of the goods and services produced? Thus, all societies must have some form of economic system to allocate resources to the production process and then to distribute the products produced. That is, the major elements of any economic system are its resource market mechanism and its product market mechanism. These two markets are probably the most basic economic elements affecting any organization.

In theory, there are only two "pure" types of economic systems — capitalism or private enterprise, and socialism. In practice, there are no "pure" economic systems;

most systems contain some mixture of both capitalism and socialism but tend to resemble one more than the other.

Capitalism—The most commonly found form of economic system is some form of capitalism. The chief features of a purely capitalistic system are (Halm 1968, p. 23):

1. The factors of production (land, labor, capital) are privately owned, and production takes place at the initiative of private enterprise.

2. Income is received in monetary form through the sale of services of the factors of production and from profits of private enterprise.

3. The members of the free market economy have freedom of choice with respect to consumption, occupation, saving, and investment.

4. The free market economy is not planned, controlled, or regulated by the government. The government satisfies collective wants, but it does not compete with private firms, nor does it tell the people where to work or what to produce.

In a capitalistic system, the price mechanism allocates resources and distributes the wealth produced. Property is privately owned, and profit is the incentive for individuals and organizations to produce. Ultimately, consumers determine what is produced by the way they spend their money.

The basic tenet of capitalism is that each contributes to the economy according to his or her ability, and each receives according to his or her contribution. Again the price mechanism is used to distribute goods and services. Consumers determine what is produced, and production processes determine what types of skills and abilities are needed. Thus, people are compensated according to the demand that exists for their personal service which is, in turn, determined by consumer demand for the products being produced.

Socialism—At the other extreme from capitalism is socialism. Some of the basic features of a pure socialistic economic system are:

1. The people's representative, government, owns all of the means for production. There is no private ownership of property.

2. The entire economic system is planned by someone or some agency. That is, questions such as what will be produced, and in what quantity, and who will produce what is decided by someone or some agency. Thus, the government regulates all aspects of production and distribution of goods and services.

Socialistic economic systems allocate resources by planning rather than depending on the price mechanism. The same is true for distributing the goods and services produced. The basic tenet of socialism is that each contributes according to his or her ability and receives according to his or her need. So, in theory, what people receive is planned according to someone's (or some agency's) perception of their needs. Further, communication channels in a socialistic state are controlled by the state. The free exchange of information is also highly discouraged.

Mixed systems—There are no pure capitalistic or pure socialistic systems. The two types of systems can be thought of as extreme opposite ends of a continuum similar to that in figure 4-2. All of the economic systems that exist today are some degree of mixture of the two pure types.

Figure 4-2 Economic System Continuum

Consider, for example, the economic system of the United States. It is probably more capitalistic than socialistic. The greatest proportion of property is privately owned, and the greatest proportion of production is through private means. Private production is, however, heavily regulated by the government. And the government does own much property and produces better than 25 percent of the total of goods and services produced in this country. So our system exists somewhere to the left of the center of the economic system continuum.

The most widely known socialistic system is that of the Soviet Union. It is probably best characterized as a socialistic system. The government owns most of the property and produces most of the goods and services. There is, however, some private ownership of property and some private production of goods for a profit. Even in governmentally owned production, prices are often used to allocate resources and to distribute products. So the Soviet system contains features of both systems but probably exists to the right of the center of the continuum in figure 4-2.

Because it is of the greatest relevance in this country, we will concern ourselves mainly with the capitalistic type system and with the forces within the system that have the greatest effects on organizations.

Economic Conditions. In a capitalistic economic system such as ours, there are always economic forces which for the most part are of a particular set of economic conditions. These conditions affect the internal organizational elements and, ultimately, organizational communication, behavior, and effectiveness. The primary economic conditions affecting organizations are: (1) the level of employment or unemployment, (2) competition in the product market, (3) wage levels, (4) interest rates, (5) tax structure, and (6) consumer preferences. For the organization to operate effectively in its relevant environment, information about these economic conditions must be communicated to decision makers in the organization.

Economic Effects on Organizations

Specific economic conditions are generally either favorable or unfavorable on balance. Whatever economic conditions exist, they tend to affect the same internal organizational elements as do cultural conditions. Thus, the economic conditions that surround any organization affect its specific goals, the technology used, the structure of the organization, and individual behavior.

Goals. The general level of economic activity and the extent to which economic conditions are favorable affect the specific goals of the organization. Similarly communication, within the organization, is influenced by economic conditions.

Technology. Economic conditions also affect the element of technology. Changes in technology, especially to more advanced and costly technologies, usually occur during favorable economic conditions and not during unfavorable economic conditions. So economic conditions can affect the organization's choice of the alternative technologies available.

Structure. Organizational structure is sometimes affected by economic conditions. Favorable conditions tend to result in "fat" organizational structures with many levels and many jobs at each level. Unfavorable conditions often result in "lean" organizational structures with fewer levels of management and fewer jobs at each level. It is not uncommon for organizations to eliminate entire levels of management during adverse economic conditions.

The Individual. Generally, whatever economic conditions exist tend to affect individuals the same way that they do organizations. Unfavorable economic conditions usually result in high levels of unemployment, and high levels of unemployment tend to cause job insecurity on the part of individuals. This insecurity can affect behavior in many ways.

Managerial Philosophy. Economic conditions also affect managerial philosophy. We know of no systematic research to support the idea, but we believe that favorable economic conditions promote tendencies toward humanistic philosophies and that unfavorable economic conditions promote tendencies toward mechanistic philosophies.

Communication Implications

The cultural and economic environment that surrounds any organization has both direct and indirect effects on communication and behavior in the organization. So far we have concentrated on understanding the indirect effects of these two external variables. Simply stated, cultural and economic conditions influence internal organizational elements which ultimately affect organizational communication. Depending on what cultural and economic conditions exist, the organization will tend to seek particular goals and use particular structures and leadership structures to achieve them. In turn how the organization is structured and led influences the quality and quantity of communication. More specifically, internal organizational elements are major determinants of the design of the formal communication subsystem and of the communication climate that prevails. Certainly the design of the formal communication subsystem and the "atmosphere" that exists influences the effectiveness of communication in the organization.

Cultural and economic conditions also influence communication in a more direct manner. The values, beliefs, and knowledge that people bring to an organization largely determine their ability to communicate with other people. In addition, the same values and beliefs influence people's willingness to communicate and, therefore, the communication climate in the organization. We will explore the effects of these values on interpersonal communication further in subsequent chapters, particularly chapter thirteen.

Summary

All organizations exist within and are a part of their environment. Organizations are heavily influenced by their environment, especially by the two elements of culture and economic conditions.

Culture is a way of life. The major elements of culture are values, knowledge, and standards of behavior. These elements have direct effects on organizations and they also shape social institutions such as government, education, and economics which affect organizations. Either directly or indirectly culture affects managerial philosophy, the individual, organizational goals, organizational structure, technology, and the leadership style used.

All organizations operate within some form of economic system and under the influence of particular economic conditions. Economic conditions influence the same organizational variables as cultural conditions.

REVIEW AND DISCUSSION

1. Explain briefly what culture is.

2. Describe the most important elements of culture, insofar as organizations are concerned.

3. What is the relationship between culture and social institutions?

4. How does culture affect organizations?

5. Explain what economics is.

6. What does the concept "economic system" mean? How do economic systems affect organizations?

7. Identify the more important cultural elements in your own culture that seem to affect organizations.

8. What significant economic conditions exist at the present time in your area? How are these conditions affecting organizations?

Chapter Five

Managerial Philosophy and Assumptions

While numerous external environmental factors influence all organizations, the basic philosophy and assumptions of the management of the organization have very significant effects on the organization. Thus, managerial philosophy and assumptions influence managerial and organizational practices and, therefore, organizational communication and effectiveness.

Our purpose in this chapter is threefold. First, we explain in more detail what managerial philosophy is, where it comes from, and why it is important. Second, the possible range of philosophies and assumptions that managers can (and probably to some degree do) hold is described. Third, the effects of philosophy and assumptions on the internal make-up of the organization is discussed.

The Nature of Philosophy and Assumptions

All people make assumptions about other people that influence the way that they perceive and communicate with each other. Whether we are aware of it or not, our social behavior is based on a set of beliefs about the way other people behave. We call these types of beliefs and assumptions *philosophy*.

In this respect managers are no different from all other people. Whether they recognize it as a philosophy or not, all managers base their actions on more or less explicit beliefs about the way people behave. Thus managerial philosophy influences managerial action and the way things are done in the organization.

What Managerial Philosophy Really Is

As we use the term, *managerial philosophy* refers to the basic attitudes, values, beliefs, and assumptions that managers hold about organizations; the work behavior of people; and how people should be managed to get the best organizational results. Not all managers call their assumptions and beliefs a philosophy, and some managers may not even be consciously aware of their philosophy, but they all have one.

Trying to identify and describe all of the elements of managerial philosophy is probably an impossibility. However, the more important elements of managerial philosophy have been identified. In their model of comparative management, Negandhi and Estafen (1965) identify six important elements of managerial philosophy — attitudes toward (1) employees, (2) consumers, (3) suppliers, (4) stockholders, (5) government, and (6) the community. These are probably the more important areas of managerial philosophy, but, for our purposes, attitudes, assumptions, and beliefs about the work behavior of employees and the best way to get work done in organizations are the most relevant elements of managerial philosophy.

So, as used here, *managerial philosophy* refers to such things as management's beliefs and assumptions about the level of people's abilities, people's initiative and motivations, how people are likely to behave in particular sets of circumstances, and the kinds of circumstances that result in the best organizational achievement. Our definition excludes several of the important elements of managerial philosophy mentioned above, but we are not directly concerned with those elements in this book.

The Source of Managerial Philosophy

Philosophies concerning anything are learned and acquired. People interact with their environment and learn from their experience. So philosophies are products of people's communications with their environments and, more specifically, their past experiences. People cling to their particular philosophy because it has helped them be at least somewhat effective by viewing the world just that way.

Strictly speaking, managerial philosophy is only a specialized part of a person's overall philosophy of life. It, too, is learned from past managerial or organizational experience, from reading and studying, and/or extrapolated from general life experiences; and, whatever the philosophy is, it is held because it is believed that it is logical and that supporting evidence is either available or could be collected.

While it is true that managerial philosophy is a specialized part of a person's overall philosophy, we should point out that it may or may not be closely related to general life values. For example, Miles (1975, p. 33) points out, ". . . a manager may have strong egalitarian values while at the same time he holds to the concept that women are emotionally unsuited for high-level executive jobs." This is possible because different experiences produce different learnings. Thus, the source of all managerial philosophy is past experiences with people in organizations and vicarious learning from other sources.

The Significance of Managerial Philosophy

This book is concerned with organizations and how they are managed generally and specifically with communication in organizations. *The effectiveness of organizational communication is determined largely by how organizations are managed and operated, that is, the way managers manage determines the quality and quantity of communication in the organization.*

The way managers manage is significantly influenced by their philosophy of management. The famous social scientist, Douglas McGregor (1960, p. vi-vii), put it this way: ". . . the assumptions management holds about controlling its human resources determine the whole character of the enterprise." What McGregor seems to be saying is that behind all managerial behavior is a philosophy — a set of assumptions, values, and beliefs. As figure 5-1 illustrates, managerial philosophy affects managerial behavior which determines how the organization is operated.

Managerial Philosophy   ⟶   Managerial Behavior   ⟶   How the Organization is Operated

Figure 5-1   The Effects of Philosophy

While it is true that managerial philosophy affects managerial behavior, it may or may not be reflected in a manager's daily activities. Miles (1975, p. 33) has argued: "For example, even though he (manager) responds warmly in contacts with his peers and subordinates, he may hold the view that good job design minimizes inter-

personal dependency. Thus, while his daily behavior may be closely tied to his theory of management, it is also possible that his concepts of how people ought to be motivated, controlled and rewarded may show up in his policy statements and directives but not in his one-to-one, face-to-face interaction with subordinates."

Alternative Philosophies

There are probably as many different managerial philosophies as there are managers. Each person's philosophy of management is indeed unique, and it would be impossible to completely describe all of the different philosophies that exist. Managers' philosophies do, however, *tend* to be similar to at least some other managers. This is not a suprising result if we consider that similar backgrounds are likely to cause people to learn at least roughly similar things. More important is the fact that, while each is unique, managers' philosophies tend to fall into general patterns.

The possible range of the patterns of philosophy will be described so that, by understanding at least the two extremes, the entire range of alternatives of managerial philosophy will become clear. Describing these extremes makes it easier to see the differences that are possible. The danger in considering only extremes is that it is easy to conclude that only two alternatives exist. We have chosen to discuss only the two extremes as if they were opposite ends of a continuum. The reader should keep in mind that this is an oversimplification and that most managers' philosophies probably lie somewhere between the two extremes.

Most writers on managerial philosophy have chosen to identify the extremes of managerial philosophy based essentially on the degree to which people are seen as having positive or negative attitudes toward work. Our approach is similar, however, we will name the two extremes. Philosophies which hold that people have negative views toward work are called mechanistic philosophies. Those including the belief that people have neutral or positive views toward work are called humanistic philosophies. Thus, as figure 5-2 indicates, the two extremes are mechanistic and humanistic.

Figure 5-2   Range of Managerial Philosophy

While he did not call the two extremes mechanistic and humanistic, McGregor (1960) was one of the first people to point out the effects of philosophy and then describe the two extreme ends of the philosophical continuum. Later writers such as Maslow (1965), Argyris (1957), Miles (1965), and Schein (1970) have modified and/or added to the original statements by McGregor. Our discussion will draw heavily on these sources.

Mechanistic Philosophies

At the heart of the mechanistic philosophy is the basic belief that most people feel work is distasteful and to be avoided if possible or at best endured only as long as the rewards it brings outweigh the pain associated with it.

Jeremy Bentham, an economist during the 1700s, was one of the first writers to advance this philosophy explicitly. Bentham believed that people sought pleasure and avoided pain. Money was believed to be the common denominator of pleasure, and work was believed to be painful. In Bentham's view, people would work only as long as the pleasure (money) received for working outweighed the pain associated with the work (Ferguson 1938). The mechanistic philosophy has deep roots in classical economics. Much practical evidence exists that these same assumptions are still widely held, at least in a slightly different form.

McGregor's Theory X.   Perhaps the most popular and widely known statement of the mechanistic philosophy is McGregor's (1960) statement of the assumptions he called *Theory X*. Theory X is, essentially, a restatement in modern behavioral terms of the classical economic assumptions about work behavior. According to McGregor, Theory X includes three assumptions about people's work behavior.

1. The average human being has an inherent dislike of work and will avoid it if he or she can.

2. Because of this characteristic dislike of work, most people must be coerced, controlled, directed, and threatened with punishment to get them to put forth adequate effort toward the achievement of organizational objectives.

3. The average human being prefers to be directed, wishes to avoid responsibility, has relatively little ambition, and wants security above all.*

Schein's Rational-Economic Man.   A more recent statement of the core of the mechanistic philosophy is the rational-economic man philosophy described by Schein (1970). These assumptions are more or less modifications and elaborations of the assumptions in Theory X. According to Schein, the rational-economic man philosophy includes:

1. Man is primarily motivated by economic incentives and will pursue that which gets him the greatest gain.

2. Since economic incentives are under the content of the organization, man is essentially a passive agent to be manipulated, motivated, and controlled by the organization.

3. Man's feelings are essentially irrational and must be prevented from interfering with his rational calculation of self-evidence.

4. Organizations can and must be designed in such a way as to neutralize and content man's feelings and, therefore, his unpredictable traits.†

Thus, the mechanistic philosophy views people as being totally selfish, motivated solely by money and placing no value on work as a source of satisfaction other than money.

Mechanistic Philosophy — A Summary.   Ultimately, the mechanistic philosophy results in people being divided into two groups that we call the "haves" and the "have-nots." "Haves" are the people with ambition, intelligence, ability, the desire to achieve and to communicate. "Have-nots" are the people with little motivation to communicate, intelligence, ambition, or ability; or if they do have ability, there is

---

*D. MacGregor, *The Human Side of Enterprise* (New York: McGraw-Hill, 1960), pp. 33-34. Used by permission.

†Edgar H. Schein, *Organizational Psychology*, 2nd ed., p. 56. © 1970. Reprinted by permission of Prentice-Hall, Inc., Englewood Cliffs, New Jersey.

certainly no way to get them to use it to help achieve organizational objectives. Obviously, it is the "haves" who must manage the "have-nots."

Amazing as it may seem, it is our belief, based on observation, that the mechanistic philosophy with its "have-have not" categories is still widely held. What is so surprising about this is that almost everyone puts himself or herself in the "have" category but seems to have serious doubts about most other people. Almost all people tend to hold these beliefs to some degree.

There is some research which suggests that these views are fairly widely held. Miles (1975) conducted an extensive investigation of managers' theories of management and found that, no matter what type of organization or level of management, managers tended to believe that they were just as capable as their boss but that they were far more capable than their subordinates immediately below them.

The above description is an extreme statement of the mechanistic philosophy. It is probably not held by many people in this extreme form, but it is fairly widely held in less extreme forms.

Humanistic Philosophy

The humanistic philosophy is an outgrowth of the behavioral sciences in general and psychology in particular. It was born with the Hawthorne studies headed by Mayo and Roethlisberger in the 1920s and popularized in the late fifties and sixties by such people as Argyris, Maslow, McGregor, Miles, and Schein.

The cornerstone of the humanistic philosophy is the belief that most people want to use their abilities to the fullest to satisfy their own needs and that work in organizations can provide opportunities for people to use their abilities. Thus, work is not necessarily painful but is more or less natural.

The humanistic end of the philosophy is often misunderstood because it is usually presented in a cursory fashion. For this reason, several writers' views of this general philosophy are presented, although the statements present extreme cases.

The Hawthorne Studies. The Hawthorne studies which began in 1927 marked the beginning of the humanistic managerial philosophy. These investigations, headed by Elton Mayo and Fritz Roethlisberger, lasted several years and covered numerous aspects of people's actual work behavior. Only the chief conclusions of the studies are important to this work.

The first general conclusion of these studies was that work behavior is socially and psychologically motivated as well as economically motivated. More specifically, the studies indicated that people had social needs which they attempted to satisfy at work; as a result, organizations were themselves social systems. A second important conclusion was that people sought, through work, to enhance their own and other's perceptions of their ability and worth as individual human beings (Scott 1965). These two basic conclusions, more or less, lay dormant in terms of further elaboration until the 1950s.

Self-Actualizing Man. During the 1950s the humanistic end of the philosophical continuum began to be popularized and publicized by Abraham Maslow and Chris Argyris. Based firmly in behavioral science, Maslow (1965) advanced the idea that people are primarily self-motivated and self-controlled and that, above all else, people ultimately seek to use their abilities to express themselves creatively and to achieve through work. People see work as a way to grow and develop into more mature individuals.

Taking a different approach, Argyris (1957) advanced somewhat similar ideas. Argyris set forth the idea that people sought to be mature on the job. Maturity was defined in terms of growth trends.

. . . The human being in our culture:

1. tends to develop from a state of being passive as an infant to a state of increasing activity as an adult.

2. tends to develop from a state of dependence upon others as an infant to a state of relative independence as an adult. Relative independence is the ability to "stand on one's own two feet" and simultaneously to achieve healthy dependence.

3. tends to develop from being capable of behaving in only a few ways as an infant to being capable of behaving in many different ways as an adult.

4. tends to develop from having private, casual, hollow, quickly dropped interests as an infant to possessing a deepening of interest as an adult.

5. tends to develop from having a short-time perspective (i.e., the present largely determines behavior) as an infant to having a much longer time perspective as an adult (i.e., the individual's behavior is more affected by the past and the future).

6. tends to develop from being in a subordinate position in the family and society as an infant to aspiring to occupy at least an equal and/or superordinate position relative to his peers.

7. tends to develop from having a lack of awareness of the self as an infant to having an awareness of and control over the self as an adult.*

Thus Argyris believes that people try to grow in these dimensions toward maturity and that they seek to do this through work as well as through other means. A similar but less complex set of ideas is McGregor's Theory Y.

McGregor's Theory Y. In discussing humanistic philosophy, McGregor (1960) set forth what he called Theory Y assumptions. These are in contrast to the Theory X assumptions of the mechanistic philosophy. According to Theory Y:

1. *The expenditure of physical and mental effort in work is as natural as play or rest. The average human being does not inherently dislike work. Depending upon controllable conditions, work may be a source of satisfaction (and will be voluntarily performed) or a source of punishment (and will be avoided if possible).*

2. *External control and the threat of punishment are not the only means for bringing about effort toward organizational objectives. Man will exercise self-control in the service of objectives to which he is committed.*

3. *Commitment to objectives is a function of the rewards associated with their achievement. The most significant of such rewards . . . can be direct products of efforts directed toward organizational objectives.*

---

*C. Argyris, "The Individual and Organization: Some Problems of Mutual Adjustment," *Administrative Science Quarterly* 2 (1957): 3. Used by permission.

4. *The average human being learns, under proper conditions, not only to accept but to seek responsibility. Avoidance of responsibility, lack of ambition, and emphasis on security are generally consequences of experience, not inherent human characteristics.*

5. *The capacity to exercise a relatively high degree of imagination, ingenuity, and creativity in the solution of organizational problems is widely, not narrowly, distributed in the population.*

6. *Under conditions of modern industrial life, the intellectual potentialities of the average human being are only partially utilized.**

Miles' Human Resources Philosophy. Taking the lead from McGregor, Miles (1965) describes the humanistic assumptions about work behavior:

1. In addition to sharing common needs for belonging and respect, most people in our culture desire to contribute effectively and creatively to the accomplishment of worthwhile objectives.

2. The majority of our work force is capable of increasing far more initiative, responsibility, and creativity than their present jobs require or allow.

3. The capabilities represent untapped resources which are presently being wasted. (p. 151)

Humanistic Philosophy—A Summary. The assumptions of the humanistic philosophy ultimately boil down to two ideas:

1. People have abilities that they seek to use to satisfy their needs through achieving.

2. Organizations can provide opportunities for people to use their abilities to achieve by allowing and encouraging people to help accomplish organizational objectives through communication.

Humanistic Philosophies in Perspective. Schein (1970) elaborates further on the humanistic philosophy and tries to set the entire philosophy in perspective:

1. Man is not only complex, but also highly variable; he has many motives which are arranged in some sort of hierarchy of importance to him, but this hierarchy is subject to change from time to time and situation to situation; furthermore, motives interact and combine into complex motive patterns (for example, since money can facilitate self-actualization, for some people economic strivings are equivalent to self-actualization).

2. Man is capable of learning new motives through his organizational experiences, hence ultimately his pattern of motivation and the psychological contract which he establishes with the organization is the result of a complex interaction between initial needs and organizational experiences.

3. Man's motives in different organizations or different subparts of the same organization may be different; the person who is alienated in the formal organization may find fulfillment of his social and self-actualization needs

---

*D. MacGregor, *The Human Side of Enterprise* (New York: McGraw-Hill, 1960), pp. 47-48. Used by permission.

in the union or in the informal organization; if the job itself is complex, such as that of a manager, some parts of the job may engage some motives while other parts engage other motives.

4. Man can become productively involved with organizations on the basis of many different kinds of motives; his ultimate satisfaction and the ultimate effectiveness of the organization depends only in part on the nature of his motivation. The nature of the task to be performed, the abilities and experience of the person on the job, and the nature of the other people in the organization all interact to produce a certain pattern of work feelings. For example, a highly skilled but poorly motivated worker may be as effective and satisfied as a very unskilled but highly motivated worker.

5. Man can respond to many different kinds of managerial strategies, depending on his own motives and abilities and the nature of the task; in other words, there is no one correct managerial strategy that will work for all men at all times.*

Schein is saying that the humanistic philosophy is not as simple as it may seem and that people must be managed as they actually are, not as the humanistic philosophy would like them to be.

---

*Edgar H. Schein, *Organization Psychology*, 2nd ed., p. 66. © 1970. Reprinted by permission of Prentice-Hall, Inc., Englewood Cliffs, New Jersey.

Effects of Philosophy

We have indicated briefly that the philosophy that management holds influences managerial action, the way that the organization is operated and, therefore, communication. We will now explain in somewhat more detail the effects of philosophy.

Generally, the philosophy of the organization is a prime determinant of the internal makeup of the organization, how it is operated, and the organizational communication system. More specifically, managerial philosophy significantly influences (1) how the organization is structured, (2) what leadership style prevails, (3) what type of reward system is used, (4) what objectives are sought, and (5) the type of technology used. Part Three will consider each of these elements. Further, managerial philosophy has a direct impact on the organizational communication system. These assumptions help determine the formal subsystem of communication, the climate in which organizational communication takes place, and the extent to which an individual is motivated to communicate (skills). Part Four will be devoted to the role which assumptions play in moderating organizational communication. However, at this point, it is sufficient to describe briefly the general approach which follows from each of the two extremes of managerial philosophy.

Management Based on Mechanistic Philosophy

The basic managerial approach based on mechanistic philosophy can be summarized in the following way: Management decides what it wants done, how it should be done, tells people exactly what to do, and then supervises people very closely to make sure that they do what they are supposed to do. People are more or less considered a necessary evil, and the total organization system is designed to compensate for and control the behavior of people so that objectives are achieved no matter how irresponsibly people behave.

More specifically, management emphasizes efficient task performance. It structures the organization so that authority can be used to control behavior. It structures jobs so that they are relatively simple and easy to perform and so that individual performance can be monitored. People are rewarded economically based on their service and obedience to organizational policies, rules, and procedures. Last, but not least, people are supervised very closely because they are either not capable of exercising self-direction or unwilling to do so.

Communication tends to be formal and guarded. As a result of its philosophy the organization designs its formal communication subsystem on a "strictly business" basis. Only essential information is supposed to be transferred. Indeed, nonessential information is suppressed. Communication tends to be closed and guarded rather than open and candid. Because of its beliefs management is likely to structure the organization, lead it, and reward people in a way that causes people to be careful about what they communicate to whom. Fear arises because people sense that unfavorable information can be used against them.

Management Based on Humanistic Philosophy

The general managerial approach based on humanistic philosophy is to create an environment that allows and encourages people to use their abilities to the fullest to help achieve organization objectives. People are seen as the greatest asset of the organization, and the basic attempt is to design a system that makes greatest use of people's most important abilities to achieve organizational objectives.

Specifically, approaches based on humanistic philosophies try to make it possible for people to have a "stake" in the organization by having some voice in what goes on. The organization as a whole and individual jobs in particular are structured to make the greatest use of people's abilities so that organizational objectives are achieved as effectively and efficiently as possible. Commitment and self-direction are attempted through the development of mutual understanding of what is being done and why. People are rewarded based on their performance and contribution toward the achievement of organizational objectives. Supervision takes on the form of guidance and help.

Communication tends to be problem centered and open and candid. Under the humanistic philosophy people tend to be respected and trusted. The result is that formal communication subsystems are designed to solve problems and achieve organizational objectives in the best way possible. Little or no distinction is made between formal and informal channels of communication. Moreover, because of the trust, respect, and support that exists people tend to feel free to communicate openly, honestly, and candidly.

Summary

The philosophy and assumptions that management holds about people's work behavior influence the way the organization is managed and other internal organizational variables.

Different managers have different philosophies, but there tend to be great similarities in philosophy. The two extreme ends of the managerial philosophy continuum are called mechanistic and humanistic. Mechanistic philosophy is based primarily on the belief that people have negative attitudes toward work and get little direct satisfaction from it. Humanistic philosophies are based on the belief that work can be a primary source of satisfaction for individuals. While behavioral science generally supports the humanistic philosophy, merchanistic philosophy still prevails.

REVIEW AND DISCUSSION

1. In your own words, state your understanding of what managerial philosophy is.

2. Briefly describe mechanistic managerial philosophy.

3. Briefly describe humanistic managerial philosophy.

4. Comment on the statement that humanistic philosophy implies that all people will in fact work for the good of the organization.

5. Write out in a page or less your own philosophy of management. Include your true beliefs about people's attitudes toward work and motivation to work.

PART TWO: Environmental Background Factors

Incidents

The Doctor's Office

Dr. Richard Charles seemed like a very amenable man when Suzanne applied for the job as his receptionist in Horton Clinic. But Christine, who has been Dr. Charles' nurse for two years, warned her differently.

"Dr. Charles is a 'workaholic'," Christine had told her during her first week on the job. "He likes to schedule in as many patients as possible, starting at 8 and with the last one leaving at 5:30. If anyone straggles in at 5:30, he wants to see him. Breaks for us are out and lunch is a half-hour — but we keep the office open and if anyone comes in during lunch, we are to take care of them."

Within the first month of her job, Suzanne found Christine's warning to be true. The other doctors in the clinic were more relaxed and easy going. Suzanne noticed Dr. Charles frowning at their occasional office conversations and reading between patients. If one of the doctors began a casual conversation with her, she would cut them off by saying, "Excuse me, I have to get back to work." The reason for this was that once she forgot Christine's advice to "keep working no matter what." Dr. Endicott stopped by her desk to be friendly. While they were discussing her previous job, Dr. Charles came out of one of the examining rooms to see about the next patient. Upon seeing Suzanne and Dr. Endicott talking, he scowled. "Hey Art. Suzanne's got work to do. She doesn't have time to chat, even if you do." Dr. Endicott, knowing the familiar patterns of Dr. Charles, left mumbling and smiled back at Suzanne as Dr. Charles began reprimanding her.

"I am not paying you for socializing. You are here to work. It has been fifteen minutes since the last patient left. Where is the next one? Let me see the appointment book." He briefly scanned the list of patients. "Why is there an hour here with no one scheduled?"

Suzanne replied timidly, "Dr. Charles, that is the lunch hour. I usually schedule patients from 12:30 to 1:00, and leave 12:00 to 12:30 open for our lunch and any patients who walk in."

"This is a clinic Suzanne, not a cafeteria. Patients should be scheduled at all times. You eat lunch when you get the chance—like I do. I don't want you setting aside time for lunch. If you're going to set aside time for anything, do it for this correspondence. There are three letters here that must go out today."

When Suzanne told Christine about this, Christine groaned. "At least you get to sit down. Dr. Charles sees to it that I'm on my feet all the time. I sat down between patients last week and he came in and humiliated me in front of Dr. Kramer. He said I was lazy and undependable. When he got through and walked out, I told Dr. Kramer how much I hated this job. He told me that he once tried to talk to Dr. Charles about his 'whipcracking.' Dr. Charles just said that Dr. Kramer was soft and even accused *him* of being lazy. I don't know what to tell you, Suzanne. The last girl quit because she couldn't stand it."

Suzanne considered following suit but decided to stick it out. Christine did quit and upon leaving told Dr. Charles her feelings. He just nodded and said he had heard it before. "You people just don't like work. It's distasteful to you. All you want to do is loaf around, drinking coffee on an eight-hour paid social visit. I admit I make the people I hire work and if they don't perform then it's good riddance. I am in charge of this section of the clinic and anyone who works for me must do so efficiently and faithfully. My policy is to work when you are at work. Anyone who does not adhere to this policy does not deserve to be employed here. I've yet to hire anyone that can meet the simple standards I have established for this clinic. If I can work a rigorous, demanding schedule, then anyone can. I am tired of the feeble complaints you girls come up with. I hope I can hire a nurse to replace you who isn't afraid of a little good, honest, hard work."

Guidelines for Analysis

1. In light of the material presented in this part dealing with assumptions, list five assumptions which you think that Dr. Charles has about people. How do the assumptions on your list compare with the assumptions that you make about people?

2. If you were Christine, what would you look for in a "boss" for your next job? Why?

3. Think of the jobs which you have had in your life. Do you think that Dr. Charles' behavior is typical of the supervisors you have had?

4. Do you think that there is an "ideal" set of assumptions that most people would like their boss to manifest? If so, what would they be?

5. Speculate about what might have gone on in Dr. Charles' life which may have made him treat Christine and Suzanne in the manner in which he did.

6. Dr. Charles seems to be saying in the incident that he feels most people are lazy and will avoid work. Do you think he is right? Why?

7. Assuming that Dr. Charles' behavior was not helpful in getting what he considered to be a high level of productivity out of his staff, what recommendations would you have for him to obtain high productivity? Do you think that one's assumptions about his or her subordinates will influence their productivity? Why?

8. Describe the climate in Dr. Charles' office. What aspects of office operations caused the climate?

The Basketball Team

The Long Beach Surfs are members of the World Basketball League, a new league with eight teams as members. The Surfs have been winning a number of games but have been averaging only 2,100 fans per game. Lane McDonald, the general manager of the Surfs, has experienced difficulty in establishing credibility with his players and the local press. Each Monday during a news conference, Lane has to meet with the press to insure them that both the team and the league are solvent and will continue to compete with the established National and American Leagues.

"We have a good product and I think the fans will begin to come around. We are in a market which is dominated by the older leagues. But we will take our time and pretty soon the league will have widespread support among the fans," Lane said at Monday's press conference. "We need to average about 5,200 fans to break even by the end of the year to meet our obligations. If we make the playoffs, I think we will do even better than that."

Headlines in Tuesday's newspaper quoted McDonald as saying that the Surfs were solvent but need to average 5,200 for the rest of the year to finish in the "black." After the stories hit on Tuesday, the team was forced to hold up paychecks to players because there was no money in the bank to cover them. Player representative Haven Malone, a former All-American forward at South Carolina A and M college, came in to talk with Lane about the checks on Tuesday morning.

"What's the deal?" Haven asked the first thing during the meeting. "We players read in the paper that the team is strong and then we are told that there is no money to pay the players. What are we supposed to believe?"

"Well, I can understand your concern. Remember this is only the first time that we have held up paychecks. You players have to remember that this is very routine in professional sports. We have to maintain a positive public posture or the fans won't come out to see the Surfs. I hope that your players will not tell the press about the delay in paychecks. We must keep our profile high if we are going to compete for the entertainment dollar here in Long Beach," Lane responded.

"I don't understand what you're saying, man. My players have got to have money to feed their families. Without the players, there is no Long Beach Surfs. It seems to me that you're lying either to the press or to the players. There's either enough money to pay the players or there is not. Which is it?" Haven argued.

"Look, Haven," Lane began to explain, "We really love our players and we want them to love us. It costs a lot of money to run a basketball team. We have travel expenses, training expenses, arena rental and sometimes we just have to establish priorities. We are in a tough market. Our competitors are very aggressive and their product is more widely known than ours. We have a public relations job to do. We want the players to help us with this job. You men have to recognize how fortunate you all are to earn your money playing professional basketball. Many people really envy you men."

Haven went back to talk with his players that afternoon. "I don't know if we are going to get our money or not. They were talking about public relations, products, markets, posture. I guess I just don't understand the situation. Mr. McDonald never did answer my questions about the paychecks. Maybe one of you men ought to go and talk with him. Maybe you can get a straight answer out of him."

"Man, Haven. They either have the money to stay in operation or they don't. They just haven't been honest with us. They tell us one thing and we read something else in the paper. I don't think that we ought to play tonight's game against Miami. Either we get our checks or we don't play. I also think that we ought to go to the newspaper and explain our view. Our fans should know how they are treating us," shouted Len Taylor, a star backcourt man for the Surfs.

"I don't know if we should do that, Lenny. Maybe they have a good reason for holding up our checks. Going to the press about this would probably only embarrass us and the team. What do the rest of you guys think? Should we play or not?" Haven asked.

Guidelines for Analysis

1. If you were a member of the Surfs, how would you have voted? To play or strike? Why?

2. What influence did the existing economic conditions regarding the local professional sports picture have on the communication within the Surfs organization?

3. Would you say that Lane McDonald was "straight" with Haven? Do you think that Lane demonstrated acceptable communication behavior? Why?

4. Is it likely that outside "environmental" conditions will influence the communication which takes place inside the organization? Why?

5. Instead of maintaining two separate positions, one for the press and one for players, what could Lane have done to reconcile the two positions?

6. Do you think, in situations such as this, that "honesty is always the best policy?" Why?

7. How would you characterize the leadership that Haven demonstrated? If you were in Haven's position, would you have behaved differently?

8. Do you think that the players understood the gravity of the financial situation facing the Surfs? Why?

The New Plant

The Baylor Food Company had grown from a small family owned producer of specialty food items to a rather large organization. Eugene Baylor began his company in the early 1940s in the garage of his suburban New York home by gift wrapping cakes and pies which his wife had baked. From that early beginning, the Baylor company expanded to include three moderate-size plants in the New Jersey-New York area. The company had grown to employ about 800 persons but the Baylor family maintained control. Eugene's sons, Harry and Brent, managed the day-to-day operations of the company. About two years ago, the company, through the help of a consulting firm specializing in marketing research, determined that there would be a national market for the Baylor line of food items. Up until this time, Baylor had distributed solely on the Eastern seaboard.

"You people can turn a nice profit by moving into other markets. No one else does exactly what you can do in producing party and picnic foods. You should think about moving southward and westward with your line of products," said a representative of the consulting firm employed by Baylor. "You may want to consider acquiring some property to build a plant in one of these areas."

This seemed like sound advice to the elder Baylor and his two sons. They took the matter up with their bankers and financial advisers. Both groups advised that it was possible to gain capital for such an expansion. Plans were made and a loan was secured. With the help of the consulting firm, a piece of property in Arkansas was purchased. There was a small factory on the property which had produced bread. Only a limited amount of reconversion was necessary to make the Baylor line of products in the plant. The location of the new plant seemed to be ideal because it offered good access to western and southern states and was located in a state with low industrial taxes. After the reconversion was complete, it was decided that Brent Taylor, Eugene's youngest son, would move to Arkansas to supervise the "start up" of the new plant. Brent took on his project with enthusiasm. He identified twelve supervisors from the Baylor's New York and New Jersey plants who were willing to assume the leadership of the Arkansas plant. Thus, Brent, the twelve supervisors, and their families moved to Arkansas. Since the new Baylor plant was located in the small town of Hilton (pop. 1,750), the move of nearly fifty "easterners" made a great impact on the community.

For the next fourteen weeks, Brent and his coworkers began the process of acquiring and training a work force. At the end of this period, some 200 local men and women were hired, trained and on the job. In the short period of three months, Baylor had become the largest employer in Hilton. The plant began operation with two shifts (7 A.M.-3:30 P.M. and 3:30 P.M.-midnight) and for the first few days things went smoothly. But then trouble began to develop. Some of the men on the day shift began showing up late for work. Efforts made by the Baylor supervisor to uncover the cause of the tardiness proved unsuccessful. Although the quality of the new workers' performance was quite high, the Baylor management noticed that the Arkansas workers were having difficulty meeting the time standards. These time standards were based on the records of the workers in the east. Continual attempts by the management to "bring the workers into line" proved unsuccessful.

Besides trouble at the plant, Brent was always being bothered by people from the community.

"They expect me to join every single organization in town. Those I don't join, they want me to contribute money to. Some guy the other day wanted me to contribute to the Sons of the Confederacy Charity Ball. Can you imagine that? Me, a New Yorker," Brent said one day to his wife. "They called from the United Way drive and wanted me to serve on the board of directors of this year's drive. I don't mind making a contribution but I don't have time for all of this. I have a plant to run. We have to make this thing go down here. They never bothered us with this stuff up in New York. I just don't know what's wrong."

"Maybe they're just being friendly and want you to feel included," his wife offered.

"We're just having more trouble than we expected down here. I've got unhappy managers, unhappy workers, unhappy people in the community. And, I'm pretty darned unhappy myself," Brent grumbled as he left the room.

Guidelines for Analysis

1. Describe what you think is wrong with the Arkansas Baylor plant. Why do you think this situation exists?

2. Had you been a member of the Baylor management team, what advice would you have given to avoid the present situation? Explain how your advice would have resolved this problem.

3. What do you think is wrong with the communication within Baylor? Why have the Baylor managers had a difficult time reaching the Baylor employees? If this continues, what is likely to happen to the Baylor product manufactured at the Hilton plant?

4. From the material presented in this part, what influence do you think cultural differences might have on communication behavior? From your own background, consider some situations in which you have experienced some cultural differences between yourself and another person. Have these differences affected communication between the two of you? How?

5. In the situation, it would seem that Brent Baylor is feeling "the walls close in around him." What might he be able to do to resolve the situation?

6. Consider the relationship between the new plant and the citizens in Hilton. What responsibility does Baylor have toward these local residents? What types of communication exchanges should have gone on, before construction of the plant, between community leaders and the Baylor management?

7. In the situation, Brent Baylor suggests that his Baylor managers are quite unhappy. Why do you think this is the case?

8. How might another organization, through good organizational communication, have avoided some of the problems facing Baylor?

PART THREE

INTERNAL ORGANIZATIONAL ELEMENTS

Chapter Six

The Individual

One of the most important and complex internal elements in any organization is the individual. In fact, individuals are the *core* element of organization. It is individuals communicating according to some structure and with some common purpose that *is* the organization. Quite simply stated, organizations are only collections of associated individuals.

Individuals are extremely complex phenomena, and their behavior is equally complex. First and foremost, all individuals are unique. Add to this fact that much behavior is influenced by the behavior of other individuals and so is socially, as well as psychologically, determined. In view of these considerations, it is not surprising to us that Berelson and Steiner (1964, p. 3) state that ". . . . human behavior . . . is so enormously varied, so delicately complex, so obscurely motivated that many people despair of finding valid generalizations to explain and predict the very actions, thoughts, and feelings of human beings."

While it is probably true that behavioral science has only scratched the surface in its attempt to uncover and understand individuals and their behavior, much knowledge is available. The explanations are incomplete and not well integrated; but useful explanations of such topics as personality, motivations, needs, and goals do exist.

Any attempt to understand organizational communication must include a basic understanding of the core element of the organization — individuals. This chapter will present and explain some of the more important concepts of individual behavior. We begin with an introduction to personality and a basic model of motivation and behavior. Next the more widely accepted descriptions of common human needs and an explanation of the satisfactions and goals individuals seek in an organization are presented. Following the general concepts the more specific subject of motivation in an organization is discussed. Last, the communication implications of these concepts are identified.

Individual Behavior

It is behavior that is important in organizations and that we are focusing on, but behavior is a product of the individual. Therefore, we begin our explanation with the individual and, specifically, with the concepts of personality and motivation. In chapter fourteen those interpersonal skills which the individual demonstrates within the organizational communication system will be considered.

Personality

Personality is a key concept in the description and understanding of human beings. Individuals in large part are characterized by their personality. In a broad sense, personality is the ultimate source of human behavior.

Argyris (1957) describes what is meant by "personality":

> Personality is conceptualized as: (1) being an organization of parts where the parts maintain the whole and the whole maintains the parts; (2) seeking internal balance (usually called adjustment) and external balance (usually called adaptation); (3) being propelled by psychological (as well as physical) energy; (4) located in the need systems and (5) expressed through the abilities. (6) The personality organization may be called "the self" which (7) acts to color all the individual's experiences, thereby causing him to live in "private worlds," and which (8) is capable of defending (maintaining) itself against threats of all types.*

This description implies that the personality of individuals is what causes behavior to be exhibited; more subtly, however, Argyris implies that the personality of individuals results in motivation and that motivation results in behavior and in individuals' communication activities.

Motivation

The terms "motivation" and "behavior" are closely related — most human behavior occurs as a result of motivation (Berelson and Steiner 1964). Human beings do not merely behave, neither do they behave randomly or by chance. There are specific reasons for their specific acts of behavior. They behave as they do in a given situation because they are usually motivated to do so. Motivation and behavior, however, are not synonymous terms. Motivation is only one (but probably the most important) class of determinants of behavior. Behavior also is influenced by biological, social, cultural, and situational determinants (Maslow 1954). In addition, not all behavior is motivated in the sense in which the term is used here. All behavior can be grouped into two classes — voluntary and involuntary. In overly

---

*C. Argyris, "The Individual and Organization: Some Problems of Mutual Adjustment," *Administrative Science Quarterly* 2 (1957): 4. Used by permission.

simple terms, voluntary behavior is motivated, while involuntary behavior is not; therefore, although an understanding of motivation is essential, it does not provide a complete explanation of all human behavior.

Motivation Defined. Motivation refers to a stimulated state of the individual (Viteles 1957). It is an inner state which causes individuals to exhibit behavior directed toward goals. The stimulated state occurs because people have needs that they seek to satisfy. These needs are most often manifested as wants and desires. The wants and desires of individuals cause them to engage in behavior, to do certain things and/or not to do certain things, designed to attain goals that satisfy their wants, desires, and needs. It is motivation, therefore, that causes and guides or directs behavior. Since we all have needs for interaction, motivation also causes us to communicate with others.

A Model of Human Behavior. Perhaps the easiest way to explain motivation and to show how it is related to behavior is with the aid of a simple model. It should be pointed out that the model in figure 6-1 applies generally to voluntary behavior and not to involuntary behavior. From this standpoint it is incomplete, but it is adequate for the purposes of discussion here.

Voluntarily exhibited behavior is the most significant and the most important. Involuntary behavior refers to behavior, such as reflexes, or behavior over which the individual has relatively little conscious control. All other behavior is voluntary and is entirely predetermined from within the individual. In other words, it is behavior which the individual consciously or unconsciously chooses to exhibit. Most acts of behavior, generally the most important ones, are voluntary. It is with this important class of behavior that this discussion is concerned specifically.

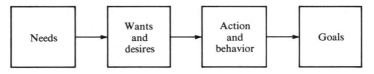

SOURCE: Aubrey C. Sanford, *Human Relations: Theory and Practice* (Columbus, Ohio: Charles E. Merrill, 1973), p. 66.

Figure 6-1   Model of Behavior

The model in figure 6-1 indicates what motivation is and how it is related to behavior. Internal needs result in wants and desires. Wants and desires stimulate behavior and actions directed toward goals. We gain information about those goals through communication.

Needs.   All individuals have inner needs or motives which create tension within them and stimulate them to action designed to satisfy the needs and relieve the tension (Scott 1965). In this discussion the terms "need," "motive," and "drive" are used synonymously. Although there are technical distinctions between them, the distinctions are highly complicated and ignoring them will not detract from the discussion. Needs or motives have their origin in the biological and sociopsychological makeup of the individual. They exist in virtually unlimited numbers in most people, so that it is almost impossible for individuals ever to satisfy fully all of their needs — there always will be needs which stimulate individuals to action.

Human needs arise from the biological and sociopsychological makeup of individuals. Although these two aspects of individuals interact, needs tend to arise and be more closely associated with one or the other of the two. Needs which arise from the biological makeup of the human organism are referred to as basic or primary needs — needs that people have for food, water, oxygen, and basic protection from the elements. Needs which arise from the sociopsychological makeup of the individual are called secondary or higher order needs — needs of the mind and spirit, rather than needs of the body (Berelson and Steiner 1964). As an example of secondary needs, all people have a need for praise from their fellow human beings. Secondary needs are much more numerous and have a much greater influence on most people's behavior than have primary needs.

Primary and secondary refer to groups of needs and not to one single need. Within each group are numerous specific needs. For example, most individuals have an unlimited number of secondary needs, among which are needs for communication, companionship, achievement, recognition, and so on. The needs in each group tend to have certain characteristics in common; primary needs must be satisfied fairly frequently, while secondary needs do not necessarily exhibit this characteristic. Primary needs, at any given time, may be relatively well satisfied; most of the secondary needs never can be fully satisfied. Secondary needs vary more in intensity — among themselves and between individuals — than do primary needs. Secondary needs may be hidden from conscious recognition, so that individuals are not even aware that their needs are affecting their behavior (Davis 1972).

Although all individuals have needs, needs exist in individuals in different degrees of intensity. Some individuals have much stronger needs in general and/or stronger specific needs than other individuals. These differences in need strength influence the behavior which results. Generally, the amount of energy an individual expends in behavior is positively related to the strength of the need he or she is trying to satisfy (Atkinson 1957). This means that the stronger the need, the greater the stimulation and, all else being equal, the more vigorous the resulting behavior. For example, a highly ambitious student who wants an A in a communication course will probably put in long hours working for the grade if he or she thinks the grade will help in gaining admission to law school, and the student sees law school as a major step toward "success." Another student, who wants high grades because getting them is "nice," will not work as hard.

Throughout this discussion an important assumption has been implied: not all needs create tension and stimulation which result in behavior. At any given point in time, individuals have some needs which are relatively well satisfied or at least partially well satisfied, and some unsatisfied needs. The satisfied needs do not motivate, rather the unsatisfied needs are the ones which create tension and motivate behavior (Maslow 1954).

Wants and Desires. Behavior is intended to satisfy needs, but needs are most often expressed as wants and desires, that is, needs usually are expressed in terms of what individuals want or desire. Although needs, wants, and desires are closely related, they are not exactly the same. Needs are more basic; wants and desires arise from needs, and there may be several wants and desires associated with the same need. For example, people may be trying to satisfy the need for nourishment, but they probably want both solid food to eat and liquid to drink.

The wants and desires which arise from particular needs may vary greatly from one individual to another. The wants and desires which arise from any given need are greatly influenced by individuals' past experiences and present situations. All individuals have needs for food, but not all individuals want similar things to eat. What individuals want to eat is primarily a result of their past experiences, which determine what they have learned to want, what they perceive as a practical possibility at the particular time, and what information has been communicated about things to eat.

It should be obvious that not all wants and desires result in behavior. Most people have many wants and desires which have little or no effect upon their behavior. As has been stated previously, there usually are many wants associated with a particular need. Some of these wants and desires are associated more closely with one certain need than with another and therefore are stronger. The strongest wants and desires are the ones which lead to behavior.

A particular want or desire may or may not result in behavior for at least two other reasons. Wants and desires may be associated with more than one need. The more needs a particular want is related to, the stronger it becomes (Berelson and Steiner 1964). For example, a person may want a particular home in which to live, because it provides him or her with basic protection from the elements and with status. A want associated with several needs may be strong enough to result in behavior, when it would not do so if it were associated with only one need. Also, it is possible that individuals realize that certain wants and desires are unrealistic and, therefore, they do not pursue them actively. Nevertheless, the stronger wants and desires result in behavior directed toward goals which satisfy needs.

Behavior. The third and, in many respects, the most important part of the model needs little explanation at this point. Behavior is the action — mental or physical — that people take in pursuit of need satisfaction. This particular part of the model is seen everywhere; it refers to almost all the behavior we see every day, exhibited by everyone with whom we come in contact. Its specific forms are so diverse that they defy complete description. What is important is that almost all the behavior we observe every day results from needs and wants and desires, and has satisfaction as its objective. The behavior is intended to achieve goals which the individuals perceive are likely to result in need satisfaction.

From another standpoint, behavior is an expression and use of the individuals' abilities such as thinking, acting, and communicating. Individuals have abilities as well as needs, and their abilities are used through behavior to try to satisfy their needs. Thus, behavior not only has need satisfaction as its objective, but it is also the means whereby individuals use their abilities.

Goals and Satisfaction. Those things individuals have received information about which might satisfy their needs and reduce tension are referred to as "goals." Goals may take one or a combination of three forms: they may be objects, conditions, or activities. To some extent, this only means that goals often can be stated in alternative ways. For example, the goal may be food, satiation, or eating. The fact that goals often can be stated alternatively as objects, conditions, or activities may not seem important, but, from an analytical standpoint, the behavior of individuals may be very difficult for other individuals to understand if they perceive the other individuals' goals quite narrowly.

Obviously, goals are quite closely related to wants and desires, but the two are not necessarily synonymous. Goals are external to individuals and are specific things which individuals perceive as being likely to satisfy internal wants and desires and needs. There probably are several goals associated with each general want or desire. For example, as will be shown later, all individuals have needs for feelings of worthiness which result in wants for status as evidence of this worthiness. Some individuals may seek the goal of a luxurious automobile to satisfy the want for status and the need for a feeling of worthiness.

The particular goals associated with any want or desire may exist in a hierarchy (Maslow 1954). A goal's position in this hierarchy depends upon the amount of need satisfaction that the individual perceives is associated with the goal. Different goals have different amounts of satisfaction power for different individuals and from time to time for the same individual.

The amount of satisfaction power that individuals attach to a particular goal is influenced by several factors. Individuals' perceptions of the satisfaction power associated with any particular goal are influenced by their past learning experiences. Since no two individuals ever have exactly the same learning experiences, the amount of satisfaction that each individual attaches to a goal varies, and, since learning is more or less a continuous process, the satisfaction power of particular goals for particular individuals changes through time (McClelland et al. 1953). The satisfaction power of goals also seems to be related to the difficulty of achieving the goal. Generally speaking, the more difficult the goal is to attain, the more need satisfaction it produces (Atkinson 1957). To some extent, this statement is merely an elaboration of the well-known proverb, "If it's worth having, it's worth working for."

The attainment of goals by individuals does not always result in need satisfaction and tension reduction. Individuals seek goals they perceive will satisfy needs, but their perceptions are not always accurate because individuals receive little or inaccurate information about a particular goal. Readers probably can recall a goal they sought and attained and, then, wondered for what reason. In addition, some needs never can be fully satisfied; therefore, although achieving a goal may result in satisfaction and some tension reduction, tension still may be present.

Some Conclusions

The fact that motivation and needs cause and guide behavior has some important implications. The first is that it applies that all people who exhibit behavior are motivated. The statement that "old so-and-so is not motivated" or "is highly motivated" is heard often. Statements such as this assume incorrectly that individuals are either motivated or not motivated to some degree. In a real sense this is not true, for all individuals are motivated; it is a matter of how highly they are motivated and in what direction. In simple terms, all people are motivated, but not to the same degree nor by the same things.

The second important implication is that the behavior of individuals is rational and selfish. Behavior is rational from the standpoint of the individuals exhibiting it, because it is intended to satisfy needs. Behavior is selfish because it is exhibited to create need satisfaction for the persons exhibiting it. The behavior exhibited may help or harm other people, but whatever its actual effect on others or on the individuals, its intended purpose is need satisfaction.

Although the model in figure 6-1 and its explanation give a sound but relatively simple explanation of behavior, its usefulness in analyzing observed behavior still is limited. The model becomes more valuable as an analytical tool if we know more about certain critical elements in it.

Common Human Needs

Earlier in the discussion we described needs by their basic origin as primary or secondary. At this point a more detailed description seems needed. In this part three different (but similar) ways of classifying and describing human needs are presented.

Before any specific needs are described, a word about the universality of needs is in order. It is probably true that no two individuals have exactly the same need structure, but if there were vast differences in needs among individuals, a general description of human needs would be impossible. To be useful, such a discussion would need to focus on each individual one at a time. Fortunately, there is enough similarity in need structures among individuals to make classification and generalized description meaningful.

Maslow's Need Hierarchy

The psychologist Abraham H. Maslow (1954) developed the most widely known and used classification and description of common human needs. Maslow feels that human beings have five general classes of needs — physiological needs, safety and security needs, social needs, esteem needs, and self-realization needs. As figure 6-2 indicates, these five classes of needs are arranged in a hierarchy, so that the appearance of one class of needs depends upon the satisfaction of the more basic classes of needs. The most basic of all the need levels, of course, is the lowest one in the hierarchy — physiological needs.

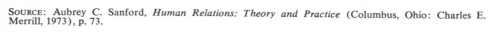
Source: Aubrey C. Sanford, *Human Relations: Theory and Practice* (Columbus, Ohio: Charles E. Merrill, 1973), p. 73.

Figure 6-2   Hierarchy of Common Needs

Physiological Needs.   The lowest level of needs on the hierarchy and the ones which individuals try to satisfy first are those which must be satisfied to sustain life. This level of needs most nearly corresponds to the primary needs mentioned earlier. It includes the needs for nourishment, oxygen, protection from the elements, and rest. These are needs of the body and are present in all people. Until these needs are at least relatively well satisfied, they tend to dominate the behavior of individuals, which means that behavior is primarily aimed at satisfying this level of needs. As Maslow (1943, p. 87) states facetiously, "It is quite true that man lives by bread alone — when there is no bread."

Safety and Security Needs. Safety and security needs are the next set of needs to have a dominant influence on the behavior of individuals. In many respects, these needs are closely related to the physiological needs; they represent needs for freedom from bodily harm and needs for security.

There are two basic types of security needs — economic security and "self" security. The needs for economic security refer to individuals' concern for the continued satisfaction of their physiological needs. As one authority states (Davis 1972, pp. 46-47), "Having met his basic physiological needs, man wants some assurance that they will continue to be met tomorrow and thereafter, and with less effort, pain, or worry if possible." The security needs also include needs for "self" security. All people need to know and understand what other people and society in general consider acceptable behavior. Unless the boundaries of acceptable behavior are known, individuals do not know how to behave in order to obtain the desired reaction from others. Individuals may disagree with the accepted boundaries of behavior, but they need and want to know what they are.

Social Needs. Social needs are the next highest level of needs in the hierarchy and have a significant influence on the behavior of individuals only after the safety and security needs have been relatively well satisfied. They include the needs for both giving and receiving love and affection, the need to accept, associate with and be accepted by others, the need to belong or to feel one's self a part of social groups, and the need to communicate with other people.

Esteem Needs. The fourth level of needs in Maslow's hierarchy are the needs for esteem — self-esteem and esteem from others. This class includes the needs for respect of others, a feeling of achievement, recognition, appreciation, freedom, status, prestige and, generally, a feeling of worthiness — the needs are normally satisfied through communication with others. Individuals have these needs for themselves and for other people. It is believed that this class of needs exerts the strongest influence on the behavior of individuals in most of the economically well-developed nations of the world today.

Self-Realization Needs. The highest level of needs in the hierarchy is for fulfillment and self-realization. Similar to all other classes, these needs influence the behavior of the individuals at all times, but they tend to dominate only after the four lower classes of needs have been at least partially well satisfied. This category includes the needs for self-fulfillment by the full utilization of one's abilities. It is believed that included in this class are the needs for creative expression and contribution to worthwhile objectives. Thus, individuals have to feel that they are using their abilities to the fullest, thereby accomplishing all they are capable of accomplishing.

As can be seen from the above discussion and explanation, the concept of a hierarchy of needs and influence is central to understanding needs and how they affect behavior.

The Concept of Hierarchy. For several reasons, the idea of needs existing and influencing behavior in a predetermined order is not as simple as has been implied in the previous discussion.

Blending of classes — First of all, needs exist within individuals, and the classes of needs are not so clear cut. The five classes of needs do not represent five distinctly different types of needs; instead, they represent five closely related general types of needs, with each class tending to overlap and/or blend into the next class.

Need interaction — Second, behavior during any given period of time or any single act of behavior probably is the result of more than one need or class of needs. It is true that the lowest level relatively unsatisfied class has the greatest influence on the behavior of individuals, but more than likely it is not the only class of needs influencing behavior. This is especially true when individuals' behavior tends to be dominated by one of the three highest levels of needs. As figure 6-3 indicates, most acts of behavior are influenced by all five classes of needs, with one of the classes (usually the lowest level relatively unsatisfied one) having the greatest effect.

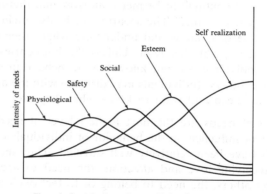

The peak of each level must be passed before the next level can begin to assume a dominant role. With self-development, the number and variety of wants increase. Note that in the esteem peak the different needs of an individual are simultaneously active.

The peak of each level must be passed before the next level can begin to assume a dominant role. With self-development, the number and variety of wants increase. Note that in the esteem peak the different needs of an individual are simultaneously active.

SOURCE: Adapted from David Krech et al., *The Individual in Society* (New York: McGraw-Hill, 1962), p. 77. Used by permission.

Figure 6-3   Level of Need Satisfaction

Threatened needs — Third, the statement that the lowest level relatively unsatisfied needs are the ones having the greatest influence on behavior at any given time should be modified to some extent. The behavior of individuals can be affected greatly by a level of needs which may be well satisfied at the time, if they perceive that the continued satisfaction of the class of needs is threatened. Thus, the behavior of individuals, at any given time, is directed toward satisfying the lowest level relatively unsatisfied needs, or assuring continued satisfaction of a lower class of needs, the future satisfaction of which is threatened.

Movement up the hierarchy — Finally, the idea that classes of needs exert their influence on behavior in a predetermined order should not be interpreted too simply. The higher order needs generally do not have a significant effect upon individuals' behavior until later in their lifetimes, but this should not be taken to mean that individuals spend a portion of their lives satisfying the first level and then a portion satisfying safety and security needs, and so on. A little reflection reveals that some of the classes, especially the lower levels, must be satisfied fairly frequently. During the course of a lifetime, or for that matter a day or a week, individuals move up and down the hierarchy, and their behavior shifts to try to satisfy the lowest level unsatisfied or threatened need at any particular time. With this in mind, it can be said that during any given period of time, the behavior of individuals is influenced more by one class of needs than by others, and that movement up the hierarchy progresses almost in a similar manner as individuals move through their life span.

Research on the Hierarchy.   Research on the validity of Maslow's hierarchy is still sparse and inconclusive. Using Maslow's hierarchy concept, Clark (1961) suggested that the results of many research studies and many case descriptions could be explained in terms of the concept of hierarchy. In a more rigorous test, Alderfer (1969) conducted a cross-sectional study of need strength. The conclusions of this study failed to support the hierarchy concept as described by Maslow. Lawler and Suttle (1972) tested the hierarchy concept with a limited range of time series data. Their results also failed to support the strict concept of hierarchy.

Does this mean that the hierarchy concept is invalid and should be abandoned? We think not. Lawler and Suttle warn that studies covering longer periods of time need to be done. In addition, there is much intuitive logic behind the idea of a need hierarchy. It is still one of the most widely known and accepted theories of motivation and behavior.

Social Motives

A second widely accepted explanation and description of common human needs is that of McClelland and Atkinson (McClelland 1953; Atkinson 1966). According to this theory only two needs are inherent — the need for pleasure and the need to avoid pain. All other needs or motives are learned. However, since many life problem-solving experiences are almost universal (such as learning to walk, talk) people tend to learn the same types of needs, but to different degrees. So people tend to have the same needs but with differing strengths and intensities.

Several different social motives have been identified and described, but only the three strongest common needs are included here. Achievement needs, power needs, and affiliation needs are described below.

Achievement Need.   In its simplest form the achievement need refers to the desire to compete against a standard of excellence. Heckhausen (1963) describes achievement in the following way:

> In its simplest form, the standard of excellence represents a classification of alternatives: passed-failed; good-bad . . . . Achievement motivation can, therefore, be defined as the striving to keep as high as possible one's own capability in all activity in which a standard of excellence is thought to apply and where execution of such activities can, therefore, either succeed or fail. (pp. 4–5)

McClelland believes (and has some research support for the belief) that the achievement need is one of the strongest common human needs.

Power Need.   A second strong common need is the need for power. The power need is described by Atkinson (1958, p. 105) as ". . . that disposition directing behavior toward satisfaction contingent upon the control of the means of influencing another person. In the phenomenal sphere of the power motivated individual he considers himself the 'gatekeeper' to certain decision making of others. The means of control can be anything at all that can be used to manipulate another person." So the need for power refers to the desire to influence, regulate, and control the actions and behavior of other people. In this context, the need for power is usually exercised through communication.

Affiliation Need.   A third important common need is the need for affiliation. Affiliation refers to needs for positive relationships with other people and is probably best described by the word *friendship* (Kolb et al. 1974). It includes such things as needs for friendship, companionship, affection, feelings of belonging and acceptance, and so on. A major aspect of the affiliation need is the need for communication. To affiliate, people must communicate. Thus, like power, the need for affiliation is satisfied through communication.

Effects of Social Motives.   Kolb (1974) and his colleagues point out that the three motives are different but interact to determine a person's interpersonal behavior. The needs for power and affiliation are both interpersonal needs. That is, other individuals are necessary for control to be exercised or for friends to exist. The need for achievement may or may not require other people for its satisfaction. Thus, to achieve a person may need other people; but the nature of the relationship established will primarily be determined by the needs for power and affiliation.

Ardrey's Territorial Theory

A third, but less widely known, description of common human needs is that from the area of cultural anthropology advanced by Robert Ardrey (1966). According to Ardrey, individuals have three types of basic needs — identity, security, and stimulation. Thus, individuals strive for ". . . identity, not anonymity; stimulation, not boredom; security not anxiety . . . . We shun anonymity, dread boredom, seek to dispel anxiety. We grasp at identification, yearn for stimulation, conserve or gain security" (pp. 334–35).

It is Ardrey's belief that "property" or "territory" is one of the prime things that satisfies these needs, so much individual behavior is directed toward acquiring property and/or staking out or defending territory. In this context, property and territory are used broadly to refer to a range of things running from real property to a favorite and customary seat in the classroom. Research (Sirota 1973) is now beginning to support the importance of territory in satisfying needs.

To summarize the discussion of common human needs, we would like to point out the similarities and interrelationships that exist between the three theories described above. Table 1 summarizes the similarities. It seems that Maslow's self-actualization need corresponds closely to McClelland's achievement need and to Ardrey's need for identity. Similarly, it seems that Maslow's esteem need might relate to McClelland's power and/or achievement motives and to Ardrey's need for stimulation. It also seems clear that Maslow's social need is closely related to McClelland's affiliation need. Finally, Maslow's two basic needs seem closely related to Ardrey's need for security.

Table 1   Comparison Common Human Needs

	MASLOW	McCLELLAND	ARDREY
	Self-Actualization	Achievement	Identity
	Esteem	Power	Stimulation
NEED	Social	Affiliation	
	Security		Security
	Physiological		Security

In concluding the discussion of common human needs, two points deserve emphasis. First, while behavior is caused by needs, individuals may or may not be consciously aware of the needs that are causing their behavior. A great many of the needs people try to satisfy are unconscious needs. Behavior is caused by needs; it is a means to the end of need satisfaction and from this standpoint it is both selfish and rational.

The second point is that there is strong evidence, based on observations of behavior in organizations and some research evidence, supporting the idea that most people in our society are significantly influenced by higher order needs. Porter (1961, 1963) found that this was true for almost all levels of employees. So, no matter which description of human needs one subscribes to, certain types of needs, achievement, esteem, power, and identity seem to be the more important ones in our society.

Need Satisfaction

Having described common human needs, we now turn our attention to need satisfaction. Individuals exhibit behaviors directed toward goals that they perceive will result in at least some satisfaction of their motivating needs. This section explains the general types of satisfaction goals provide and the important institutional sources of need satisfaction.

Goals and Satisfaction

Generally speaking individuals seek goals through their behavior that provide satisfaction in one or both of two ways — intrinsically and extrinsically.

Intrinsically Satisfying Goals. Some goals that people seek are simply satisfying within themselves. Take, for example, the pride and satisfaction associated with completing and doing a particular job or task well. The mere act of doing this produces satisfaction. Thus, intrinsically satisfying goals tend to produce need satisfaction symbolically by what they represent, e.g., achievement in the illustration above.

Extrinsically Satisfying Goals. Some goals produce satisfaction not so much within themselves or by what they represent but by what other satisfactions they can provide. In one sense, extrinsically satisfying goals are only intermediate goals which can be used to attain the real need satisfaction desired. One prime example of this type of goal is money. While it is valued for other reasons (often symbolically as a measure of achievement), money provides the means of satisfying other needs through the goals it will buy.

Many goals are capable of providing both intrinsic and extrinsic satisfaction. Whether a particular goal is intrinsically or extrinsically satisfying or both depends on individual needs, perceptions, and available alternative goals. For example, depending on past experiences, money may or may not be seen as a symbol of achievement. Another possibility is that in the absence of other meaningful indicators of achievement, individuals may use money symbolically as a measure of achievement. The above are some ideas that apply to many goals other than money. The important points to remember are that the goals individuals seek provide satisfaction in different ways and that the type of satisfaction associated with a goal depends on individual needs, past experiences, and the communication individuals have received about alternatives.

Sources of Satisfactions

Whether they are intrinsically or extrinsically satisfying, there must be some potential source of the goals for individuals. The different potential sources of goals and, therefore, need satisfaction are almost endless, but, especially in modern industrial societies, interdependence is a fact and way of life. The result of such interdependence is that individuals tend to be dependent in some way on other people and social institutions in particular as sources of goals. Many of the goals sought by individuals are either available only through social institutions or they are more easily achieved through social institutions. Three of the more important of these potential sources of goals — the family, organized religion, and work in organizations — are discussed below.

Work in Organizations. It is through work in organizations that individuals satisfy many of their needs. For the great majority of people, it is through work that extrinsic goals are achieved and basic needs are satisfied, and it is through work and organizational affiliations that much social satisfaction is attained. One authority (Levinson 1965) believes that work in organizations is now challenging the traditional extended family as a source of social goals and need satisfaction. Work in organizations also seems to be an important source of satisfaction for the higher order psychological needs. Also, it is believed that work now is the principal means by which individuals seek to achieve goals which enhance their human dignity (Levinson 1964). The belief that work in organizations is an important source of goals and need satisfaction is indicated by the conclusion that approximately 75 percent of all psychiatric patients suffer from lack of work satisfaction (Levinson 1965). Although it is possibly the most important potential source of goals, work is certainly not the only source.

The Family. In many societies and especially in the United States, the family and the extended family have traditionally been important sources of goals and need satisfaction. At the minimum, the family offers social goals and social satisfaction; equally important, as an institution it offers goals capable of satisfying needs and, to a lesser degree, psychological needs. The family is an important source of need satisfaction for many individuals, but its relative importance seems to have diminished as the institution of work in organizations has grown more important. Today, for many people, the family is a significant source of goals and satisfaction for social needs and, to a lesser degree, for security needs.

Organized Religion. Any discussion of important social institutions providing need satisfaction for individuals would be incomplete without mentioning religion. Organized religion in the past has been and continues to be an important source of security and social and psychological satisfaction.

Although religion and the family are important sources of need satisfaction, the number of goals they offer is more limited than the potential number available through work in organizations. From the standpoint of the number of goals and the absolute amount of potential satisfaction available, work is the most important source of need satisfaction for most individuals.

Motivation in Organizations

The question of what goals and satisfactions people seek through work has been the subject of numerous research studies (Brayfield and Crocket 1955; Herzberg et al. 1959). It continues to be an issue today. No definitive answers have been found, but some practically useful answers have been developed. In this section two of the more widely known work motivation models — the Vroom Expectancy Model and the Porter and Lawler Model — are explained.

Vroom's Expectancy Model

The model of work motivation set forth by Vroom (1964) concentrates on goals and outcomes rather than internal needs. The idea is that motivation is a function of three factors: (1) the strength or desirability of the goal, (2) perceived ability to exhibit the required behavior, and (3) the perceived probability that the behavior will result in the goal. Figure 6-4 illustrates the relationship among these three variables.

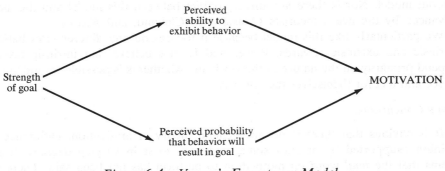

Figure 6-4   Vroom's Expectancy Model

An example helps us understand the model. Suppose that an individual desires a raise in pay or a promotion. Whether this goal is translated to behavior depends partially on whether the individual believes that certain behavior (higher performance) will result in the goal (salary increase or promotion) and partially on whether he or she believes he or she can exhibit the behavior (higher performance) required. Thus motivation to work tends to depend heavily on the individual and people are motivated to perform to the degree that they believe that performance will result in the goals that they are seeking.

Behavior can be motivated by weak as well as by strong goals. Relatively weak goals might motivate behavior if there is a strong belief about the behavior resulting in the goal and that the behavior can be successfully exhibited. Research (Galbraith and Cummings 1967) on Vroom's model indicates that performance is positively related to pay and supervisory support.*

The Porter and Lawler Model

The Porter and Lawler Model (1967) developed from investigations of the relationship between satisfaction and productivity. A commonly held conclusion of the Hawthorne studies was that satisfaction led to productivity (performance). This model hypothesizes that performance leads to satisfaction and that the variable of rewards intervenes between performance and satisfaction. Figure 6-5 illustrates the relationship in the Porter and Lawler model.

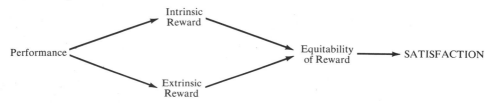

SOURCE: E. E. Lawler III and L. W. Porter, "Antecedent Job Attitudes of Effective Managerial Performance," *Organizational Behavior and Human Performance* 2 (1967):122-42. Used by permission.

Figure 6-5   Porter and Lawler Model of Motivation

The implied assumption in the Porter and Lawler model is that *perceptions* of rewards, which include the amount of information about the rewards, and their equitability determine performance. So, this model is not entirely different from the Vroom model. Nor is there any direct conflict between this model and the model advanced by the needs theorists (Maslow, McClelland, and Ardrey).

We particularly like this model because it focuses on and differentiates between intrinsic and extrinsic rewards. Porter and Lawler believe that intrinsic rewards depend primarily on the nature of the work and whether is is possible for individuals to see and feel for themselves the rewards.

Some Conclusions

It is obvious that there is no one general theory of motivation. Differences of opinion (supported by at least some evidence) exist in varying degrees. It also seems that the *final word* on motivation to perform has not been said. There still remain many questions, and there is still much work to be done before many of the models are valuable practical managerial tools.

---

*See also P. Mitchell and A. Bigland, "Instrumentality Theories: Current Uses in Psychology," *Psychological Bulletin* 76 (1971): 432-54 for a review of the literature in the area.

Organizational Implications

Several factors about the individual seem especially significant. One is that the degree to which needs are satisfied is a prime determinant of individual behavior, satisfaction, and performance. Organizational effectiveness and these things are greatly influenced by the types of goals organizations make available. Another factor is that the other internal organization variables (the reward system used, technology and the design of jobs, intergroup relations, organization objectives, and the leadership style used), in large part, determine the goals that are available to individuals and, therefore, individual behavior. An individual's communication activity is, in reality, a main part of behavior. Thus, these organizational variables can encourage or discourage effective interpersonal communication and development and improvement of communication skills.

Communication Implications

Perhaps the most obvious implications that the above concepts and theories have for organizational communication deal with individual satisfaction and communication climate. Much of the need satisfaction people seek in organizations is actually achieved and experienced through interaction (communication) with others. In turn, the degree to which people experience satisfaction in organizations would seem to affect their attitudes toward effective communication. In other words, the degree to which people experience satisfaction influences their willingness (communication climate) to communicate.

Summary

The individual is the core element in organizations. Behavior is a product of the personality and motivation. This implies that behavior is caused and directed toward goals.

The driving force producing behavior is unsatisfied internal needs. Maslow believes that five classes of needs — physiological, safety and security, social, esteem, and self-actualization — tend to affect behavior in a predetermined order. McClelland believes that the three strongest common needs are achievement, power, and affiliation. Ardrey advances the idea that strong common needs are identity, security, and stimulation.

Other theorists concentrate more on goals than needs. Vroom believes that the overall probability of achieving the goal combined with strength of the desire for the goal determine the level of motivation. Porter and Lawler indicate that performance depends on the perceived equitability of both intrinsic and extrinsic rewards.

REVIEW AND DISCUSSION

1. Explain how motivation and behavior are related.

2. Explain Maslow's Need Hierarchy concept.

3. Describe the three most important social motives advanced by McClelland.

4. Explain Vroom's Expectancy Model of motivation.

5. Explain Porter and Lawler's Model of Motivation.

6. Point out similarities and differences in the Vroom Expectancy Model and the Porter and Lawler Model.

7. Explain your grade point average in this class in terms of the Porter and Lawler Model.

Chapter Seven

Organizational Structure

The individual is the most important and complex internal element of organization, but organizations also have structure. That is, individuals in organizations act and interact according to some defined plan or pattern. This structure is both an important part of the formal communication subsystem and an important influence on the other elements — climate and interpersonal skills — of organizational communication systems.

This chapter will explain this important internal element of organization as it relates to organizational behavior and communication. First we discuss the purpose of structure, what structures really are, some of the basic concepts of structure, and the determinants of structure. In the second part of the chapter some of the more relevant research focusing on the effects of structure on behavior and communication is presented.

The Nature of Organizational Structure

All organizations have a more or less well-defined structure of relationships. The purpose of this structure is to provide a means for coordinating all of the individual efforts necessary to achieve organizational objectives. Organizational structures are

95

actually systems of activity and authority created by the application of certain concepts. The particular way in which any given organization is structured depends on both external environmental factors and on other internal organizational elements. Structures require information to operate efficiently. To obtain and transmit requisite information, they create formal mechanisms for communication. The formal mechanisms, which we have labeled the formal subsystem, will be considered in detail in chapter twelve.

The Purpose of Structure

Organizational structures are not ends in themselves; they are one of the means to the end of coordinated individual and organizational activity. In a very simple sense, the purpose of structure in organizations is to help everyone know who is supposed to do what and who reports to whom, so that necessary activities can be meshed together in the best way. Thus, structure is one of the primary tools used to make sure that all of the activities necessary to achieve organizational objectives are performed in a coordinated fashion and that there is no unnecessary duplication of activities. This is accomplished through communication via the formal subsystem.

What Organizational Structures Really Are

In their most basic form, organizational structures are activity-authority systems. If we focus on just the structure of organizations, we find that they are made up of activity groups (at the lowest level these activity groupings are more commonly known as jobs) tied together or related to each other by authority.

The first comprehensive, and now classic, description of organizational structure was that by Weber (1946). Weber's analysis is relevant here not so much for the analytical insight it provides, but because it is a good description of many of the important aspects of organizational structure. A brief summary of Weber's model is presented in the following outline.

OUTLINE OF WEBERIAN BUREAUCRACY

General Principles

I.   There is the principle of fixed and official jurisdictional areas, which are generally ordered by rules, that is, by laws or administrative regulations.

   A. The regular activities required for the purposes of the bureaucratically governed are distributed in a fixed way as official duties.

   B. The authority to give the commands required for the discharge of these duties is distributed in a stable way and is strictly delimited by rules concerning the coercive means, physical sacerdotal, or otherwise, which may be placed at the disposal of officials.

   C. Methodical provision is made for the regulation and continuous fulfillment of these duties and for the corresponding rights. Only persons who have the generally regulated qualifications to serve are employed. . . .

II. The principles of office hierarchy and levels of graded authority mean a firmly ordered system of super and subordination in which there is a supervision of lower offices by the higher ones. . . . Once established and having fulfilled its task, an office tends to continue in existence and be held by another incumbent.

III. The management of the modern office is based upon written documents ("the files") which are preserved in their original or draught form. . . .

IV. Office management, at least all specialized office management, . . . usually presupposes thorough and expert training. . . .

V. When the office is fully developed, the official activity demands the full-working capacity of the official, irrespective of the fact that his [or her] obligatory time in the bureau may be firmly delimited. . . .

The Position of the Official

I. Office holding is a "vocation." This is shown, first, in the requirement of a firmly prescribed course of training which demands the entire capacity for work for a long period of time, and in the generally prescribed and special examinations which are prerequisites of employment. . . . It is decisive for the specific nature of modern loyalty to an office, that, in the pure type, it does not establish a relationship to a *person*, like the vassal's or disciple's faith in feudal or in patrimonial relations of authority. Modern loyalty is devoted to impersonal and functional purposes. . . .

II. The personal position of the official is patterned in the following ways:

   A. Whether he [or she] is in a private office or in a public bureau, the modern official always strives and usually enjoys a distinct *social esteem* as compared with the governed. . . .

   B. The pure type of bureaucratic official is *appointed* by a superior authority. . . .

   C. Normally, the position of the official is held for life, at least in public bureaucracies, and this is increasingly the case for all similar structures. As a factual rule, *tenure for life* is presupposed even when the giving of notice or periodic reappointment occurs. In contrast to the worker in a private enterprise, the official normally holds tenure. . . .

   D. The official receives the regular *pecuniary* compensation of a normally fixed salary and the old age security provided by a pension. The salary is not measured like a wage in terms of work done, but according to "status," that is, according to the kind of function (the "rank") and, in addition, possibly, according to length of service. . . .

   E. The official is set for a "*career*" within the hierarchical order of the public service. He [or she] moves from the lower, less important and lesser paid, to the higher positions. . . .*

Basic Concepts of Organizing

Organizational structures are products of the process of organizing — of grouping activities and relating these activities with authority. The organizing process is a universal process built primarily on the work of Weber. Organizational structures are developed through the application of particular concepts and principles. The

*From *From Max Weber: Essays in Sociology* edited and translated by H. H. Gerth and C. Wright Mills. Copyright 1946 by Oxford University Press, Inc. Renewed 1973 by Dr. Hans H. Gerth. Reprinted by permission.

cornerstones of organizational structure are the concepts of specialization of work; unity of command; span of supervision; and authority, power, and responsibility. Each of these concepts is described and explained below.

Specialization of Work.   Perhaps one of the most basic and widely used concepts of organization is the economic principle of division of work and specialization. This principle and its use dates back at least to the 1700s (Smith 1937, orig. 1776).

Basically the principle of *division of work* and *specialization* states that greater efficiency is achieved when work is divided so that people perform simple activities and jobs rather than complex activities and jobs. Thus, the principle of division of work refers to dividing work up into small tasks so that individuals can specialize in the performance of a relatively limited set of activities.

General benefits of specialization — The general reason for using the principle of division of work and specialization is that it makes performance of tasks that are too large or complex for one person possible. Many jobs (in fact, the overall job of most organizations) are simply too big for one person physically to do. Dividing the job up among many different people makes its performance possible. Closely related to this is the fact that many jobs (again, almost all of the overall "jobs" of all organizations) require more knowledge than any one person is likely to possess. Dividing the total job into parts and, therefore, the knowledge required to do the job makes performance possible. In this sense, specialization allows individuals to overcome their physical and mental limitations, and it makes large-scale organizations possible (Barnard 1938).

Specific benefits of specialization — The more specific benefits of division of work and specialization are that it makes higher levels of individual performance possible. Both research and experience indicate that a person's level of performance on a job is determined by two things — one is the person's level of ability, and the second is the person's motivation to use his or her ability to do the job. Stated another way:

$$Performance = ability \times motivation$$

When work is divided so that a person can specialize in the performance of a limited range of activity, it has the effect of increasing ability. In the equation above, if motivation remains constant and ability is increased, then performance will increase. So division of work and specialization increase performance by increasing people's abilities to do the jobs required of them.

Limitations of specialization — While it is believed that the principle of division of work and specialization is valid, research and experience indicate that extremely high degrees of specialization may decrease rather than increase individuals' levels of performance. The evidence (Herzberg 1959; Myers 1964, 1966) suggests that when work activities are divided into extremely small units, people tend to have difficulty relating their performance to meaningful achievement. That is, when people's jobs become highly specialized and very small in scope, they have difficulty seeing the real worth of the job. When this happens, motivation to perform the job is likely to decrease; if there is a large decrease in motivation, performance may not be as high as it otherwise would be. Whether the resulting decrease in motivation actually lowers performance or not depends on whether the decrease caused by less motivation is larger than the increase resulting from a higher level of ability.

It should be pointed out that some degree of division of work and specialization probably increases motivation to perform. Take, for example, work which is entirely too difficult for a person to do or jobs which, because of their size, are beyond the scope of one person's ability, such as building a hydroelectric dam. It seems reasonable to conclude that some division of work and specialization of these types of jobs, assuming people have appropriate information about them, would tend to increase people's motivations to perform.

In light of all its effects, it seems that division of work and specialization are a necessity for large organizations to exist and perform efficiently. It also appears that better performance might result from more motivation brought about by less specialization, especially where jobs are very narrow and routine.

Application of the principle — Application of the principle of division of work actually takes place in the organizing process through the grouping of activities into positions and jobs. There is not one but several different bases for grouping activities or dividing work so that specialization results.

Unity of Command.   A second fundamental concept of organizing is the principle of *unity of command*. The principle states that coordination of activities is easier when each person has only one superior. Simply stated, everyone in the organization should have only one boss and each boss is responsible for communicating with his or her subordinates.

Like the principle of division of work and specialization, unity of command is not a recently recognized principle of organization. It dates back to at least biblical times. Luke 16:13 states, "No servant can serve two masters: for either he will hate the one, and love the other; or else he will hold to the one and despise the other."

The application of the principle of unity of command is related to the division of work and specialization. While division of work makes large-scale jobs possible and promotes efficiency through specialization, it also results in some problems. It makes the coordination of activities difficult because the activities are divided into relatively small groups performed by different people. The activities of any group of subordinates are easier to coordinate if the subordinates have only one boss.

The reasonableness of this principle is difficult to argue. At some time or another almost everyone has either had two bosses or has tried to share authority over subordinates with another and is familiar with the usual consequences. Confusion, unhappy subordinates and superiors, lack of coordination and communication, and generally ineffective performance are not uncommon results.

The real difficulty with the application of unity of command is that it is almost impossible to apply without exception in large complex organizations. The need for consistency of action and the need for expert knowledge in many areas of decision making cause organizations to divide authority over some things among several people. The result of this is that people have more than one boss, and it seems necessary that this be the case. In actual practice, the application of the principle of unity of command focuses on trying to assure that each person will have only one primary boss and that the authority of secondary bosses be clearly communicated and understood by all.

The application of the unity of command principle takes place in the organizing process with the delegation of authority. Thus, the degree to which the principle is applied or violated depends on how well task assignments and authority delegations are made. The subject of delegation of authority is covered in more detail below.

Span of Management.   Achieving coordination through application of the principle of unity of command and having only one boss for each person is limited by the fact that no one can supervise an unlimited number of people. The term *span of management,* or span of supervision, refers to the number of people a manager supervises. The concept of the span of management refers to the determination of how many people a manager can supervise and communicate with effectively.

Limitations of the span of management — To supervise and coordinate the activities of a large number of people, the work must be divided up among a number of people (managers), who in turn may themselves require a manager above them to supervise and coordinate their activities. Since any one person can supervise only a limited number of people, the effective supervision of large numbers of people and activities may require more than one level of management. Thus, the end result may be that there are managers who supervise managers who supervise workers.

Size of the span affects structure — The number of levels of management and the number of managers needed in an organization depends on the size of undertaking (and, therefore, the number of activities that must be supervised) and on how many people each manager at each level supervises.

For a particular organization with a given number of people, the number of levels of management and the number of managers needed depends on the span of management for each manager at each level. If broad spans of management (with each manager supervising a relatively large number of people) are used, the organization structure will have fewer levels and fewer managers than if relatively narrow spans of management are used.

Consider the example in figure 7-1. If there are sixty-four workers to be supervised and the span of management is eight at each level, then eight supervisory managers are needed and at least one manager to supervise the eight supervisors. Thus, two levels of management and nine managers are needed. In contrast, if the span is four, then three levels of management and twenty-one managers are needed — sixteen supervisors, four managers to supervise the sixteen supervisors and one top manager to supervise the four middle managers.

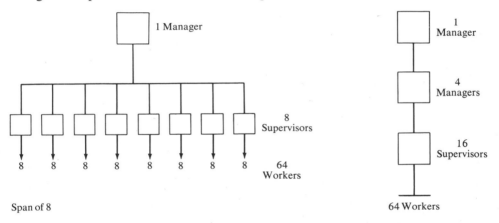

Figure 7-1   Effects of Span of Management on Organizational Structure

The number of levels of management and the number of managers have important effects on the organization's effectiveness and efficiency. If there are too few managers and levels, ineffective supervision results. On the other hand, the more levels and managers an organization has, the larger is its salary cost and the more difficult effective communication becomes. So, the important question is how wide the span be, not whether it should be relatively wide or relatively narrow.

Factors affecting the span — There are a number of factors which appear to affect the number of people that a manager can supervise effectively. Among the more important of these factors are (1) supervisory ability, (2) subordinate ability, (3) complexity of activities supervised, (4) degree to which the activities are interrelated, (5) adequacy of performance standards, (6) amount of authority delegated, and (7) availability of staff assistance.

Certainly the number of people that managers can supervise effectively is influenced by their ability and their energy level. Managers have different levels of knowledge and understanding of the management process. Within reasonable limits, the higher the level of supervisory ability the greater the number of people the manager can supervise. Two important aspects of supervisory ability — performance standards and authority delegation — have important effects on the span and are discussed separately below. People also have different energy levels and certainly people with relatively high energy levels can supervise a large number of subordinates than people with lower energy levels.

The levels of ability of the subordinates being supervised also have important effects on the number of people a manager can supervise. The higher the level of subordinates' abilities, the more people the manager can supervise. This is true because more authority can be delegated to such subordinates and because their work will require less of the supervisor's time for orientation, instructions, and control. The success of the delegation will depend on the extent to which communication is effective between the boss and his or her subordinate.

A third factor affecting the size of the span is the *complexity and diversity* of activities supervised. The simpler the activities and the more similar subordinates' activities are, the wider the span can be. When activities are very complex and when subordinates are doing entirely different types of activities, the narrower the span needs to be for effective supervision and the greater the communication needs.

The degree to which the activities of subordinates are *interrelated* also has important effects on the number of people a manager can effectively supervise. Where subordinates' jobs are interrelated and the activities of one subordinate affect the activities of other subordinates, more of the manager's time is required to coordinate activities among subordinates. Therefore, fewer people can be supervised where subordinates' jobs have significant impact on each other.

The quality and adequacy of the methods used to measure and evaluate subordinate performance are another factor influencing the span of management. The better *performance standards* are, the less time the manager has to spend in direct contact with subordinates. In contrast, if performance standards are poor, or are communicated poorly, more of the manager's time is likely to be needed for direct observation of subordinate performance. So, the better the standards of subordinate performance, the wider the span of management can be.

Another factor — *amount of and clarity of authority delegated* — that is related to both subordinate ability and supervisory ability has a significant effect on the number of people a manager can supervise. Generally, the more authority delegated, the wider the span can be because less of the supervisor's time will be needed in decision making and face-to-face communication. In addition, the more precise and accurate the communication about the delegation has been, the wider the span can be because there is less room for doubt and less need for checking with the supervisor by the subordinate. The amount of authority delegated, however, should be related to the level of ability of the subordinate, so this factor should operate within limits. The clarity and preciseness of the delegation communication depends, to a great degree, on the supervisor's managerial and interpersonal communication skills.

Last, the width of the span is affected by the quality and quantity of staff assistance available to the manager. Naturally, a manager with good staff to assist him or her in the form of both advice and service can supervise more people than one who must do everything related to the job himself or herself.

Considering how each of the seven factors affects the span of management, several conclusions can be drawn. First, there are no precise rules concerning the appropriate span of management. Second, the appropriate span ultimately depends upon the specific manager, his or her subordinates, and the work supervised. It must be determined for each manager in each situation. So, deciding on the appropriate span is a subjective, situational decision.

Spans in practice — While there are not and probably never will be any hard and fast rules which state how many people managers at any level can supervise effectively, experience has produced some rather rough conclusions and broad guidelines. It seems generally true that spans need to be narrower the higher the level of the position in the organization. In practice, spans of three to eleven at the top of organizations are commonly found, while spans from six to thirty are not unusual at lower organization levels. Again, determining the span is a subjective, *situational decision.*

Authority, Power, and Responsibility. Application of the concepts of specialization, span of management and especially unity of command are closely related to a fourth important set of organizing concepts — authority, power, and responsibility. Limiting the number of people reporting to one person, having people perform a specialized set of tasks, and preserving unity of command is made possible through authority relationships.

Authority is the thread that ties the different groups of activities (jobs) in the organization together. An organizational structure is a system of activity-authority relationships. Application of the concepts of specialization and span of management result in an activity system. Through the use of authority, power, and responsibility relationships, the different parts (job activity groupings) of the organization are linked to each other and to the total organization in some fashion. The result of the application of all four concepts is a hierarchical organization, illustrated in figure 7-2.

Authority is a right — From a management standpoint, authority is the right that a manager has to make decisions and require subordinates to do the things necessary to accomplish the organization's goals. "In an organization, the manager's authority consists of his right to such things as: (1) make decisions within the scope of his

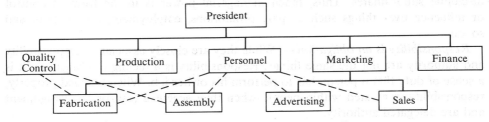

Figure 7-2   A Hypothetical Organization Structure

authority, (2) assign tasks to subordinates, and (3) expect and require satisfactory performance from subordinates" (Hicks 1972, p. 272).

Authority is a managerial right delegated from above and has its legal origins in the rights of ownership of private property. In theory, the owners of property (in the case of corporations, stockholders) delegate some of their authority to a board of directors, who in turn delegate to top level executives, who further delegate some of their authority downward. Thus, as figure 7-3 illustrates, the scope of authority is broad at the top of the organization and it becomes narrower at lower organizational levels. This results because no one can delegate more authority than he or she has and because not all of the authority held by a manager is in turn delegated downward to subordinates. Thus, communication dealing with authority (or things to be done) is primarily *downward,* as we shall see in chapter twelve.

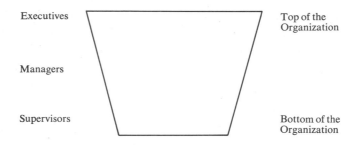

Executives — Top of the Organization

Managers

Supervisors — Bottom of the Organization

Figure 7-3   Scope of Authority

Power is a force — Power and authority are closely related, but they are not the same things. Authority is a right; power is a force that backs up the right. Stated another way, authority is the *right* to do something; power is the *ability* to do something. Managers may have the right to do something but may not be able to because they lack the power and influence to exercise or enforce the right. On the other hand, managers may have the power to do things, but not the right. You probably have seen both of these situations.

Power in organizations comes from several sources. It may come from recognized knowledge or competence, from personality, from level in the organization, and from the right to give or withhold rewards and punishments. One of the main sources of power for managers is delegated authority. Delegated authority of managers usually includes the right to provide or withhold rewards and the right to discipline subordinates. Thus, much managerial power is in the form of control or influence over things such as pay, promotions, employment, termination, and so on.

Responsibility is an obligation — While they are closely associated, responsibility and authority are not the same things. Responsibility is a feeling of obligation; it is a sense of duty that a person has to perform his or her job. When handled properly, responsibility is created within people when they accept a task or job assignment and are delegated authority.

Unlike authority, responsibility cannot be delegated. A person may delegate authority to you to do a certain thing, but since that person had the authority and the corresponding responsibility initially, that person is still responsible for the use of the authority delegated to you. "Delegating" responsibility, in the same sense as authority is delegated, is actually abdicating responsibility.

Types of authority — So far we have talked about authority as if there were only one type of authority. When authority is delegated from one person to another person, an authority relationship exists. There are, in fact, three different types of authority, or more specifically, three different types of authority relationships — line authority, staff authority, and functional authority.

Line authority is decision-making authority that exists between all superiors and all subordinates. If the principle of unity of command (one person, one boss) is not violated, there is a line of communication running from the top of the organization to each person at the bottom of the organization. Line authority and line relationships are the kind generally shown as solid lines as in figure 7-4. As can be seen, there is a line relationship (supervisor-subordinate) running from the top to the bottom of the organization. In the figure, the board of trustees of the university is connected to the graduate assistant via a line relationship running through a vice-president, a dean, a department chairperson, and a faculty member.

Staff authority is the authority to serve. It is the right to advise, assist, and help other people; it is not decision-making authority over others. When staff authority is delegated, a staff relationship is created. Line authority flows vertically, is implemented by *downward* communication, and creates supervisor-subordinate relationships. Staff authority is characterized by *lateral* communication, can flow in any direction, and creates advisory relationships. Staff relationships are most likely to be used to provide managers with expert advice. No manager can be a specialist in all of the areas that he or she needs to be. The next best thing is to provide expert help and advice to all managers through staff relationships.

Some departments, such as personnel, usually exist primarily in a staff capacity — their relationship to other departments is advisory. For example, a personnel department with staff authority might look like that shown previously in figure 7-2. Here staff relationships are shown as dotted lines.

A third type of authority relationship is functional. Functional authority is decision-making authority that is limited to an activity or aspect of an activity no matter who performs the activity or where it is performed in the organization. So functional authority results in a superior-subordinate relationship, but it is limited

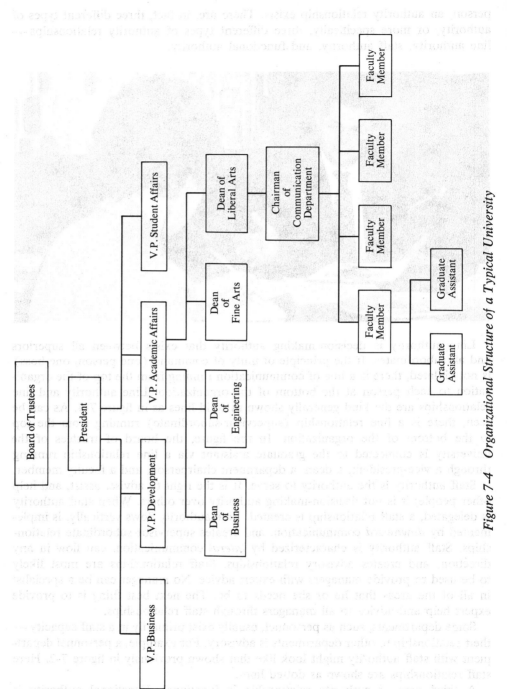

Figure 7-4 Organizational Structure of a Typical University

authority that results in a secondary rather than primary superior-subordinate relationship. Functional relationships are usually shown on organization charts as broken lines as in figure 7-2.

By now you may have recognized that the use of both line and functional authority relationships results in more than one boss for some people in the organization. If only one manager has functional authority in the organization, somebody has a primary superior to whom he or she reports for most of his or her work and a second boss because of the functional authority. This is a major disadvantage of functional authority. There are situations where this is necessary, however. In many cases the need for uniformity of decision making and action are so great (for example, in safety or accounting practices) that one person needs to have authority over the activity no matter where it is performed. So, while functional relationships are valid and useful, they should be used sparingly or else everyone in the organization ends up having several bosses and receiving contradictory communication.

Positions or departments are not limited to one type of authority. They may have all three types of authority. For example, the vice-president of finance has line authority over his or her subordinates and may have staff authority (advises others) relative to financial analysis and functional authority (requires action) relative to accounting records. Other departments may only have one type of authority. The delegation process determines the number and type of authority relationships.

These are the basic concepts upon which all organizations are structured, but the specific manner in which the concepts are applied determines the basic character of the structure, i.e., the nature of jobs, the amount and type of authority delegated, and how jobs are related.

Determinants of Structure. The way that the concepts are actually applied in practice and the nature of the structure created is the result of several interrelated forces. At the most basic level, the application of the organizing concepts is influenced by managerial philosophy and assumptions. At a more practical level, the particular structure of any organization is a function of its goals, the technology used to achieve the goals, the leadership style of the organization, the individual, and intra- and intergroup behavior. We will comment further where appropriate on the way these other internal organizational variables affect organizational structure in the chapters that follow.

Chapter twelve explains in depth the implications that the organizational structure has for the formal communication subsystem. At this point we turn to some of the research and theory dealing with the effects of structure on behavior.

Effects of Structure

In the last few years, much research has been done with the objective of finding out how organizational structure affects behavior and communication. We have not attempted to include an exhaustive review of the research and literature in this area, but some of the classic literature on the subject and one fairly comprehensive review of research in the area are included.

The Sears Roebuck Study

One of the earlier attempts to systematically study the effects of formal structure on behavior was the Sears Roebuck Study reported by Worthy (1950). In this empirical study, retail stores of similar size were classified as having either tall or flat organizational structure. In the tall structure stores, with narrow spans of management, there were three levels of authority above the salespeople. In the flat structure stores, there were only two levels of authority above the salespeople. Results of these studies indicated that the flat structures were superior to the tall structures in profits produced, satisfaction of individual members, and proportion of promotable personnel produced.

Thus, the studies seem to indicate that flat structures with wide spans of control were more effective than the tall structures with narrower spans of control. Worthy attributed this to the fact that the wide spans were so wide that superiors were forced to delegate authority and allow subordinates greater discretion, freedom, and independence in decision making and action.

Argyris' Conflict Thesis

In the late 1950s Chris Argyris (1957) reported some rather dramatic conclusions drawn from a relatively large research project in which he was engaged. Argyris' major conclusion was that there tends to be an inherent conflict between the needs of a healthy, mature individual and the requirements of formal organizational structure. This thesis stimulated controversy which continues to the present. A summary of Argyris' position is presented below.

First, some basic properties of human personality are presented. Next, some basic properties of formal organizational structure are outlined. Last, the conflict between these two sets of properties is identified.

A word of warning is in order before studying the individual-organization controversy. Argyris' statement of the conflict is an extreme and dramatic one. Argyris himself pointed this out and warned that certainly not all real-life situations fit the extreme. Also, all Argyris maintained is that there is the tendency for the conflict to exist when organizations are structured according to the concepts explained earlier in the chapter.

Characteristics of Personality. Argyris begins his discussion with a definition of personality and a description of the major growth trends of maturing personalities.

> Personality is conceptualized as: (1) being an organization of parts where the parts maintain the whole and the whole maintains the parts; (2) seeking internal balance (usually called adjustment) and external balance (usually called adaptation); (3) being propelled by psychological (as well as physical) energy; (4) located in the need systems; and (5) expressed through the abilities. (6) The personality organization may be called "the self" which (7) acts to color all the individual's experiences, thereby causing him to live in "private worlds," and which (8) is capable of defending (maintaining) itself against threats of all types.*

The self, as defined above, tends to develop along certain important dimensions. According to Argyris, the individual:

---

*C. Argyris, "The Individual and Organization: Some Problems of Mutual Adjustment," *Administrative Science Quarterly* 2 (1957): 4. Used by permission.

(1) tends to develop from a state of being passive as an infant to a state of increasing activity as an adult. (2) tends to develop from a state of dependence upon others as an infant to a state of relative independence as an adult. Relative independence is the ability to "stand on one's own two feet" and simultaneously to acknowledge healthy dependencies. It is characterized by the individual's freeing himself from his childhood determiners of behavior (e.g., the family) and developing his own set of behavioral determiners. The individual does not tend to react to others (e.g., the boss) in terms of patterns learned during childhood. (3) tends to develop from being capable of behaving in only a few ways as an infant to being capable of behaving in many different ways as an adult. (4) tends to develop from having erratic, casual, shallow, quickly dropped interests as an infant to possessing a deepening of interests as an adult. The mature state is characterized by an endless series of challenges where the reward comes from doing something for its own sake. The tendency is to analyze and study phenomena in their full-blown wholeness, complexity, and depth. (5) tends to develop from having a short-time perspective (i.e., the present largely determines behavior) as an infant to having a much longer time perspective as an adult (i.e., the individual's behavior is more affected by the past and the future). (6) tends to develop from being in a subordinate position in the family and society as an infant to aspiring to occupy at least an equal and/or subordinate position relative to his peers. (7) tends to develop from having a lack of awareness of the self as an infant to having an awareness of and control over the self as an adult. The adult who experiences adequate and successful control over his own behavior develops a sense of integrity and feelings of self-worth.*

Thus, barring blockages, individuals tend to develop and mature along these dimensions.

Characteristics of Organizational Structure. In describing formal organizational structure, Argyris focuses on four concepts of principles — specialization, chain of command, unity of direction, and span of control. As described by Argyris, these concepts are very similar to those described earlier. For the sake of continuity of discussion, a brief summary of each is included here.

Specialization — By specialization, Argyris means dividing work up so that it requires less individual skill and/or that more and more skill is transferred to machines. The result of specialization is that "it inhibits self-actualization and provides for the expression for few, shallow, superficial abilities that do not provide the 'endless challenge' desired by the healthy personality" (p. 571). Thus, specialization requires relatively mature individuals to behave in relatively immature ways.

Chain of command — By chain of command, Argyris means the delegation of authority to create superior-subordinate relationships so that individual subordinates' behavior can be controlled and coordinated. The impact of this is to make individuals dependent on others (superiors), and passive with a short-time perspective because they have little control over either the information they receive or their everyday work surroundings.

Unity of direction — "The principle of unity of direction states that organizational efficiency increases if each unit has a single activity (or homogeneous set of activities) that is planned and directed by the leader" (p. 574). The result, again,

---

*Ibid., p. 3. Used by permission.

is that individuals have little or no control over the goals toward which they work in the organization. Thus, people experience little sense of achievement, worthiness, and, consequently, physiological success.

Span of control — "The principle of the span of control states that administrative efficiency is increased by limiting the span of control of a leader to no more than five or six subordinates whose work interlocks" (p. 575). This allows close supervision and, ultimately, little direction, independence, and freedom for individuals.

The Conclusions.   Two basic conclusions complete this analysis. First, there is a conflict between the needs of healthy individuals and the demands of formal organizational structure. Second, because the individual is more or less dependent on some organization for a livelihood, the result is that people experience psychological failure and frustration.

We think some concluding statements about Argyris' thesis are in order. First, his conceptions of personality and maturity (self-actualization) are, for the most part, consistent with our discussion of the individual in chapter six. Second, the concepts of organizational structure that Argyris is so critical of are the same ones described earlier in the chapter. Also, the tendency for conflict between mature individuals and formal organizations exists. However, we want to make two things clear. First, we are not "indicting" formal organizational structure. It may have some disadvantages, but as yet there is no better alternative than the formal hierarchial organizational structure. Second, while what Argyris says does tend to apply to many organizations, it is because of the *way* the concepts are applied rather than the concepts themselves. An analogy might be that automobiles are bad because they can be used to kill people. Automobiles, like organizational structures, are not, in themselves, bad; it is the way that they are developed and used that counts. They can be used constructively or destructively. We think (as he points out) that Argyris is describing extreme, somewhat naive, applications of organizational structure (which exist all too often in the real world). The point is that it does not have to be this way.

Review of the Literature

In a fairly comprehensive review of the literature dealing with the relationships between several selected elements of organizational structure and job attitudes and behavior, Porter and Lawler (1965) conclude that some elements of structure have much greater effects than others and that a great deal more study needs to be done. Because it does include at least a large representative share of the research, a summary of their review is included here.

The Study.   This review investigated the relationship between seven elements of organizational structure and job attitudes and behavior. The seven elements of structure were organizational levels, line and staff hierarchies, span of control, size of subunits, size of total organization, shape (tall or flat), and shape (centralized or decentralized in decision making). The variable attitude referred generally to opinions about some object, while behavior was defined to include performance, output, absenteeism and the like.

The Conclusion. Porter and Lawler concluded that five of the seven elements of structure have some significant relationship to either attitudes and/or behavior. The more significant of these conclusions are:

1. Greater need satisfaction is associated with jobs at higher organizational levels than with lower levels;

2. Greater need satisfaction is associated with line-type jobs as opposed to staff-type jobs;

3. Less job satisfaction is associated with large subunits than with small subunits;

4. Greater absenteeism and turnover are associated with large subunits than with small subunits;

5. The evidence is inconclusive concerning whether tall or flat structures and whether large or small organizations produce greater satisfaction.

6. Neither span of supervision nor decentralization-centralization were significantly related to either attitudes or behavior.

While the review supports these conclusions, the authors point out that these conclusions, as a group, do not necessarily fit any of the particular individual studies included.

One obvious inconsistency exists between the conclusions of this study and the Sears study. In the Sears study, flat structures were found to be superior to tall structure in terms of both satisfaction and performance. This conclusion was not supported by the review above. For this reason, one additional study of the effects of structure is presented.

Effects of Tall and Flat Structures

Carzo and Yanouzas (1969) report the results of a laboratory experiment aimed specifically at determining the effects of tall and flat organizational structures on organizational performance.

The Experiment. This experiment involved four organizations of fifteen members each — two tall and two flat organizations. Tall organizations had four levels; flat organizations had only two levels. The experimental design was a complicated factorial one with each organization making fifteen decisions, so both structure and experience were dependent variables.

The Conclusions. Several conclusions were supported by analysis of the data, but only selected ones are important to this discussion. Structure seemed to have no effect on either learning or decision time; however, tall structures with narrower spans of control showed significantly higher levels of organizational performance.

Implications. The strongest statement that can be made about the effects of structure on behavior is that some types of structure are more appropriate than other types in particular situations. Certainly, the available evidence indicates that structure affects behavior and communication, but the specific effects of particular aspects of structure and of particular combinations of aspects of structure are not completely clear.

Structure and Communication

Organizational structure has tremendous effects on organizational communication. First of all, the structure created forms the basic outline of the formal communication subsystem. Lines of authority, especially superior-subordinate relationships, are primary lines of communication in the organization's communication system. In addition, how activities are grouped and divided and how activity groupings are related through authority relationships to a large degree determines who needs to communicate what to whom.

Based on both research and practical observation, it also seems safe to say that the structure influences the communication climate that prevails in the organization. Certainly structures which promote dissatisfaction or fail to provide much satisfaction result in negative attitudes toward communication and negative climates. Structures also tend to create status hierarchies. We will explore some of the more specific effects of these status hierarchies on communication in chapter ten.

Summary

Organizational structure is one of the more important internal organizational elements affecting organizational communication, behavior, and effectiveness. Structure is the major tool used by organizations to coordinate individual and group activity toward organizational goals. Structure is primarily a function of managerial philosophy and other internal elements such as goals, technology, leadership, and so on.

All organizational structures are built on some form of application of the four concepts of specialization, unity of command, span of management, and authority. These four concepts are applied to create activity-authority systems.

Research on the effects of structure on behavior is still inconclusive. Argyris argues that the four concepts, as they are often applied, conflict with the needs of a mature individual. Some studies indicate that flat structures are more effective than tall ones, while other studies indicate the reverse. It does seem that level in the organization and size of the organizational subunit affect both satisfaction and performance. Unfortunately, much is yet to be learned of the effects of various types of structure.

REVIEW AND DISCUSSION

1. Briefly explain what an organizational structure is.

2. Explain whether Weber's description of formal organization fits the organizations with which you are familiar.

3. Briefly explain each of the four basic concepts of organization.

4. In your own words, explain Argyris' conflict thesis.

5. Based on your own experience in organizations, explain how you think structure affects behavior and communication in organizations.

6. Are there any alternatives to the hierarchical organizational structure? What are they?

Chapter Eight

Technology
and
Job
Design

Organizations are systems which combine human abilities and physical resources to produce outputs and attain goals. Communication is the vehicle through which this combination takes place. Of the many internal organizational elements that affect behavior and organizational communication, technology and the design of jobs are two of the more important. There is now some systematic evidence that technology and job design affect not only behavior and communication but also other internal elements (such as structure) as well.

The objective of this chapter is to explain the effect that these two related variables have on behavior and communication. In the first part of the chapter, we explain the concepts *technology* and *job design*. Next we will deal with the concept of specialization as it relates to technology and job design. The third part of the chapter presents some of the more relevant research focusing on the effects that technology and job design have on behavior.

Technology

Technology refers generally to the way work is done, i.e., the methods of task performance and the way tasks are related to each other. The type of technology used ultimately affects the nature of the specific jobs and tasks that individuals perform.

No widely accepted definition of technology exists. Burack (1975, p. 76) defines technology as ". . . the human employment of an aid, physical or intellectual, in generating structures, products, or services that can increase man's productivity through better understanding, adaptation to, and control of his environment." Miles (1975, p. 13) states: "The technology of an organization includes not only the visible machinery, tools, and equipment used in turning out its product or service but also the specific human skills, knowledge, and procedures used to operate the devices." For the purposes of this book, technology is defined simply as the way tasks and work are done.

Alternative Technologies

Unfortunately, there are no clear-cut concepts of all of the different types of technology that exist. Technology differs depending on the product or service being provided. There are, however, some general explanations and descriptions of the range of technology available. In her research on technology and organizations, Woodward (1965) developed a technological continuum similar to the one in figure 8-1. The Woodward continuum is based primarily on the degree to which the skill, effort, and attention required to use tools or operate machines is actually transferred to and contained within the machine itself. Thus, technologies on the left-hand side of the continuum use tools and machines which tend to require higher levels of attention, effort, and skill, while technologies on the right-hand side of the continuum tend to embody tools and machines which have much of the skill and effort required built into them.

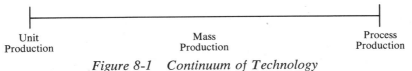

Figure 8-1   Continuum of Technology

Another way to look at various technologies is by the degree to which they use human labor and the degree to which they use capital equipment such as machines. Generally the more technologically advanced the organization is, the more use it makes of machines as opposed to human effort. This type of technological continuum might look like that in figure 8-2.

Figure 8-2   Human to Machine Continuum

An example may help illustrate the continuum. Suppose we wanted to build another canal connecting the Atlantic and Pacific Oceans somewhere in Central America. We could approach this task in several different ways. We could conceivably use people and simple shovels. This would certainly be a relatively simple technology making extensive use of human effort and skill and would be on the extreme left-hand side of the continuum. Another possibility would be the use of power machines such as bulldozers. This technology would employ machines which embody much of the effort and skill needed. Today we could conceivably use laser beam technology where most of the effort and skill needed has been transferred to the machine.

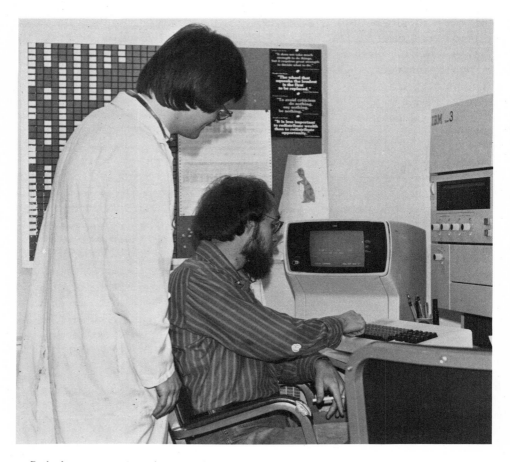

It is important to point out that we have been using the term technology in a very general fashion. Technologies are more advanced in some areas than in others. For example, the technology of space flight is more advanced than that of the more conventional air flight. So, the above explanations of technological alternatives always have to be viewed in the narrower context of the products and services being produced.

Technology and Other Internal Elements

Organizations are systems whose parts or elements communicate with each other, and technology both affects other internal elements and in turn is affected by the other elements. Highly technical organizations require mechanized formal subsystems to transmit information rapidly. Less technical organizations need different types of subsystems.

Determinants of Technology. The particular technology that an organization uses is probably influenced by several factors — the general level of development of the technology available, the specific objectives sought, managerial philosophy, and leadership practices.

All organizations have more or less specific objectives that they try to achieve. The nature of these objectives influences the technologies that are available to the organization because the level of technological development differs for specific types of work and processes, and all technologies do not advance at the same rate. Cultural conditions tend to be a major determinant of the level of technology available for any given process at any given time. Therefore, the level of technological development that exists for any given process obviously limits an organization's choice of technology.

Management chooses from among the technological choices available in light of general economic conditions. At any given time, some technologies are more economically practical than others. Take, for example, the production of electrical energy. Two of the more advanced technologies available for producing electricity are nuclear production and solar production. Prior to the petroleum energy shortage in 1974, both of these technologies were less practical than other less highly developed means for producing electricity. In short, they were for the most part too expensive to use. However, the shortage of petroleum increased petroleum prices to the point that nuclear production became much more economically practical.

Managerial philosophy and leadership style also influence the technology used. Dependent on its particular philosophy, management may choose either simpler or more advanced forms of technology. We know of little research to support the ideas, but it seems reasonable that either humanistic or mechanistic philosophies might result in the selection of either simple or advanced forms of technology. For example, a humanistic organization that wanted to eliminate routine repetitive, boring jobs might mechanize and automate them. On the other hand, a mechanistic organization that wanted to be sure people did not interfere with organizational achievement might also automate jobs to minimize dependency on human effort.

The technology used by an organization is influenced first by the objectives sought and the general level of technological development in the particular area of activity, and second by both economic conditions and management's philosophy and leadership style.

Interaction with Other Variables. Technology affects organizational communication both indirectly and directly. There is rather strong evidence that the type of technology chosen influences the organizational structure that is used (Woodward 1965). In short, particular technologies tend to require that organizations be structured in certain ways. And, the type of organization structure used influences the formal communication subsystem — that is, how work is divided and who needs to communicate what to whom.

The type of technology used also influences the organizational communication system directly. Aside from its effect on the organization structure, technology is a prime determinant of other aspects of the formal communication subsystem — it has direct influence on who needs to communicate what to whom. Technology also seems to affect the communication climate in the organization by creating assumptions and rules which must be followed for people to communicate. These effects are discussed in greater detail in the last section of the chapter. It is sufficient to say that technology is an important internal element in the organizational system which affects organizational communication and effectiveness.

Technology and Job Design

Perhaps the most significant effect of technology is its influence on the design and nature of the specific jobs and tasks that people in organizations do. The nature of specific jobs in any organization depends heavily on the type of technology used.

Take, for example, the manufacture of men's clothing. With a simple technology, a person's job could involve making an entire suit of clothes. With an assembly line operation, a person's job could involve only cutting out one small piece of a coat or sewing two small pieces of a coat. Certainly the two jobs are drastically different in nature. The first job involves a total product requiring high levels of personal skill. The second type of job involves only a relatively small simple job requiring much lower levels of personal skill.

Research today indicates that the nature of work that people do significantly influences their attitudes and motivations (Herzberg 1959). That is, the design of jobs in the organization affects the communication climate that exists. In highly mechanized jobs people do not have the freedom to interact spontaneously. On the other hand, jobs requiring communication tend to produce positive communication climates (La Follette et al. 1975).

Specialization

While the concept of specialization was discussed in chapter seven in connection with organizational structure, it also has important implications here. Basically, specialization of tasks and division of work are central themes in technological development. Much, but by no means all, technological advance results from dividing tasks up into more and more specialized, simplified parts.

"Specialization is basically a program aimed at achieving maximum efficiency of the productive activity by subdividing the work assignments and machine utilization to capitalize on specific skills of the worker and/or techniques of production."* As such, specialization is a significant influence on the nature of the jobs that people do.

The logic of specialization is that an individual's level of performance on the job is a function of both ability and motivation. Specializing and dividing complex work up into smaller, simpler parts reduces the level of ability needed to perform the job. This has the effect of increasing the level of the individual's ability to do the job. And, if ability increases while the level of motivation remains the same, performance increases. While this logic is reasonable, research today indicates that at least extreme specialization results in meaningless jobs and tasks that reduce individuals' intrinsic motivation to perform and limit their opportunities for communication. Dunn and Rachel cogently point out both the advantages and disadvantages of specialization.

---

*J. D. Dunn and F. M. Rachel, *Wage and Salary Administration* (New York: McGraw-Hill, 1971), p. 120. Used by permission.

Advantages:

(1) A minimum skill level required of the worker;
(2) Easy recruiting for these simple skills;
(3) Ease of training for these simple skills;
(4) Centralized control of the production process and employee workload;
(5) Considerable flexibility of employee assignments;
(6) Little mental effort required of the worker;
(7) Little responsibility required of the worker.

Disadvantages:

(1) Boredom and monotony of work assignments;
(2) Mental fatigue, generally resulting in a lack of responsibility on the part of the worker for the product;
(3) Occasional difficulty in controlling quality;
(4) Increased rates of employee turnover and absenteeism;
(5) General employee dissatisfaction with the work.*

It seems that these advantages and disadvantages can be summarized, respectively, as minimizing the skill required and reduction of intrinsic motivation to perform.

We are not necessarily for or against specialization. We see the issue similarly to Leavitt and his colleagues (1973, p. 45) who state: " 'Are we for specialization or against it?' We might better ask, 'Under what conditions is specialization desirable? At what cost? And in what form?' " It is now time to consider some of the more relevant research findings on technology and job design.

Research on Technology and Job Design

After reviewing the research on technology and job design, we find that there is no orderly classification that helps place the results in perspective and make sense of them. The fact is that studies vary in their scope and because they are usually done by different people with different needs and interests, they are not always easily related to other studies.

In this part we will somewhat arbitrarily classify studies into either general studies of technology and job design or more specific studies dealing with the nature of the actual job that individuals perform. The discussion is limited to studies dealing with potential impact on these elements and communication behavior.

The Impact of Technology

Several studies have investigated the general impact of technology on behavior. The dominant conclusion arising from most of these studies is that the technology used definitely influences behavior as indicated by both performance and morale (with morale being measured by individual reports, absenteeism, and turnover.)

The general idea is that the technology used affects the nature of the jobs people perform and the relationships which exist between the jobs and the people performing the jobs and that ultimately all of these things affect behavior. This conceptual approach is most often referred to as *socio-technical systems analysis*. The general conclusions of several important studies in this are presented below.

The Long-Wall Coal Studies. Perhaps the earliest systematic studies of the gen-

---

*Ibid. Used by permission.

eral impact of technology on behavior in the organization were those of Trist and Bamforth (1951). These studies investigated the impact of a significant technological change in the technology associated with mining coal in England.

The comparison was made between the conventional system of mining and a team composite system. Under the conventional system, jobs were specialized and accorded different status and pay. Jobs and the organization of work tended to be sequential and performance on each job was highly dependent on the performance of the previous job. This was compared to a team shift type technology where specialization was minimized and compensation was tied to group shift productivity. Under this arrangement, groups were allowed to determine the skills that they needed, select members, and allocate jobs according to skills.

The results were, by today's standards, not too suprising. Under the group composite technology, productivity increased while turnover and absenteeism decreased. These results were produced under very similar physical mining circumstances. It was, in fact, these studies which produced the idea that the technical, physiological, and sociological aspects of organizations are inextricably woven.

The Indian Weaving Mills Studies.   Studies of a similar nature conducted by Rice (1958) tend to support the idea of the socio-technical system. These studies began with an investigation of why automatic looms did not increase production in an Indian weaving mill. It appeared that worker morale was favorable and that good relationships existed between superiors and workers. Essentially, the studies showed that introduction of the new technology created a great deal of ambiguity among the roles assigned to workers.

Changes were made in the way work roles were related. Basically, a group of workers with a designated leader was made responsible for a group of the automatic looms. Previously, the different jobs associated with each loom were specialized and looms were unrelated to each other in terms of work roles. After the change, specialization still existed, but with work groups responsible for the total operation of a particular set of looms. The results were higher productivity and higher quality.

Both of the above studies embodied the establishment of an identifiable "territory" that a work group controlled and for which it was responsible. It seems reasonable to conclude in light of what we know about individual motivation and work group behavior that the greater productivity and satisfaction resulted from identification with and control over the territory.

Some Recent Evidence.   More recent evidence also supports the effects of the technological concept of territory reported above. Sirota (1973) reported an experiment where machine territories were assigned to particular employees. Previously, machine operators had rotated among the different machines because some were older, in worse condition, and had more frequent downtime. Two changes in the technological set were made — employees were assigned to particular machines and they were allowed to do minor maintenance and adjustments themselves and to determine when qualified expert maintentance was needed. The results were that after the changes were made, production increased on both old and new machines and quality improved as well. Indications were that individual satisfaction increased.

Woodward's Research.   Joan Woodward (1970) investigated the structure and technology of over 100 British organizations in the 1950s and while her research on the effects of technology on behavior was general, it is relevant here. The general conclusions that can be drawn from her studies support the idea that the level of technology does, in fact, interact with organization structure to affect behavior in the organization.

The Effects of Assembly Lines.   Van Beck and his associates (1964) systematically studied the effects of assembly line technology on output, quality, and morale. They compared two assembly lines — one long unbroken line of 100 people and one line of 100 people somewhat artifically divided into small groups, all producing the same product. Their general conclusion was that small work groups were the most effective approach in the long run. This conclusion was based on the fact that satisfaction and morale were low in both of the lines and that the assembly lines were extremely vulnerable to the consequences of poor morale and satisfaction.

Thus, technology in general seems to have important effects on the behavior of individuals in organizations. To the degree that the technology used results in socio-psychologically satisfying roles and work relationships, it promotes productive behavior and satisfaction. To the degree that it fails to do these things or interferes with these things, it promotes dysfunctional behavior for the organization.

Research on Job Design

Based on the quantity of research and literature, job design occupies a more important place in the study of organizations than technology in general does. In this section, we will report on some of the more important research on job design and the impact that the resulting nature of the job has on individual behavior.

The Motivator-Hygiene Theory.   Frederick Herzberg's Motivator-Hygiene Theory (1959) has probably created more controversy and stimulated more discussion and research than any other single theory in recent times. The theory developed from systematic research, but much of its criticism is based on the methodology employed.

The basic assumption underlying the Motivator-Hygiene Theory is that individuals are motivated to work in organizations to the degree that they perceive that satisfaction of their needs will result. In addition, the theory asserts that individuals seek two types of goals and satisfactions and that these two types tend to affect behavior in different ways.

The contention is that job satisfaction (motivation) and dissatisfaction are not opposites. The opposite of job satisfaction and motivation is not dissatisfaction; it is simply no job satisfaction. The opposite of dissatisfaction, in turn, is not job satisfaction, but simply the absence of dissatisfaction. The significance of this distinction is that job satisfaction and dissatisfaction seem to be caused by two entirely different sets of factors. The factors which influence job satisfaction and motivation center in the job and seem to have relatively little effect upon dissatisfaction. The factors which influence dissatisfaction are peripheral to the job and seem to have relatively little effect upon satisfaction and motivation.

The significance of the distinction between job satisfaction (motivation) and dissatisfaction becomes clearer when the two are related to levels of performance. Figure 8-3 indicates that there is a neutral or zero point in performance level where employees are not dissatisfied with their jobs, but neither are they experiencing job satisfaction. At this point, people simply perform at the minimal acceptable level necessary to maintain their jobs and employment. The goals which have the greatest effect upon job satisfaction and motivation are achievement, recognition, the work itself, responsibility, and growth and advancement.

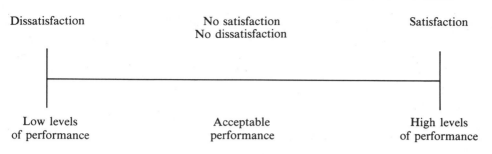

SOURCE: Aubrey C. Sanford, *Human Relations: Theory and Practice* (Columbus, Ohio: Charles E. Merrill, 1973), p. 174.

Figure 8-3   Relationship Between Job Satisfaction, Dissatisfaction, and Performance

Achievement — Achievement refers to the competition against a standard of excellence. It represents goals, such as successfully completing a job, solving problems, seeing the results of one's work, and, generally, the outcomes of situations which can be classified as good or bad, successful or unsuccessful, or pass or fail.

Achievement, as a motivational goal, can affect employee performance positively or negatively. Feelings which stem from the outcomes of the above types of situations can lead to job satisfaction and motivation to produce above mere acceptable levels, or to the absence of job satisfaction, with performance at or below acceptable levels. Whether the situations result in job satisfaction or the absence of it depends upon whether the outcomes produce a feeling of achievement or lack of achievement. You probably can recall times when you have performed extremely well and others when you have done extremely poorly on tests, and the general motivational effect that these two outcomes had on you.

Recognition — As a motivational factor, recognition refers to some act of notice, praise, or blame for outcomes of achievement situations. Recognition can be positive or negative, but it must be deserved recognition before it can have much positive motivational effect. Whether the motivational effects of recognition are positive or negative depends upon whether or not recognition occurs, and upon whether or not it is deserved. Deserved recognition for a job well done or a job not well done has a positive motivating effect, while undeserved positive or negative recognition has either a negative effect or little effect at all. If you think for a minute about your own experiences with recognition, you will likely be able to verify personally the above statements.

Work itself — Work itself, as a motivational factor, refers to the nature of the job or task that employees do. The actual work that employees do can be routine or varied, interesting or uninteresting, challenging or dull, easy or difficult, or creative or stultifying. The effects of the nature of the work itself on motivation can be either positive or negative. Work which employees perceive as any combination of interesting, challenging, varied or creative results in job satisfaction and motivation to produce above acceptable levels, while work perceived otherwise does not produce satisfaction and motivation.

Responsibility — Responsibility refers to employees' accountability for their own work, the work of others or increases in such accountability. Employees may feel that they have too little responsibility and that they deserve increased responsibility. Whether or not responsibility has a positive or negative motivational effect depends upon the way in which people feel about the responsibility that they have. Being responsible for jobs or people, and especially increases in such responsibility, tend to have a positive effect on job satisfaction and performance. A feeling of too little responsibility or lack of any responsibility leads to no job satisfaction and no motivation above the neutral point.

Growth and advancement — Growth and advancement refer to changes in individuals' positions in organizations and to opportunities to grow in terms of ability. The motivational effects of growth and advancement are what readers logically would expect. Advancement up the organizational ladder and the provision of opportunities to grow and develop lead to job satisfaction and motivation above the neutral point, but lack of advancement and opportunity for growth results in little or no job satisfaction and motivation.

As can be seen from the definitions of the motivational goals, they are closely related to job content and performance of the job. The motivating factors tend to have a significant influence on satisfaction and motivation to perform above mere acceptable levels; on the other hand, they do not seem to have much influence on dissatisfaction. The goals which have the greatest influence on dissatisfaction and motivation to perform below acceptable levels are company policy and administration, supervision, salary, working conditions, and communication relations with supervisors.

Company policy and administration — This hygiene factor refers to the adequacy or inadequacy of company organization and management and to the effectiveness of the basic personnel policies, including areas such as the equality of authority and responsibility and the effects of personnel policy and fringe benefits. When company policy and administration are inadequate, they produce dissatisfaction and may cause people to restrict performance; but, when they are good, people are not dissatisfied, but they are not necessarily motivated to produce above acceptable levels. For example, when organizations do not have adequate fringe benefits, such as paid holidays, employees probably will be dissatisfied; but when employees are paid for holidays, they are not highly motivated — they are merely no longer dissatisfied.

Supervision — As a hygiene factor, supervision refers to the competency of the supervision received. Supervisors are either competent or incompetent to some degree in their jobs, and this factor relates to how well supervisors do their jobs. The hygiene effects of supervision can have a positive or negative effect upon dissatisfaction. When supervision is good, there is little dissatisfaction; but, when supervision is poor, there is much dissatisfaction. When dissatisfaction is present, people tend to perform at or below acceptable levels; however, its removal does not create high levels of motivation.

Salary — Salary refers to the compensation that people receive for their jobs and expectations about increases. It may be adequate or inadequate, and expected increases may or may not become reality. When people feel that their salary is inadequate or that they should have received an increase, they are dissatisfied; feelings of adequate salary and the acquisition of expected increases remove dissatisfaction, but they do not motivate. If salary increases do create satisfaction and motivation, production in the United States should have increased drastically in the winter of 1972 because of the increased motivation when the wage-price freeze ended.

Working conditions — This factor refers to the actual physical conditions under which employees perform their jobs. It includes elements, such as temperature, light, ventilation, space, and so on. The effects of working conditions are no different from any of the other hygiene factors. When employees have pleasant working conditions, they are not highly dissatisfied; but they also are not highly motivated. When working conditions are poor, there is dissatisfaction and productivity may be restricted.

Because these factors are more closely related to the context or surroundings in which employees perform rather than the actual jobs performed, they are referred to as hygiene factors. As Herzberg explains it, medical hygiene operates to remove health hazards from people's environment. It is preventive and not curative; it does not make people healthy — it tries to remove those things that cause illness. The hygiene factors operate in a similar manner because they keep people from being dissatisfied, although they do not necessarily motivate people highly.

The Motivator-Maintenance Theory. M. Scott Myers (1964, 1966) replicated and extended somewhat Herzberg's dual factor theory of motivation. Myers' research included several thousand workers and several hundred managers. Generally, his results support those of Herzberg — that two distinct sets of factors operate to affect motivation in the organization. Myers' findings do indicate, however, that some people tend toward being either motivation or maintenance seekers in that they tend to respond more to one set of the factors than the other. Myers' research used essentially the same methodology as did Herzberg's, so it, of course, is subject to the same controversy.

The Effect of Individual Differences. Hulin and Blood (1968) investigated the relationships between individual differences such as age and personal backgrounds and the validity of the Herzberg-Myers theory. While their research does not deny the existence of a positive relationship between satisfaction and performance and the intrinsic content of the job, it does indicate that different reactions to the two sets of factors are associated with differences in age and personal background. So, their research seems to indicate that some refinement of the theory may be in order.

The Controversy. Much of the controversy surrounding the dual factor theory arises from the lack of methodological rigor employed in its research basis. Reviews of the literature seem to draw one conclusion. Studies that use Herzberg's methodology generally produce Herzberg's results, and studies that use other methodologies tend to produce less consistent results (Behling et al. 1968).

The two-factor controversy is complicated by the fact that it has some empirical support. A set of practical techniques known as job enrichment (or more broadly as job enlargement) has developed to implement the theory. Studies of the effects of implementing the theory abound and generally tend to support the theory (Herzberg 1966; Myers 1970; Foulkes 1969; Paul and others, 1969; Sirota 1973).

At least one other study (Hackman and Lawler 1971) utilizing a rigorous methodology produced conclusions similar to the Herzberg dual factor theory. Hackman and Lawler report overall job satisfaction is strongly related to "the opportunity for independent thought and action on the job, (2) the feeling of worthwhile accomplishment derived from working on the job, (3) the opportunity for personal growth and development provided by the job, and (4) the self-esteem and self-respect a person can get from working on the job" (p. 321). Overall satisfaction was only slightly related to (1) pay, (2) the opportunity to develop close friendships on the job, (3) promotion opportunities, and (4) the amount of respect and fair treatment received from the superior.

Certainly the results are not conclusive, but it does seem that the design of jobs and the nature of the work that individuals do influences their motivation and behavior on the job. Herzberg's theory may or may not be complete or completely valid, but the important message seems clear — what people actually do on their jobs makes a difference in their satisfaction and their behavior.

Technology and Communication

Systematic study of the effects of technology and job design on behavior and communication has only recently received attention. It would seem that technology and job design affect both behavior and communication in that where there is a "good match" between the individual and his or her job, he or she is motivated to communicate and tends to express satisfaction.

The type of technology employed does seem to influence behavior and, more specifically, organizational communication. To begin with, technology influences organizational structure which forms the basis of the formal communication subsystem. In additional, the type of technology used, in conjunction with the way activities are grouped, is a prime determinant of who needs what information, when. The evidence is not yet totally clear but it also seems that the general technology used also influences satisfaction and probably people's communication attitudes. Technology also has significant impact on the climate in the organization. Further, technology also operates to encourage the individual to acquire the interpersonal skills required in his or her job.

Research dealing specifically with the effects of job design on organizational communication is limited. But some research focuses on satisfaction and performance. Certainly the way jobs are designed influences the design of the formal communication subsystem. The evidence also suggests that job design affects performance and satisfaction and, therefore, attitudes. Thus, it seems reasonable to conclude that job design and the attitudes that result affect people's willingness to communicate.

Summary

Technology and job design are two of the important internal organization elements that have significant effects on the organizational communication system. Technology refers generally to the way work is done and to the relationships between jobs. Types of technology range from those making intensive use of human effort and skill to those making intensive use of machines embodying much of the skill and effort required by the process.

The technology used by an organization influences other internal variables and is, in turn, influenced by other internal variables. The chief determinants of the technology used are the specific goals sought by the organization, the alternative technologies available, and management's philosophy and leadership. Technology is also a chief determinant of the design and nature of jobs that people do.

Specialization is a major concept in technology. Basically, specialization and division of work have advantages and disadvantages. Disadvantages are negative attitudes and reduction of intrinsic motivation. Advantages are reduction of the skill required to perform jobs. The moral is to try to strike an appropriate balance between advantages and disadvantages. Research on technology and job design indicate that both of those variables have significant effects on attitudes and behavior that affect performance and individual satisfaction. Studies investigating the general impact of technology and work role relationships indicate that technology interacts with organizational structure to produce significant effects on employee satisfaction. Generally, the research indicates that technology and structure which provide an identifiable work group "territory" produce the best results. Studies of the effect of job design indicate that jobs which are meaningful in terms of the effects that they have enhancing the human dignity and self-respect of the individual produce greater satisfaction and performance. Certainly the behavioral effects of technology and job design have important influences on the formal communication subsystem and the communication climate that prevails in the organization.

REVIEW AND DISCUSSION

1. Explain what the term *technology* means.

2. Explain why specialization is a central concept in technology.

3. What are the advantages and disadvantages of specialization?

4. What were the conclusions of the Long-Wall Coal studies? What implications do these conclusions have for managers in organizations?

5. How are technology and job design related?

6. Explain the Motivator-Hygiene Theory.

7. Explain whether or not the research findings on the effects of technology in general are consistent with the research findings on the effects of job design.

Chapter Nine

Leadership Style

Leadership style is another internal organization variable shaped by the external background factors discussed in Part Two that affects the effectiveness of organizational communication both directly and indirectly. The leadership style which prevails in the organization is primarily a result of managerial philosophy and cultural and economic conditions. Whatever the style is, it influences organizational communication and effectiveness indirectly through influencing other internal organizational variables (such as organizational structures and reward systems); it also has direct effects on the organizational communication system.

Leadership occupies a central place in the literature of organizations. The role and impact of leadership in organizations has long been recognized, but there are still no clear-cut answers to all of the questions surrounding leadership effectiveness. This chapter will summarize the most important aspects of leadership in organizations.

The Nature of Leadership

Concerning the nature of leadership, Douglas McGregor (1960) stated the questions succinctly:

> Are successful managers born or "made"? Does success as a manager rest on the possession of a certain core of abilities and traits, or are there many com-

binations of characteristics which can result in successful industrial leadership? Is managerial leadership — or its potential — a property of the individual, or is it a term for describing a relationship between people? (p. 179)

We will try to provide some general answers for these questions in this part of the chapter.

Influence

Modern theory defines leadership as interpersonal influence toward the attainment of specific goals in specific situations. This definition contains three related, important elements.

Interpersonal Influence. The objective of leadership is to influence the behavior of others toward some goal. Tannenbaum and Massarik (1968, p. 413) state, "The essence of leadership is interpersonal influence, involving the influences in an attempt to affect the behavior of others." Thus, leadership is behavior that attempts to influence through communication; it can be effective or ineffective in varying degrees.

Since influence is such a key concept in the definition of leadership, a distinction needs to be made between influence and power. Power refers to the potential for influence. Influence is then the product of using power. Any given leadership act may reflect that part of the leader's power that he or she chooses to use.

Power for influence, which is exercised through communication, may come from several sources. Gibson and his associates (1973) contend that power, which can be used to influence, derives primarily from two sources — the organization and the individual. Power is derived from such organizational factors as position in the organization and the ability to both give and withhold rewards. Power can also arise because of administration and the recognition of expert knowledge.

Situational. The second important component of the leadership definition is the situation. Leaders do not try to influence people in general; they try to influence particular individuals toward specific goals. A particular attempt at leadership (influence) may have one effect in one situation as with one group of people and an entirely different effect in another situation and/or with another group of people. Thus, the effect that leadership behavior has is determined not only by the leadership behavior itself but also by the situation in which the influence is attempted.

Specific Goals. The objective of leadership is the achievement of specific goals. Although all leadership behavior is goal oriented, there are at least four classes of goals which may be the objective of such influence — organizational goals, followers' goals, group goals, and leaders' personal goals. In our definition the reference is usually to organizational goals, but we should recognize that not all attempts at influence have organizational goals as their object.

Leadership Functions

Our definition of leadership implies that leadership is a function or process performed by individuals through communication rather than a prescribed role or set of personal traits or behaviors. Some of the communication behaviors required to exercise leadership will be covered in chapter fourteen. The general manner in which leadership is exercised constitutes a "leadership style."

Leadership Styles

The term "leadership style" refers to the pattern of communication behavior which an individual manifests in attempting to influence another person. Whether they recognize it or not, all individuals have a leadership, or more generally an inter-personal influence style, and it is through the leadership style that much communication takes place.

There are no universally agreed on classifications and descriptions of leadership styles. Different researchers and theorists use different categories and descriptions. It does, however, seem that most of the style descriptions focus on the functions of leadership, but in different ways. We will examine some of the more widely accepted and used descriptions of alternative leadership styles.

The Leadership Style Continuum

One of the first and still most widely used leadership style description continuum was developed by Tannenbaum and Schmidt (1958). As figure 9-1 indicates, there is a range of behavioral styles that leaders can and do use in their influence attempts. The way in which authority (power arising from the organization and position) is used is the main characteristic which determines the general leadership style. The use of authority varies from extreme usage on the left to nominal usage on the right. Stated another way, the use of authority on the left-hand side of the continuum is predominantly to coerce, entice, persuade, and reward people; the use of authority on the right is predominantly shared with the followers.

From an influence point of view, the continuum illustrates leadership according to the distribution of influence between leaders and followers. If we consider that the vertical distance from the top to the bottom of the rectangle is the leader's total amount of influence (authority) or decisions, then the diagonal line represents the division of the influence between the leader and the "lead." Moving from the left to

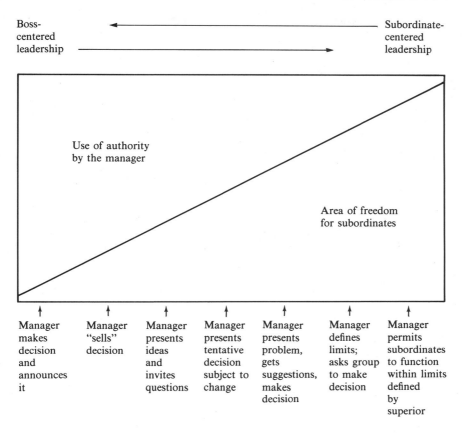

Boss-centered leadership						Subordinate-centered leadership
Manager makes decision and announces it	Manager "sells" decision	Manager presents ideas and invites questions	Manager presents tentative decision subject to change	Manager presents problem, gets suggestions, makes decision	Manager defines limits; asks group to make decision	Manager permits subordinates to function within limits defined by superior

SOURCE: Robert Tannenbaum and Warren H. Schmidt, "How to Choose a Leadership Pattern," *Harvard Business Review* 36, no. 2 (March-April 1958): 96. Used by permission.

Figure 9–1   Continuum of Leadership Behavior

the right on the continuum, management leadership styles change as less and less authority is used to lead and as subordinates are allowed greater amounts of freedom and influence on decisions.

While there are, in reality, probably more than the seven styles indicated on the continuum, we can group several of the styles together to simplify the discussion. It seems more meaningful to divide the continuum into three general styles in the manner shown in figure 9-2. The three general styles are fairly typical of the types of leader behavior we see in most of today's organizations. By examining only three leadership styles, the essential differences among types are readily identifiable. In the Autocratic style, which would encompass the two points to the left on the Tannenbaum and Schmidt continuum, the leader controls final decision-making power. He or she decides on a course of action and communicates the decision to subordinates. Participative styles, the three midpoints on the Tannenbaum and Schmidt continuum, require the leader to encourage communication from subordinates about a possible course of action before a decision is made. But, *final* decision-making power still rests with the leader. Variations on the Participative style are the most commonly used approaches to leadership in today's organizations. When a leader attempts to use a Democratic style, he or she must agree to give up final veto power over the decision made. The participating group, usually composed of subordinates, makes the decision with the presumption that the superior will support it. Communication in the Democratic style must be spontaneous and status differences between the superior and subordinates are de-emphasized.

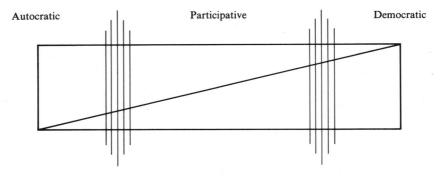

SOURCE: Aubrey C. Sanford, *Human Relations Theory and Practice* (Columbus, Ohio: Charles E. Merrill, 1973), p. 149.

Figure 9–2   Three General Leadership Styles

The Grid Styles

Another widely accepted classification of leadership styles is that developed by Blake and Mouton (1964). Their "Managerial Grid Theory" describes five general leadership styles. The "Grid" style descriptions are basically in terms of the task and group maintenance functions, and these classification and description schemes correspond closely to our earlier general explanation of leadership.

The Grid Theory hypothesizes that leadership styles are primarily determined by three common elements or dimensions: (1) production orientation, (2) people orientation, and (3) the manner in which the two orientations are meshed or combined. Production orientation and people orientation roughly correspond to task and group maintenance functions, respectively.

As the Grid in figure 9-3 indicates, five different styles result from different combinations of degrees of the two orientations.

1,1   Impoverished style — very low concern for people coupled with very low concern for production.

9,1   Task style — low concern for people coupled with extremely high concern for production (task accomplishment).

1,9   Country Club Style — extremely high concern for people matched with very low concern for production.

5,5   Middle-of-the-Road Style — moderate concern for people mated with moderate concern for production.

9,9   Team Style — very high concern for production combined with very high concern for people (strong emphasis on both task and maintenance functions).

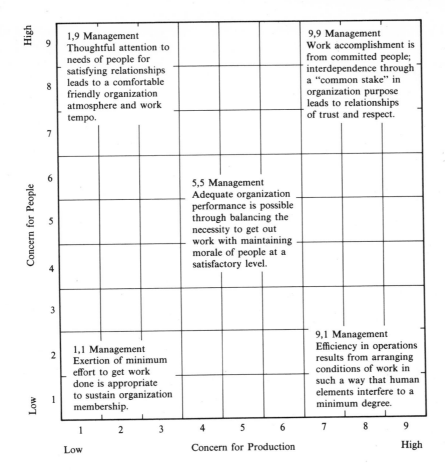

SOURCE: Robert R. Blake and Jane S. Mouton, "Managerial Facades," *Advanced Management Journal* (July 1966), p. 31. Used by permission.

Figure 9–3   The Managerial Grid

An important element of each of the Grid style descriptions is the *way* in which the two orientations are actually put together in practice. For this reason, we include some brief examples of each of the styles.

Impoverished Style.   The impoverished leadership is one where very low degrees of concern for both people and production are combined. The basic approach is almost an abdication of the real leadership function with little or no real attention paid to either task or maintenance functions. The basic strategy is never to make noticeable "waves" of any kind (either good or bad). Steinmetz and Todd (1975, p. 112) describe an individual using this style in the following way: "This individual might best be characterized as both unfriendly and lazy, if he is having a good day, and grouchy and obstinate on a bad day."

Task Style.   The task-centered style includes lots of emphasis on task functions and little or no emphasis on group maintenance functions. The main concern in this style is results. Anything, even people, is sacrificed for the sake of task accomplishment. People are more or less machines to be dealt with fundamentally or on an impersonal level. An additional feature of this style is that most people cannot be trusted to act in the best interests of task accomplishment, so they must be directed and controlled closely. Simply stated, the task style (in numerous more or less obtrusive ways) is to decide what must be done, make sure people understand what must be done and then be sure that they do what must be done for effective task accomplishment.

Country Club Style. In the country club style great emphasis is placed on group maintenance functions and little or no emphasis on task functions. The general approach here is to keep people happy enough so that they will accomplish the task. The basic idea behind this style is that "You can lead a horse to water, but you can't make him drink." The country club style seeks to keep people happy enough to "drink." Thus, lots of effort is devoted to the development of pleasant working conditions and to an atmosphere of friendliness, informality, and lack of pressure.

Middle-of-the-Road Style. The middle-of-the-road style places emphasis on both task and maintenance functions. The idea behind this style is that people's satisfactions must be balanced against the organization's needs for production. The approach is one of persuasion coupled with "tactful prodding." Compromise is the "key" to balancing concern for people and for production.

Team Style. The team style combines strong emphasis on task functions with strong emphasis on group maintenance functions. The general approach is to involve people and give them a "stake" in the organizational achievements and to generate commitment by using their abilities to get the best possible results. This is a problem-solving approach where the mutual trust, respect, and support develop through the use of people's abilities to solve problems interfering with organizational results.

All five of the above styles take on more meaning when the underlying beliefs about the relationship between task and maintenance functions is made explicit. With the exception of the team styles, the implied belief is that task functions and maintenance functions exist at opposite ends of a continuum. That is, task functions and maintenance functions contradict each other. More emphasis on one necessarily means less emphasis on the other. The implied assumption in the team style is that not only are task and maintenance functions independent of each other but also they are complementary.

The Continuum and the Grid Compared

The Tannenbaum and Schmidt style continuum and the "Grid" style descriptions cannot be matched easily. They simply describe somewhat different styles. The most obvious relationship exists between the autocratic style and the task style. The participative style corresponds rather roughly to the middle-of-the-road style; the team style corresponds generally with intelligent Democratic (but not laissez-faire) styles. We recognize that this is subject to question and encourage you to decide for yourself.

The above discussion of leadership and leadership styles implies that individuals, not organizations, exhibit leadership and, therefore, have leadership styles. Organizations also can exhibit leadership styles.

Organizational Leadership Styles

Only individuals actually produce leadership styles but organizations tend to take on leadership styles, which affect organizational communication and effectiveness.

The Concept of Organizational Leadership Style

Literally, organizations are abstractions; they are individuals interacting in some structured fashion, and they do not exhibit leadership behavior and, therefore, have no real leadership style. There is some research evidence and fairly strong evidence from casual observation that organizations do tend to take on leadership styles. For whatever reasons, one leadership style tends to be predominant in the organization. Thus, organizational leadership style refers to the way members are directed on an organizational-wide basis.

An organization's leadership style, like many other internal features of the organization, tends to be heavily influenced by the philosophy and assumptions and resulting leadership styles of the top levels of management. Certainly the policies and practices of the organization affect the general manner in which leadership functions are handled in the organization. So, much of the organization's leadership style is determined for all managers on an organizational basis.

While we know of little research support, we also believe, based on limited observation of the real world of organizations, that the "trickle-down theory" does tend to exist. The idea is that people tend to manage (and lead) similarly to the way that they are led. This seems quite logical because subordinates probably realize that one way to "look good" to superiors is to do things (like lead) in similar ways. Thus, while leadership is actually exercised by individuals, there is normally enough similarity (either required or by choice) in the way leadership functions are handled that we can meaningfully speak of organizational leadership styles.

Descriptions of organizational leadership styles are in some ways similar to individual style descriptions and in other ways different. Obviously, both deal with the emphasis placed on leadership functions and the way they are carried out. Unlike individual styles, however, organizational styles contain elements that are not so easily identifiable in individual styles. Some of these elements are manifested mainly in organization policy, practice, and procedure and in other internal elements such as reward systems and the way they are administered. There are two somewhat different approaches to organizational leadership styles and their description: the "Grid," with which we are already familiar, and Likert's Four Systems.

Organizational Grid Styles

We described the basic concepts of the Grid in the discussion of individual leadership styles. Grid styles are characterized primarily by the emphasis placed on leadership functions and by the way these functions are integrated or synthesized.

Our approach to explaining organizational grid styles is a little different. For each of the Grid styles, we will explain how an organization generally approaches and handles such critical elements as (1) goals, (2) decision making, (3) planning, (4) control, (5) rewards, (6) conflict, and (7) communication.

The Task Organization. This organization tends to be relatively autocratic with fairly tight control exercised from the top through policies, practices, and procedures. People are more or less regarded as resources to be used to achieve organizational objectives, and the interests of individuals are almost always subordinate to the needs of the organization. Emphasis is placed on individual performance. The general approach is to engineer the work environment so that "people" do not get in the way too much.

Goals — Strong emphasis is placed on organizational goals. Little attention is paid to individuals' personal goals and to whether these "fit" with organizational goals. If necessary, individuals are expected to sacrifice their own personal goals to help the organization. The emphasis placed on goals clearly indicates that the "organization" is more important than the individual.

Decision making — Most decisions of any real significance are made at relatively high levels in the organization. The criterion base for making decisions is whatever is in the best interests of the organization. Established policy and practice are rarely violated. There is usually relatively little effect exerted to gain acceptance of decisions; they are either dictated or "sold" convincingly from above.

Planning — Most planning occurs at the top of the organization with people at lower levels basically excluded. There are usually only superficial attempts to allow people at lower levels to help decide what the organization tries to accomplish. In addition, their acceptance of plans is rarely sought. The emphasis in planning is on making sure that people know what (not necessarily why) should be done.

Control — Tight control is exercised to see that people do what they are supposed to do. Control takes the form of close supervision and extensive reporting to see that people adhere to a comprehensive set of policies, rules, regulations, and budgets. Thus, control emphasizes control of people's behavior to see that it is consistent with that believed necessary for effective organizational performance.

Rewards — Rewards are designed to promote loyalty to plans; obedience to policies, rules, and procedures; and high levels of effort. Results produced are only factor-affecting rewards. Rewards tend to be based on the dependability with which assignments are carried out with no trouble.

Conflict — Conflict is generally seen as destructive and is undesirable. As a consequence, it is either ignored, squashed, or decreed out of existence. No real attempts are made to face and resolve differences and/or to use them to benefit the organization.

Communication — Communication tends to be formal, limited to essential information, and guarded. Much communication is either written or followed up and verified in writing. People are informed about what should be done and provided the essential information that they need to do their job. Communication tends to be closed and guarded rather than open and candid.

In summary, the task organization operates on the assumption that most people are not to be trusted and must be closely guided and controlled.

The Country Club Organization. The Country Club organization tends to be really "loose" and relaxed; it is an extremely pleasant place to be. People are regarded as the most important asset. Emphasis is placed on maintaining harmonious interpersonal, intragroup, and intergroup relations. The general idea is to create a set of working conditions and social environment that promotes loyalty and inhibits unpleasantness. Thus, the organization tries not to interfere with people's happiness.

Goals — Strong emphasis is placed on people's personal goals. Little attention is paid to whether or not people's personal goals fit the organization's goals. If necessary, organizational goals can be sacrificed in the interests of people's happiness. The emphasis placed on goals clearly indicates that people are more important than the organization.

Decision making — Most decisions of significance are made after careful checking with people and consideration of the impact on people's morale. The criterion used for decision making is whatever is in the best interests of the organization affords the most happiness or least dissatisfaction. Numerically unpopular decisions are infrequent. Unpleasant decisions are usually "coated with sugar."

Planning — Most planning occurs on a local basis after careful informal surveys of people's opinions. The idea is to find out what people want and then plan it (or let it happen). The emphasis in planning is on making sure that plans are acceptable to the great majority and are not disquieting.

Control — Most control is informal and positive. It takes the form of gentle persuasion, admitted illegitimate requests for help, and appeals to sympathy. Control is based on personal and organizational loyalty. Official reporting is minimized. So, control focuses on maintaining harmonious interpersonal relations; there is a general looseness and/or laxness in the enforcement of policies, rules, and procedures.

Rewards — Rewards are designed to promote goodwill among people in the organization. Performance is only one of several factors affecting rewards. Rewards tend to be based on impersonal things such as length of service and/or highly personal things, like need, in order to keep competition, conflict, and dissatisfaction to a minimum.

Conflict — Conflict is considered extremely destructive and is to be avoided because it can cause tension and destroy good morale. Conflict is rarely faced directly. Efforts are made to avoid conflict if possible and to smooth it or "shuffle it under the table" if it arises. The approach to conflict is to blot it out by focusing on good things and/or on things on which everyone does agree.

Communication — Communication is usually friendly, informal, and highly social in nature. Most communication focuses on positive things. Unpleasant subjects or subjects which might cause dissatisfaction are avoided or handled in an informal social manner. Social non-job related communication is frequent.

In summary, the country club organization operates on the assumption that people must be kept happy, and the organization is run with that in mind.

The Impoverished Organization.   The impoverished organization is really a rare phenomenon. It is an organization that has "given up" on really trying to accomplish something and instead does only what is required for survival. People are more or less left on their own with only broad ideas of what should be done. Emphasis, if it can be called that, is placed on surviving and maintaining the status quo. The general approach of the organization is to survive by being as inconspicuous as possible.

Goals — Little emphasis is placed on either personal or organizational goals. As a result, there is little or no attention paid to individuals' personal goals and whether they are consistent with organizational goals or not. The goal of all concerned is maintenance of the present organizational position so as to maintain present personal positions. Specific goals, either organizational or individual, receive little attention.

Decision making — Decision making in the impoverished organization is more or less by default. Rarely are concrete decisions made at any level. Things are allowed to just "drift along." The criterion for decision making is that most problems will solve themselves or go away if ignored long enough; those that do not, somebody can decide. There is little established policy and practice except that which originates elsewhere and over which the organization has little control.

Planning — Planning consists mostly of not really planning at all but of waiting to let things work out as they will. The general idea is that planning does not make much difference and that everyone can plan for himself or herself. What planning is done is usually very broad and general to provide people lots of freedom. Thus, planning is the individual responsibility of everyone and the real responsibility of no one.

Control — Real control is a myth in the impoverished organization. Control takes the form of letting individuals "do their own thing" except in real emergencies. As long as severe problems do not arise, people are free to control themselves. What control is exercised is so broad and general that it is almost meaningless.

Rewards — Rewards in the impoverished organization are a matter of course. They bear little or no relation to either organizational or individual performance. In fact, rewards are likely to be simply taken for granted under the assumption that the organization has little or no power to really influence the rewards people receive. Thus, rewards also tend to be left to the dictates of the specific situation.

Conflict — True conflict is indeed rare in an impoverished organization because it focuses attention on things detrimental to survival. Conflict is a thing to be avoided or sidestepped because it can force taking a stand that brings attention to the organization and puts it "on the spot."

Communication — Communication of any kind is minimal in this type of organization. It consists mainly of relaying that which has been communicated down from above (somewhere). Little or no attempt is made to interpret or determine the significance of what is communicated. In addition, little attempt is made to seek out and collect information. People are more or less on their own, in terms of job-related information.

In summary, the impoverished organization takes little responsibility for its own destiny. It assumes the fatalistic attitude that it has little or no control over its own fate and that it is at the mercy of higher powers. In this situation, the best thing to do is never make "waves" of any kind. "Lay low" is the password and key to survival.

The Middle-of-the-Road Organization. The middle-of-the-road organization tends to be a compromise between the task organization, the country club organization, and the impoverished organization. Both people and production receive moderate degrees of attention fairly balanced between the two. Emphasis is placed on following precedents or tradition to achieve a working compromise between the organization's needs and the satisfaction of people.

Goals — Emphasis on goals is usually overly balanced between the organization and people. People are expected to sacrifice some of their goals in the interests of the organization and, in turn, the organization makes only "reasonable" requests of its people. The tendency usually is to balance the good with the bad so that the two offset each other.

Decision making — Decision making in this organization is a matter of balancing of interests. Precedent and tradition are relied on heavily. Decisions tend to be made democratically. Compromise on problem solutions is the order of the day.

Planning — Planning is usually short range and an extension of past performance. The general approach is to determine what performance is really needed, communicate this tentatively and then negotiate a compromise between what is needed and what people will reasonably agree to.

Control — Control in the middle-of-the-road organization is equally balanced between positive and negative. People are expected to be reasonable and are treated as equals with the organization.

Rewards — Rewards in this organization are designed to compensate people for what they do for the organization — produce results and endure some sacrifice. Thus, rewards are seen as a big positive factor which serves to balance or offset the negative aspects of organizational life. Thus, rewards are used as carrots to dangle in front of people to entice and encourage agreement and performance.

Conflict — Conflict is seen as a win-lose situation that most often should be faced discreetly and indirectly. The general approach to conflict is to let the smoke "die down" and then search for some acceptable solution with which everybody can live. Compromise — give a little, take a little — is used to reach solutions that are at least equally fair to the organization and to all other parties involved.

Communication — Communication in the organization is rather evenly balanced between official information communicated through the formal subsystem and informal, unofficial information passed through informal channels such as the grapevine. Unofficial communication is used to temper and supplement formal communication. Generally, the approach is to monitor the grapevine closely to really find out what is really going on and then use either formal channels or the grapevine to get the message across.

In summary, the assumption of the middle-of-the-road organization is that people are just as important as the organization and, therefore, deserve equal emphasis. Equality of emphasis is achieved by democracy and compromise between reasonable people and reasonable requests of people.

The Team Organization.   The team organization tends to make the fullest use possible of the abilities of its people in an effort to produce the best organizational results possible. People are regarded as individuals with important abilities. Emphasis is placed on teamwork. The general approach is to make it possible for people to satisfy their needs to achieve and feel worthwhile by using their abilities to achieve the best organizational results possible. Interests of employees and the organization are seen as complimentary and shared.

Goals — Strong emphasis is placed on organizational goals and on aligning and integrating these with individual goals. Much attention is focused on goals (organizational and individual) which are mutually beneficial and reinforcing. The emphasis placed on goals clearly reflects the belief that what is really best for the organization is also best for individuals and vice-versa.

Decision making — Decisions are made by the people (whoever or wherever they are) who have the information and ability to make them effectively. Their criterion used for decision making is the best and most effective result for the organization. Decisions are made in light of the specific situation and their analyzed effects on goal achievement. The decision-making process focuses on gaining commitment to decisions through involving people in the process and allowing and helping people understand the rationale behind the decision.

Planning — The responsibility for planning at all levels is shared throughout the organization. The emphasis in planning is on using all of the knowledge and ability available to take full advantage of whatever opportunities exist. Thus, planning is shared because it affects all concerned.

Control — Tight control at all levels is exercised to ensure that planned goals are achieved as efficiently as possible. Control takes the form of individual self-control exercised because people understand and agree on the goals sought and the means being used to reach them. Thus, the general approach is to strive for understanding and agreement and then provide help and guidance.

Rewards — Rewards in this organization are shared, consistent with organizational performance and personal contributions. Rewards are closely related and tied to individual, team, and organizational performance. Rewards are shared to the degree that they are earned.

Conflict — Conflict is seen as neutral in this organization. In any case, it is an issue to be faced head on. It is either something that gets in the way of performance or something that can be used constructively to produce better performance, but it is dealt with and resolved if at all possible.

Communication — Communication tends to be open, honest, and candid. Effective communication is sought because it is the only way effective organizational performance is possible. The atmosphere is one of respect, support, and trust where people feel free to voice their opinions. The idea is that only when people feel free to "speak up" will they contribute their best to the greatest degree possible. To inhibit the free flow of communication stifles creative contribution.

In summary, the team organization tries to create an environment where people are involved and committed to the organization because they are using their abilities in a meaningful way and because their own satisfaction is interlaced with organizational goals.

The organizational leadership styles described by the Grid theory are in some important respects similar to those described by Likert.

Likert's Four Systems

Likert (1967) has identified four different systems of organization. While Likert's systems may be more encompassing than our concept of organizational leadership styles, they are, in fact, descriptions of such styles. Each of the four systems is explained in terms of its approach to (1) goal setting, (2) decision making, (3) motivation, (4) interaction among levels, and (5) communication. Based on these elements, Likert identifies an exploitative authoritative system, a benevolent authoritative system, a consultative system, and a participative system.

Exploitive Authoritative. The exploitive authoritative system essentially seeks to "use" people to achieve organizational goals. People are generally regarded as essential impersonal resources to be manipulated for the good of the organization with little or no regard for the individuality and feelings of people. People are likely to be viewed as not trustworthy and not capable of determining what is in their own best interests.

Goals — Goals in the exploitive authoritative organization are normally dictated from above. Organizational goals receive almost all of the emphasis and there is little or no participation in the development of these goals at any level by the people who are to achieve the goals. Individuals' personal goals are considered irrelevant.

Decision making — Most decision making of any significance whatsoever is at the top of the organization. Decisions at lower levels are relatively insignificant and/or closely channeled from above. Decisions are made with relatively little input from lower organization members or from people with expertise in the area.

Control — Control in this style is exercised from the top of the organization. Control is exercised through substantial reporting to higher organizational levels and the issuance of orders to correct conditions believed to be out of control.

Motivation — Motivation is one of the "big sticks — little carrot" variety. The general approach to this is to use the negative motivators of threats, punishments, and fear combined with occasional enticements (rewards) to coerce people in the direction desired and to the level of performance required.

Interaction — Interaction between levels in the organization is usually limited to what is essential and takes place in a formal impersonal atmosphere. Influence flows mainly downward with lower levels being passive, particularly in the interaction. Interactions take place in a climate of fear and distrust.

Communication — Communication is mainly formal, being initiated at the top of the organization and flowing downward. Little real communication begins at the lower levels and flows upward. Little attention is paid to whether information is actually accepted at lower levels. Formal communication is supplemented by a "spy system."

In summary, the exploitive authoritative organization operates under the assumption that people at lower levels need strong guidance and control from above, and that management is best when it is strong and impersonal.

Benevolent Authoritative Style. The benevolent authoritative style of organizational leadership is probably best characterized as authoritarian but one which recognizes the feelings of people. People are regarded as resources like machines but different in that they have feelings and emotions. And, these must be considered and compensated for along with other important elements.

Goals — Goals in the benevolent authoritative organization are normally dictated from the top of the organization with lower levels being allowed to respond back to goals. Responses are usually allowed to let people "blow steam" and have little effect on organizational goals. Individuals' personal goals are recognized and accepted as long as they do not interfere with organizational goals.

Decision making — Major decisions are made at the top of the organization with little input from below. Lower levels are allowed to make decisions affecting them within clearly prescribed limits from above.

Control — Most control is exercised from the top of the organization. As in the exploitive style, reporting and close supervision are used to provide a basis for control. Some control (usually of a relatively insignificant nature) is exercised at lower organizational levels.

Motivation — Motivation is of the "small stick — big carrot" and/or of the big stick used discreetly and tactfully variety. The general approach is to reward with such enticements as money and status and to use threats and punishment when such rewards fail.

Interaction — Interaction between levels in the organization is limited and formal with higher levels making sure that all concerned know who is the boss. Most of the influence lower levels have upward is through informal unofficial channels.

Communication — Communication is mostly formal and downward. Upward communication occurs with lower levels being allowed to voice their opinions and gripes, but few changes result. Acceptance of decisions and information is promoted through letting people engage in moderate amounts of "bitching" without retaliation. Communication is rarely open, frank, and candid.

In summary, the benevolent authoritative organization is dictatorial but recognizes that people are people, and as such people's irrational nature must be planned for and siphoned off so that it does not interfere with the organization.

Consultative Style. In the consultative style of organizational leadership people's opinions are considered along with all of the other relevant information. People are regarded as resources whose behavior influences organizational goal achievement and, thus, their opinions should be considered.

Goals — Goals are set primarily at the top of the organization after considering inputs from lower levels. Goals at lower levels are set by people at lower levels as long as they are consistent with overall organizational goals.

Decision making — Decisions are made throughout the organization within broad limits imposed from the top. Limits within which decisions must be made become narrower the lower the organizational level.

Control — Control originates from the top of the organization, but review processes are delegated downward to some degree. The general approach to control requires reporting of "exceptions" or deviations from expected results. Thus, control focuses mainly on problem areas of performance.

Motivation — Motivation is mainly of the economic and "ego" variety. The general approach is to make people at lower levels feel important through some limited participation and involvement and to reward them with recognition and other ego satisfiers, and when these fail, to resort to threats and punishment.

Interaction — Interaction between levels in the organization is fairly frequent and moderately personal and informal. Lower levels have some influence on upward levels through the consultation process.

Communication — Communication flows both upward and downward but with more emphasis on downward communication. Downward communication tends to be patterned after that which originates from the top of the organization. Lower levels feel "reasonably" free to communicate upward. The atmosphere is one where moderate levels of trust, openness, and candor exist.

In summary, the consultative organization recognizes the abilities of people, respects their inputs, and considers them to generate feelings of participation which oil the gears through which authority is exercised.

The Participative Style.   The participative organizational leadership style is based on the principle of supportive relationship. Likert (1967) states it as follows:

> The leadership and other processes of the organization must be such as to insure a maximum probability that in all interactions and in all relationships within the organization, each member, in the light of his background, values, desires, and expectations, will view the experience as supportive and one which builds and maintains his sense of personal worth and importance. (p. 47)

Thus, the general approach is to build a situation where the most effective organizational results are achieved through people who make full use of their abilities in their own best interest.

Goals — Goals are set in participative organizations through true group participation. At various stages all levels are involved in group and individual goal setting. Goals are accepted by all concerned because involvement and personal contribution create feelings of "ownership" of the goals.

Decision making — Decisions are made throughout the organization. The important criterion for where decisions are made and who makes them is access to the relevant information and expertise in the problem area.

Control — Control is exercised by all levels. Where control occurs and who controls is a function of what will produce the best results. Raw authority is seldom a control device. People control their own areas of activity and help others with control of their areas of activity. This control is shared at all levels.

Motivation — Motivation is internal and arises from within people. The general approach of motivating people is to totally involve them and let them develop feelings of ownership by allowing and encouraging them to use their abilities fully to participate in and contribute to organizational excellence. Accordingly, the full range of economics, ego, and self-actualization rewards are utilized.

Communication — Communication flows freely in all directions and may be initiated anywhere. Little distinction is made between formal and informal channels. No subjects are taboo. People communicate freely, openly, and candidly with little fear of reprisal. The atmosphere is one of respect, trust, and support.

In summary, the participative style, similar to the team style, seeks to allow feelings of ownership of organizational results by supporting people in the use of their abilities to satisfy their needs. It tries to integrate organizational needs with individuals needs to enhance people's dignity and worth.

The Grid and Systems Compared

Certain parallels between the Grid styles and Likert's systems seem clear. The task style is very similar to the exploitive and authoritative, and in a slightly modified form similar to the benevolent authoritative style. The middle-of-the-road style corresponds generally to the consultative style. There is little doubt that the team style and the participative style are simply two slightly different ways of describing the same general organizational leadership style.

Descriptions of individual leadership styles and their corresponding organizational counterparts are essential to fully appreciate the influence of leadership style on communication and organizational effectiveness. However, leadership styles must be evaluated in terms of leadership effectiveness.

Leadership Effectiveness

Research on Individual Style Effectiveness

The University of Michigan Studies. Based on a relatively large amount of research, Likert and his colleagues (1961) at the Institute for Social Research succeeded in differentiating between more and less productive managers on two related bases.

Based on the way they led, managers are classified as either job centered or employee centered. The job-centered managers tend to structure the jobs of subordinates highly, supervise closely and use incentives to stimulate effort. The employee centered managers tend to focus on the human aspects and on teamwork. They provide considerable freedom to subordinates to do their tasks once goals are specified. Figure 9-4 shows the results of one of the studies. Clearly, the employee-centered leaders tend to be more effective.

Number of Supervisors Who Are:

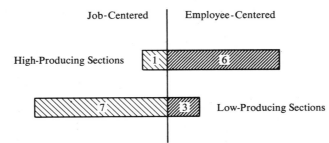

SOURCE: J. H. Donnelly et al., *Fundamentals of Management* (Dallas: Business Publications, 1971), p. 218. Used by permission.

Figure 9–4   Leader Orientations

Another of the studies classified leaders as either close supervisors or general supervisors, as figure 9–5 demonstrates. Again, general supervision tends to be more effective than close supervision.

The Ohio State Studies. A team of researchers at Ohio State University (Stogdill and Coons 1957), after extensive research, has added some more information to the data on leadership effectiveness. The researchers were successful in isolating two dimensions of leadership — initiation of structure and consideration which seemed to

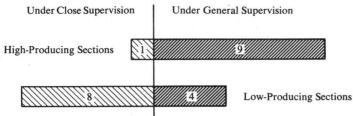

SOURCE: J. H. Donnelly et al., *Fundamentals of Management* (Dallas: Business Publications, 1971), p. 218. Used by permission.

Figure 9-5   Close and General Supervision

be related to effectiveness. The two dimensions are somewhat similar to those identified in the University of Michigan studies. The initiating structure dimension refers to the degree to which managerial leaders structure theirs and their subordinates' roles. The consideration dimension refers to the degree to which leaders have developed a work atmosphere where there is mutual trust and respect for subordinates' ideas and feelings and good two-way communication. Those low in consideration tend to be more impersonal in their dealings with subordinates.

The results of the Ohio State studies may be somewhat confusing. Based on performance ratings by superiors, production managers high in initiating structure and low in consideration were more productive. The reverse was true for managers in nonproductive areas. In both types of situations, however, managers high in initiating structure and low in consideration had higher rates of such things as absenteeism, tension, and grievance. While their immediate superior saw them as successful, they did not have good results when the other criteria variables (absenteeism and so on) were examined.

Contingency Theory.   The research of Fielder (1967) and his associates is more easily related to the style continuum of Tannenbaum and Schmidt in that it includes styles similar to the two ends of the continuum. The results of these studies indicate that effectiveness of general leadership is contingent on the three broad situational factors of leader-subordinate relations, task structure, and power position. Leader-subordinate relations refer to the degree to which subordinates accept, like and have confidence in the leader and can be either good or bad. Task structure refers to the degree to which jobs and routine are defined and can be highly or lowly structured. Power position refers to the degree to which leaders have the authority (power) to give or withhold rewards and punishment, and it can be strong or weak.

After exhaustive study of varying combinations of these three variables, Fielder concluded that different styles were more effective with different combinations of the three situational factors. Table 2 summarizes the results.

Some Conclusions.   The above research indicates that there is no one *best* style of leadership for all individuals. It is our belief that the most effective style for any particular person is the one in which the person really believes. Adopted styles which do not fit with a person's values seem sure to fail because they result in "acting" which people usually recognize as manipulation. Two points must be made, however. First, leaders need to continually experiment with different styles to test their per-

Table 2   Summary of Fiedler Investigations of Leadership

| Condition | Group Situation | | | Leadership Style Correlating with Productivity |
	Leader-Member Relations	Task Structure	Position Power	
1	Good	Structured	Strong	Directive
2	Good	Structured	Weak	Directive
3	Good	Unstructured	Strong	Directive
4	Good	Unstructured	Weak	Permissive
5	Moderately poor	Structured	Strong	Permissive
6	Moderately poor	Structured	Weak	No Data
7	Moderately poor	Unstructured	Strong	No relationship found
8	Moderately poor	Unstructured	Weak	Directive

SOURCE: Adapted from Fred Fiedler, *A Theory of Leadership Effectiveness* (New York: McGraw-Hill, 1967), p. 146. Used by permission.

sonal fit and effectiveness. Second, all styles depend on skills such as communication, analytical problem solving, and the like, which can be acquired and improved.

Research on Organizational Style Effectiveness

Research on the effectiveness of organizational leadership styles is even more piecemeal than that on individual style effectiveness, but there is some helpful evidence. Some of the research relevant to the organizational leadership styles described previously in the chapter is now presented.

Effectiveness of Grid Styles.   There are basically two types of evidence concerning the effectiveness of organizational Grid styles. One type is symbolic, and the other is an overall empirical test.

While it tends to be piecemeal, there is substantial evidence that the team style is the most effective organizational leadership described by the Grid, if it is a true, sincere style and not a facade. Evidence also indicates that other styles are less effective, but concrete data on the relative effectiveness of the various styles are still not available. Common observation leads us to believe that all of the styles, with the possible exception of the impoverished style, can achieve some measure of effectiveness.

One partial test of the organizational Grid styles was done by Blake et al. (1964a). The managerial personnel of a relatively large organization were trained in an effort to move the organizational style toward the team style. Rough measurements indicated that the organization did move significantly toward this style. There is also evidence that this move increased the effectiveness of organizational communication and organizational effectiveness, as measured by several factors. The data are certainly not conclusive and more tests of the other Grid styles need to be done, but it does seem that organizations can change styles and that some styles are more effective than others.

Effectiveness of Likert's Systems.   An empirical test of Likert's (1967) system styles, similar to that of the Grid, has also been done. Since the actual test covered a long period of time and was rather complicated, only the major conclusions are important here. Attempts to move toward a participative style were initiated and, at least by rough indicators, were successful in moving the style toward participative. Measures of effectiveness indicated that the further the style moved toward participative, the more effective communication and the organization were. Thus, the participative style would seem to be the more effective style. Before any definite conclusions are drawn, however, more research on all of the styles in different situations needs to be done.

Implications

Organizations do tend to have leadership styles, and these leadership styles influence communication and ultimate organizational effectiveness both directly and indirectly. There are direct influences on the formal subsystems of communication used to provide information for the producing and decision-making process and there are obvious effects on the climate (degree of openness and candor) that exists. In addition, the leadership style affects both of these elements indirectly through influencing other internal organizational variables such as the rewards system, objectives, organizational structures, and technology and job design.

The point seems clear: more research on organizational style needs to be done, and organizations themselves need to be conscious of their style and to experiment with changes to see how both communication and effectiveness are influenced.

Summary

Leadership style is an important internal element of the organization affecting communication and organizational effectiveness. Leadership is interpersonal influence. The chief functions of leadership are task functions and group maintenance functions.

Leadership style refers to the general behavioral approach to influence and to the way in which the leadership functions are carried out. The Tannenbaum and Schmidt continuum identifies and describes individual leadership styles based on the way in which authority is used to influence others. Three general styles are identified — autocratic, participative, and democratic. The "Managerial Grid" identifies five different managerial styles based on the degree of concern shown for production, the degree of concern shown for people, and the way in which the two concerns are combined.

Organizations also tend to exhibit leadership styles similar to individual leadership styles. Five organizational styles are identified by the "Managerial Grid." Likert and his associates identify and describe four organizational styles.

Research on leadership effectiveness indicates that some types of leadership behavior are more effective than other types. More research has been done on individual style effectiveness than on organizational style effectiveness. More research on both individual and organizational style effectiveness needs to be done. What evidence is available definitely indicates that leadership style affects communication and organizational effectiveness.

REVIEW AND DISCUSSION

1. In your own words, explain task functions of leadership.

2. Explain group maintenance functions.

3. Describe the central concept on which the Tannenbaum and Schmidt Continuum distinguishes different leadership styles.

4. In the Grid theory what is meant by the way the two concerns are put together?

5. What are the similarities and differences between the organizational style descriptions of the Grid and Likert's four systems?

6. What is the best individual leadership style? Explain why.

7. Describe your own leadership style in terms of the Grid. Be honest and specific.

Chapter Ten

Intergroup Relations

Groups are a fact of life, especially in organizations. People have social needs which require other people to satisfy. Even other types of individual needs are more easily satisfied through group membership than otherwise. In addition, anyone even vaguely familiar with any type of organization is probably aware that organizations are almost always structured to divide (or collect, if you prefer) people into groups, i.e. departments, divisions, units, and so on. So groups make up a significant part of organizations and their behavior is an important element affecting organizational communication.

When we stop to think about it, most of us are already aware of the pressures and influences that groups have on our own behavior and also of how group membership affects the behavior we exhibit toward members of other groups. At one time or another each of us has probably experienced some anxiety over whether we should or should not do something we want to do when we know it is considered a "no no" in our group. As Lawrence (1965, p. 47) and his colleagues point out ". . . the meaning of the group to its members is very frequently a more direct influence on behavior than any other single set of factors."

Not only group membership affects individual behavior, but the relations which prevail between groups also affect individual behavior. As Athos and Coffey (1968, p. 208) suggest: "The pressures that exist between individuals . . . exist also among the various groups in the organization." The nature of the relations between various groups in the organization have a significant impact on other internal organizational elements and most importantly on the effectiveness of organizational communication.

This chapter will explain these two interrelated variables and how they affect behavior. The first part of the chapter presents an overview of some basic terminology and concepts associated with groups in organizations. Next we explain with the aid of a model small work groups and their effects on behavior. Finally, we deal with the subject of intergroup relations and their effects on behavior. The nature of the interpersonal skills necessary for group communication will be considered in chapter fourteen.

Groups: An Overview

Although we are primarily concerned with the way in which groups and intergroup relations affect behavior and communication, we believe knowledge and understanding of more basic group concepts and characteristics are a necessary beginning.

Definition

Almost everyone is familiar with the term "group" and has some idea of what a group is; but most people are hard pressed when it comes to giving a good, concise, specific definition. Perhaps a fully adequate definition of groups is impossible, but any meaningful discussion of groups should begin with an explicit conception of what the term means.

Most definitions of groups focus on the element of interaction. One noted authority defines a group as "a number of persons who communicate with one another often over a span of time, and who are few enough so that each person is able to communicate . . . face-to-face" (Homans 1950, p. 1). The same author emphasizes, however, that defining groups based on communication does not mean that such communication is the total of group behavior. In this discussion, we use the term "group" to refer to a relatively small number of people that engage in interpersonal communication frequently.

Elements of Group Behavior

While we have used and will continue to use the term group behavior for the sake of convenience, it should be kept in mind that it is individuals that behave, not groups. There is no such thing as group behavior. Groups are abstractions — they are collections or associations of individuals — and abstractions do not exhibit behavior; it is the individuals who make up the abstraction "group" who behave. In this context, behavior is the product of individuals influenced by group membership through interaction with other individuals.

While they do not literally behave, we can identify some of the more important aspects of behavior in groups. In his now classic work, Homans (1950) describes three related but different elements of group behavior — activity, interaction, and sentiment. Activity refers to something that individuals do — something that results in movement of the muscles (walking, working, for instance). Interaction is communication or contact between two or more people in which the activity of one is in response to the behavior of the other(s). All communications are interactions, but interaction, or influence, can occur without verbal communication. A sentiment is an idea, belief or feeling about something or someone; and it is not directly observable because it is internal to the individual.

These three elements are the most important components of group behavior and are by no means independent, but are in fact interrelated. Figure 10-1 illustrates the interrelationships among the three elements. The way in which the elements are related, and the reasons why, are explained later in the chapter.

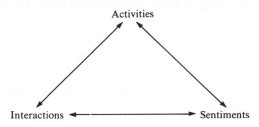

SOURCE: Aubrey C. Sanford, *Human Relations: Theory and Practice* (Columbus, Ohio: Charles E. Merrill, 1973), p. 90.

Figure 10-1   Elements of Group Behavior

Characteristics of Groups

Groups, similar to individuals, have certain characteristics in varying degrees. The more important of these characteristics are (1) identity, (2) status, (3) formality, and (4) cohesion.

Identity.   All groups are unique and thus have an identity. While we know of little research support, we believe that group identity is a composite of several factors, among which are such things as the status of the group, the objectives it strives for and the methods used to achieve objectives, and norms and codes of conduct of members. Just as individuals use their behavior to establish and maintain their identity, groups regulate the behavior of members to establish the group identity.

Status.   One important part of a group identity is its relative status, especially its occupational status. In ours and most other cultures, different types of jobs and occupations tend to have different statuses. More status is attributed to some occupations than to others. In most organizations, work is divided and organized so that people doing similar types of jobs and, therefore, with similar occupations are grouped together. Occupational status tends to be associated not only with individuals but also with entire work groups (Turner 1961). It is, for example, well known that greater occupational status is associated with medical doctors than with used-car salespeople. These same types of status differences exist in varying degrees between work groups in organizations. Their relative status rankings have significant effects on organizational communication.

Formality.   The degree of formality exhibited by groups is another characteristic included in group identity. Groups are classified as formal when they have a well-defined, highly developed and durable structure of authority and internal status and role relationships. They are considered informal when their structure of authority status and roles is not well defined or highly developed and is spontaneous rather than deliberately established.

The classifications of formal and informal are relative rather than absolute. As figure 10-2 illustrates, the formal and informal classifications described refer to the extremities of a continuum of formality. In reality, it would be difficult to find completely formal or informal groups, because almost all groups exhibit varying degrees of structure — they exhibit some degree of both formality and informality. Most groups, therefore, exist at some point between the two extreme ends of the continuum.

Formal   Informal
Well defined   Vague
structure   structure

SOURCE: Aubrey C. Sanford, *Human Relations: Theory and Practice* (Columbus, Ohio: Charles E. Merrill, 1973), p. 85.

Figure 10-2   Continuum of Group Formality

Although it is relative and imprecise, the classification of groups according to their formality is useful because it is based on important common group characteristics. To say that a particular group is formal or informal connotes certain important characteristics and provides an idea of the internal nature of the group.

Cohesion.   Another important characteristic of all work groups is the degree of cohesion, established through communication, among members of the groups. Cohesion refers, here, to the degree to which groups are "close knit" and "stick together." As with the degree of formality, cohesion is not an all or nothing feature. All groups exhibit, by definition, more or less cohesion, with some groups being more tightly knit than others.

In summary, work groups of various types exist in all organizations and forces within these groups have significant effects on the behavior of individuals in the organization.

Intragroup Behavior and Communication

Although descriptive information about work groups and their characteristics is useful to fully appreciate the effects of group membership on behavior, we need to understand the *hows* and *whys* of groups. One of the most useful ways of looking at and understanding groups was developed by Homans (1950). Homans' approach is applicable to all groups, but it has been applied specifically to work groups in organizations by Turner (1961).

A Way of Thinking About Groups

In figure 10-3 we have modeled the basic Homans approach to group behavior. It includes four major parts and indicates that group behavior is understood best through a sequential analysis of cause and effect. In outline form, the model hypothesizes that background factors determine the group's external system. The external system is the set of activities, interactions, and sentiments required of the

group by its environment. The external system (Required and Given System), in turn, determines the internal system (Emergent System) of group behavior (activities, interactions, and sentiments) that actually results. Thus, the internal system of behavior produces consequences which have some effect on the group as a whole,

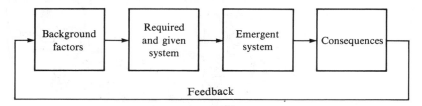

SOURCE: Aubrey C. Sanford, *Human Relations: Theory and Practice* (Columbus, Ohio: Charles E. Merrill, 1973), p. 91.

Figure 10-3   Intragroup Behavior Model

and individuals within the group (Homans 1950). The basic intragroup behavior model can be used to describe and explain in detail the behavior of work groups.

The Hows and Whys of Work Groups

Anyone who has studied or observed the behavior of work groups is aware that such groups invariably exhibit behavior which is different from that required for job performance. The behavior of work groups contains what is absolutely necessary for some acceptable level of job performance but almost always includes behavior in addition to what is required. Turner (1961) has argued that communication behavior manifested by the work group not only may not be required in the situation but also may not even be officially allowed. He has developed a model, shown in figure 10-4, which diagrams all of the important steps which are common to work group behavior. The reader will note that Turner has built on the Homans approach to intragroup behavior which we examined earlier in figure 10-3.* In a summary statement of reverse order, the consequences of group behavior are determined by the internal system (the actual behavior exhibited); the internal system of emergent communication behavior is determined by the external system; and the external system is a product of particular background factors.†

Background Factors of the External System

The external system refers to the behavior which is required of individuals for job performance and to the behavior that group members bring to the work group

---

*This discussion is based on a paper prepared by Arthur N. Turner of the Harvard University Graduate School of Business Administration and first published in P. R. Lawrence et. al., *Organizational Behavior and Administration,* 2d ed. (Homewood, Ill.: Irwin-Dorsey, 1961), pp. 213-23. The paper is based primarily on the work of George C. Homans, *The Human Group* (New York: Harcourt Brace Jovanovich, 1950), and H. W. Riecken and G. C. Homans, "Psychological Aspects of Social Structure," in *Handbook of Social Psychology,* ed. Gardner Lindzey (Cambridge: Addison-Wesley, 1954), vol. II, pp. 786-832.

†You are probably aware by now that there are striking conceptual similarities between the work group model and the organizational communication model summarized in chapter two. We acknowledge our debt to Turner and his work, and particularly to this model which significantly influenced our thinking in general and this book in particular.

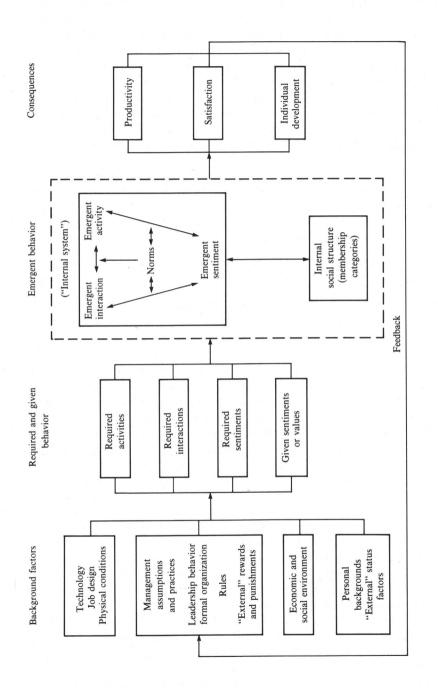

| Background factors | Required and given behavior | Emergent behavior | Consequences |

Background factors

Technology
Job design
Physical conditions

Management
assumptions
and practices

Leadership behavior
formal organization

Rules

"External" rewards
and punishments

Economic and
social environment

Personal
backgrounds
"External" status
factors

Required and given behavior

Required
activities

Required
interactions

Required
sentiments

Given sentiments
or values

Emergent behavior

("Internal system")

Emergent
interaction

Emergent
activity

Norms

Emergent
sentiment

Internal
social structure
(membership
categories)

Feedback

Consequences

Productivity

Satisfaction

Individual
development

Figure 10-4 Work Group Behavior

SOURCE: Arthur N. Turner, "A Conceptual Scheme for Describing Work Group Behavior," in Paul R. Lawrence and others, *Organizational Behavior and Administration*, 2d ed. (Homewood, Ill.: Richard D. Irwin, 1961), p. 158. © 1961 by the President and Fellows of Harvard College. Reproduced by permission.

from the outside. All jobs require certain behavior for successful performance; thus, the external system includes required activities, required interactions (or, communications) and required sentiments. Although it is obvious that job performance always requires certain activity, it is not as obvious that it also always requires certain interactions and sentiments. There are few work group jobs which can be performed so completely in isolation that they require no communication whatsoever. Further analysis of most jobs reveals that particular sentiments also are required for their performance (Turner 1961). For example, an individual may drop out of medical school because he cannot tolerate the risks of failure in the job; certain sentiments are required to perform the job of a doctor and he feels he does not possess those particular sentiments.

The external system also includes those aspects of behavior, particularly sentiments, that work group members bring to the group from the outside. This behavior is referred to as "given" behavior, or, in this case, as "given" sentiments. The external work group system, therefore, is made up of required activity, required interaction, required sentiments and given sentiments.

Background Factors and Effects. The particular external system of any work group results from four sets of background factors: technology and job design; management assumptions, policy, and practice; the economic and social environment; and the personal backgrounds of work group members.

Technology and job design refer to the methods and procedures of work; they influence the nature of the activities, interactions, and sentiments required to perform jobs. Organizations generally have alternative choices concerning the technology used, and different technologies and different job designs require different behavior for job performance. One technology may result in jobs requiring one set of activities, interactions, and sentiments, while another technology may require entirely different activities, interactions, and sentiments (Turner 1961).

The behavior required for job performance also is influenced by management assumptions, policies, and practices, including specifically those of the immediate supervisor of the work group. Within the same technology, two identical jobs might require different behavior because of management's assumptions about the abilities of people and the most effective use of these abilities. When management assumes that work group members have little ability and must be coerced to use whatever ability they have, jobs will likely require different behavior than when management assumes that work group members have high levels of ability and will use it without coercion. Together with its direct effect upon the external work group system, it seems logical that management's assumptions about people and the ways in which they should be managed might influence its choice of alternative technologies and effect required behavior through the factor of technology.

The economic and social environment is a third background factor, for it differs from place to place and from time to time. Different economic and social environments are likely to result in different required behavior and different internal systems (Turner 1961).

The last major background factor—the personal backgrounds of work group members—may have some indirect influence on the behavior required for performance, but it is also the major determinant of the second part—given sentiments—of the external system. Given sentiments are those which members bring to the work group from the outside (Turner 1961). At any point in time, the given sentiments of work group members are the result of their past and present overall environment and learning experiences. No two individuals ever have the same personal backgrounds, but the members of any work group tend to have similar jobs and similar backgrounds which result in similar given sentiments.

These, then, are the background factors which determine the work group behavior required by the external system and the sentiments work group members bring to the work group. The background factors vary in different situations and they produce different external systems, but the external system always can be understood better as the product of these forces. The external system must be understood, therefore, before the emergent work group behavior of the internal system can be understood, because the internal system is a product of the external system.

Relation Between the Internal and External System. The actual behavior that emerges in work groups almost always is different from and much more complicated than that which is required. The accomplishment of the organizational goals of the work groups requires that their behavior include at least the bare outline of that which is required, which must be communicated to each group member. Only rarely is this required behavior all the behavior that occurs in work groups. Additional behavior emerges that is different from but related to the required behavior. Work group research and observation have produced several tentative, general hypotheses concerning the manner in which the external system affects the internal system and the nature of the internal system. These hypotheses are useful and valid but are not universal laws. The most useful of these hypotheses are explained below.

Given Sentiments and Their Effects. The values, beliefs, and opinions that workers bring to work groups as a result of their past experiences always affect the behavior that emerges in work groups. The more similar the given sentiments of work group members, the more likely they are to communicate more than required, and the more likely it is that more favorable sentiments will exist between the work group members. Moreover, the status of work group members in the overall external environment seems to influence, at least initially, their status and rank in the emergent internal social system and the emerging interpersonal sentiments (Turner 1961).

These are not necessarily profoundly surprising propositions. In many respects, they are logical common sense deductions, but they do explain particularly how the "given" behavior of the external system affects the emergent behavior of the internal system. It also should be kept in mind that these propositions are only a small part of the total explanation of work group behavior. When the propositions are viewed in light of the entire system and the contribution they make to it, they take on even more meaning.

Required Behavior and Its Effects. The second major part of the external system, required behavior—activities, interactions, and sentiments—also exerts a major influence on emergent behavior. First of all, the required behavior makes up at least the foundation and starting point for the behavior that actually results. Beyond this, however, members whose jobs are close together and members whose jobs require that they communicate are likely to interact more than other work group members. The emergent behavior is also likely to be influenced by the technology and physical working conditions, including things such as noise, heat, dullness and routiness of jobs. This proposition goes a long way toward explaining much of the "horseplay" in which assembly line workers frequently engage—it helps compensate for the dullness and breaks up the boredom of the job. Finally, the degree to which particular sentiments are required for job performance affects emergent behavior (Turner 1961).

As with the previously mentioned propositions, these seem disappointingly simple, but they are capable of explaining the reasons why work groups engage in much— though not all, by any means—of the behavior they do. The test of the value of the statements is not whether or not they are revolutionarily startling, but whether they make a useful contribution to understanding work group behavior. Observation of work groups reveals that they indeed are useful.

Thus far, we have concentrated on explaining the ways in which background factors affect the required and given behavioral system and on the way the external system influences the emergent internal system. Now we move to the composition of the internal system itself.

The Internal System

In all work groups, an internal system emerges that contains an interrelated set of activities, interactions, sentiments and social structure. The internal system is where the face-to-face communication among members takes place.

Interaction and Sentiment. Within the emergent internal system, member communications and sentiments are related. All else being equal, favorable sentiments result between members who interact frequently, and, vice-versa, more frequent interaction results from favorable sentiments. Under some conditions, increased communication results from less favorable interpersonal sentiments, but this is not usually the case (Turner 1961). The conditions which cause this are described more fully later on.

While the relationships between communications and sentiments among work group members seem both logical and expected, the fact that, all else being equal, members who like each other talk more than those who do not is the key to understanding the emergent behavior of work groups. Many of the most important aspects of work group behavior occur because the "other things" are not equal. This proposition, therefore, provides some guidance when events do occur as expected.

Activities, Sentiments, and Norms. The activities, sentiments, and norms of work groups tend to be related in certain ways. A norm is merely a special type of sentiment; it is an idea or belief concerning what the activities, interactions, and sentiments should be in a particular work group. It is related to both the emergent group activities and sentiments. Normally, members who violate the generally accepted norms of the group are the objects of unfavorable sentiment; moreover, the unfavorable sentiments directed at members who violate group norms frequently lead the work group to engage in activities designed to punish the violators. In turn, the punishing activities often cause the violators to retaliate with defensive or aggressive activity. The result is a circular pattern, in which the sentiments of both the work group and the violators become less and less favorable toward each other (Turner 1961). In other words, a self-sustaining and growing detrimental force is created in the work group.

The hypotheses relating activities, sentiments, and norms are capable of explaining many aspects of work group behavior. For example, in light of these hypotheses it is much easier to understand why most work group members "stick together" and are reluctant to do things contrary to group opinion. It is also easy to see why unfavorable sentiments and conflict between the majority of group members and norm violators may tend to get worse before they get better.

Activities, Norms and Interactions. The quality and quantity of communication between any two work group members are affected by the sentiments which prevail between them, but also they are influenced by the degree to which each group member perceived the other's activities as violating accepted group norms. When members violate group norms, efforts are made to "bring them back into line." Communication toward them, therefore, increases as a result of their violations. If groups' corrective activities fail to bring the violators back into compliance, they become the object of increasingly unfavorable sentiments and decreasing communication (Turner 1961). In this way work groups have the power of social ostracism with which they can effectively control most members.

These hypotheses, too, go a long way toward explaining much of the behavior that work groups exhibit. They explain both how and why work groups can control effectively the behavior of their members. They also explain why particular members of certain work groups never "get along" with the rest of the group— they are not willing to live up to its norms of behavior.

The Social Structure of Work Groups. Together with the complicated, interrelated set of activities, interactions, sentiments, and norms, the emergent work group system also contains a well-defined social structure: " . . . there usually emerges in a work group a core of regular members which includes the informal leader or leaders of the group" (Turner 1961, pp. 162-63). Status and rank in groups are determined by the degree of faithfulness to group norms. Informal or unofficial work group leaders are the ones most faithful to group norms and, therefore, are the highest status members. The informal leaders also tend to be the most frequent initiators of communication among group members.

In most work groups there are some who are not regular members, who interact with the "regulars" only as required by their jobs. In many cases, there are also some work group members who are on the fringe area of regular membership. These "deviates" talk fairly frequently among themselves and with regular group members, but full acceptance and regular group membership are denied to them because of their less than whole-hearted adherence to group norms and values (Turner 1961). From a relatively simple set of required and given behavior, therefore, work groups develop an intricate system of activities, interactions, sentiments, norms, and social structure designed to protect themselves from perceived detrimental forces and to preserve their norms and values.

The Consequences of Work Group Behavior. It is obvious that the behavior of work groups has some significant effects upon work groups' productivity and the achievement of their organizational goals and the satisfaction and development of individual members. The behavior of the work groups may be functional or dysfunctional from each of these three standpoints. In work groups characterized by stability and high rates of communication, member satisfaction is usually high; on the other hand, the same things that cause member satisfaction to be high may result in the restriction of productivity and of the development of individual members. Of course, other combinations of favorable and unfavorable effects are also possible. It is possible that the behavior of work groups is functional from all three standpoints (indeed, that is the hoped-for ideal) or, unfortunately, dysfunctional for individuals and the overall organization (Turner 1961).

As figure 10.4 indicates, the consequences—no matter what they may be—feed back and affect the most basic parts of the model—background factors. This feedback process closes the circuit in the model and means that the consequences of work group behavior tend to reinforce the very elements that caused the behavior in the first place. When conditions are such that the resulting internal system restricts productivity, then it is likely that the feedback will alter the background factors to produce an internal system which results in even further productivity restriction. Thus, work group behavior tends to create forces which not only perpetuate its consequences but reinforce them. All is not hopeless, however, because the same reinforcing dynamics work when the consequences of the internal system are favorable for all parties.

While the model and explanation deal with work group behavior in general, work group membership has significant effects on individual behavior and other internal organization variables that ultimately influence the effectiveness of organizational communication.

Certainly the degree to which groups feel that their norms and values and even their very existence is threatened is the degree to which they defend themselves by communicating only those things that help maintain and/or enhance their position. On the other side, when groups perceive support rather than threat, they are likely to feel more freedom to communicate openly and candidly and, consequently, more effectively.

In addition, group membership has enormous effects on the way individuals communicate with individuals in other work groups.

Intergroup Relations and Communication

Communication in organizations is made even more complex and difficult to understand because it is influenced not only by work norms and values but also by the relations which prevail between and among groups. As stated previously, the same type of pressures that exist between individuals are present between groups (Athos and Coffey 1968). As a result of these pressures, the nature of the relations which exist between work groups can run the gamut from almost open warfare to collaboration and teamwork.

As is the case with individual behavior in work groups, both research and observation indicate that the behavior which occurs between groups in organizations rarely conforms only to that which is required or expected. Unfortunately, the relations which prevail between groups are not always in the best interests of the organization or of the groups and individuals involved. "It is a common complaint, for instance, that the sales department is having a running feud or cold war with the production department, with occasional shots being fired by other interested groups" (Seiler 1961, p. 534). Many students may be familiar with the controversy that exists between line and staff in some organizations.

The actual nature of the relationship which prevails between any two work groups is influenced by several factors—small group norms and values, intergroup communication, technology, and the way work and the organization is structured. We will present one systematic way of making sense of intergroup relations. That is, we seek to determine the *hows* and *whys* of behavior and its effects on communication between and among groups.

A Way of Thinking about Intergroup Relations

The intragroup and work group approaches described in the preceding section have also been adapted by Seiler (1961)* to explain intergroup relations. It makes use of the same basic model and terminology and builds upon the intergroup as illustrated in figure 10.5. In fact, small group norms and values are one of the major background factors affecting intergroup relations.

Background Factors and the External System

All organizations of any significant size include many small work groups of the type discussed in the preceding section, and the effectiveness of organizational communication depends heavily on the patterns of behavior that exist between these groups. For example, we may think of organizations being composed of *groups of groups.* But these diverse groups must communicate among themselves for the organization to be effective. Sometimes particular channels, or *networks,* link these groups within the organization. Some of the typical networks will be examined in chapter twelve devoted to the formal communication subsystem.

The External Intergroup System. Organizations accomplish things by the application of human effort through technology to physical resources, that is, organizations perform interrelated sets of activities. These activities usually are organized into sets performed by small work groups; moreover, the activities performed by different small work groups are interrelated and the activities of the different groups must be coordinated for effective organizational performance. This necessity for coordinated performance of the activities of work groups requires that groups behave in some defined pattern with respect to other groups.

As figure 10-5 indicates, the intergroup behavior required by organizations includes required activities, required interactions, and required sentiments. This means that it is necessary for all groups to engage in particular activities in relation to certain other groups, to interact (or communicate) with certain other groups, and that certain more or less obvious attitudes or sentiments are necessary for achieving the organization's objectives. These required elements of intergroup behavior make up the intergroup required system. This required system is a product of certain

---

*This discussion is based on a paper prepared by John A. Seiler of the Harvard University Graduate School of Business Administration. It also appears in Lawrence et al. (1961). The discussion of the intergroup model draws heavily from this source.

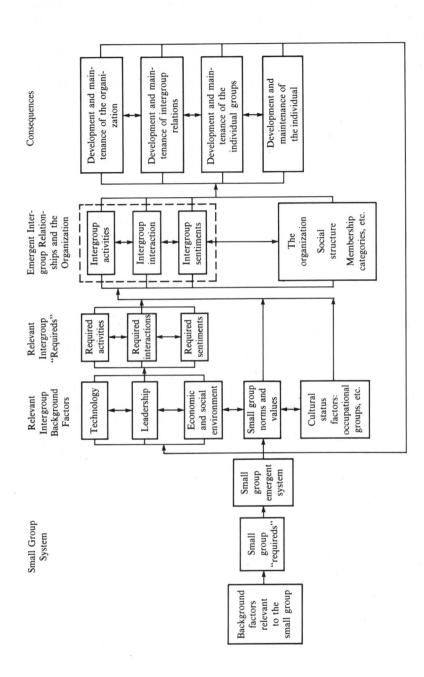

Figure 10-5 *The Intergroup Conceptual Scheme*

SOURCE: John A. Seiler, "A Systematic Way of Thinking about Intergroup Behavior," in Paul R. Lawrence et al., *Organization Behavior and Administration*, 2d ed. (Homewood, Ill.: Richard D. Irwin, 1961), p. 537. © 1961 by the President and Fellows of Harvard College. Reproduced by permission.

background factors, and it forms the general framework within which the emergent intergroup system develops (Seiler 1961).

The Relevant Background Factors. The most important background factors affecting intergroup behavior are similar to those affecting intragroup behavior. There are actually three sets of intergroup background factors: two sets, small group norms and values and cultural status factors, have direct effects upon the emergent work group system; the third set, technology, leadership, and economic and social conditions, determines the required intergroup system, which, in turn, influences the character of the emergent system.

The three background factors of technology, managerial leadership, and economic and social conditions are the chief determinants of the required intergroup system.

> What products or services the organization is to produce and under what physical circumstances, how its formal leaders conceive of their jobs, and what kinds of competitive and other environmental pressures are exerted upon the organization will tend to define, in broad terms, the required activities, interactions, and sentiments of a multigroup organization: which group will assume responsibility for what task, where that task will be performed, which group will pass on its product to what other group (or otherwise initiate activity for other groups), within what time limits the task must be completed and with what level of quality and what physical equipment will be available to each group or cluster of interrelated groups for the performance of the task. (Seiler 1961, p. 538)

The set of background factors labeled small group norms and values is the product of the emergent small work group system discussed in the previous section and included in an abbreviated form in figure 10-5. It indicates that a complex set of background factors, similar to those which affect the intergroup required system, produce a required and given system of small group behavior. This required and given system produces an emergent system of small group behavior that is related to but different from that which is required (Seiler 1961). Each small group emergent system contains a unique set of norms and values, and these norms and values affect the nature of the intergroup behavioral system that emerges.

The third set of background factors—cultural status factors—is the result of the cultural environment surrounding the organization. Whatever the particular culture is, it contains some clear ideas and beliefs about the relative status and prestige rankings of particular personal backgrounds and especially of particular occupational categories, such as salespeople, production line workers, and others (Seiler 1961).

The Emergent System. The required intergroup system, together with the small group norms and values and cultural status factors, determines the system of intergroup communication behavior that emerges. We shift now to the way in which these factors affect the emergent system to explain the system of intergroup communication behavior that actually emerges.

The Effects of the Required System. The environmentally determined system of required activities, interactions, and sentiments forms the basic framework and boundaries within which the emergent intergroup system develops. The emergent system almost always differs significantly from the required system, but it must contain at least the bare outline of the system which is required for the organization to function. Thus, the required system of intergroup behavior is at least the starting point for the emergent system. The required system also establishes the limits for the degree of mutuality of values which occurs across group boundaries. Members of small work groups tend to have similar backgrounds, values, and aspirations, because similar skills and abilities tend to be required in particular work groups. In fact, similarity of background and values is one of the chief criteria for selecting members for particular small groups (Seiler 1961). This means that the required system frequently results in work groups where members tend to have similar values but where values differ greatly between work groups.

The Effects of Small Group Norms and Values. The norms and values of small groups also affect the nature of the relations which prevail between them. The particular norms and values of any group influence the expectations of its members about both intragroup and intergroup behavior. Thus, the small group's norms and values govern the behavior of members and their communications with members of other groups. As it is within groups, the more similar the norms and values of two groups are, the more likely it is that members of the two groups will communicate more frequently, and the more likely they are to develop even more favorable sentiments toward each other. Conversely, the less similar the norms and values of two groups, the less likely they are to communicate frequently (Gouldner 1960).

The Effects of Cultural Status Factors. The ideas and beliefs about the relative status and prestige rankings of particular occupational categories which individuals bring with them to organizations also affect the character of relations between groups. Because the required system usually results in small work groups with similar backgrounds and values, it also tends to result in small work groups in which members have similar occupational status and prestige, but in which there are significant differences between the occupational status and prestige of particular groups. All else being equal, groups which must communicate will try to avoid contact with each other when their occupational status ranks are vastly different and especially when their status ranks are inconsistent with the authority relationship between them (Seiler 1961).

The two factors mentioned above—the degree to which group values are similar and the degree of consistency between the occupational status of the groups and the direction of authority and activity initiation—are primary determinants of the nature of the relationship that exists between any two groups. The nature of the relationship depends upon what particular combination of these two factors exists.

Figure 10-6 illustrates four different combinations of these two factors and the nature of the intergroup relationships produced. As shown, when groups have many shared values and the activity initiation sequence is consistent (from high to low) with the status ranking of the groups, there will be frequent communication and collaboration between the groups. When there are few shared values but the activity initiation sequence is considered proper, intergroup relations will tend to be formal, distant, and only as necessitated by the required system. When there are many shared values but low status, groups initiate the activity for higher status groups; intergroup relations will tend to deviate from those required formally and be replaced by more informal ones. Finally, when there are few shared values and low status, groups initiate the activity for high status groups, severe conflict results, and groups tend ultimately to withdraw from each other (Seiler 1963).

	Many Shared Values	Few Shared Values
Initiation from high status group to low status group	Free collaboration	Formal distinct relationship
Initiation from low status group to high status group	Informal relationships replace formal ones	Withdrawal from each other

SOURCE: John A. Seiler, "A Systematic Way of Thinking about Intergroup Behavior," in Paul R. Lawrence et al. *Organizational Behavior and Administration,* 2d ed. (Homewood, Ill.: Richard D. Irwin, 1961), p. 542. © 1961 by the President and Fellows of Harvard College. Reproduced by permission.

Figure 10-6   Determinants of Intergroup Relations

These are not the only types of possible intergroup relationships; there are certainly more than two degrees of each of the two factors and, therefore, many more variations of the four types of relationships described. It should be pointed out that the degree to which values are shared among groups and the consistency of status and activity initiation is determined primarily by the nature of the required system. It should not be assumed, however, that required systems always can be designed so that collaboration results in all intergroup relations; conflict will result even in the best structured organizations.

The Consequences of Intergroup Behavior.   It is obvious that whatever the quality and quantity of intergroup relations, they always produce some consequences for all of the parties concerned. The intergroup behavior that actually emerges in organizations may be beneficial or detrimental for the total organization, for intergroup relations, for individual groups, and for individuals within groups, or it may have varying effects upon each depending on the behavior involved (Seiler 1961). For example, intergroup behavior might be detrimental to the existence and improvement of intergroup relations, but it may be beneficial to organizations in the short run. Probably conflict is more commonly found, which is beneficial to some groups and some individuals, but which is detrimental to many individuals, groups, intergroup relations in general, and the entire organization. It is obvious also that conflict is generally detrimental to the organization's growth and development, for it results in the detrimental consequences of intergroup behavior. If intergroup relations were characterized by collaboration, there would be few dysfunctional consequences from any standpoint.

The nature of the relations which prevail between groups has extremely important communication implications. These relations have a great influence on individuals' motivations and actions. Thus, intergroup relations tend to exhibit or promote effective intergroup communication.

Feedback.   As in the small group model, the consequences of intergroup behavior —whatever they are—feed back upon the background factors and the required system and cause changes to occur in the system. Fortunately or unfortunately, as the case may be, the tendency is for the feedback to result in changes which reinforce the consequences which produced it. When the consequences are dysfunctional for one party, therefore, the changes resulting from the feedback are likely to cause future consequences to be even more dysfunctional. Fortunately, the same reinforcing mechanism tends to occur when the consequences of intergroup behavior are functional, as well as when they are dysfunctional. Whatever the consequences, they feed back upon the background factors in the small group systems and cause changes in them in the manner described in the preceding chapter. Because of this feedback, the required system changes and, consequently, the small group emergent system changes and its inputs to the intergroup system change accordingly.

In the intergroup system, feedback has a kind of double effect. It feeds back not only upon the small group systems and directly affects small group requirements, but also upon the intergroup background factors of technology, leadership, and social and economic conditions. Although feedback affects the intergroup model in the same manner as it does the small group model, its effects tend to be magnified in the intergroup model and, as a result, the intergroup model, if anything, is even more dynamic than the small group model. Fortunately, intergroup relations do not have to be left to chance; there is much that can be done to develop effective intergroup relations and communication (Seiler 1961).

Communication and Groups

The effects that intra- and intergroup relations have on organizational communication are clear. These two sets of relations are one of the most important internal elements affecting the communication climate that exists in the organization. In short, the relations that prevail within groups and between groups in the organization, i.e. small group sentiments and sentiments that exist between groups, result in forces which affect people's willingness to communicate with each other. All too often these forces inhibit rather than promote favorable communication climates in organizations. An approach to developing skills as a group member will be presented in chapter fourteen.

Summary

Behavior and communication in organizations are influenced by social as well as psychological and organizational forces. Work groups develop complicated norms of behavior and status systems which guide their behavior and communication. These norms both promote and inhibit communication within groups.

Just as groups develop norms to regulate internal behavior, they also develop norms to regulate their relations with other groups. The relations which prevail between any two groups are chiefly a result of the occupational status of the two groups and the activity initiation sequence which prevails between the two groups.

The relations which prevail within groups and the relations which prevail between groups are one of the major determinants of the communication climate that exists in the organization.

REVIEW AND DISCUSSION

1. According to the text, what is a group?

2. How are informal groups distinguished from formal ones?

3. Pick some work group with which you are familiar and analyze it in terms of the small group model presented in the text.

4. Explain briefly how the intergroup model works.

5. Use the intergroup model to analyze the relations between two groups with which you are familiar.

6. Explain the ultimate determinants of small group behavior. What are the most basic determinants of intergroup relations?

PART THREE: Internal Organizational Elements

Incidents

The State Champs

The Holtville Lions are the state "Class A" football champions. Holtville High, a school with an enrollment of only 600 students, has been a football power among small schools for the last twenty years since Joe "Mighty Joe" Jefferson has been the football coach and athletic director. Holtville, an agricultural community, located in the center of the state, has a population of 3,500 and every one of the local citizens is proud of the accomplishments of Mighty Joe and the Lions. When the Lions play a home game on Friday night in the fall, over 6,000 people, many from surrounding farms and villages, fill the brand-new Holtville Stadium to watch the Lions demolish another opponent. No stores, restaurants, or filling stations dare remain open for business when the Lions are playing. It is the dream of every young man born around Holtville to grow up and wear the "black and gold" of Holtville High.

Last year's Lions were Mighty Joe's best. The team led by all-state quarterback Galen Coggin won fourteen games, including four playoff contests, without a loss. Although Mighty Joe had won three state titles before, this was his first undefeated team. Nearly 25,000 people turned out to watch the finals in the state capital. Holtville defeated the Santa Raphael Gauchos, 34-6, for the state crown. Local sportswriters called this the best small high-school football team ever assembled in the state. College recruiters rated six Lion players off last year's team as "sure-fire" collegiate All-Americans. In all, it was a great year for Mighty Joe.

As he assembled his players for fall practice this year, Mighty Joe had to fill fourteen spots in his offensive and defensive teams because of graduation. None of the sophomore players had ever encountered anything like Mighty Joe in their young lives. He was an awesome man, standing nearly 6'4" and weighing close to 260 pounds. Rumor had it that he had been a war hero as a Marine officer in Korea. After the war, he was supposed to have played professional football in Canada before returning to college to obtain his teaching license. Since coming to Holtville, Mighty Joe had turned down many offers to move on to larger high schools and colleges to remain at Holtville High. Mighty Joe's wife had been killed in an automobile accident about ten years ago and he had raised his son, Joe Jr., alone. Joe Jr. had been a respectable football player at Holtville High but had given it up when he went off to college. The son was now serving as an assistant district attorney in Dallas after graduation from law school.

"There are some rules which you will follow if you are going to be a Holtville Lion this year," barked Mighty Joe to open practice on a hot mid-August day. "Everybody on the team will get a haircut, no sideburns, no hair coming out from behind the football helmet. There will be no dating for football players during the season. Anybody dating will be immediately off the team. Everybody will be in bed by 10 P.M. on week nights and 11 P.M. on weekends, except after games. There will be no booze, no drugs, and no smoking. If you're going to play for me, you play by my rules."

After the first practice, Billy Joe Washington, a sophomore running back, walked out of the locker room with Mike Seaver, a starting guard from last year's team. "Mike, is he really as tough as he sounds? Half the guys in school go out on a country road on weekends for a beer. And, man! No girls! That's unbelievable."

"Well, yeah, it's tough. The coach does ask you to give up a lot of thing but it's worth it. There is no greater thrill than winning the state championship before 25,000 people. It's a once-in-a-lifetime chance. And, listen, nine guys off last year's team won college scholarships for football. Not one of those guys could have afforded to go to college on his own. I think I have a good chance for a scholarship myself. I'd be crazy to blow that for a night out with the boys or for a date."

Billy Joe did a lot of thinking between the first practice session and the second, held the next day. What Mike had said the previous day had made a lot of sense to him. As the season progressed, Billy Joe became more and more a believer in Mighty Joe Jefferson and the Holtville Lions. When the coach called him a loafer, he answered, "Yes Sir" and tried to hustle that much harder. When the coach told him to run, he ran. And, when the coach laid down rules, he followed them. As he continued to play football as a member of the team, Billy Joe kept telling himself that his personal sacrifices were worthwhile for "the good of the team."

Guidelines for Analysis

1. What do you think are the components of Mighty Joe Jefferson's leadership style? Would this style work in an industrial organization as it did for a high school football team? Why?

2. List the advantages and disadvantages of a leadership style like Mighty Joe's.

Would you work comfortably in an organization practicing this kind of leadership? Why?

3. Describe the organizational communication which you think might exist on the Holtville Lions. Do you think that this type of communication is the product of Mighty Joe's philosophy? Why?

4. In your life, have you ever been asked to give up your own identity for the "good of the team"? What are the advantages (to the organization) gained when this happens? What disadvantages result?

5. Are there certain goals which can only be obtained by the individual through the "team" (or organization)? What are these? Discuss the relationship between individual and organizational goals.

6. Often the "organization man," the individual who goes along with the organization regardless of circumstances, has been criticized. Do you think being an "organization man" is good for the organization? For the individual involved?

7. It would seem that Mike Seaver, in the situation above, saw his own individual goals as being in concert with the goals of the team. When this occurs, what is likely to happen?

8. Using the leadership style of Mighty Joe as a springboard, speculate about the *ideal* leadership style. Is there such a thing? What might it be ?

The Reprimand

Don George is a Vietnam veteran who works for Faraday Manufacturing Company in Mooring, an eastern seacoast community of about 80,000. Don works on the #1 assembly line at Faraday as a quality control supervisor. Faraday makes electronic motors for lawn mowers, washing machines, and dishwashers. On a routine day, the three lines at the plant will produce about 1,400 electronic motors. Nearly 900 are employed on the three lines.

When Don graduated from high school he married his sweetheart, Gloria Jenson, and went to work at Faraday, thinking that he would be there about two years to gain enough money to go to college to study mechanical engineering. But before he could pick up the money for college, he was drafted into the Army and spent eighteen months in Vietnam. When he returned to the United States, Don was stationed in Washington for a year where a son was born to him and Gloria. After he had completed his service obligation, Don and Gloria talked about Don using his GI benefits to begin college. But, during this time, Gloria found out that she was pregnant for the second time and Don felt that he should return to his job at Faraday. That was nearly six years ago and since then Don has been one of the best workers at Faraday. He was promoted off the assembly line about two years ago to the quality control department. His job requires him to move up and down the assembly line to make sure that each motor produced in his unit passes minimum quality standards. Don has adjusted to his job and is in line for another promotion to foreman. Occasionally, however, he has complained to his wife about the routine and boredom associated with his work at Faraday.

Since returning to Faraday from the service, Don has noticed quite a change in the attitudes of the men on the line. When he first began to work eleven years ago, Faraday offered men in Mooring security. He thought that he was lucky to have a good job making good money close to home. During coffee breaks the "oldtimers" rarely "badmouthed" the company and most of the conversation was about sports and sex. Now things are very different. Most of the older employees have retired and a great majority of the younger men on the line are military veterans who have worked at Faraday for only a few years. Much of the talk now during coffee breaks and lunch periods is devoted to attacks on Faraday and its management. Some of the talk has impressed Don as quite hostile and destructive.

Recently a problem developed involving Don's unit. On a routine inspection, he noticed that one of the important rotary bars on the Faraday engine was being attached incorrectly. He immediately went to the work station responsible for the attachment of the bar. When he arrived he saw Harold Bradshaw and Grif Raymond, who were both supposed to be occupying the station, out of their places engaged in conversation and smoking cigarettes.

"Hey, what's going on here? Why aren't you guys at the station?" Don asked. "One of you is supposed to be in that station at all times. You both know that. Unless one of you gets back in there, I am going to have to write you up." But Don's advice did not have any effect. Both men remained out of the station.

"Look, George, you're only the quality control guy. You have no authority over us. We are just talking and that rotary bar will get attached anyway. Those engines don't mean a damn to us. You get the foreman or write us up if you want. But for now, just don't bug us," responded Bradshaw with Raymond nodding in agreement.

Don left and went to the quality control office. He submitted reports to both his own foreman and the foreman of the two men. As he left that night he was physically shaken. "I have known those guys all my life. I was in the fourth grade class with Grif and we played football together in high school. I just don't understand it. I have been having all kinds of trouble with some of these younger guys. I just can't see it. We get good money. We need to work. I am just like they are. How can they refuse to work like that?" Don said to Gloria that night.

"Don, you were just doing your job in ordering the men back to their stations, weren't you?" Gloria asked. "Yes," Don responded. "I don't know if I want to be a foreman or not if I have to put up with this kind of guff. How can those guys risk losing their job to stand there and talk? Gloria, I just don't understand it."

The next day at work, Don learned that Howard and Grif received official reprimands for their behavior which meant that any other reports would constitute immediate dismissal from Faraday. In addition to the reprimand, the men were split up and assigned to different work stations.

As Don walked down the assembly line that day he noticed a few icy stares directed his way from men on the line. A couple of Don's attempts to converse with some of his longtime friends on the line were met with silence. He did not understand what he had done to warrant this behavior from his "friends."

Guidelines for Analysis

1. What do you think Don George had done to his friends to cause their "cold shoulder" treatment? Was this treatment deserved? Why?

2. What relationship do you see between the nature of the task (or job) and organizational communication? What terms might be used to describe the communication within Faraday?

3. Do you think that the nature of assembly line work inherently restricts communication? Why?

4. Consider some of the jobs which you have held. Discuss the nature of the task. Did you handle the task well? Did you like it?

5. Speculate about some of the reasons why Don was no longer sure that he wanted a management position within Faraday. After what had happened to him in the situation above, do you see reasons for his hesitancy?

6. Suggest some other strategies which Don might have used to handle the situation differently. How would you have handled this situation?

7. What do you think of the punishment Raymond and Bradshaw received? What punishment would you had given them if you had been their supervisor?

8. Speculate about some of the reasons why Don may be presently unhappy in his job.

New Rules, New Regulations

Rod Goings, twenty-four, has been employed by the Northern States Sporting Goods Manufacturing Company for two years since his graduation from Midlam University with a B. S. degree in marketing. He is a sales representative for Northern States products to dealers, retail stores, and schools. The best-selling line of products of Northern States is baseball and basketball uniforms. Customers have noted that Northern States uniforms tend to launder and wear better than their competitors. Besides uniforms, Northern States also sells a line of sporting equipment such as balls, tennis rackets, and golf clubs.

Since Rod went to work at Northern States, he has had the Pacific Northwest sales territory. He has a company car and attempts to call upon ten to twelve clients per day. In his last appraisal, Ty Harold, the Northern States sales manager, told Rod that he was doing a "fine job" and that the company had been very pleased with his performance over the last two years. But in recent weeks, Rod has been developing some dissatisfaction with his job. Since Warren Keltz took over as vice-president of marketing six months ago, salespeople in the field have had to change many of their methods of operating. Before Keltz took the position, salespeople were very free to report their expenses in a mannner which was appropriate to them. Now each expense over $1.00 has to be recorded on a company form. Up until Keltz was promoted, each salesperson was free to establish his or her own work day. Now each salesperson must call upon at least twelve customers per day regardless of circumstances. Recently, the vice-president for marketing has implemented a new sales procedure news sheet. The news sheet is sent to each salesperson every Monday and contains new procedures which were adopted during the week at Northern States. Before Keltz, each salesperson reported to Ty Harold once a week. Now each salesperson is expected to report to the sales manager every day.

During the regular bi-monthly sales meeting, Keltz spoke to the salespeople about the new procedures. "We have been rather loose in our sales methods over the past few years. Although we have had a rather good sales record, many of us in the head office want to insure that we continue to maintain the good record. I don't think anything which we have done causes any unusual hardships on our sales force," concluded Keltz.

The talk did not set well with the sales staff. Before the promotion of Keltz, the Northern States representatives prided themselves in the fact that they were pretty much their "own boss." The policy had been to let the salespersons do as they pleased as long as they remained productive. Rod had appreciated his job at Northern States because it gave him the freedom to do his job, his own way. Since he had heard from his superior only once or twice a month, he considered himself his own boss. As he talked with his fellow salespersons, he found that many of them agreed with him.

"I don't mind the increase in rules and regulations," said Larry Palmer, the California representative, after the Keltz speech at the sales meeting. "I will play by the rules as long as I can agree that they are important. But I don't know here. I have been going over my quota for the last five months and I never had to call into Harold. Now every Friday, I have to check in. I just don't understand it."

"I'm spending more time filling out expense reports and production reports than I am calling on customers. I had been selling that new double knit uniform for about two weeks before I had time to read the *Newssheet*. I read in the *Newssheet* that we are no longer marketing this uniform. I know that I should have read the *Newssheet* but when do I have time to read it and call on fifteen customers a day? They don't seem to care how much we sell just so we meet the twelve customers," said Janice Wilson, a Northern States sales representative who covers the eastern territory. "We are going to have to do something about this. I feel like a teenager having to account for all the change to his father after coming home from the market."

After the meeting, most of the sales representatives met together at a nearby restaurant. "Let's go to Ty Harold to complain about this. Why don't we elect a representative? Rod's a good man. How would you feel about Rod as our representative? Okay?" Larry suggested. Rod did not actually have an opportunity to decline. But he was not sure that he would have if he could have. He felt that the company had made some bad changes and he was good as anyone to point these out. Rod called Ty Harold for an appointment.

Guidelines for Analysis

1. What approach would you take if you were meeting with the sales manager about the changes? What approach do you think Rod took? Why?

2. What do you consider to be the problem among the Northern States sales staff? What was responsible for the problem?

3. In light of the material in this part on structure, how would you characterize the structure within the sales division of Northern States?

4. Why do you think Keltz decided to implement the changes in the sales division?

5. What reaction would you have had to the changes in the sales division if you had been Rod?

6. Consider the effects of the new structures within the sales division on the behavior of the sales representative. Discuss what you consider to be the relationship between behavior and structure.

7. Do you think that the changes implemented by Keltz helped or hindered the communication within the sales division? Why?

8. What do you think Ty Harold's (the sales manager) reaction would have been to the meeting with Rod? Why? What constraints are likely to govern the communication between Rod and Ty?

The Miss Middleburg Contest

Over the years, the Miss Middleburg contest has become a tradition in town. The winner of the contest is invited to the Miss Knox County contest en route to the Miss United States pageant. Normally, Miss Middleburg is sponsored by the North Middleburg and South Middleburg Junior Chamber of Commerce clubs (Jaycees). The clubs meet together for about five months before the contest to plan the event. Last year, nearly 500 people crowded into the Middleburg Junior High auditorium to watch Jaynee Robinson be crowned Miss Middleburg. Jaynee went on to be named Miss Knox County and she finished as first runner-up in the state pageant. Nearly $1500 was raised for charity through last year's contest and it was judged a success by all in attendance.

This year Gary Issac, a local advertising executive, was elected by the North Jaycees as the chairman of its Miss Middleburg four-member delegation. Darrell Parker, head of the local Ford dealership, was named as the leader of the South Jaycee contingent. Gary called his club's committee members together before the official joint committee meetings were to begin.

"Guys, we have to maintain our own club's identity during this pageant. Since we were the first club in Middleburg and we first began the contest, people in the community still feel as if the pageant is really our project," said Gary. "I was on the committee last year and it was Dave Springhorn, our current president, who did the major share of the work. If it weren't for our club, last year's pageant would not have been successful. I think that one of the reasons why Dave was elected president was because the club recognized what a good job he did on the pageant. We have to be just as prepared to do that kind of work this year. O.K.?"

As representatives from the two clubs met for the first time, on the surface, relations were quite good. All joint committees seemed to want to work together to achieve a successful pageant. On various aspects of the contest such as entries, ticket sales, entertainment, and judges, each joint committee member seemed to exercise leadership. But as the weeks rolled by, it became apparent that the joint committee was depending increasingly on Darrell Parker for ideas and inputs. He agreed to supply automobiles to the pageant officials. He volunteered space in his daily advertisement in the Middleburg *Guide,* the local newspaper, to publicize the contest. Later, in joint committee meetings, Darrell said that he would underwrite the rental of the junior high auditorium in exchange for some advertising in the entryway. He even went so far as to arrange for his brother-in-law to donate printing services for the pageant program. In all, Darrell was responsible for saving the joint committee over $1200 in expenses.

Aside from the donations, it was apparent that the joint committee was depending heavily on the South Jaycees for direction. During the meetings, it was also clear that Darrell was the guiding force. He dominated the group discussions, he always seemed to have good ideas about what the joint committee should do, and he was obviously the most enthusiastic member. Gary really became concerned about the North Jaycees' identity when, with one North member voting in favor, the joint committee elected Darrell as the Master of Ceremonies for this year's pageant. Since the welcoming address would be given by Ray Baker, the South Jaycee president, there would be no North club member in a prominent position in this year's pageant. This was the first time that something like this had ever happened.

As Gary reported on the activities of the joint committee to Dave Springhorn, he said, "I just don't understand it. I had all my plans laid out. We were going to keep the record of the North Jaycees prominent in the pageant. Now look, it's going to be an 'all-South' show. I really let the club down."

Guidelines for Analysis

1. What happened to Gary's well-laid plans? Was there anything he might have done to change the outcome of the joint committee? What?

2. In terms of the models of group behavior presented in this part, what do you think happened? Attempt to develop a model of the relationship among members of the joint committee.

3. From the information contained in the incident above, do you think the joint committee *acted* as one or two committee(s)? Provide a rationale for your answer.

4. Do you think that Gary had a "hidden agenda" in going into the joint committee meetings? Discuss what you think happened to the agenda. Why?

5. What conditions are necessary for two groups to integrate their behavior to act as a single group? What has to happen for integration to occur?

6. Speculate about the goals of the joint committee. Make a list of five possible goals. Do you think that the joint committee reached its goal(s)?

7. Do you think the structure above was appropriate for the task of putting on the Miss Middleburg contest? What other structures might have been used?

8. What type of interpersonal skills do you think are necessary for members to possess for this type of joint committee to be successful?

The Work Slowdown

Larry Harmon, thirty-two, works as a first-line foreman at Porter Tool Company in Centerberg, a small town in Maryland. Larry was a Vietnam veteran and went to work at Porter as a machinist when he returned from the war. Under Larry's supervision are fourteen machinists and two maintenance men. Larry's team normally works the second shift (3:30 P.M. to midnight). At Porter, Larry is responsible for appraising each of his subordinates but union rules provide their pay scale. Union rules prevent Larry from making any recommendations regarding salary increases for his men. Normally, the foremen at Porter are selected by the General Plant Superintendent on the basis of their educational qualifications

(Larry had graduated from Centerberg High and had picked up some college credits in the service); leadership capacity (in the Marines, while in Vietnam, Larry had obtained the rank of staff sargeant); and work record (since coming to Porter, Larry had been considered one of the best machinists in his department.)

In the last few months, there has been some unrest among workers at Porter. Contract time was coming up in six months and the union was preparing to include some issues related to work safety, work hours, and vacation scheduling part of its bargaining plan. Within Larry's department his men had not been meeting their work quota. Jack Smitter, a twenty-two year Porter employee, had become one of Larry's most trusted friends among his subordinates. Over a beer after work one night, Jack said to Larry, "Lar, I don't know what's wrong with the men. They just don't want to work. They don't give a damn about their quota and their loyalty is to the union and not to the company. Timmy Jacobson, the union president, passed the word that we should slow down and let the company know what we can do if they don't budge a little bit on some of those issues."

This bothered Larry after he got home that night. He had always felt that the union had been good for the men. It had made the hourly employees among the best paid in Centerberg. It had also been responsible for securing excellent fringe benefits. But the company had also been very good to him and he felt much loyalty toward Porter. He also felt that the company had been good to the men. There had never been any strikes or hostility between the union and Porter, even at contract time. Larry knew that his superiors thought that his machinists were important to Porter and made a significant contribution to the company. Larry was in a state of conflict.

The next afternoon, the situation got even worse. Before the second shift, Larry's boss, Carl Horton, the general foreman, called the second shift foremen together for a meeting. "We have got to get these men working again. Production is falling down all through the plant. We have to make the men realize that their slowdown behavior is only hurting themselves in the long run. We must do something right away. We have lost about 300 man-hours of production the last week. I'm going to get our personnel department to speak to Timmy Jacobson directly about this situation," Carl said during the meeting.

Larry had some reservations about what was taking place but he kept them to himself through the shift. Again in Larry's team, that night only one machinist met his quota. Production was down over 50 percent from what it was just three months ago. Obviously, something was wrong with the men on his shift, but Larry did not really know what to do about it. That night, his wife was waiting up for him and he welcomed the opportunity to talk about the situation at work.

"I really don't know what to do about this. This is the first time that something like this has come up. I respect the men and I know that they like me. The union has made some good points, there are some safety problems and the men need more freedom in selecting their vacation. But, they also are being hurt if they don't meet their quota. They are part of Porter, too. We all get hurt when the company loses money. I feel like the company will meet the union's terms when they start negotiating. If they would just wait until then. Man, this has really got me down."

"I can see that you're bothered by this. It seems to me that you're going to have to talk to the men," his wife advised.

"You're right. I think I'll have all my men into the conference room tomorrow to hash this thing out once and for all. We'll stay there till we get it resolved," Larry said decidedly.

Guidelines for Analysis

1. What do you think happened at the meeting? Suggest some possible strategies which Larry could have taken with his men. Which of these strategies would, upon first glance, appear most viable?

2. In your own words, try to formulate the position being expressed by the union in the situation above. What do you think of this position?

3. In your own words, try to formulate the position being expressed by the management of Porter in the incident above. What do you think of this position? Do you see the union's position as being in direct conflict with management's? Why?

4. In terms of the material presented in this part related to motivation, what factors seemed to be motivating the union members? What factors were motivating Larry? What about Larry's superiors?

5. What do you think about the group meeting as the vehicle for motivating employees? What are some problems associated with the group meeting? During the meeting, what counterproductive things might occur?

6. Speculate about the feelings that Larry might have before the meeting. Where do you think his *primary* loyalties were? With his men? With his organization? Is it possible that this split loyalty could influence Larry's communication behavior? How?

7. Do you think that the work group influences the motivation of the individual? How?

8. If you had been in Larry's position, how would you have handled this situation? Provide a rationale for your behavior.

The Job Change

Rick Williams, twenty-one, works as an electronics assemblyman at Craig Electronics, a firm which produces television and radio circuits. Rick works the second shift (3:30 P.M. to midnight) and his job requires him to assemble the electronic pads used in televisions and radios. He has worked at Craig for two years. Rick's primary motivation for being at Craig is to support himself and his wife Beth while they attend college. Beth is a senior at West Coast State University and she will graduate next June with a B.S. degree in Nursing. Rick, who had dropped out a year, is a junior in the School of Social Work at West Coast State and wants to stay in school to obtain his M.S.W. degree, to enable him to work with juveniles as a social worker. After graduation, Beth plans to go to work as a nurse to allow Rick to quit his job and concentrate on school full-time.

When he was looking for employment, Rick selected Craig because the job as an assembler was at night and did not require much preparation or thinking. He simply came to work, did his job, and left when his shift was over. The job did not require any mental energy and he could almost do the work with his eyes closed. It paid fairly well and Rick liked most of his coworkers. He felt that the job was more than tolerable until Beth's graduation the following year, after which he could devote all his time to his work at college.

But things had begun changing at Craig over the past few weeks. Rumor had it that an "efficiency expert" had been called in by the company to improve production. Later another rumor said that the jobs within Craig were going to be restructured. Eventually, the early rumors proved accurate. One day, a member of the Personnel Department, Mike Powers, came into Rick's department and introduced Sheila Druker, a representative of Management Consultants, who was going to help the department improve its performance. During the next few weeks, many changes were made. Rick, instead of working alone on his own projects, was now working as a member of a team. His job was now quite different. Before, he just assembled electronic components. Now, he was in group meetings with his team, discussing production schedules, and filling out reports. One night, the worst happened: *Rick was elected team leader.* As team leader, he was expected to go around making sure that each member understood his task, to turn in all production reports, and to meet with other team leaders to talk about common problems. All this was getting Rick down.

"Man, I'm really up against it. Before, all I had to do was put in my eight hours and go home to sleep. I had mornings free for class, afternoons for study and then work. Now everything is all messed up. I'm always in meetings and filling out reports. Last night I didn't get out of there until 2:00 A.M. and I didn't get any overtime for it. I find myself thinking about things related to work while I'm in class. It should be the other way around. They've got to understand that I'm not going to make my career at Craig," Rick complained to Beth one night after work.

"Well, honey, why do you think they did this? It seems to me that they are just messing with things that were going along pretty well down there," Beth responded. "It's just a few more months until I graduate and you can quit."

"I don't know, but some of the older people down there really like the new program. They say now that they are able to spend their time doing what they like. Production seems to be up, so I guess Miss Druker knew what she was talking about. But I just don't have enough energy to devote to this job. I just want to punch the clock, put in my eight hours and leave. I don't want to have to think about my job when I leave it," Rich said. "Maybe I should just quit and look for another job."

Guidelines for Analysis

1. What do you think Rick did about his job at Craig? Why? In his situation, what would you have done?

2. From the information contained in the incident above, what do you think was going on within Craig?

3. What impressions do you have about the manner in which information about the new program was communicated to Craig workers? How could this have been improved?

4. In your own words, describe what you think was happening to Rick. What new responsibilities were given him?

5. Do you think that a compromise between the requirements of his job and the requirements of school is possible? How?

6. From the information contained in the situation above, what do you think motivated Rick? What were his primary goals? How do you think those motivations influenced Rick's job performance?

7. In terms of the material covered in this part, what do you see as the major difference between Rick's task before the change and after the change?

8. Again referring to the difference in task before and after the change, which type of task required the most sophisticated communication behavior from Craig workers?

PART FOUR

The Organizational Communication System

Chapter Eleven

Components of the Organizational Communication System

In chapter two, we presented a model of organizational operations which focused on the communication system of organizations. This model was developed to demonstrate how the communication system will help to produce successful organizational results, or *organizational effectiveness*. Put simply, we have built a case for the relationship between organizational communication and *functional organizational outcomes* such as goal attainment, satisfaction, and development. This relationship was examined further in chapters three and four.

In this part of the book we will consider each of the subsystems of the model, the formal subsystem, the climate in which communication takes place, and the interpersonal skills demonstrated by individual organizational members. Each of the subsystems will be examined in chapters twelve, thirteen, and fourteen from the perspective of its unique role in the organizational communication system.

This chapter will introduce each of the subsystems in the model, consider the relationship of each subsystem to the other two, and suggest some ways in which the subsystems help achieve organizational effectiveness. But first, it may be helpful to return to that part of the organizational operations model which diagrams the elements of the organizational communication system.

The Model

You may remember the model first presented on page 16. It demonstrated the proposed relationship between the system and other important aspects of the

183

organizational communication process. The system component of the model is presented in figure 11-1. The model lists three subsystems which are related to each other and which influence the decision-making and producing processes in the organization. This influence occurs since both decision making and production depend on good and accurate information. A breakdown in any one of the subsystems is likely to produce negative results within these important organizational processes. This influence will be examined later in this chapter.

Since this model represents *human organizational communication,* we *expect* failures in each subsystem. No organization can create a perfect communication system, because people must operate the system. A rational approach to organizational communication would be to expect the system to operate effectively to the extent to which its human operators are effective. As humans fail, the system will fail.

The Formal Communication Subsystem

Since humans first organized themselves to accomplish certain prescribed group tasks, various types of hierarchical configurations have emerged to diagram the organizational relationships among people. In large organizations, a person must ultimately be responsible to a board at the top of the hierarchy. Similarly, there

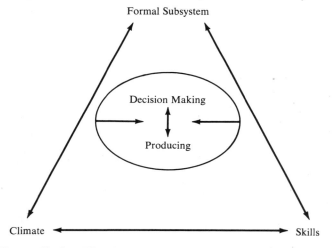

Figure 11–1   The Organizational Communication System

must be people employed at the bottom of the hierarchy to perform the specific tasks of the organization. Obviously, there are more people at the bottom than at the top. In these configurations, the level "above" is responsible for the supervision and direction of the level "below." These configurations, called structures, were the topic for chapter seven. Structure is important in the organization, and it helps determine the patterns of interaction among members. *The official communication linkages from the top of the structure to the bottom constitute the formal communication subsystem.*

The decision makers at the top of the structure create a variety of positions which are assigned specific organizational tasks, or jobs. The hierarchy develops relationships ("above," "below") which accompany each of these positions. People are then selected to occupy the positions.

As each position in the structure is created, there is an accompanying *need* for communication associated with that position. The person in the position, in order to perform his or her job adequately, needs information from positions above, below, and equal with his or her own. This need exists because the organization operates as a social system with each position influencing each other position. To illustrate, let us examine the role of the teacher in a typical high school organization. If the school board adopts a new policy on teacher grooming, the policy will affect teachers and they *need* to know about it. Organizations, recognizing this inherent need for communication, create a variety of formal techniques, or *channels*, which are used by the structure to transmit information to all positions. The school board may use the teacher's supervisor (the assistant principal) and the weekly employee newsletter to communicate the new grooming policy. There is a wide variety of available mechanical (newsletter) and human (supervisor) channels within the formal subsystem.

In an organization, there is an established formal communication subsystem which is one of components of the organizational communication system. It consists of all the official and recognized communication channels in the organization, including the interpersonal relationship between superiors and subordinates. The formal subsystem is most widely used for the transmission of work-related information to various positions throughout the structure. As a supervisor communicates with one of his or her subordinates in a required salary review session, the exchange becomes part of the formal subsystem. The success of this exchange will depend upon the organization's environment (climate) as well as on the interpersonal skills demonstrated by both the superior and subordinate. In this way, the formal subsystem is both influenced *by* and influences the other two components of the organizational communication system.

The Climate in the Organization

The concept of climate refers to the attitudes held by members about the immediate environment in which communication takes place within their organization. In interpersonal situations, the individual's communication is greatly influenced by the behavior occurring around him or her. This behavior is part of the climate of the organization. Climate is determined by the managerial philosophy and assumptions considered in chapter five and by the external cultural and economic conditions examined in chapter four. Also, all of the organizational elements which composed Part Three would certainly be expected to have an impact upon climate.

We assume that people will have very strong feelings about their organizations, and we assume that those feelings will have an impact on the organizational communication system. For example, if, in a local industrial plant, rumors had been circulating about an impending layoff, we would expect these rumors to affect the information transmitted on the formal subsystem. In place of accurate information about the organization's tasks flowing up the structure for decision making and production, we might observe employees initiating only inquiries to their supervisors about the layoff. If the primary decision makers do transmit information intended to disconfirm the layoff, it will only be believed to the extent to which the company has been *truthful* with employees in the past. *Attitudes about the organization held by members can be said to significantly influence the information transmitted on the formal subsystem.*

Climates are part of the composition of every work group, operating division, and organization. Sometimes the climate of a particular work group is better (or worse) than the climate of the organization as a whole. The typical member relates most readily to the climate of the unit closest to him or her. We occasionally hear an employee say, "This plant is really a hole, but I really like working for my boss." In this situation, the worker is expressing a negative reaction to the climate of his or her organization but reacting positively to the climate of his or her own work group.

What Causes Climate?

There has not been total agreement among social scientists about the cause and composition of climate in an organization. This lack of consensus makes it necessary for us to speak speculatively about climate. But it is possible to make some general comments about the concept.

(1) *It would appear that climate is an attitudinal dimension involving one's relationship to his or her organization.* It may not always be possible to identify the exact cause of one's feelings about his or her organization, but a reaction to climate seems to be based in one's feelings. To improve a "bad" or negative climate in an organization, one would work at changing the perceptions of individual members.

(2) *Climates are determined by a wide variety of organizational elements.* It would be highly unusual for one single organizational element (supervision, decision-making procedures, and so on) to be the only determinant of climate. Instead, climate is likely to be caused by a reaction to a variety of elements associated with the work place. Although not yet established in the research, climate may be caused by the "little things," either good or bad, associated with an organization.

(3) *The supervisor is a major factor in establishing climate.* Leader behavior, or supervision, in the work group does play a major role in setting the climate. In chapters four and nine we suggested that a leader has, at his or her option, a wide variety of possible "leadership styles." As the leader uses one style (or combination of styles), it initiates a reaction from his or her subordinates. This reaction, be it positive or negative, helps determine the climate of the work group.

(4) *Climate is both influenced by and influences the flow of communication within the organization.* This may seem circular, but it does seem to describe the situation. When climates can be characterized as "structured and formalistic," the flow of communication appears highly structured. On the other hand, loosely structured climates seem to be related to spontaneous communication. Whether climate is an independent, dependent, or intervening variable has yet to be determined definitively in the research.

(5) *Individuals appear to work best in a variety of climates.* There is not one "best" climate for all work groups. Instead, the best climate depends on the individual personalities and attitudes of the people who compose the group. Some work best in climates where there is much pressure to produce, while others prefer low-pressure environments. Thus, the optimum climate must be thought of as a *situational variable.*

These five observations about climate are intended to establish the phenomenon as a concept. The literature on which they are based, along with some of the elaborate approaches for analyzing climate, will be reviewed in chapter thirteen.

As a Subsystem of the
Organized Communications System

As with the formal subsystem, climate becomes part of the organizational communication system by composing its attitudinal component. As the formal subsystem transmits work-related information, climate provides the background in which individuals formulate a reaction to the information they receive. The same message transmitted will probably have different effects on each member of the intended audience. Climate is but one of a number of variables likely to influence this effect. The organizational elements considered (e.g. the job, inter- and intragroup behavior, organizational structure) in Part Three also play a role in determining the message effect.

Interpersonal Skills in the Organization

Often those who are interested in organizations become so caught up in the study of structure that an important point is neglected—*organizations are made up of people*. People manage organizations for the purposes which other people have established to provide goods and services to be consumed by still other people. We have touched on this point earlier in our consideration of organizational communication as a people phenomenon.

Within any organization, there are members who manifest a wide variety of interpersonal communication skills. If a member is a good communicator, he or she would be expected to influence organizational communication positively. As people assume roles of increasing responsibility, the communication prerequisites associated with the position similarly increase. In chapter fourteen, we shall examine the seven most important interpersonal skills for organizational members. Later, in chapter sixteen, methods will be presented which can be used to improve members' skills.

There are several ways in which interpersonal skills influence organizational communication:

(1) *Individuals must make decisions about which messages are to be transmitted through the formal subsystem.* A member at a strategic position in the hierarchy must decide which messages are sufficiently important to transmit. This decision is based on the individual's sensitivity and perceptions about the needs of his or her organization.

(2) *Individuals must make decisions about which medium or channel is most satisfactory for message transmission.* A variety of channels, ranging from the grapevine to an official interoffice memorandum, are available to the communicator for message sending. The member must decide which channel is likely to produce the appropriate response to his or her message. This decision should be based on his or her understanding of the function of each of the available channels and the requirements of the message (speed, accuracy, size of intended audience, and so on.)

(3) *Individual receivers must be able to interpret and apply a message which has been communicated.* The individual, in the organization, is exposed to many potential messages. Those messages which are most meaningful to him or her will be processed, but he or she must also apply them to his or her unique organizational situation. The individual's skill at accomplishing this task will depend on his or her perceptual and listening abilities.

(4) *The accuracy of information transmission will depend upon the individual's abilities to articulate an understandable message.* The individual who sends a score of memoranda about a pressing organizational problem will have no impact unless his or her memoranda are understood by potential receivers. Message articulation is a product of the sender's skill at analyzing the needs and requirements of the intended audience(s).

Interpersonal Skills as a Subsystem

As with the formal subsystem and climate, the combination of interpersonal skills demonstrated by members is an important component of the comprehensive organizational communication system. The formal subsystem constitutes the mechanism of official information within the organization while the climate involves the attitudes of members toward that information. Interpersonal skills determine the degree of effectiveness of the formal subsystem for transmitting the information. When the formal subsystem is operated by skillful communicators, it should communicate understandable and trustworthy information, influencing the climate and, in turn, help achieve organizational effectiveness. All three subsystems are integrally linked and must operate at relative peak efficiency to produce an effective organizational communication system.

The Organizational Communication System and Organizational Effectiveness

The model developed in chapter two hypothesized that the organizational communication system facilitates two important organizational processes, decision making and producing.

Decision Making

Good organizational decision making depends on satisfactory information being available on which to base decisions. Primary decision makers depend on information flowing up to them from the extremities of the organization. This information must be relatively accurate and free of distortion. For this to take place, all three subsystems must operate properly. There must be a mechanism within the organization which can transmit information (the formal subsystem), the individual must want to transmit this information (the climate), and he or she must be able to articulate an understandable message (interpersonal skills).

Producing

A primary objective of each organization is the satisfactory production of its goods and services. But production can be accomplished only if people *know* what they are supposed to do and *want* to do it. Before a member can do his or her job, he or she must understand the nature of that job. This understanding depends upon the formal subsystem transmitting useful job-related information. A sender (generally, a supervisor) must know what information is needed by his or her subordinates and must be able to articulate an understandable message for them. Finally the climate must be such that the worker wants to apply this information to his or her job. If one subsystem breaks down, production losses may result.

Organizational communication is one of the processes which enable the organization to achieve *functional outcomes*. Our model has specified three of these functional outcomes. As the organizational communication system operates proficiently, a sufficient degree of decision making and production is achieved producing goal attainment, satisfaction, and development.

Goal Attainment

In chapter three dealing with effectiveness, we suggested that organizations have self-preservation as one of their primary goals. Those organizations which meet their goals will survive and those which do not will disappear. As good decisions get made and as satisfactory production is achieved, the organization survives. But survival depends upon its abilities to accurately monitor changing conditions in its relevant environment. This information about changes must be transmitted to employees by means of the organizational communication system. As the system operates effectively, the relevant information from the environment reaches the appropriate places in the hierarchy. At this point, the information can be used by the organization to adapt to changes to produce organizational survival.

Satisfaction

Social scientists agree that when employees are free to produce in a comfortable working environment with sufficient information to do their jobs, they will be satisfied. Of course, individuals are satisfied for different reasons. However, as organizational communication operates effectively, individual satisfaction will increase because the work situation has become a pleasant place to be. Ambiguity and uncertainty, prime causes of dissatisfaction, have been removed.

Development

Attempts must be made to enable members to develop the necessary skills to grow with their organization. Training and personal growth programs need to be based on accurate information. Further, individuals must recognize the positive outcomes associated with their participation in these programs. By offering these opportunities for growth, the organization is atttempting to insure its future survival by developing in its members the talents which will be needed tomorrow.

Summary

This chapter has considered the three components of the organizational communication system: (1) the formal subsystem, (2) the climate in which organizational communication takes place, and (3) the interpersonal skills of organization members. Each of these components must operate effectively for good organizational communication to be achieved.

REVIEW AND DISCUSSION

1. Provide some examples of how breakdowns in one of the subsystems considered in this chapter are likely to influence the other two components of the organizational communication system.

2. Explain the differences among the three subsystems. What functions does each subsystem fulfill in the organization?

3. Discuss the ways in which climate is likely to influence organizational communication. Speculate about some of the "little things" in the organization which may affect climate.

4. Why are interpersonal skills important in the organization? What skills are likely to help the organization become more effective?

5. We have suggested three possible organizational effectiveness criteria (goal attainment, satisfaction, and development). Can you think of some other criteria to judge the effectiveness of organizations? In those you select, explain the role which communication plays.

Chapter Twelve

The Formal Communication Subsystem

In chapter seven we examined organizational structure as one of the important elements which influences organizational communication. Structures help organization members know who is supposed to do what and who reports to whom, so that necessary activities can be meshed together in the best possible way. For structure to fulfill this required coordination, organizations have established *linkages, patterns, and devices* which transmit the information required by the structure. These linkages, patterns, and devices are the *formal communication subsystem.*

It is important to understand the relationship between structure and the formal subsystem. This may be clear if we return to the Weber model first presented on page 96. The model suggests that the *person* in the organization is much less important than the *position* which the person occupies. The position prescribes the exact duties required by the structure which must be accomplished by the officeholder. Similarly, the position holder is expected to *communicate* in a manner and about the things prescribed by the structure. The hierarchy, not the officeholder, determines *who talks to whom.* For example, in a rigidly bureaucratic organization, an individual would not be free to talk to his or her boss' boss about job-related matters without permission. On the other hand, a superior would not attempt to supervise someone else's subordinate. Spontaneous communication, that which is out of the normal structure, is discouraged in the traditional pyramidal organization. The formal subsystem is delegated the responsibility of carrying the routine communication throughout the structure.

In this chapter, we shall examine those communication activities which are part of the formal subsystem. First, the flow of information within the subsystem, including the important communication networks, will be considered. Second, the various shapes of structures and their influence on communication will be treated. Finally, several devices created by the structure to enable the subsystem to transmit information will be examined.

Message Flow and the Subsystem

On first glance it may appear that all members of an organization are completely free to communicate with each other. But such is not the case. Instead, communication travels in fairly well-defined *networks*. Leavitt (1972) explained:

> [it might appear that] ... in most face-to-face industrial groups only one communication network seems possible, and that is a fully connected network in which everyone can communicate directly with everyone else. But the argument that this is the only actual network, even in committee, does not hold water. A clear, albeit informal, notion about who can talk to whom exists in most groups. In fact, in most face-to-face meetings, although the *official* network is a fully connected one, the *actual* network may be some other one altogether. Communication networks are much like organizational charts; there is likely to be a formal, officially charted organization, and there is likely also to be an informal, uncharted organization that nevertheless plays a significant role in the functioning of the company.*

Farace and MacDonald (1974) suggest that the membership of such networks changes depending on the topic under discussion:

> One readily discernible feature of an organization's communication system, as it is examined over time, is that repetitive patterns of information and communication exchange take place. Some members of the organization interact with one another, but not with other members. They interact more often some times than at other times. Their interaction may cover certain topics; at other times it doesn't. Certain topics never occur in the interactions among some members of the organization. When management sends out messages to subordinates, the messages travel various pathways or networks — some intended and some not.†

We may conclude that these networks, generally similar across organizations, guide the flow of information within the formal subsystem. Guetzkow (1965) has attempted to label the standard networks, or channels, and we shall borrow his paradigm to learn more about these as they occur in organizations.

Authority

It is through the authority network that the messages which enable the exercise of authority, as described in chapter seven, are communicated. Normally, orders, directives, and commands are transmitted on this network. Characteristic of this

---

*Harold J. Leavitt, *Managerial Psychology,* 3rd ed., p. 195. Copyright 1972 by the University of Chicago Press. Used by permission.

†R. V. Farace and D. MacDonald, "New Directions in the Study of Organizational Communication," *Personnel Psychology* 27 (1974): 7. Used by permission.

network is that most of the information flows *downward* (i.e. the boss giving orders to a subordinate). Organizations often develop special devices, such as group meetings and instructional packets, to facilitate information exchange within this network. Barnard (1938) has suggested six elements of the authority network:

(1) The channels of communication should be definitely known.

(2) The line of communication must be as direct or short as possible.

(3) Objective authority requires a definite formal channel of communication to every member of the organization.

(4) The complete line of communication should usually be used.

(5) The line of communication should not be interrupted during the time when the organization is to function.

(6) Every communication must be authenticated. To Barnard, the control of the authority network was a major responsibility of management. The authority network provides the channel for the members at the top of the pyramidal organization to control the behavior of those at the bottom.

Information

As the authority network primarily transmits information downward, the information network enables persons at the top of the organization to obtain information from those at the bottom. The content of the information transmitted normally deals with internal organizational operations and changing conditions in the environment. This network provides the information necessary for good decision making. There are two kinds of informational networks within the organization: formal and informal.

Formal. Organizations routinely develop information sources through formally established *reporting procedures.* Periodic progress reports, staff meetings, and newsletters are examples of these procedures. The devices are attempts to provide the required official information on which to base decisions.

Informal. Unofficial information is also communicated within the structure of organizations. The mechanism for this unofficial transmission is the *grapevine.* The grapevine operates to supplement the formal channels, sometimes accurately, and, at other times, inaccurately. Grapevine communications are very difficult to control but can be extremely effective in communicating highly interesting information rapidly. Research has demonstrated that the grapevine is the least preferred communication channel when it was compared to other official written and oral channels (Dahle 1954).

Task Expertise

This network is responsible for providing the technical know-how which enables the organization to accomplish its unique purpose. Information about performing the variety of tasks of the formal structure is communicated via this network. As tasks become increasingly complex, the importance of this network increases. Skilled professionals develop special languages and codes which can only be understood by other members of the profession. About this tendency, Guetzkow (1965) said:

> The trades and profession, existing in the larger society within which the orga-
> nization is embedded, provide an important basis for the development of task-
> expertise networks. Occupational groups socialize employees into the use of
> specialized jargon in handling tools and techniques of their trades. (p. 545)

New information about task specialities must continually be transmitted on this
network for the organization to meet changing conditions in the environment.

Friendship

Within the organization, members develop a series of friendship relationships,
not necessarily produced through the three networks mentioned above. These
friendships may be built through routine organizational operations (i.e. secretaries
who work at adjacent desks). Or, these friendships may be the product of nontask-
related organizational activities (i.e. membership on an after-hours bowling or
softball team). Within the structure, it is conceivable that friendships may develop
between a person at the top of the hierarchy and someone at the bottom. Thus,
a linkage results between two people from entirely different organizational backgrounds. However, it is likely that their communication will be constrained because
of the differences in position. Communication in the friendship network tends to
be more informal and less directly purposeful than in the other three networks. The
friendship network makes it possible for the organization to accomplish many
functional outcomes which will be considered later in this chapter.

Status

The status that accompanies positions of high authority is part of the daily
reality of organizational life. Networks exist to carry information about status to
all organizational members. Often this information is transmitted nonverbally
through such things as the size of one's desk or the location of a person's office.
It may be argued that the person who is able to use the other networks with ease
probably possesses some degree of high status.

There appears to be interaction between the status network and the structure
of the organization. For example, it has been shown that those who perceive themselves at the top of a structure are more likely to use communication networks
than are those at the bottom (Borgatta 1954). Further, those at the top of a
structure are more likely to receive communication than are those at the bottom
(Barnlund and Harland 1963). There is also a tendency for the number of levels
of the structure to distort information going to those at the top (Barnlund and
Harland 1963; Guetzkow 1965). It is logical to assume that those high in the status
network will also be influential in other networks. One's status, or more precisely,
one's position in the status network, would be expected to alter the messages the
person receives through the authority, informational, and task-expertise networks.

Networks: An Afterword

The five types of communication networks, presented above, are not intended
to be an exhaustive list. Instead, they are examples of the types of networks in
operation within the structure of an organization. In reality, organizations are networks of networks, each operating with specific purposes. Individuals are likely to
be members of a wide variety of different networks.

There is great pressure on the individual to conform to the rules of the particular network of which he or she is a member. If not, the person is isolated from the network. If one violates the rules by talking to someone out of the network, about the subject matter of the network, or by not following the content within the network, the person may loose personal credibility among other organizational members. Communication networks will play an important role as we consider the other aspects of the formal subsystem in the rest of this chapter.

The Shape of Organizational Structures and the Subsystem

In chapter seven, we introduced the concept of structure and considered its effect upon behavior in the organization. Some alternative structures were presented to help the organization achieve some degree of specialization of work, unity of command, span of supervision, and authority. But there is another aspect of structure which is very important for organizational communication. In this section, we will reexamine structures in terms of their *shapes*. As organizations begin to structure themselves, two general shapes are available. The relative *complexity* of an organization can be determined by its *flatness* or *tallness*. In terms of the formal subsystem, each represents widely different approaches.

The Flat Organizational Structure

In the flat structure diagram of figure 12-1, we can see that there are only three hierarchical levels present. This type of structure tends to equalize the status of positions and gives each level relatively the same communication access to the person at the top. Also, in the flat structure, the authority, information, and task-expertise networks are small with little opportunity for distortion to occur. Positions in the structure are such that information going up the structure is not "buffered" below. Relatively, the person at the top can have direct communication with almost every position holder in the structure.

There are some problems inherent in the flat structure, however. In our diagram there are seven position holders competing for the president's time. In times of crisis, it may be impossible for the top person to work directly with all seven subordinates. When things become difficult, one or two subordinates may be delegated out of the authority network causing conflict and interpersonal problems.

In the flat structure, the second-level position holders have little "clout" in terms of power because, with some exception, each only speaks for his or her own department. In a situation requiring the department head to compete for access to the top person, his or her chances might be enhanced if he or she represented a large constituency.

The Tall Organizational Structure

Communication is complex in the tall structure since there are eight distinct levels through which a message must pass before it reaches the top person. Downward communication may be facilitated, however, because of the opportunities to delegate communication duties downward. Individuals can be assigned the responsibilities to pass the word throughout their level.

The tall organization does tend to structure the kind and amount of information going into the top person's office. In figure 12-1, only three position holders have access to the top and only that information judged relevant by these three will be

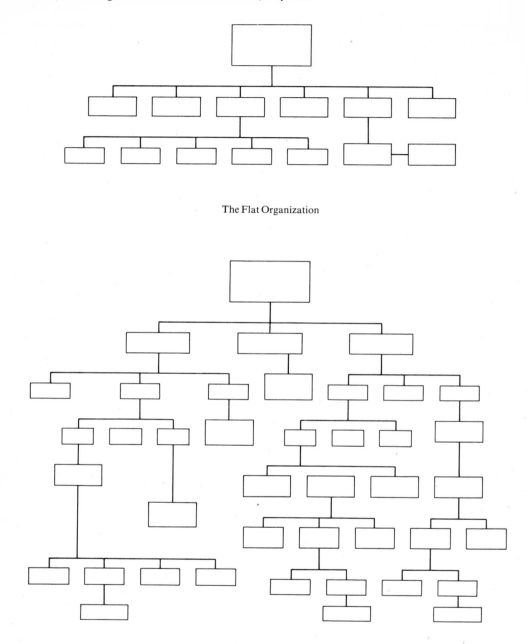

The Flat Organization

The Tall Organization

Figure 12–1   Flat versus Tall Organizations

passed upward. They act as *gate-keepers* in influencing the information getting to the top-person. The gate-keepers are very much part of the authority and information networks in the tall organization. In large organizations it is sound management practice to limit access to the top person, otherwise the person would have little time for anything but seeing employees. It would appear that the optimal formal subsystem would allow some access to the top, by lower-level position holders, while still enabling the top person to have time to accomplish other managerial duties.

Filtering: A Communication Problem

We have suggested that it is difficult to transmit accurate information up the structure to appropriate levels for decision making. The difficulty is present because *people* occupy positions in the structure and people are imperfect communicators. As people attempt to transmit information up the structure, they tend to leave out important aspects of the message they send. This tendency is called *filtering* (Davis 1972). Certainly a position holder does not want to transmit information upward which reflects badly on him or her. As a result, a position holder is likely to send only that information which is very positive. When filtering occurs often, it may be counterproductive to the organization. This may be clear if we return to figure 12-1. If all seven levels of the tall structure systematically remove negative aspects of the information they send upward, by the time the information reaches the top, it will not represent a clear picture of life at the lower levels of the structure.

Redding (1972) has suggested that filtering also occurs downward, in that a superior may not be able to "level" with a subordinate. This leaves the subordinate with an inaccurate view of his or her role in the structure. Ultimately, something may occur to "wake up" the subordinate, perhaps leaving the person with a negative view of the supervisor and the organization.

Lateral Relationships in the Organization

It may appear from the previous sections that only *horizontal relationships* (superior to subordinate) exist in the organization. But these horizontal relationships represent only a small portion of the total communication linkages in the formal subsystem. Much communication takes place among position holders who occupy hierarchically similar jobs. *Lateral relationships,* often nurtured through the friendship network, provide an important vehicle for organizational communication. In figure 12-2, we can see that individuals on one level often depend on some-

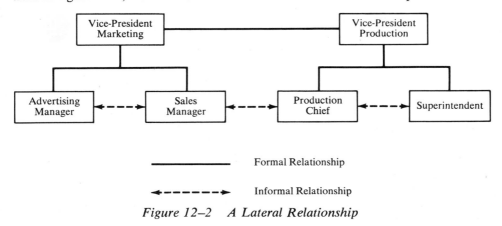

Figure 12–2   A Lateral Relationship

one else on the same level for job-related information. This is demonstrated by an example of a sales manager, who while visiting one of her company's accounts in the field, encounters a possible market for a new product. One approach would be for her to write a memorandum on the subject to her boss, who, in turn, would bring the matter up in executive session with other vice-presidents. Eventually, the matter would be routed to the production supervisor for a response. This rather strict adherence to the structure would be very costly in terms of time. Normally, a sales manager simply picks up the telephone to ask the production manager, who is on her or his same level in the structure, about the *feasibility* of a new product. Some of the devices which *facilitate* this lateral communication and are part of the formal subsystem are treated below.

The Gangplank. Fayol (1949), a French management theorist, perceived that organizations were using a ladder of authority such as the one depicted in figure 12-3 where the ladder had to be climbed F to A and then descended A to P for communication between F and P to take place. To solve the problem, Fayol suggested a "gangplank" which allowed F to go directly to P when the occasion arose. To enable the gangplank to work, managers E and O had to authorize their respective subordinates to handle the problem directly while keeping them informed as to any agreements reached. The gangplank was intended to be part of the formal subsystem to improve lateral communication within the structure.

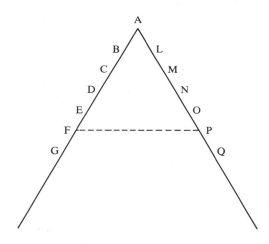

SOURCE: From Henri Fayol, *General and Industrial Administration* translated by Constance Storrs (1949, Sir Isaac Pitman & Sons Ltd.). Reprinted by permission of the publishers.

Figure 12–3   Fayol's Gangplank

The Linking Pin. In many organizations, there is a tendency among work groups to become needlessly specialized and narrow in their tasks. But this specialization can lead to provincialism which hampers organizational communication. There are really two, sometimes contrasting, processes which work groups must maintain. They must achieve their own unique identity while, at the same time, integrating their activities with those of other groups in the organization. Lorsch and Lawrence (1972) explained:

> While the processes of differentiation and integration seem to be basically antagonistic between pairs of units within one organization, we have found in comparing several organizations that an organization can achieve both the high differentiation required for individual unit performance and the effective integration required for organizational total performance. The key to the achievement of both high differentiation and integration seems to reside in the development of what we have conceptually identified as integrative devices, which function effectively. These integrative devices can be managers in linking roles, a separate department entity which has a coordinating function, or cross functional committee which are intended to facilitate the resolution of conflict and decision-making between functional units. (p. 276)

They, along with Likert (1967), suggest a device which is intended to encourage the necessary interaction among departments, *the linking pin*. The linking pin is *a method for organizing work groups which places one member in more than one lateral group to encourage interaction between the groups.* Figure 12-4 demonstrates how the linking pin operates. On the left side of the figure we observe two groups operating with little regard for the other. Possibly, each is considering policies which might have great impact on the other. This lack of integration happens because there is nothing inherent in the formal subsystem of most organizations to generate communication across lateral work groups. On the right side of figure 12-4, the

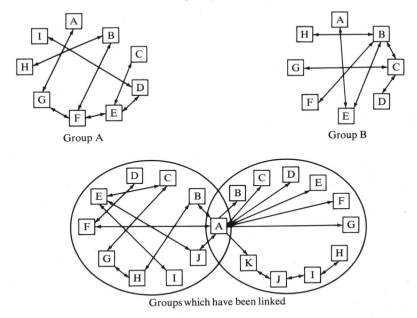

Figure 12–4   The Linking Pin Concept

same groups have been organized into a linking pin structure. Member A has joint membership in both groups with responsibilities of keeping his or her group informed about the other's activities. Thus, each group is able to maintain its own uniqueness while still achieving integration with others in the organization.

The Friendship Network and Functional Organizational Behavior

As suggested in the first part of this chapter, when individuals, in the organization, use the friendship communication network, they begin to form a series of social contacts, not constrained by authority. These social contacts, or peer relations, can prove very functional to the organization.

Peer relations are very effective in providing the following positive outcomes for individuals: (1) they work to fulfill the socioemotional needs of workers,* (2) they provide an important source of job satisfaction, (3) under appropriate conditions they can influence the individual to contribute to the goals of his or her work group, and (4) they provide an important source of job-related information. The friendship network, an important part of the formal subsystem, provides a functional element which may improve organizational effectiveness.

Bypassing: A Communication Alternative to Rigid Structure

The more numerous the levels created by the structure, the more difficult it is to get a hearing at the top for an idea or grievance. Early in this century, when most Americans worked in very unsophisticated organizations or on the farm, communication with the top person may have been a simple yell to get the person's attention. Today, however, the average worker is employed in very large corporations with numerous structural levels where communication "up the line" becomes quite complicated. In these corporations, control over the authority, information, and task-expertise networks is maintained by those at the top. This control by legitimate authority is understandable since the organization must maintain some level of order. But, occasionally events at the bottom of the structure demand the immediate attention of those at the top. When this happens, the formal subsystem must be *bypassed*.

A variety of methods are available, such as the suggestion box and the question-and-answer column in the employee newspaper, for bypassing. But these methods are cumbersome and sometimes do not provide the direct attention necessary. Organizations are increasingly instituting an office of the *ombudsman* to bypass the formal subsystem when necessary.

Communication and the Ombudsman. In an organization, an individual who has been employed to bypass the formal subsystem is playing the role of the ombudsman. Although the title may change in different contexts, the ombudsman is a creation of the structure to allow information to be exchanged (especially from lower to higher levels) which is not presently exchanged through the normal communication networks. Figure 12-5 demonstrates how the ombudsman works to encourage com-

---

*See the chapter on job satisfaction in J. Tiffin and E.J. McCormick, *Industrial Psychology,* (Englewood Cliffs, N.J.: Prentice-Hall, 1973), for a complete treatment of the role of co-workers and the fulfillment of socioemotional needs in contributing to job satisfaction.

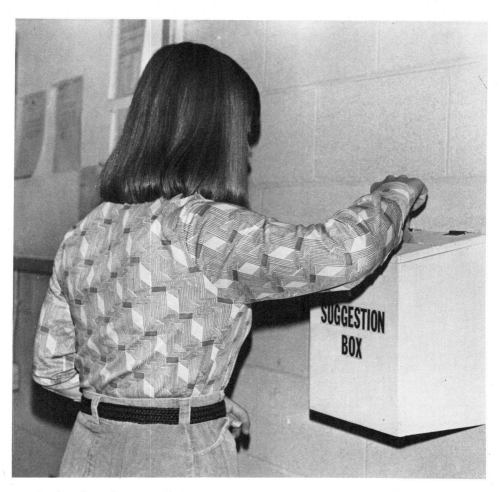

munication from lower to higher structural levels. In carrying out typical communication duties, the ombudsman would be expected to:

(1) provide a channel for receiving complaints and suggestions not transmitted through the formal subsystem.

(2) channel information from lower points in the structure to points above.

(3) funnel information, not presently reaching appropriate places in the structure to those places.

(4) act as an investigator to deal with legitimate complaints and suggestions.

(5) provide feedback about results to those who have initiated communication to the ombudsman.

(6) relay information about decisions made at the top of the structure to lower points.

(7) provide a channel for members to "sound off" outside the structure.

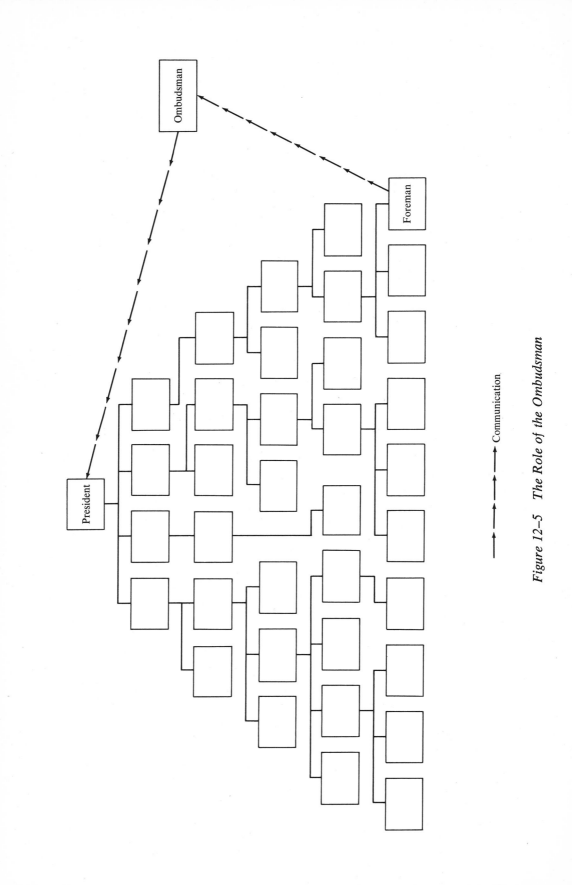

Figure 12–5 The Role of the Ombudsman

(8)   resolve counterproductive conflict which may occur among individuals, groups, or departments.

The Authority Network and the Ombudsman.   It may at first appear that the ombudsman serves a very important function within the organization. But this generalization may be tenuous. Although such duties of the ombudsman, as those listed above, are very valuable, there is a telling admission present when the organization is forced to create an ombudsman. It suggests that the authority and information networks are not generating an acceptable level of upward communication. If there are serious human problems in the organization, it is doubtful that the mere appointment of an ombudsman will resolve them. When the ombudsman replaces the immediate supervisor as the primary "sounding board" and first contact point of the authority network, severe communication problems may result.

Structured Communication Devices of the Subsystem

Various devices have been developed to facilitate downward communication within the authority network. The type of devices and their effectiveness will vary across organizations depending on their suitability and the attitudes of members. In this section, we will briefly examine four of these: (1) group meetings, (2) appraisals and appraisal interviews, (3) house organs, and (4) message system.* We can then make some observations about the potential effectiveness of each device considered.

Group Meetings

Meetings of various sorts are routine in most organizations. These meetings normally have two purposes: (1) to pass along directions and orders generated at the top of the structure (i.e. the authority network) and (2) to obtain information from position holders at lower levels about their jobs (i.e. the information network). Chapter fourteen will deal with the interpersonal skills necessary to participate successfully in meetings, so our purpose here will be to examine the group meeting as a communication device of the formal subsystem.

Group meetings are popular in organizations because they allow moderate interaction among members while not requiring many man-hours in preparation time. Supervisors hope to obtain feedback about what is happening to their subordinates on the job, but few managers have the time to sit down and talk with each employee every time the situation calls for it. The group meeting represents an effective balance between a sterile memorandum and time-consuming interviews with employees. It must be pointed out, however, that the meeting does not guarantee interaction and feedback. Employees will respond favorably only if a positive climate exists and leaders have the required skills to conduct meetings. The group meeting does at least provide the opportunity for this important interaction and feedback.

Appraisals and Appraisal Interviews

We might define the appraisal interview as a *dyadic exchange between a superior and subordinate which attempts to provide information to the subordinate about*

---

*Other devices such as bulletin boards, employee magazines, daily production reports, television and radio programs, and videotape presentations are also used by the authority network to pass information to employees. However, we have selected for treatment what we consider to be the four most widely used.

how the organization evaluates the subordinate's job performance. Appraisals normally take one of two forms.

Unprogrammed Appraisals.   An example of the unprogrammed appraisal might be:
   Boss: (walking up to subordinate) "Mike, how are you today?"
   Mike: (the subordinate) "Fine, Mr. Everett."
   Boss: "I want to tell you that management was very pleased with the on-the-job training you gave Jon, the new man, last week. We appreciate it."
   Mike: "Thanks, Mr. Everett."

In this brief exchange, the supervisor *elected* to provide some informal appraisal of Mike's work. Much of the typical supervisor's time may be spent on this kind of appraisal. Normally, the communication subsystem does not require the supervisor to interact with his or her subordinates in this way. This device, unprogrammed by nature, can help provide need satisfaction to the employee.

Programmed Appraisals.   In many organizations, the formal subsystem requires the supervisor to officially appraise the work of each subordinate in some systematic way within a stipulated time period. The title of this type of appraisal varies (year-end review, performance appraisal, salary interview, and so on) but the employee's performance and upcoming salary are almost always matters of discussion. Often elaborate forms and reports are completed based upon these appraisals, sometimes becoming part of the employee's permanent record. The following example may help the reader understand how these interviews are routinely conducted.

Boss: "Hi, Mike. Come on in and sit down. As you know from our discussions last week, it is time for your annual review."

Mike: "Yes, Mr. Everett, I have been thinking about the review."

Boss: "I have completed this appraisal form which I discussed with you last week. As you can see, I have marked you very high in individual motivation and supervisory potential."

Mike: "I see that, Mr. Everett, and I am pleasantly surprised. As you know, I had some trouble with the Haskell project and I thought my review might reflect that."

Boss: "I think that you are being unfair to yourself there, Mike. The trouble with the Haskell project was not limited to your team. The whole department had its share of troubles, but it came out profitably anyway."

Mike: "Thanks, but I think my team can do better next time."

Boss: "Mike, there is one area here where I have marked you "need improvement" and I would like to discuss that with you."

Mike: "I think I know what you are going to say . . . I need to improve my written reports."

Boss: "Right. You are a good employee with excellent management potential but your reports are too infrequent. When they do come, they are difficult to follow. Do you know what these reports are used for?"

Mike: "Aren't they used to evaluate the production process?"

Boss: "Yes, they are, but about five levels of supervision will see them and we use them to see if the engineering department needs to get involved."

Mike: "Yes, I know they are important and if I am assigned to a department, as a manager, I will have to do a better job of reporting. That is why I have enrolled in a business letter writing course at the university. I think that it will help me improve."

Boss: "Well, good. I am glad that you have spotted this weakness yourself and are trying to do something about it. Now about your salary. . ."

Mike: ". . . I thought that we would never get around to it."

Boss: "I have recommended you for a salary of $13,400 for next year. This represents an increase of nearly 15 percent. I think that the increase tells you what the company thinks about you. Of course, you know this form and a report of the interview will become part of your work file, but do you have any questions?"

Mike: "No, Mr. Everett, just thanks for going to bat for me. See you later."

Boss: "Right. Goodbye, Mike."

The programmed appraisal is the vehicle which the formal system uses to communicate highly relevant performance and salary information to employees in a fairly systematic way.

House Organs

In larger organizations, various types of employee newspapers, or *house organs,* are published to transmit information to members. These are usually edited by the communication or public relations staff and distributed within the organization. As is the case with most newspapers, it is difficult to maintain timely and interesting stories. The boss will sometimes use the house organ to preach his or her own brand of organizational gospel through a regular column. Such events as a 300-game at the local bowling alley by an employee, a scholarship won by the daughter of an em-

ployee, or the upcoming company picnic are sure to receive extensive treatment in the house organ. The potential value of the house organ as an integral part of the authority network, in disseminating highly valuable job-related information, is dubious. The newpaper may, instead, build an *espirit de corps* in the structure. Assuming the limitation of the newspaper in transmitting current information, its value may be in: (1) providing recognition to the indivdual employee who has made a worthwhile contribution to the organization and (2) explaining fully a policy already adopted and communicated by management. As an organization becomes large, it is difficult to publicly note every individual accomplishment but this recognition may be provided in the employee newspaper. Also, the full story, in terms of background, explanation, and detail, on new policies and decisions may be presented in the house organ.

Message Systems

Organizations often spend money on various kinds of *message systems* to communicate to members. These systems, some highly mechanical, are generally integrated with the internal telephone system in the organization to enable the member to dial a number to receive a message from management. A variation of this approach is a "hot-line" which allows the member to ask a question about the organization and have it answered rapidly. Other message systems utilize films, video and audio tape recorders, and slide presentations to transmit information.

Effectiveness of Communication Devices

All of the devices considered in this section are aimed primarily at facilitating downward communication. The emphasis here has been on devices which do not encourage face-to-face communication, with the possible exception of the appraisal. The advantage of all of these devices is that they allow the rapid, and generally very accurate, transmission of information. Figure 12-6 diagrams the relationship between time expended and opportunities for communication in some of the devices treated above. Since communication is a two-way process, we can assume that more information will be generated when the receiver is given the opportunity to participate in the exchange.

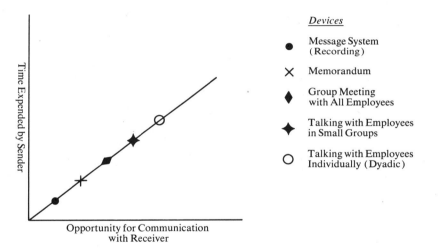

Figure 12–6   Communication Devices and Interaction

Those devices which lend themselves to much communication tend to be very costly in terms of man-hours expended. The most effective devices are those which allow some opportunity for give-and-take while not requiring exorbitant man-hours.

Summary

This chapter has investigated the elements of the formal communication subsystem which transmits the information required by the organization's structure. Five types of communication networks—authority, information, task-expertise, friendship, and status—were studied as they provide the framework through which communication flows within the organizational structure. The shape of structures and their impact upon communication in the formal subsystem were examined. Finally, four important communication devices of the formal subsystem, group meetings, appraisals, house organs, and message systems, were discussed.

REVIEW AND DISCUSSION

1. Discuss the relationship between the organization's structure and the formal subsystem. How do they work together?

2. What constraints exist in the organization to prevent an individual from communicating openly with any other person? Why are these constraints necessary? What are some problems associated with the constraints?

3. Discuss each of the five communication networks which exist in the organization. What information does each carry? What is the relationship between the networks and the formal subsystem?

4. Consider the effects on organizations that "tall" and "flat" organizational structures are likely to produce. Why would a flat structure be used? Why would a tall structure be used?

5. What is bypassing and why is it necessary, under certain conditions, in the organization? What techniques can be used to institutionalize bypassing?

6. Formal devices within the structure are often used to transmit information in the organization. What assumptions do we make about these devices? What are some important devices? When should they be used?

7. Which devices of the formal subsystem are likely to produce interaction between the sender and receiver? What criteria should be used to judge the effectiveness of these devices?

Chapter Thirteen

The
Climate
for
Communication

Most of us, at one time or another, have detected *something* not quite right about our immediate environment. The source of these feelings is sometimes not easily definable. We may have searched our consciousness attempting to explain what is wrong, but the exact cause of our uneasiness remains undiscovered. This point is made by the following example of the new girl in town who is forced to go to a new school. The exchange below takes place as the girl comes home from her first day at her new school:

MOTHER: "How did you like your new school?"

GIRL: "I hated it, all the kids stared at me and no one wanted to talk to me."

MOTHER: "Did someone *say something* which hurt your feelings? Did *something happen* to make you dislike the place?"

GIRL: "No! No one did *anything*. I just felt that no one there liked me."

In our example, the young girl was perceiving a *climate* of dislike at her new school. Inherent in the composition of every organization and group is the presence of one or more climates. The concept of climate has been given a variety of labels. Such phrases as "psychological atmosphere," "organizational climate," "psychological climate," "communication climate," and "growth atmosphere" have all been used to describe this construct. In organizational research dealing with climate, each of these labels has specific definitions, but a common thread is that they all involve attitudes of individuals about their organizations.* For our purposes, climate will be defined as the *subtle, sometimes implicit, attitudinal assumptions and postulates individuals have formulated about their organization and immediate work group.* The nature of the assumptions that managers make about people was investigated in chapter four. These managerial assumptions get communicated over the "long haul" in organizations. The sum of these assumptions and postulates form the attitudinal environment in which communication takes place.

This chapter will consider some of the historical antecedents of the study of climate and will suggest a number of perspectives from which climate might be viewed. The purpose here will be to help you understand how climate operates in the organization and how it is related to the formal subsystem and to the skills of organizational members to compose the organizational communication system.

Climate: Historical Antecedents

Lewin (1938) was one of the first to conduct research to study the relationship between the individual and his or her environment. Lewin's (1951) early climate research studied the concept which he described as follows:

> To characterize properly the psychological field, one has to take into account such specific items as particular goals, stimuli, needs, social relations, as well as more general characteristics of the field as the atmosphere (for instance, the friendly, tense, or hostile atmosphere) or the amount of freedom. These characteristics of the field as a whole are as important in psychology as, for instance, the field of gravity for the explanation of events in classical physics. Psychological atmospheres are empirical realities and are scientifically describable facts. (p. 241.)

Lewin suggested that the behavior of the individual in an organization is influenced by his or her own personality and the environment or climate of the organization.

Brunswik (1939) in another early attempt to propose an approach to climate classified variables as to whether they were inputs (stimuli) or outputs (responses). To some extent, he was able to specify how the quality of a climate influences the individual's behavior in the organization.

Gibson et al. (1973) summarized a number of the major historical, theoretical, and research trends which have attempted to establish the parameters of climate. They developed the table on page 211 which brings together the contributions of a number of important theories and concepts related to climate. In discussing the theories of the early writers, they concluded:

> . . . the major emphasis of these writers was on developing a highly rationalized system of organization. They concentrated on such concepts as division of labor,

---

*This view is consistent with a conclusion reached by L.R. James and A.P. Jones, "Organizational Climate: A Review of Theory and Research," *Psychological Bulletin* (1974), pp. 1096–1112, who suggest that, in organizations, there are numerous *climates* operating. Some deal with the elements of the organization, others with a member's reaction to the elements, while still others with the individual's reaction to his or her work group, department, and so on. Yet, all of the climates involve primarily the individual's attitudinal evaluation of *something* in the environment.

Table 3   Summary of Historical Climate Literature

Theory or Concept	Focus	Use of Climate concepts
Taylor (scientific management)	Upon a "one best way" system of management by encouraging specialization and formal structuring of jobs.	Showed how structuring the job and developing a line of authority leads to working in an environment of certainty.
Woodward and Lawrence and Lorsch	Upon the interrelationships of environmental forces, technology, structure, and performance.	Attempted to show how structural-technical demands describe climate influence largely through job expectations.
Cybernetics	Upon the fact that man can control and modify his environment.	Showed how information significantly modifies the climate in which the employee operates.
Lockheed span of control model	Concerned with developing a model that highlights the optimal span of control.	Used weighted scale to assess the importance of various climate factors such as degree of training of managers and the planning atmosphere within the firm.
Decentralization	Upon the downward delegation of decision-making latitude.	The amount of delegation that is allowed depends upon the trust and faith that exists within the organization.
Likert (System 4)	Process of group interaction as related to participation, communication, and motivation. Leadership style is a crucial factor in determining the degree of interaction.	Attempted to show how a work atmosphere that perpetuates a supportive climate leads to better performance.
Job enrichment	Seeks to improve task efficiency and human satisfaction by means of improving the intrinsic features of a job.	Attempts to create a climate that provides the employee with responsibility, recognition, and opportunities for advancement.

SOURCE: Adapted from James L. Gibson, John M. Ivancevich, and James H. Donnelly, Jr., *Organizations: Structure, Processes, Behavior*. (Dallas: Business Publications, 1973), p. 316. Used by permission.

studying jobs via motion and time study, and structuring the total organization. This type of emphasis prohibits extensive consideration of such personalistic and subjective phenomena as organizational climate. However, these concepts interact and create a climate with the organization.*

A significant consideration from the early studies which have touched on climate is the interrelationship among climate and such structural variables as span of control, division of labor, time and motion of jobs, all of which have been detailed in chapter seven dealing with structure and chapter twelve which was concerned with the formal subsystem. There is an interrelationship between these structural variables and climate which will be examined later in this chapter.

---

*J.L. Gibson et al., *Organizations: Structure, Processes, Behavior* (Dallas: Business Publications, 1973), p. 315. Used by permission.

Climate: How It Works

In the daily routine of the organization, the individual encounters many aspects of human behavior within his or her environment. He or she must learn to deal with various elements of the organization such as production, supervision, compensation systems, the nature of the work task, and the informal and formal structures of the organization. All of these variables have an impact upon the individual and cause him or her to form a series of subtle attitudes about his or her job and coworkers. Sometimes he or she may not even be fully aware of these attitudes until they are tested in a crucial situation such as a strike vote or an exit interview. The worker must deal with his or her attitudes daily, they are likely to influence his or her ability to do his or her job, and they will be communicated to his or her coworkers (Redding 1972).

Job Satisfaction and Climate

Some scholars have suggested that the individual's perception of climate is the same as what the industrial psychologists call *job satisfaction* (Johannesson 1973; Guion 1973; Lawler et al. 1974). A possible method for distinguishing the two, however, is that climate appears to involve a perception by an individual of his or her work environment. Job satisfaction, on the other hand, tends to be tied closely to the nature of the task and is measured by investigating individual job components, as Katz and Kahn (1966) explain:

> . . . job satisfaction is used loosely to cover overall liking for the job situation as well as intrinsic job satisfaction deriving from the content of the work process. Hence the greater gratification of the higher occupational levels can be due to the higher pay, the greater the prestige of the calling, the hours, or working conditions, and the like. It is important, therefore, to hold constant factors other than the nature of the work in comparing the satisfaction derived from jobs varying in level of skill and complexity. (p. 370)

The relationship among climate, job satisfaction, and performance is extremely complex. It appears that climate is related to job satisfaction but they are both related to performance in different ways. There is some research to suggest that climate causes satisfaction rather than the reverse (Lee 1975; LaFollette and Sims 1975). We might conclude from these findings that when the individual member likes the climate in his or her organization, he or she will also express satisfaction with his or her own job.

For our purposes in this chapter, as we consider climate, we are focusing on an individual's *overall* reaction to his or her organizational environment including, but not limited to, his or her own job.

A Model of Climate

Figure 13-1 is a model to explain how we perceive that climate in the organization is communicated to the individual. Any number of organizational elements in the environment can be included as part of the climate. In this case, eight have been placed on the model (the left-hand side). The climate screen on the model sums relevant information about the elements to the individual's perceptual field. From the perceptual field of the individual, the information is communicated through the attitudinal set of the individual to his or her value set where response to climate in his or her organization is formulated.

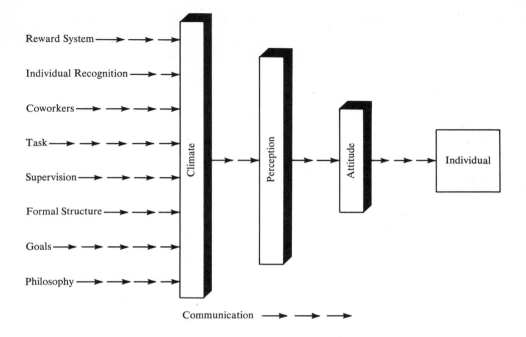

Reward System

Individual Recognition

Coworkers

Task

Supervision

Formal Structure

Goals

Philosophy

Climate

Perception

Attitude

Individual

Communication

Figure 13-1   A Model of Climate

The role of perception in communication will be considered further as an interpersonal skill in the next chapter. The perceptual and attitudinal screens work to filter the elements of the organization depending on the unique personality of the individual. By the time the individual has formed an opinion about the climate, it is probably the product of many logical and illogical unique personality traits of the individual. It would be rare, therefore, for two individuals to have exactly the same opinion about climates. Climates, then, are likely to vary from one individual to the next, and from one group to the next.

Climate: Three Approaches

Because climate is an extremely complex variable, there is some disagreement among organizational specialists as to exactly how the concept should be viewed. Some have suggested that the climate in an organization should be approached from *a perceptual viewpoint.* (Pritchard and Karasick 1973; Lawler et al. 1974). Others have proposed that the variable can be viewed by very *objective criteria* within the organization (Lawrence and Lorsch 1967; Guion 1973). This part shall consider each of these approaches, but there are inherent limitations associated with each, so a third viewpoint will also be presented.

The Perceptual Approach

This approach implies that the response to climate in an organization depends entirely on the individual who is perceiving. This view was summarized in the definition of climate offered by Campbell (1970):

> [climate is] . . . a set of attributes specific to a particular organization that may be induced from the way the organization deals with its members and its environment. For a member within the organization, climate takes the form of a set of attributes and expectancies which describe the organization in terms of both the static characteristics (such as degree of autonomy) and behavior-outcome and outcome-outcome contingencies. (p. 390)

The logic of the perceptual approach goes something like this: each individual member of the organization has his or her own perceptual field of relevant variables related to his or her organization. As such, each individual has his or her own unique response to climate in his or her organization. This approach is appealing because we know that it is difficult to achieve agreement between even two people about relatively simple concepts. For example, when we go to an art gallery with a friend to look at paintings, some disagreement will probably emerge when we begin to discuss the merits of a particular piece of art. The same problem occurs when two people communicate about a new organizational policy. As we know, people tend to view reality from their own unique perspective.

It is not uncommon in a large organization to encounter two members of the same department who both work under the same supervisor. One subordinate may view his or her boss as "open and participative" while the other worker may perceive the superior to be "closed and autocratic." In this situation, each employee is "right" because it is his or her accurate perception of reality. The conclusion is obvious: *one's own unique perception of the climate of the organization is influenced by his or her set of attitudes about the organization.*

There are some important implications for management in the perceptual view of climate. If it is a viable managerial task for the supervisor to help his or her employees improve their perception of the climate, he or she would need to evaluate the expectations and attitudes of each of his or her subordinates. The manager would develop habits enabling him or her to take into account the individual differences of subordinates. By having his or her supervisor's approach catered directly to him or her, in that supervisory style is an important dimension of climate, the individual's perception of the climate should be significantly improved.

The Objective Approach

To return to our climate model on page 213, we will focus on another part of the model, the organizational elements. The nature of the elements have been treated extensively in Part Three of this book. The emphasis in those chapters was on providing background for each element. Here we are concerned with demonstrating how the element influences climate. Any single aspect of an organizational element might be referred to as *objective* because, in theory, it can be isolated and measured. It is possible to obtain a copy of the pay scale for a given organization and compare it with other organizations. In doing this, we assume that an objective measure, to be used for comparison, of the "reward structure" is obtained. It follows that there are other objective elements in any organization, department, or work group which can be isolated. These elements are common to each individual in the work unit. Such characteristics as the number of *written rules* present in the work unit, the type of *leadership* present in the work unit, and the degree to which the individual is encouraged to be a *self-starter* have been cited as aspects of the organizational elements which would allow the climate to be viewed objectively. The assumption of this approach is that since these elements tend to be generalized throughout the work unit, those individuals in the unit should have somewhat similar responses to them. The objective view of climate is explained by Guion:

> Objective measures of physical climate (i.e. of something external to the people who experience it) are possible and commonplace. One may examine an almanac and find that climatologists have recorded variations in daily mean temperature in, for example, Cleveland and Honolulu, the mean of the mean temperature is perhaps higher in Honolulu than in Cleveland, while the variance of such readings is higher in Cleveland. At any given point in time and at any given location, the climatologist can observe both temperature and wind velocity. From these measures he can compute a "derived score" to measure objectively a psychological factor known as the wind-chill factor. The wind-chill factor is logically related to the human experience of being cold, but it is nevertheless empirically a function of objective measures of external climate variables . . . . The actual perception of being cold is clearly something different from the wind-chill factor and they probably have distinguishably different networks of correlates. The one is an attribute of a person, the other an attribute of the world he is in. They differ but should be related to some degree.*

Guion is suggesting that, like the wind-chill factor, the climate in an organization can be measured objectively *apart from the individual's perceptions*. Even the neophyte student of organizations recognizes that attitudes about the organization often get communicated in extremely subtle but objective ways. For example, the informal group network in an organization plays a major role in establishing the climate. Probably more attitudinal responses to climate become soldified in the lunchroom than at the work place. When workers get together at the water cooler or at the bowling alley after work, the communication often turns to work-related matters. Gossip, personality conflicts, and gripes about the job become the communication content for these informal networks. If a particularly persuasive worker thinks that the organization has not been treating him or her fairly, he or she is likely to "sound off" about it during these "bull" sessions. This informal structure exists throughout the work unit and may influence the individual's response to climate. The informal structure is an objective aspect of the organization which does not depend on the individual perceiver for existence.

In addition, there is within every organization a set of formal rules, codes, and expectations which constitute the organization's operating *prescriptions*. These are part of the organization's structure and are communicated through the formal sub-system by means of the authority communication network. The prescriptions and the way in which they are communicated all work to establish an objective climate in an organization. Those advocating the objective approach argue that the attitudes of all members of the work unit are established by the presence (or absence) of these prescriptions.

A partial list follows of some of the objective aspects of organizational elements likely to establish the climate in an organization:

(1)   The nature of the expectations placed upon supervisors in terms of motivating employees to produce

---

*R.M. Guion, "A Note on Organizational Climate," *Organizational Behavior and Human Performance* 9 (1973): 121-22. Used by permission of the journal and the author.

(2) The number of formal rules existing

(3) The degree to which jobs are tied to existing descriptions in the organization

(4) The nature of the relationships between labor union and management

(5) The nature of the performance appraisal system in the organization

(6) The orientation procedures for new employees

(7) The productivity standards placed upon each employee

(8) The dress and conduct standards placed upon each employee

(9) The punishment procedures existing in the organization

(10) The assumptions about people manifested by management

Although quite appealing logically, there are some difficulties associated with this approach to climate. It suggests that any of thousands of aspects of organizational elements may cause climate. This approach is so general that specific statements about climate become impossible as James and Jones (1974) have explained:

> In fact, almost any study focusing on organizational or group characteristics would be included in the general area of organizational climate. In this respect, organizational climate appears to be synonymous with organizational situation and seems to offer little more than a semantically appealing "catch-all" term. (p. 1099)

In the previous two sections, approaches to viewing the nature of climate in the organization have been presented. Although both approaches contain important contributions as we seek to understand the concept, neither should be taken as definitive. In an attempt to draw together the salient features of both approaches, we present a third.

The Process Approach

An influential social psychologist, Weick (1969) presents a rather innovative approach to organizations. He argues that organizations are primarily information processing units attempting to remove equivocality (uncertainty) from informational inputs:

> If the relevant environment for the organization is described in terms of information, then it is possible to argue that organizing is directed toward resolving the equivocality that exists in informational inputs judged to be relevant. Such an interpretation is consistent with the basic concept in information theory that information results when uncertainty is removed. Any item of information contains several possibilities or implications. It is more or less ambiguous and is subject to a variety of interpretations. If action is to be taken, the possibilities must be narrowed and the equivocal properties of the message made more unequivocal. Organizing is concerned with removing equivocality from information and structuring processes so that the removal is possible.*

*K.S. Weick, *The Social Psychology of Organizing* (Reading, Mass.: Addison-Wesley, 1969), p. 29. Used by permission of the publisher.

Later he specifies the role of the individual in the process of organizing:

> . . . the task of managing equivocality requires that stable interaction patterns be activated. It is in this sense that we are talking about cycles. Interstructured behaviors are the crucial element of organizing, and the removal of equivocality is predominantly an interpersonal activity.*

The Weick theory will be useful if we return to the model of climate in figure 13-1. The perceptual approach to climate focused at the perceptual screen of the model, while the objective approach involved the selection of organizational elements which establish the climate. However, an important aspect of that model, dealing with the arrows which guide the respective elements through the perceptual and attitudinal screens to the individual, has been ignored by both approaches. These arrows represent the communication process in the organization. Communication helps determine an individual's response to an element because that response will depend on how much information about the element has been transmitted.

If one accepts Weick's logic, the argument can be made that thousands of potential stimuli exist in the environment. These stimuli deal with aspects of organizational elements and the pool of stimuli is available to all members. However, the individual will *process* those stimuli which are relevant to him or her at a given time. The model in figure 13-2 has broken down one aspect of the organization's structure, the compensation system. There are thousands of potential inputs about the compensation system which may exist in the organization. On the model only ten have been included, but these become informational inputs as they are processed by the individual. The illustration on the model involves an organizational member who has just experienced a job-related injury which threatens to put him out of work for a long period of time. Up until this time, our injured employee may have expressed generally positive responses to the climate of his organization. But because of his injury, he will now only process those information inputs in the climate dealing with sick leave (c_4) and insurance systems (c_7). These then become, for this individual at this particular time, the major determinants of his response to climate. *The organizational element and the aspect of that element are both determined by the situation.* The individual's response to climate in the process approach is a function of (1) what informational inputs (about respective elements) are relevant to him or her, (2) how these inputs are communicated to him or her, (3) what attitudinal values the individual places on these inputs, and (4) at what point in time the individual is doing the processing. The response will vary because it is continually "in process." Like the perceptual approach, the process approach does suggest that each individual will perceive the climate differently but the individual's perception is based on the objective structure of the organization.

A Summary of the Three Approaches to Climate

This part has outlined three approaches to the concept of climate and proposed a model which diagrammed the variables which determine climates in organizations. The perceptual approach has suggested that climate depends on how the individual

---

*Ibid., p. 76. Used by permission of the publisher.

ORGANIZATIONAL ELEMENT

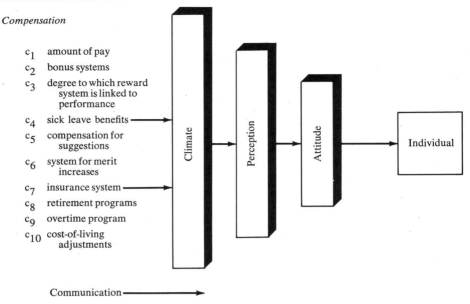

Compensation

c_1 amount of pay

c_2 bonus systems

c_3 degree to which reward system is linked to performance

c_4 sick leave benefits

c_5 compensation for suggestions

c_6 system for merit increases

c_7 insurance system

c_8 retirement programs

c_9 overtime program

c_{10} cost-of-living adjustments

Climate   Perception   Attitude   Individual

Communication ⟶

Figure 13-2   A Model of the Process View of Climate

member perceives his or her environment and, as such, each member is likely to possess a unique set of responses to the climate. In the objective approach, the individual's response to climate is a product of the aspects of the organizational elements. A third approach was proposed based on the theories of Weick. The process approach suggested that the individual's response to climate is a function of which aspects of the organization's elements are most relevant to him or her and of how these were communicated.

Climate and Organizational Effectiveness

We have used considerable space thus far attempting to explain how climates operate in organizations, but we have yet to provide a rationale as to why climates are important. In this part, we would like to suggest some ways in which climate can help achieve effective organizations.

Redding (1972) has suggested that the climate of an organization is the major determinant of the organizational communication system and is more important than communication skills or techniques in creating effective organizations. Later in discussing McGregor's (1960) definition of climate as "subtle behavior manifestations" of assumptions and attitudes, Redding concluded:

> These assumptions and attitudes, in turn, refer to ways in which the managers and supervisors define the goals of the organization, ways in which they believe an organization should be run, and ways in which they regard the motives and talents of the employees. As a number of observers have affirmed, there is a high probability that underlying feelings or attitudes will be communicated, at least

over the "long haul," whether or not the message-senders are aware of what is happening. *

Redding appears to be suggesting that despite attempts by the individual to hide his or her own negative response to the climate in his or her organization, this negative response will inevitably be communicated in the work place.

An even stronger case for the importance of climate in organizations was made by Guion:

> The construct (or perhaps, family of constructs) implied by the term organizational climate, may be one of the most important to enter the thinking of industrial-organizational psychologists in many years. Ecological problems are at the fore in contemporary social concern; psychological pollution of the work environment may be as serious a source of some kinds of human misery as chemical pollution of rivers. Discovery and development of environmental factors at work that facilitate human well-being and productivity deserve high priority. Psychology has long contended that individual behavior is a function of a pervasive environment, yet industrial psychology has yet to define or to isolate invariant environmental variables that impinge upon all those who work.†

Both writers have implied that the work environment will influence the communication system as well as the individual's rate of productivity. They have provided theoretical evidence for the conclusion that as workers react positively to their environment, the organization becomes effective.

A Research Argument

There has been some research which has attempted to support empirically the relationship between climate and organizational effectiveness (Brayfield and Crockett 1955; Frederiksen 1968; Johannesson 1973), but one of the most creative approaches to study the relationship was done by Indik et al. (1961). They broke climate down into four parts and examined the relationship between the job performance of organizational members and each of four aspects of climate: (1) openness of the communication channel between the superior and his or her subordinate, (2) degree to which subordinates are satisfied with their superior's supportive behavior toward them, (3) the degree of mutual understanding among interacting supervisory and nonsupervisory organizational members, and (4) the degree to which subordinates feel that they, and their superiors, have influence over organizational operations which affect them. This research attempted to determine if, when a worker has a positive feeling about climate, he or she will also have high work performance. The data were collected among 27 "stations" (offices) and 925 individual employees of a moving distribution firm.

The results demonstrated that in the organization, as a whole, a high level of job performance tended to be positively associated with (1) openness of communication channels between superiors and subordinates, (2) subordinates' satisfaction with supervisors' supportive behavior, (3) a relatively high mutual understanding of

---

Communication Within the Organization, p. 112, © 1972, by Purdue Research Foundation, West Lafayette, Indiana. Used by permission.

†Guion, "A Note on Organizational Climate," p. 120. Used by permission of the journal and the author.

viewpoints and problems among those who work together, and (4) a relatively high degree of local influence and autonomy on work-related matters.

Although the writers argued against widespread generalization from their data, there does not appear to be consistent evidence that *the climate in an organization is positively associated with the job performance of the individuals who work in that organization.* Or, put another way, people seem to work well when they manifest a positive view of their work environment. More recent research (Lee 1975; La Follette and Sims 1975) has also reported data which suggest that there is a high correlation between high job performance and positive perceptions of climate.

Dimensions of Climate

A number of attempts have been made in the research literature to catalog, both theoretically and empirically, the various dimensions of climate.* These attempts have been based on the assumption that by breaking down the concept into its smallest parts, it will be less difficult to understand how it operates in the organization. In this part, we would like to present four dimensions of climate, all based on research previously reported. Each dimension involves very different kinds of organizational behavior, but together they represent *the* climate in an organization.

Dimension No. 1: Structure, Rules, Control

The nature of the structure and its importance in communication were considered extensively in chapters seven and twelve. It will not be our purpose here to review material already covered. Instead, we will deal with those highly relevant aspects of structure which influence the climate in an organization.

The Organization and Rules. Organizations vary greatly in the number of rules, regulations, and procedures which they maintain. Various levels of government have been criticized for establishing bureaucracies which tend to do little but sustain themselves. One only has to battle the red tape to transfer an automobile title or try to obtain a satisfactory answer to an inquiry about income taxes from the Internal Revenue Service to be enlightened about the government's tendency to rigidly formalize even the most minor aspect of organizational operations. Two popular books have been written, *The Peter Principle* (Peter 1970), and *Up the Organization* (Townsend 1970), which are "tongue-in-cheek" attempts to poke fun at the tendency of organizations to develop a rule, manual, or prescription for every occasion.

---

*Recent attempts to look at the Dimensions of climate include J.P. Campbell and E.E. Beatty, "Organizational Climate: Its Measurement and Relationship to Work Goal Performance," paper presented at the Annual Meeting of the American Psychological Association, Washington, D.C., 1971, who identified: (1) individual autonomy, (2) the degree of structure placed on a position, (3) reward orientation, and (4) consideration, warmth, and support. H.S. Dennis III in a paper entitled "The Construction of a Managerial 'Communication Climate' Inventory for Use in Complex Organizations" presented at the International Communication Association annual meeting, Chicago, 1975, hypothesized the following components of what he called "communication climate": (1) managerial supportiveness, (2) participative decision making, (3) trust, confidence, credibility, (4) openness and candor, (5) high performance goals, (6) information adequacy/communication satisfaction, and (7) semantic distance (perceptual disparity between two people about an attitudinal object). For a thorough treatment of climate in an organization, as it relates with other behavioral variables, see J.L. Gibson, J.M. Ivancevich, and J.H. Donnelly, Jr., *Organizations Structure, Processes, Behavior* (Dallas: BPI, 1973), chapter 11.

An appropriate amount of structure is indispensable to organizations. The organization which does not have some rules and regulations cannot operate. If the university does not have a workable structure to collect and record grades, it is cheating the student. The organization without a functional method for recruiting and training employees will eventually be without employees. Rules and formal procedures provide the roadmaps which the organization uses to chart its progress toward its objectives.

As we pointed out in chapter twelve, organizations tend to formalize rules by writing them down and making them a part of the organization's authority network. However, there are also other important rules and codes which do not get written down. Sometimes these unwritten rules are quite covert and only get communicated haphazardly. An example would be a young male high school teacher who is *expected* to report for work the first day with a necktie, fresh haircut, and no beard. The teacher who violates this unwritten rule runs the risk of experiencing his principal's wrath and after a number of such violations will probably no longer be with the organization.

The Climate and Structure. In the typical organization, the individual has to live within the rules of the organization. We tend to comply with the structure because we want the end result rewards such as pay, status, and security. If an organization can be characterized as possessing too many rules, it may be counterproductive to the growth and development of members. If, in a given organization, a member has a very specific job description but continues to violate it, even to the benefit of the organization, he or she may eventually become suspect. The structure of the organization becomes dysfunctional when it negatively restricts the behavior of the individual.

Structure, Climate and Communication Flow. The structure of an organization certainly influences the flow of communication. If the structure is characterized as "formal and rigid," there is evidence to suggest that the communication flow will also be formal and constrained (Frederiksen 1966; Litwin and Stringer 1967; Lawler et al. 1974). On the other hand, when the structure can be characterized as "informal and flexible," the communication flow is more spontaneous.

Dimension No. 2: Responsibility, Challenge

This aspect of climate is related to the discussion of structure above. The focus there was on the quantity and quality of the formal rules and regulations. But here we are concerned with whether or not *the member, working within the existing structure, feels challenged to put forth maximum effort at his or her task and to acquire new skills and competencies at his or her job.*

Individual Responsibility. One method which might distinguish organizations would be the degree to which they encourage the individual to think and act for himself or herself. Some organizations reward conforming behavior and punish deviation by exerting pressure on the individual to "play by the rules." The presence of many rules and regulations tends to restrict creative organizational behavior. Parameters of behavioral alternatives, drawn tightly around the individual, may restrain his or her ability to accomplish a task, as demonstrated in figure 13-3.

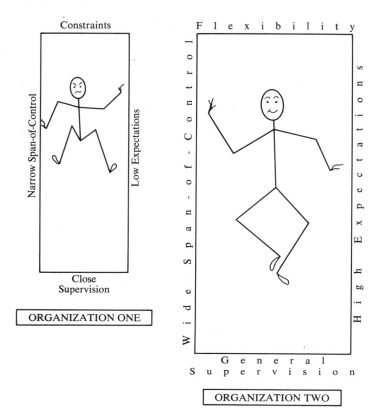

Figure 13-3   Narrow and Wide Parameters

The climate in Organization One has boxed in the worker in the figure. The constraints and expectations placed on the individual make it difficult for him or her to be a self-starter. Management is always looking over his or her shoulder to make sure that he or she accomplishes what he or she is supposed to when he or she has been assigned. As pressure increases our harried worker is likely to feel cramped, uneasy, and unmotivated to work (Herzberg 1959). It can be argued, perhaps, that some people work best under the climate diagrammed in Organization One since some people seem to produce best when "all eyes" are on them. But for many of us, working in this kind of high-pressure situation every day may produce emotional and psychological stress.

In the climate of Organization Two, the worker appears to be able to cope with the existing structure. He or she seems to be able to grow and develop in his or her job and there is much room within the existing structure for him or her to move around to find the best work techniques and schedules for him or her. The worker is able to do his or her job in his or her own way with the organization's encouragement.

We might conclude by suggesting that the *individual responsibility* component of climate consists of *the degree to which the individual perceives that he or she is autonomous and able to exercise his or her own judgment about the techniques and emphasis of his or her job.*

Individual Responsibility and Supervision.   The major determinant of this responsibility dimension of climate is the behavior of the supervisor toward the subordinate. Even within the most highly structured climates, the individual supervisor is able, by granting sufficient latitude, to help his or her subordinates achieve their optimum level of responsibility. The work by Likert (1967) on creating "participative" climates and McGregor (1960) on Theory X and Theory Y, both discussed extensively in chapter four, helps us understand how the manager is able to create climates which help the individual reach his or her maximum potential. Managers make certain assumptions about their subordinates and those assumptions do get communicated. In many cases, the manager creates the climate in which his or her subordinates must work. He or she may improve this aspect of climate by: (1) allowing the subordinate to develop responsible behavior by providing him or her with opportunities for training and growth. If the individual has never been given the chance to prove himself or herself, his or her true potential has never been tested, and (2) rewarding responsible behavior in the organization equitably. The individual who makes an unexpected and significantly positive contribution to his or her organization, but finds that the contribution was unrecognized, will probably be less likely to contribute in the future.

Dimension No. 3: Risk, Risk-Taking, Tolerance

Building upon the previous section, we can see that individuals can only be responsible and grow and develop in their jobs if the climate of the organization allows them to take *risks* to communicate when they have a creative idea or contribution. Risk in this context means that the individual perceives that he or she is able to *communicate possibly threatening messages about his or her job without fear of retribution.* Organizations vary greatly in the degree to which they will tolerate negative communication. This concept is roughly analogous to the citizen's right of free speech under the United States Constitution. Under optimal conditions, the individual can, within certain constraints, say anything he or she wants about the country, even if what he or she has to say is critical. The citizen who exercises his or her right of free speech does it without fear of penalty for his or her action.

The free speech analogy holds when we are considering the composition of a climate within an organization as to whether or not the individual employee feels free to criticize, make suggestions to, and argue with the management of his or her organization. Climate determines the degree to which a member at a lower point in the structure feels that he or she can initiate communication to a point higher in the hierarchy. The diagram in figure 13-4 will help the reader focus on the relationship between "risk-taking tolerance" and "upward communication" in the organization.

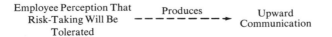

Figure 13-4   Upward Communication and Risk-Taking

There are many organizational situations where risk-taking is important, all of which cannot be considered here. We have chosen to focus on three risk-taking situations only: (1) job level, (2) interpersonal level, and (3) superior-subordinate level. These situations have been arranged in reverse order of their likelihood to create threat for the individual who engages in risk-taking communication.

Risk-Taking at the Job Level.   Taking a risk to initiate communication about one's job is often encouraged in the organization. Many employees offer suggestions and ideas through various suggestions systems, as considered in chapter twelve. Suggestions which are likely to save the organization money are often rewarded financially. When suggestions are written down and placed in a suggestion box limited threat is present. By writing down the suggestion, the employee may not have to test his or her ideas in front of doubting peers and supervisors.

Risk-Taking at the Interpersonal Level.   An aspect of risk-taking involves the initiation of threatening communication when that information is *not expected.* Sometimes we find ourselves covering our real feelings because we want to protect ourselves or someone else when we communicate. The instructor who asks a student the rhetorical question, "How did you like my examination?" may not be prepared when the student responds, "It was a lousy test and didn't test my knowledge at all." It would have been less difficult for the student to have provided a socially accepted response in this situation. The student, instead, apparently decided to risk his or her true feelings. This aspect of climate is concerned with conditions under which the typical individual perceives that he or she is able to "go out on a limb" and open up when the situation calls for it.

Risk-Taking at the Superior-Subordinate Level.   Since it is the member's immediate supervisor who will usually be the vehicle through which suggestions are transmitted, the relationship between the two will mediate upward communication. Later in this chapter, we will examine superior-subordinate communication, but some attention to this relationship will be given here. For a member to approach his or her superior with a suggestion, he or she must feel that his or her boss will respond openly and honestly. If continually turned off by the superior, the individual will probably discontinue risk-taking behavior. Since upward communication will depend on the subordinate's ability to take a risk without fear of reprisal, the communication channel between the two should not only tolerate but also encourage risk-taking.

Risk-taking, in most situations, is highly functional to the organization and should be encouraged because it generates new data for decision making. Risk-taking communication should occur when the organization demonstrates the behaviors tional feedback:

Provides Feedback.   In communication, feedback helps us gauge the effectiveness of our message sending. The person who risks making a suggestion in the organization needs feedback about the results and effects of his or her suggestion before he or she will risk others. Redding (1972) described the significance of organizational feedback:

> No doubt, both interpersonal and organizational feedback are crucial to the
> successful functioning of any large organization. For example, the subordinate

in the conventional performance appraisal receives interpersonal feedback from his superior concerning his effectiveness on the job. And, obviously, managers must receive feedback reports concerning the ongoing operations of the enterprise if they are to secure information on which to base decisions.*

Feedback about suggestions or ideas initiated by the employee may take either oral or written form but must explain why the suggestion was or was not implemented. The feedback process acts to satisfy the ego needs of the individual by recognizing the contribution to the organization made by that individual with his or her suggestion.

Encourages Productive Conflict. The existence of conflict in the climate is neither harmful nor injurious to the organization. In fact, individuals will engage in risk-taking when a "productive climate" is present. Deutsch (1969) has suggested that existing conflict in the climate provides four very useful functions: (1) it stimulates curiosity, (2) it is the medium through which problems can be aired and solutions arrived at, (3) it is the root of personal and social change, and (4) it is the process of testing and assessing one's self. Coser (1956) provides a rationale for why conflict should be present in the organization:

> In loosely-structured groups and often societies, conflict, which aims at a resolution of tension between antagonists, is likely to have stabilizing and integrative functions for the relationship. By permitting immediate and direct expression of rival claims, such social systems are able to readjust their structures by eliminating the sources of dissatisfaction. The multiple conflicts which they experience may serve to eliminate the causes for disassociation and to re-establish unity. These systems avail themselves, through the toleration and institutionalization of conflict, of an important stabilizing mechanism. (p. 154)

The individual will feel comfortable in risking threatening communication when the climate is flexible enough to allow this type of conflict.

Discourages "GroupThink." Organizational members, similar to members of small groups, have a tendency to take on the attitudes and beliefs of the management of the organization or group. This characteristic has been labeled as *GroupThink*. Brilhart (1974) in explaining Janis' (1971) concept defined it this way:

> The term "GroupThink" refers to the conformity to the belief of a head person or group which sometimes occurs when members begin to think they are infallible, or that the ideas of high status members should not be challenged. Leaders who promote their own solutions invite GroupThink, but this phenomenon can occur in any group. (p. 108)

During the early 1970s, the United States went through a great political upheaval commonly referred to as the Watergate affair. An American president, popularly elected in 1968 and 1972, was forced to leave office under a cloud of suspicion that he engaged in illegal activities. This president was criticized for surrounding himself by a group of "yes men" who would go to any lengths to keep themselves in power and who labeled anyone who disagreed with them "enemies." Conflicting opinions

Communication Within the Organization, pp. 40-41, ©1972, by Purdue Research Foundation, West Lafayette, Indiana. Used by permission.

or deviant behavior was not tolerated. These men used the federal bureaucracies to implement their own unique brand of GroupThink. The climate of the organization must be such that occasional nonconformity is tolerated. If GroupThink does exist in an organization, there is little likelihood of unique and creative ideas coming from its members.

These three characteristics are suggested as preconditions which should be present in the climate before the individual member of the organization will risk nonconforming or threatening communication.

Dimension No. 4: Support, Warmth, Consideration

As organizations continue to grow, there is a tendency for them to develop impersonal characteristics which stifle the individuality of the member. When the organization has 20,000 members and must satisfy numerous internal and external constituent groups, it is difficult to provide the recognition and support desired by most people. Sometimes when the individual does not obtain the level of support he or she is seeking from his or her place of employment, he or she will search for it elsewhere. It is not uncommon for an employee low in the structure of his or her organization to assume an important leadership position in his or her church, bowling league, or lodge. These outside organizations may provide the individual with the psychological support missing through his or her regular employment.

Although three terms (support, warmth, and consideration) were used to describe this aspect of climate, perhaps it can be clarified if we refer to it simply as "supportive climate." This is consistent with the work of McGregor (1960), Likert (1967), Redding (1972), and Dennis (1975).

Supportive Climate: A Definition. Likert has written extensively on the characteristics of what he calls "participative organizations" which have supportive climates. Of these characteristics, seven are particularly helpful as we attempt to establish a definition of this aspect of climate. According to Likert, a *supportive climate* would be one in which: (1) there is reciprocal confidence and trust between the manager and his or her subordinates, (2) a sincere effort is put forth by the manager to secure good pay for his or her subordinates, (3) an effort is made by the manager to understand his or her subordinates' problems, (4) the manager helps the subordinate accomplish his or her task by providing such things as coaching, help in problem solving, and budgeting, (5) the manager keeps the subordinate informed about work-related matters, (6) the manager is perceived of as "friendly and approachable," and (7) the manager appears willing to give credit to others rather than attempting to take credit for himself or herself. At the core of Likert's approach is the relationship between the supportive climate and the "participative organization." Likert is convinced that when the employee is given the opportunity to participate in the making of important decisions which affect him or her, he or she will become a productive employee.

The Work of Jack Gibb. After many years of observing therapeutic and educational small groups, Gibb (1961) developed a paradigm which distinguishes between supportive and what he calls "defensive" climates:

Defensive Climates	*Supportive Climates*
1. Evaluation	1. Description
2. Control	2. Problem Orientation
3. Strategy	3. Spontaneity
4. Neutrality	4. Empathy
5. Superiority	5. Equality
6. Certainty	6. Provisionalism

Climates in which there exists a characteristic of judgment, with people thinking in terms of "goods" and "bads," are described as *evaluation. Control* would describe climates which have tightly structured rules or are manipulated by a strong person. Climates in which tricks or hidden agendas are common would be described as *strategy. Neutrality* defines climates in which individuals display little genuine concern for each other. Climates in which the manager "talks down" to subordinates can be described as *superiority. Certainty* is characteristic of climates where the manager has all the answers, leaving little room for possible error. The supportive climate is based on the "here and now" and contains few behavioral restrictions. In this type of climate, the individual is encouraged to be himself or herself.

Lateral Support.   As the individual worker is on the job for a period of time, he or she begins to develop close personal relationships with his or her peers in that organization. These relationships often grow to such an extent that employees spend after work and weekend hours together. Even some jobs which society purports to be unattractive such as assembly-line and deep coal mining work are made appealing because of the tight personal relationships which tend to develop among individuals who hold these positions.

Peer groups in the organization are often engaged in such nontask related, but very functional, activities as helping with babysitting for each other, exchanging clothes, presents, and personal advice, and aiding in the household duties if a member becomes incapacitated. Strong communication bonds and behavioral codes often develop among peers in the organization. These strong peer groups can be functional to the organization to the extent to which they accept its goals.

This section described the four dimensions of climate: (1) structure, rules, and control, (2) responsibility and challenge, (3) risk, risk-taking, and tolerance, and (4) support, warmth, and consideration. Each dimension plays a role in establishing the climate in which organizational communication takes place.

Climate and Superior-Subordinate Communication

Thus far in this chapter, we have made many references to the communication relationship between the superior and subordinate as a function of climate. Since this relationship is critical to organizational communication, it will be examined further.

A diagram of the communication channel between the superior and his or her subordinate is presented in figure 13-5. As the diagram indicates, A is placed higher

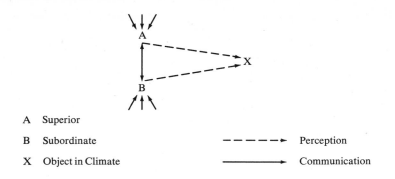

A   Superior

B   Subordinate   – – – – –▶   Perception

X   Object in Climate   ————▶   Communication

Figure 13-5   Superior-Subordinate Communication

in the structure and is party to more official communication than is B. Within the structure, it is often the responsibility of A to communicate this information to B, as part of the authority network. B, on the other hand, is aware of much information about his or her own job. It is necessary for the organization to acquire this information for good decision-making. Theoretically, this information about B's job should be transmitted to A through the information network for relay up the structure. The degree of success of this communication linkage will depend on their individual perceptions about the object under discussion (X). Since differences of perceptions are likely to occur regardless of the object under discussion, accurate communication is constantly being hampered by these differences. It would be rare for A and B to agree fully on the composition of B's job. This may cause an inherent communication barrier between the two.

Research on Superior-Subordinate Communication

A number of the important studies dealing with communication between the superior and the subordinate have been summarized in table 4. The reader will observe from the studies cited that, although good communication between the superior and his or her subordinate is highly functional to the organization, various intervening variables (mobility, aspirations of subordinate, trust, job security, and the like) are likely to hamper communication between the two. Two of these will be given consideration here, *trust* and the *upward mobility* of the subordinate.

Trust.   Giffin (1967a) offers the following definition of trust in the interpersonal situation:

> Reliance upon the communicative behavior of another person in order to achieve a desired but uncertain objective in a risky situation. (p. 105)

He goes on to establish the following five dimensions of trust:

(1)   *Expertness* on the topic being discussed.

(2)   *Reliability* as an information source which involves the communicator's dependability, predictability, or consistency.

(3)   Favorable or unfavorable *intentions* of the speaker toward the listener.

(4)   *Dynamism* (activity) of the speaker as perceived by the listener.

(5)   *Personal attraction* of the speaker for the listener.

Central to Giffin's explanation of trust is the dependency of one individual on the behavior of another. This dependency can characterize the relationship between the boss and his or her subordinate. The boss depends on his or her worker to produce and to provide information about problems associated with the subordinate's job. The subordinate depends upon his or her manager for information about general policies of the company and to "go to bat" for him or her for promotions and merit salary increases. Trust appears to be an important precondition for satisfactory communication between the manager and his or her subordinates (Read 1962; Roberts and O'Reilly 1974a).

Mellinger (1956) studied the communication between two people when one person did not trust the other. He found that when person A did not trust person

Table 4   *Important Research Studies Dealing with
Superior-Subordinate Communication*

Researcher(s)	Major Variables	Major Findings
Pelz (1951)	Superior's influence upon the subordinate	1. Superiors vary greatly to the degree to which they can exert influence on their subordinates. 2. Superior's influence is related to the degree to which subordinates perceive that their boss has influence with *his* or *her* superiors.
Read (1962)	1. Mobility aspirations of the subordinate for his or her boss' job and the resultant tendency to distort communication going from himself or herself to his or her superior. 2. Subordinate's trust of his or her superior as a mediator in upward distortion.	1. Upward mobility aspirations appear to be related to the tendency to distort information. 2. Trust does, to some degree, modify upward distortion.
Indik, Georgopoulos, and Seashore (1961)	Relationship between superior-subordinate communication and subordinate productivity.	"Open" communication between superior and subordinate does appear to be related to subordinate productivity.
Athanassiades (1973)	Relationship between tendency of the subordinate to distort information going to superior and his or her own job security and need achievement.	1. Subordinate is likely to distort information when he or she has high needs to achieve. 2. Subordinate is less likely to distort information when he or she has high job security.
Roberts and O'Reilly (1974b)	Relationship among trust, upward influence, and mobility.	1. Trust appeared to be major predictor for upward communication. 2. Mobility aspirations of subordinates not related to upward communication. 3. Relationship between upward communication and influence not clear.

B, person A tended to conceal his or true feelings about a particular issue when communicating with B about the issue. A concealed by being:

(1) very *evasive* in his or her communication with B.

(2) very *compliant* toward B in his or her communication.

(3) *aggressive* in his or her communication with B.

As concealment occurs, B obtains a very distorted perception of the issue under discussion. He or she may either *under-* or *overestimate* the areas of agreement or disagreement between himself or herself and A.

Mobility Aspirations.　The second major intervening variable likely to influence communication between the manager and his or her subordinate involves the degree to which the subordinate would like to have the boss' job. If he or she wants the job, he or she may intentionally distort information going to the boss. Read (1962) explained:

> The stronger the mobility aspirations of subordinates, the more they will communicate to their superiors in a way that will maximize positive, and minimize negative aspects. Thus, they will be likely to withhold, restrict, or distort information about problems, current and unsolved which they experience in their day-to-day work. (p. 4)

Read, in a study of fifty-two superior-subordinate pairs, found that when the subordinate was upwardly mobile, he or she did tend to distort information going to his or her superior. This occurred even when the subordinate trusted the superior. Some contradictory results on the relationship between distortion and mobility aspirations of subordinates were reported by Roberts and O'Reilly (1974b). They found no relationship between mobility and communication behavior:

> the lack of strong correlations between mobility aspirations and communication behavior suggests that the impact of mobility may operate only in certain groups. Recall that the subjects sampled in this study are drawn from a variety of work settings and positions in the organization hierarchy. Read focused on a set of 52 executive pairs. Perhaps with highly mobile managers communication may be altered more. . . . For the larger picture, however, the impact of mobility (in our study) was not great. (p. 214)

It may be that upward mobility aspirations of subordinates will influence their communication with the superior, but the nature of that influence is not yet clear.

Summary

This chapter began with the premise that climate is one of the major components of the organizational communication system. A number of historical antecedents to the construct of climate were examined. Three approaches to climate were proposed: (1) perceptual, (2) objective, and (3) process. It was suggested that employees' attitudes about climate were related to their rates of productivity in the organization. A number of dimensions of climate were presented: (1) structure, rules, and control; (2) responsibility and challenge; (3) risk, risk-taking, and conflict; and (4) support, warmth, and consideration. A final section dealt with the communication relationship between the superior and subordinate.

REVIEW AND DISCUSSION

1. Of the dimensions of climate presented in this chapter, which is the most important to you as an organizational member? Why?

2. Discuss the relationship between the structure and climate of an organization. What role does each play? How are they similar? How are they different?

3. In terms of the research presented in this chapter dealing with superior-subordinate communication, what observations can you make? What do you see as the most important principles of superior-subordinate communication?

4. Which organizational elements (presented in Part Three) are likely to have the most influence in determining climate? Support your position with examples from your experience as an organizational member.

5. Of the three approaches to viewing climate (perceptual, objective, and process), which do you think best explains the construct? Provide reasons for your answer.

6. Climate appears to be related to organizational effectiveness. Suggest some ways in which this relationship might be manifested. How can "good" climate help the organization achieve its goals?

7. What relationship do you see among upward communication and risk-taking by subordinates in the organization? Which is the precondition? How do they work together?

Chapter Fourteen

Interpersonal Skills in Organizational Communication

The component of the organizational communication system to be considered in this chapter is the range of interpersonal skills displayed by the individual members of the organization. Gibb (1961) called communication essentially a "people" variable and since people vary greatly, the communication skills possessed by them also vary. As a result, the communication system is different from one organization to another, and from one subunit to the next within organizations, depending on many things, including the communication skills demonstrated by members.

This chapter will investigate seven important interpersonal skills which can be utilized by individuals. Those skills associated primarily with message receiving will be examined in the first part which will be followed by a consideration of those skills associated with message sending.

Receiver Skills in Interpersonal Communication

This part will deal with four interpersonal skills which are very important in receiving communication: (1) listening behavior for recall, (2) listening behavior for understanding, (3) communication perception, and (4) group awareness.

Listening Behavior for Recall

Probably no skill in communication has been as neglected in the research as listening behavior. Most of us develop sending skills (e.g. talking, writing) very early in life, but rarely are we taught to listen. Listening is the attribute which allows one to *receive and interpret communication messages.* It is really a *psychological process* which is more inclusive than the physiological state of simply *hearing* a sound wave. The individual "listens" with his or her eyes while observing a nonverbal stimulus or by perceiving that a particular interpersonal situation is hostile. The ability to listen has to be developed over time by practice. For the past twenty years, surveys dealing with communication have revealed that corporation presidents feel that the ability to listen is the most important communication tool for their subordinates to possess (Lull et al. 1955; Trent and Redding, 1964; Hunt et al. 1974). Many people would rather talk than listen, however. Talking is fun but listening involves work. Listening means that we must focus upon someone else's behavior instead of upon our own. It is this ability to focus upon someone else which is the key to success in the communication process. Good listening enables us to reach mutual understanding in our communication relationships with others.

The human being is a *processor of information* who is constantly being bombarded with information inputs which must be "handled." These inputs come from many sources and in many forms. Since many of our organizations are so complex, it may be impossible for one individual to be an expert on all areas within the organization's domain. The individual, faced with the realization that potential information inputs are mushrooming all around him or her, must begin to sort relevant stimuli. Those stimuli which have the most meaning to the individual are those which get processed. For example, let us assume that Rachel takes a job in a factory. A number of written manuals, instruction sheets, and oral directions are available to show her how to do her new job. The ability to listen for recall enables Rachel to select and interpret those potential inputs in such a way to complete the task. *Listening behavior for recall allows the individual to organize and synthesize potential information and direct it toward a specific purpose.*

In the industrial situation, orders, given as part of the authority network, are supposed to be implemented by the subordinate. He or she is charged with the responsibility of remembering the details of the directions. If the subordinate acts upon only a part of his or her directions, he or she is open to charges of incompetence. In the illustration of Rachel above, we witness a breakdown in communication if she is unable to sort through the directions to accomplish her particular assignment. Because of the quantity and complexity of oral and written communication in most organizations, breakdowns are inevitable in most routine operations.

Communication Overload. Like a computer, humans can only process so many information inputs at one time. If a particular input is so new that our cognitive structure cannot associate it with something with which we are familiar, it will not compute new inputs. Overload can produce three kinds of counterproductive organizational behavior.

Hostility — When an individual is forced to input more information than he or she can handle, he or she may react with hostility toward the source of the new input. The hostility is produced as a reaction to the confusion over what to do with the new information. The resultant hostility will influence the subsequent communication between the sender and the receiver. Counterproductive conflict may result from the hostility.

Withdrawal — Upon the realization that new and potentially threatening information is present in one's cognitive structure, an individual may withdraw from a communication exchange rather than attempt to reconcile the conflict which has been created. When withdrawal, whether it be physical or psychological, occurs the channel between the sender and the receiver is broken.

Tension — Unfamiliar inputs may produce a feeling of uncertainty or uneasiness in the receiver. This may lead to disorientation and frustration. Tension in these circumstances would make it difficult for the receiver to concentrate on the rest of the sender's message.

The negative aspects of overload are understandable in light of people's attempts to control their environment. When a person is not in control, he or she may become threatened or upset. Overload, when not corrected, becomes a major blockage to successful communication. Some steps to correct overload and improve listening behavior will be presented.

Improving Listening for Recall. Over the past twenty years, Nichols (1961) has been concerned with teaching people to improve their listening skills. His guides are presented in the outline below. From the outline, you should be able to observe that listening requires hard work and the kind of concentration that few of us are willing to give. Listening involves a commitment to communication because there are no short cuts to improving listening skills.

NICHOLS' GUIDE TO LISTENING

(1) *Find Areas of Agreement*

Often when listening, we tend to "turn off" a speaker after the first sentence if we find him or her dull. This guide suggests that the listener should attempt to find areas of common interest, even if he or she finds the topic dry.

(2) *Judge Content, Not Delivery*

People tend to judge a speaker's content by his or her personality or the appeal of his or her delivery. This guide recommends concentrating on the content of the speaker's message.

(3) *Hold Your Fire*

The tendency is for a listener to find areas of agreement or disagreement after the speaker's first few words, and then spend the rest of the time mentally supporting or attacking the speaker. This guide posits that the listener should hear the speaker out before making an evaluation of him or her.

(4) *Listen for Ideas*

There is a major difference between the speaker's main ideas and the materials (or facts) which he or she uses to support those main ideas. Unfortunately, sometimes people only hear the supporting material and entirely miss the central ideas. This guide argues that a good listener should concentrate on ideas.

(5) *Be Flexible*

Note taking sometimes helps the individual become a good listener. However, since all messages are different, this guide suggests that the technique of note taking should be adjusted to the particular communication situation.

(6) *Work At Listening*

Bad listeners tend not to expend much energy at listening. This guide recommends devoting full attention to listening.

(7) *Resist Distractions*

The poor listener is one who is bothered easily by outside distractions, while the good listener can tolerate even the worst physical surroundings for communication. This guide advises the good listener to fight distractions.

(8) *Exercise Your Mind*

Some listeners are inexperienced in dealing with difficult, expository material. Good listeners, on the other hand, relish the challenge of this type of material. This guide proposes mind exercises to develop experience in handling difficult material.

(9) *Keep Your Mind Open*

Some people have psychological "blind spots" which prevent them from perceiving and understanding some emotional concepts. This guide argues that the good listener will bring a level of objectivity to his or her listening behavior.

(10) *Capitalize on Thought Speed*

Since thinking is a much faster process than talking, we should have "spare time" as we listen to someone. This guide suggests that the listener should use this time to anticipate what a speaker is going to say, summarize what the speaker has said, question the speaker's evidence, and listen between the lines.*

Listening and Organizational Codes. In large organizations, codes are often present which allow the communication process to be shortened. Instead of a project to design and build a new supersonic transport, the job becomes "Project A." The electrical engineer's title is reduced to simply "EE." The codes are designed to allow the organization to structure many diverse potential inputs into manageable forms. However, serious problems result when all parties to an exchange are not familiar with the code. One cannot communicate about Project A unless he or she knows what the project is all about. These codes are often neglected during training programs for new employees.

Codes and the climate — The climate of the organization, in terms of listening behavior, is extremely important. It must be such to allow the individual to ask and have answered all relevant questions which enable him or her to break organiza-

---

*Adapted from Ralph G. Nichols, "Do We Know How to Listen? Practical Helps in a Modern Age," *Speech Teacher* 10, no. 2 (March 1961). Used by permission.

tional codes. Information, on which codes are based, must be available to the individual. Codes, which remain unbreakable, become a serious roadblock to effective communication.

In concluding this section, we should mention that the ability to process and utilize appropriate information is an important method for assimilating new members into the organization. As new members learn the language (codes) of the organization, they can then become productive.

Listening Behavior for Understanding

There is a different, but still very important, kind of listening behavior for organizational members. Kelly (1974) defined this listening as occurring:

> . . . when the person participates in the spirit or feeling of his environment as a communication receiver. This does not suggest that the listener is uncritical or always in agreement with what is communicated, but rather, that his primary interest is to become fully and accurately aware of what is going on.*

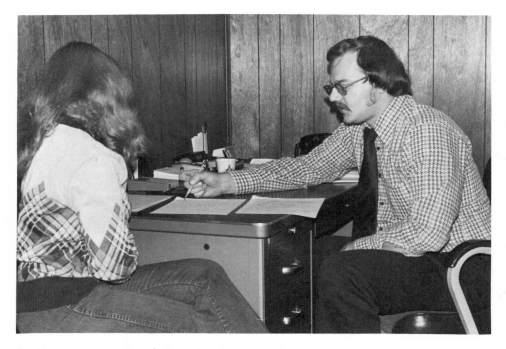

In his attempt to distinguish what he called listening as a *critic* and listening as a *receiver*, Kelly developed the model reproduced in figure 14–1. The model suggests that the receiver must attempt to *understand* what the sender is saying and be willing to take part in the communication exchange as an active participant. Kelly describes empathic listening as follows:

> The differences between empathic listening and deliberative listening are primarily motivational. Both listeners seek the same objective: accurate under-

---

*Charles M. Kelly, "Empathic Listening," in *Small Group Communication: A Reader,* ed. R.S. Cathcart et al. (Dubuque, Iowa: Wm. C. Brown, 1974), p. 341. Used by permission of the author.

standing of the communication from another. The model suggests that the motivation to receive information is superior to the motivation to use critical skills. The empathic listener lets his understanding of the speaker determine his modes of evaluation, which are automatic; the deliberative listener's understanding of the speaker is filtered through his predetermined modes of selective listening, and actually spends less time as a communication receiver. The empathic listener is more apt to be a consistent listener, and is less prone to his own or other distractions. This theory is correct, only if the assumption is true that persons can and do think critically without deliberate effort — *while listening.* (Of course, if persons do not make the effort to listen *per se,* little or no understanding will occur.) *

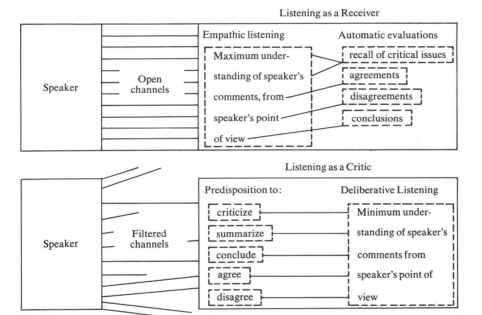

Source: Charles M. Kelly, "Empathic Listening," in *Small Group Communication: A Reader,* ed. R.S. Cathcart et al. (Dubuque, Iowa: Wm. C. Brown, 1974), p. 341. Used by permission of the author.

Figure 14–1   Kelly Model of the Listening Process

The essential differences between the two types of listening behavior are illustrated by the following situations.

LISTENING AS CRITIC

Supervisor (A): (walking by the subordinate) "What's wrong with you today?"

Subordinate (B): (stopping from work at his machine) "Oh, I don't know. Not feeling too well, I guess."

A: (walking on by) "Well, whatever's wrong, you better get it straightened out. Your work quota is really down."

---

*Ibid. Used by permission of the author.

LISTENING FOR UNDERSTANDING

A: (walking up to his subordinate at the machine) "Hey, how ya doin' today?"

B: (turning to A) "Oh, just fair."

A: (stopping and giving his undivided attention) "What's the problem? Anything I can do?"

B: "I've been having some trouble with my back and I didn't get much sleep last night."

A: "Do you want to go up and have the company nurse look at your back?"

B: "No, I'm planning to see my doctor tomorrow and he'll probably have to x-ray it."

A: (putting his hand on B's shoulder) "Look, I know you've been having a lot of back trouble. If it starts giving you too much pain, why don't you go home early today. We can cover for you. O.K.?"

B: "Thanks."

A: "Listen, keep me posted on how you're feeling, all right?"

It is clear in the second situation that the supervisor is willing to participate in the communication exchange with his subordinate. In this way, he appears to be expressing genuine concern for him. In the first situation, we cannot determine if real communication between the superior and subordinate has taken place.

Listening Behavior and Supervisory Practices. In chapter four, we considered the role of the supervisor and the part which his or her *assumptions* about people play in his or her supervision. One technique which a supervisor may use to become more "people-oriented" is to practice listening for understanding. By appearing actively involved in the communication exchanges with his or her subordinates, the supervisor is able to manifest an interest and regard for them. Rogers (1959) has outlined what he called "elements of a helping relationship" which all deal with listening behavior and have significant implication for the supervisory style of managers. The elements are: (1) understanding of others, (2) sensitivity to others' meaning and feelings, (3) warm interest in others, (4) mutual liking and respect for others, and (5) warm acceptance of others. A recent study by Dunlevy (1973) conducted under the direction of one of the authors found that the degree to which the supervisor practices these principles of listening for understanding was positively related to his or her subordinates' job satisfaction. Or, put another way, subordinates seemed to like their jobs when they perceived that their supervisor was practicing listening for understanding.

Listening Behavior and Nonverbal Communication. Individuals vary greatly in the degree to which they are able to manifest nonverbal involvement in communication exchanges. Yet it is by nonverbal communication that we most easily demonstrate the principles of listening for understanding. If an individual is extremely sincere and genuine in his or her concern for others but maintains an objective "poker face" in his or her interpersonal relationships, he or she will likely be perceived of as uninvolved. Below are some techniques which might be used by the listener to demonstrate personal involvement in the communication exchange.

Eye contact — One of the fundamental principles of good communication is that the listener and sender should establish and maintain a high degree of direct eye contact throughout the communication exchange.

Proximity — A good listener will determine and establish an appropriate distance between himself or herself and the sender. The distance between the two should be close enough to allow verbal communication and good eye contact.

Facial expression — The listener can help the sender "get out" difficult information by displaying a facial expression which demonstrates personal interest and empathy and encourages further interaction.

Verbal punctuation — The listener can facilitate communication by inserting verbal punctuators such as "tell me more," "I see," and "uh huh." These should occur during appropriate points in the exchange and be supported by nonverbal action.

Positive evaluation — While listening, the individual should be careful to keep his or her nonverbal evaluations positive to insure that the channel of communication remains open. A frown or other obviously negative nonverbal cue may block further communication.

Communication Perception

Once we receive input through our listening behavior, we must then manage it. The process of managing input is referred to as *perception*. Patton and Griffin (1974) explained:

> The first step in communicating with another person is to form some impression of him/her. This impression directs our reactions to that person and thus influences the course of our interpersonal communication. This process of forming impressions of others and making judgments about them we have labeled interpersonal perception; our characteristic responses to people are our orientations. (p. 157)

In our interpersonal communication, we are continually making evaluations of other people. People are selected for jobs and important work assignments on the basis of what is sometimes the briefest personal encounter. The ability to draw first impressions, which later tend to be substantiated through further interaction, is an important interpersonal skill.

In his book on human communication, Berlo (1960) suggested that we receive communication inputs through our hearing, smelling, seeing, touching, and tasting. Perception involves taking these inputs and making an accurate evaluation of their importance. Perceptual skills vary widely among individuals. When cast into the same interpersonal situation, it would be very unlikely for two individuals to perceive the same details of the situation. In courtrooms, two purported "eyewitnesses" to the same event are likely to present conflicting reports on what took place. Most of us make our evaluations in interpersonal communication based upon our own unique *value sets*. Since we have very different value sets, it is inevitable that we will perceive events differently.

Patton and Giffin have suggested that the human perception process can be examined in two distinct stages: (1) people *recode* various information inputs which they receive into some form which can be managed by the human brain, and (2) after recoding, people use the data to predict the future to enable them to minimize surprise. Within the organization, there are a wide variety of potential stimuli. In order to deal with the complex environment, the individual will process those inputs which he or she values as important to him or her. As we have argued in the previous chapter on climate, each person perceives the elements of his or her organization's climate differently. Generally, this perception will be based on (1) the amount and type of inputs available and (2) how the person recodes those inputs.

Some Common Perception Errors.   Most of us are so actively engaged in perception behavior that we are unaware that it is even taking place. By examining some of the most common errors in perception, we may be able to better understand how our perceptual skills work.

Selectivity — It is almost a truism that people see what they want to see in a given situation. People have a natural tendency to want to maintain a state of psychological balance (Festinger 1957). When a person perceives a stimulus which causes him or her to be uncomfortable or uneasy, he or she will stop perceiving that stimulus, disassociate the stimulus with what makes him or her uncomfortable, or change his or her negative attitude about it. In the organization, a highly cohesive work group occasionally may perceive only the good things about its labor union while processing only negative inputs about management. When left uncorrected, selectivity may lead to counterproductive conflict as different factions perceive different aspects of the same situation differently.

Stereotyping — Because it takes less effort, some people tend to perceive others in terms of the role they *think* that the other person plays. It is easier to have a set of predetermined evaluations for the role "boss" since one does not have to get to know each boss to evaluate. Stereotyping is often apparent in people's reactions to individuals of a particular occupational class. For example, we may have stereotypes built up for such roles as "IRS agent," "minister," or "housewife." Yet the conclusion should be obvious: *each person is unique and should be reacted to as such.*

Abstracting — Rarely does a person have infinite knowledge about a particular subject. But some people have difficulty distinguishing between what they *think* to be true and what they *know* to be true. We *abstract* details in every situation. Our collectives of abstractions constitute our *inferences* about the situation. There is a major difference between an inference, a set of inputs which we *think to be true,* and a fact, a set of inputs which we *know to be true.* Some people *know* they are right in a given situation instead of thinking that they *may* be right.*

These three types of errors in perception can work to cause difficulties as we encounter new communication situations. By realizing that we do perceive uniquely, we leave room for the possibility that our perception of reality may not, in fact, accurately reflect such reality.

Group Awareness

It might be argued that group awareness skills are misplaced in this part devoted to the receiver. However, successful participation as a member of small groups comes from the utilization of the skills considered previously, and as such, group awareness has been included in this part focusing on message receiving.

The old slogan, "two heads are better than one," describes much of the decision making practiced in contemporary organizations. One study of decision-making practices concluded that today's younger managers are increasingly willing to allow their subordinates to participate in the making of the decisions which affect them (Ewing 1971). Organizations have adopted such decision-making models as task forces, executive committees, and organizational families.† The movement for wider distribution of decision making appears solidly grounded in theory and research. Research in the area of small groups has found that people tend to accept a decision and implement it, if they have had the opportunity to participate in making it. We assume that groups make high-quality decisions since four or five (or even more) people, with information about a particular problem, possess more inputs on which to base that decision than does any single individual. A negative "trade-off" is that group decision making takes more time than does individual decision making (Maier 1963; Vroom 1968).

Small groups can be studied from many perspectives and all of these cannot be treated in this section. Instead, we shall consider three general approaches to small

---

*These are only three of numerous perception errors which may hamper organizational communication. A group of scholars called General Semanticists have developed a body of principles which deal with the relationship between perception and behavior. For a thorough treatment of perception in the organization, as well as the role of general semantics in organizational communication, see W.V. Haney, *Communication and Organizational Behavior* (Chicago: Irwin, 1973), Part III.

†For a comprehensive treatment of the wide variety of group decision-making models, including the organizational family, see W.L. French and C.H. Bell, *Organizational Development* (Englewood Cliffs, N.J.: Prentice-Hall, 1974).

groups: (1) interactional, (2) situational, and (3) structural. Our focus here will be on the identification of those facets of each approach which help small groups work to facilitate organizational communication.

Interactional. This approach suggests that groups can be analyzed on the basis of what members say during group discussions. A precondition of success in any small group is that a satisfactory level of communication among participants must be achieved. Some important group theorists have developed systems for analyzing this interaction process (Benne and Sheats 1948; Bales 1970). Probably the best of these was developed by Benne and Sheats and has been summarized in the outline below. A *process-observer* can use this system to analyze each interaction which occurs in a group discussion. The assumption on which the system is based is that groups which have more task and maintenance than self-centered interactions will be successful. It is important for the listener to be a sharp perceiver of his or her group's interaction pattern to determine the type of input which is needed at a particular time.

BENNE AND SHEATS GROUP ROLES

Group Task Functions

(1) *Idea initiation:* proposing new ideas, new goals, possible solutions.

(2) *Information seeking:* asking for facts, clarification of information from other members, or suggesting that information is needed.

(3) *Information giving:* offering facts and information, personal experiences and evidence that are pertinent to the group purpose.

(4) *Opinion seeking:* asking for convictions, opinions, beliefs, values, and judgments of others.

(5) *Opinion giving:* stating own belief, opinion, judgment, value or conviction.

(6) *Elaborating:* developing an idea expressed previously, explaining, clarifying with examples, illustrations and explanations.

(7) *Coordinating:* developing, describing or clarifying relationships among facts, ideas, and suggestions, or suggesting an integration of ideas.

(8) *Orienting:* clarifying purpose or goal of group, defining position of group in relation to its task, suggesting direction for the discussion to take, suggesting procedures for the group to follow.

(9) *Energizing:* prodding the group to greater activity, stimulating activity, reminding of importance of task or time available.

(10) *Recording:* keeping written records on paper or chalkboard, serving as group memory, preparing reports and minutes of meetings.

Group Maintenance Functions

(1) *Supporting:* agreeing, praising, indicating warmth and solidarity with others.

(2) *Harmonizing:* mediating differences between others, finding common ground of values or beliefs, reconciling disagreements, conciliating, suggesting compromises.

(3) *Tension relieving:* joking and pointing out humor in a situation that relieves tensions among members, reducing formality and status differences, putting others at ease.

(4) *Gatekeeping:* encouraging others to speak, stopping the overly talkative and dominating from interrupting or blocking others from speaking, opening channels of communication.

(5) *Norming:* suggesting standards of behavior for members, challenging unproductive ways of behaving in a group, "punishing" behaviors which violate group rules of conduct.

Self-Centered Functions

(1) *Blocking:* preventing progress toward group goals by constantly raising objections, repeatedly bringing up the same topic or issue after the group has considered and rejected it.

(2) *Attacking:* attacking the competence of another, name-calling, downgrading the motive of another instead of describing own feelings, joking at expense of another, attempting to destroy "face" of another.

(3) *Recognition seeking:* boasting, calling attention to one's own experience when it is not necessary to establish credibility or relevant to group task, relating irrelevant experiences, game-playing to elicit sympathy or pity.

(4) *Horseplaying:* making tangential jokes, engaging in horseplay that takes the group away from serious work or maintenance behavior.

(5) *Dominating:* giving orders, interrupting and cutting off, flattering to get own way, insisting on own way.

(6) *Advocating:* playing the advocate for the interests of a different group, thus acting as its representative, apologist, or advocate counter to the best interests or consensus of the current group.*

In the case of managerial leadership, it is imperative for the discussion leader, generally the supervisor, to be able to recognize self-oriented interactions emitted by members of the work group as they occur. He or she can deal with these by (1) attempting to provide the necessary maintenance interactions or (2) encouraging and training his or her subordinates to provide the maintenance interactions. It should be obvious that from the viewpoint of the future growth of the organization, the second managerial behavior has great appeal.

Situational. The second approach suggests that each group needs to be analyzed on the basis of its own leadership style, agenda, rules, and standards. In that each group is unique, its reaction to a particular situation is extremely significant. Often individuals go into the group discussion with pre-established purposes and goals, only to discover that they were unable to accomplish them. What results are feelings of hostility and conflict on the part of the participants because they perceive that they have failed in their cause. Groups, in their normal patterns of communication,

---

*Adapted from John D. Brilhart, *Effective Group Discussion*, 2d ed. (Dubuque, Iowa: Wm. C. Brown, 1974), pp. 22-23. Used by permission.

tend to modify the preconceived purposes held by individuals. To counter this tendency, the situational approach suggests that the group has the ability to decide what it is going to accomplish *during a particular meeting*. One group meeting may be devoted to a discussion of policies or facts and the next may be given over to a discussion of implementation. But the decision as to the appropriate course of action is up to the group.

The variable of leadership style in a group may illustrate how the situation approach can work. At a given time, based upon the group's goals, a particular group may work best under an *autocratic* leadership style in which one or two members direct the behavior of other members. A different group may function best under a *democratic* style characterized by all members having an equal say in what action is to be taken. Not only do groups differ, but within the same group, situations may arise where the style of leadership may change from one time period to the next. But the decision about leadership style, as well as other group variables, is made by the group based on the requirements of the particular situation.

Structural.   This approach suggests that a group can be analyzed by means of the pattern it uses for solving problems. Beginning with the work of John Dewey (1910), group theorists have suggested particular *structures*, or typologies, which can be used by groups to solve problems. Typologies have been offered which can be "plugged into" just about any group problem-solving situation. Phillips (1973) has called these various typologies "standard agendas" because they are capable of being generalized to any group situation. Brilhart (1974) considers these typologies as *maps* which can overcome the obstacles faced by the group in solving a problem. He explains:

> Every problem can be analyzed into three basic components: a present situation, a goal, and some obstacles to the goal. Problem solving is the process by which we find a way to remove or get around the obstacles. A goal to which there are no obstacles is not a problem. Members of a group who have different goals cannot engage in problem solving until they first agree on the goal to be achieved. So a cooperative group must first agree on what the discussants hope to achieve, then understand where they are at present in relation to that goal and what obstacles lie between them and the goal. A solution question leads to looking at a means before the obstacles have been fully mapped out; effective solutions are those which overcome real obstacles which the group has power to do something about.*

In this passage, Brilhart argued that a group must first reach some agreement about its goal and then begin to select a pattern of interaction which will allow it to overcome obstacles to its reaching its goal.

The oldest and perhaps still the best of these structures was developed by Dewey (1910). He assumed that there were chronological stages to solving problems in groups:

Felt need — The group shows some recognition that there is something not quite right in a particular situation.

---

*J.D. Brilhart, *Effective Group Discussion*, 2d ed. (Dubuque, Iowa: Wm. C. Brown, 1974), pp. 105-6. Used by permission of the publisher.

Definition of the problem — The group makes some attempt to determine and identify the source of the difficulty.

Suggestions for possible alternative solutions — A full consideration is given to all possible alternatives which might solve the problem as it has been defined after appropriate data have been gathered.

Selection of best alternative—Agreement among group members is reached as to which solution is best.

Evaluation of solution selected — Continual evaluation and review is undertaken to examine the effects of the solution selected.

After analyzing the interactions of various groups, Bales and Strodtbeck (1950) suggested that Dewey's chronological structure may be reduced to just three steps: (1) *orientation*, involving giving information, orientation behavior, and repetition; (2) *evaluation*, involving giving and seeking opinions, evaluation, and analysis; and (3) *control*, involving action and expressing levels of agreement and disagreement.

Other Typologies.　There have been attempts to develop other structures for group problem solving. Of these, two have come into widespread use in the organization.

PERT

Phillips (1973) has suggested that PERT (program review and evaluation technique) can be used to work out complexities in problem solving. PERT helps groups specify the details of schedules, time requirements, resources and personnel. It offers a number of chronological steps which the group can follow to insure problem solution. The major advantage in using a system such as PERT is that it allows the group to make some attempt to prepare plans for a variety of contingencies.

Delphi

The Delphi is a problem-solving structure which attempts to minimize potential interpersonal biases which may be present in face-to-face communication. There are five steps in the process: (1) group members state *in writing* their opinions about the problem and possible solutions, (2) results are tabulated and sent to all members, (3) members who do not agree with the majority are asked to state in writing their objections, (4) after all members have read the minority report, they are asked to state their opinions again independently, and (5) summaries are sent again to all members and deviant members are again asked to state their objections.

The various structures which have been considered in this section are designed to produce quality problem solving. In each structure, the emphasis is on the *typology* and not on the *individual* group members who must implement the structure. The structure does provide a seemingly logical approach to group interaction. However, since the implementation of the typology is left up to the individual interactants, the success will depend on how well they are aware of it and on how committed they are to using it.

Sender Skills in Interpersonal Communication

Communication involves both sending and receiving messages, and the individual can be an effective communicator only if he or she can do both. In this part, we will consider three kinds of message-sending skills: (1) dyadic, (2) presentational, and (3) writing.

Dyadic Skills

Dyadic skills enable the individual to interact effectively in groups of twos and threes. An important type of dyadic skill involves the ability to conduct interviews. The interview is a *dyadic exchange where at least one of the participants has a preconceived purpose for the exchange* (Goyer et al. 1963; Stewart and Cash, 1974). Most dyadic exchanges in the organization tend to be interviews, since routinely one decides to interact with another for a *reason.*

Elements of Successful Interviewing. Because the interview is used widely for a variety of purposes in the organization (e.g. employment, appraisal, training, termination), it would be appropriate to examine some of the *abilities* which produce successful interviews.

Ability to put the other person(s) at ease — The sender's effectiveness in the dyad depends on his or her skill at systematically evoking meaning in the person(s) with whom he or she talks. Since communication occurs most readily in contexts which are free of distraction, the physical surroundings of the interview are very important. If the assembly-line foreman is forced to reprimand one of his or her workers for poor productivity, the roar of the machines and the knowing stares of other workers make the worker station an unacceptable location for an interview. These elements would work to make both the interviewer and the interviewee uncomfortable. It is the responsibility of the sender to select a physical location which is conducive to interaction. Of course, in the organization, this may not always be achievable, but it is a goal which should be maintained. Before the sender begins the interview, it may be appropriate to engage in some rapport-building communication, unrelated to the specific purpose of the interview. A brief discussion of an upcoming sports event or the weather may reduce uncertainty for the interviewee. If the receiver knows beforehand how long the interview is going to take, one possible source of uncertainty has already been removed.

Ability to conduct a systematic interview — Since the major responsibility for the flow of the interview rests with the sender, he or she needs to maintain an appropriate level of control. This control allows the interview to proceed in some systematic fashion. Some degree of spontaneous and tension-relieving communication should be encouraged; however, good dyadic communication requires reasonable adherence to the goals of the interview. The sender can establish a level of moderate progress which will allow him or her to proceed through his or her prepared interview format.

Ability to ask insightful questions — At the heart of successful interviewing is the talent for asking good questions. The interview rises or falls on the sender's use of nonthreatening inquiry. Many managers are unable to obtain accurate information from their subordinates because they have never mastered the skill necessary in formulating penetrating questions.* There are many kinds of questions which can

---

*Among other types of questions are the funnel, the mirror, the leading, and the loaded. For a thorough treatment of the use of questions and questioning techniques in the interview, see C.J. Stewart and W.C. Cash, *Interviewing Principles and Practices* (Dubuque, Iowa: W.C. Brown, 1974).

be used in the interview, but we would like to examine briefly one approach, *open* versus *closed*. An *open* question is one which broadens the range of response for the receiver while a *closed* question narrows the alternatives. For example, the question, "How do you feel today?" provides a wide range of possible responses. In contrast, a question such as "Do you drink beer?" provides only for three or four possible responses. Both kinds of questions have their place in an interview. As a rule, however, there is increased likelihood of spontaneous communication being achieved between the sender and receiver if the interviewer asks good open questions.

Ability to summarize — Two people can sit through the same interview and each may have entirely different perceptions of what went on. Accurate summaries by the interviewer before the session adjourns will help reduce the likelihood of completely unrelated perceptions. Although there will always be some disagreement on the content of any communication situation, the summary does help mutual understanding.

The interview and other forms of dyadic exchanges are a major type of oral communication in the organization. The perceptive dyadic communicator will consider the effect that his or her interviewing will have upon receivers. He or she should be able to develop a dyadic style which focuses upon the needs of those receivers.

Presentational Skills

In organizations, information is often passed by means of the public oral presentation. These presentations may take various forms ranging from the weekly meeting between the first-line supervisor and his or her hourly employees to the annual address by the company president to the board of directors. Although there are inherent problems such as low attention and retention by the receivers, the oral presentation still serves as an important channel for transmitted information to organizational members. The oral presentation is also used by officials in speaking to various audiences "outside" the organization for public relations. Although this section is not intended to be a treatise on public communication, we shall examine the oral presentation to gain a perspective as to how it fits into the organizational communication system.

What Is Said. Generally, the *message* to be communicated should determine the *channel*. When the content is fairly straightforward, is relevant to most of the members of the audience, and the need exists to communicate rapidly, the public presentation can be used quite effectively. The content should be general enough *not* to require complete mastery by the audience. Other channels such as the interview may be called for when we want to insure the complete internalization of our message by the audience. In terms of what is said, two important considerations should prevail.

Audience analysis — The sender, in this case, the public communicator, has the responsibility to consider the attitudes, beliefs, and personal orientations of his or her audience before he or she decides what to say. It is common in American industry for costly standardized training programs to be developed with little attention given to the needs of the specific group to which it is being directed. The composition of audiences differ widely. Some public communicators fall into the trap of reading standard notices from company headquarters to subordinates during group meetings. After listening to a number of such "speeches" most members would be expected to be turned off because the information is not particularly relevant to them. The content of standard notices must be related to the specific audience facing the communicator if a high level of interest is to be obtained.

Credibility — The concept of credibility, or trust, has been considered in the previous chapter on climate. But the personal credibility of the public communicator will determine whether or not he or she will be believed. Research on credibility (Hovland et al. 1953; Andersen and Clevenger 1963; Giffin 1967a) has found that the audience will tend to believe speakers who are perceived, by the audience, as trustworthy. The supervisor who is not trusted will not make an effective public communicator because his or her subordinates will be unable to disassociate even the most believable message from the mistrusted source.

Content for oral presentations should be selected on the basis of the level of understanding and knowledge of the audience. Since many oral presentations in the organization may be quite technical, the speaker should be aware of the technical capability of the audience. This capability should govern the speaker in his or her selection of materials for presentation and his or her treatment of the subject.

How It Is Said. It is rare to find a polished orator on the supervisory staff of the typical organization, but one does not have to be an orator to be effective as a public communicator. Instead, if the speaker sincerely attempts to communicate with his or her audience, within its level of understanding, he or she should have some success. To judge the effectiveness of the oral presentation, two important elements should be considered.

Delivery — The unsophisticated audience is sometimes swayed by how a communicator sounds instead of by what he or she says. In the organizational context the delivery which is relaxed and conversational will be appropriate for most audiences.

Organization — Since the threat of miscommunication is always present in the public presentation, the sender should attempt to structure his or her ideas as clearly as possible. The public presentation should be organized with the needs and expectations of the audience in mind.

Writing Skills

As organizations become more bureaucratic, there is a tendency on the part of members *to write everything down*. The memorandum, a written message for distribution internally within the organization, has become a widely used communication channel. Since most organizations maintain elaborate filing and record-keeping systems, many written documents have to be written in triplicate. Purportedly, the vast record-keeping procedures enable the organization to reduce uncertainty and control its environment. The procedures do help in this regard, but there are some negative aspects to them. Many corporation executives, college administrators and professors, and governmental officials complain about not having enough time to keep up with the reading required by their jobs. The phrase, "I sent you a memo on that," makes it easy to assume that communication has taken place, when in fact it has not. The memo can only communicate if it has been read. Townsend (1970), in his humorous look at American organizational life, *Up the Organization*, wrote the memo shown on page 250.

If the memorandum is going to continue to be with us (and the evidence is over-whelming that it will be), it should reflect good writing skills. Often the writer does not give adequate attention to the memo he or she is writing in terms of the *receiver who will eventually be reading it*. Some writers feel that the more verbose and elaborate their writing style, the better. But such is *not* the case in the organization. Good memoranda are those which are clear, concise, straightforward, easily under-stood, and free of unnecessary words.

Summary

This chapter has considered important interpersonal skills which can be used by members to influence organizational communication. Four types of message-receiving skills—(1) listening for recall, (2) listening for understanding, (3) percep-tion, and (4) group awareness—were investigated as they help improve organizational communication. Three message-receiving skills—(1) dyadic, (2) presentational, and (3) writing—were also treated.

MEMORANDUM

Use them for dissemination of noncontroversial
information. Write them to yourself or organize
your thoughts. But keep in mind that a memo is
really a one-way street. There's no way to
reply to it in real-time, or to engage it in a
dialogue. Murder-by-memo is an acceptable crime
in large organizations, and a zealous user of
the Xerox machine can copy down dozens of
otherwise productive people. The small company
cannot survive such civil war games.

When two of your departments or divisions start
arguing by memo and copying you, call them in and
make them swear never to write another memo on
that subject. Then listen to both sides and if
they won't work it out then and there, decide it.
When the conflict between the State and Defense
departments was at its peak, it was rumored that
20 percent of the employees of each department
were there just to throw memo grenades at each
other.

Memos and all other documents should always bear
dates and initials. One of my colleagues once
spent a twelve-hour night working on an undated
document which turned out not to be the current
draft. Why he was not convicted of mayhem
remains a mystery.

If I were ever again sentenced to run a bank, I
promise you one of my first official acts would
be to write a memorandum to everybody, beginning,
"This is the last memorandum...".

SOURCE: From *Up the Organization,* by Robert Townsend, pp. 110-11. Copyright © 1970 by Robert Townsend. Reprinted by permission of Alfred A. Knopf, Inc.

REVIEW AND DISCUSSION

1. Can you provide some examples of where overload hampers organizational communication? What can be done to prevent overload in the organization?

2. Discuss essential similarities and differences between the two types of listening behavior considered in this chapter. Under what conditions would each skill be important in the organization?

3. Provide examples of perception behavior in the organization. Explain how perception skills can help improve organizational communication.

4. Consider the three approaches to small groups presented in this chapter. Under what conditions in the organization would each approach be important? Are there additional approaches to small groups? Identify them.

5. Why are dyadic skills important to organizational communication? Think of some situations, in the organization, where the interview might be used.

6. What are presentational skills? What important elements lead to successful oral presentations? Under what conditions might an organizational member use an oral presentation?

7. If too many memoranda are sent in the organization, what communication problems might result? What are some things which can be done to cut down on the use of the memorandum in the organization?

Incidents

The Youth Group

Terri Linden was elected president of the Youth Group of the First Community Church of Mayfield. The youth group normally meets on Monday evenings through the school year. About forty-five high-school students attend the weekly meetings. There are two major projects for the youth group this year. During last year's election, the group decided to raise money for Christmas presents for underprivileged children in Mayfield. The other project involves a variety of programs to sponsor scholarships to send developmentally disabled children to summer camp. In campaigning for the presidency of the youth group, Terri supported each of the projects in discussions with other youth group members.

Within the youth group at First Community, and among her friends at Mayfield High, Terri is well liked and seems to have many friends. She was also a candidate for office at school. Terri lost the race for student body vice-president by only 14 votes (of nearly 400 votes cast). Terri has been dating Clint Zimmer for the last three months. Clint attends First Community youth group and supported Terri in both of her candidacies.

Over the past few months, Terri has been so involved in school activities that she has not devoted very much time to youth group activities. One night she received a telephone call from Art Karlin, adult sponsor of the youth group. "Terri, I'm a little concerned about the youth group program. It's already October 15 and we don't have more than $20.00 in our treasury. I'm afraid that we are not going to have any money to contribute to the Christmas presents program. Do you have any suggestions?"

"This is a good project. We'll make it, Art," Terri answered confidently. Down inside though, Terri was worried about the youth group. The next night, she called Clint to talk over the situation with him.

"Clint, I'm worried about the youth group. We don't have much money and I'm not sure how hard the kids want to work between now and Christmas," she told him.

"Terri, I think that we can get the contributions from local merchants. After all, this is a worthy cause," he tried to reassure her.

The next week, Terri called the executive committee of the youth group together. "We must get the kids on the ball. We have to get going with fund-raising activities. How about a car wash? I'll appoint a committee of Karen Brownley and Rob Atwood to look into projects which might raise money. You guys report the results to me by Monday."

Over the next two weeks, Terri rushed around to youth group members to ask them to get going on the fund-raising project. She did not meet with much enthusiasm among the members with whom she talked. "Look, I'm busy with my school work and I just don't have the time to devote to the youth work program," one member told Terri during one of these meetings. "You should have started the planning earlier. I'm not even sure that the younger members of the group even know what the money-raising projects are. All we do during meetings is talk about social activities. We never talk about money-raising projects."

This attitude startled Terri. She felt that she had a good deal of support among members. "I thought all I had to do was ask the members to work on the projects and they would. Now, I don't know what to do. Here we are in October and we don't have any money. I'm so discouraged," Terri told Clint one evening.

During the next Monday's meeting, Karen and Rob came back with a report. They concluded that the best idea would be to approach members of the church for funds. They also said that a drive to do odd jobs for people in the community would probably raise enough money to buy some presents for needy children.

"I don't like those suggestions much. I don't think that either of those will work. Besides, going to the congregation for money would be embarrassing our youth group. The executive committee just isn't doing a good job at coming up with ideas. I'm going to have to go to the membership of the entire youth group. I think that maybe they will come up with some other suggestions. I don't know why, but we are failing. We just have to go out and do something. Let's get going. We just can't sit here and flounder between now and Christmas," Terri said at the close of the executive committee meeting.

Rob was discouraged. "What do you want us to do?"

"I don't know," Terri answered.

Guidelines for Analysis

1. Using the elements of the organizational communication system detailed in this part, analyze the communication within the youth group of the First Community Church. What were its strengths? Its weaknesses?

2. If you had been a member of the youth group, what would your view have been of the climate within the organization? Why?

3. What is your opinion of the formal communication subsystem within the youth group? Why?

4. In terms of those communication skills presented in this part, how would you have characterized the skills demonstrated by Terri? What type of skills should she have demonstrated?

5. Speculate about what you think happened within the youth group. Do you think that they raised enough money for the projects? Why or why not?

6. List five things that the youth group should have done to insure the success of their projects. Explain how you think the things which you have suggested would have helped.

7. In terms of earlier chapters related to assumptions and leader behavior, how would you characterize Terri's leader behavior? Do you think that her behavior influenced communication within the youth group?

8. What behavior would you have expected from the members of the youth group? Would this behavior have been productive or counterproductive to the groups goals? Why?

The Silent Supervisor

Frank Caufield, business manager of the Carlton Chemical Company, has eaten lunch alone in his office every day for the twelve years he has been with the company. Donna James, the bookkeeper, and George Lloyd, the assistant treasurer, have both become accustomed to his closed door and lack of social conversation during their tenure of eight years at the company. They generally eat in the lunchroom with the other employees or go out to a local restaurant together. When Kay Anderson was hired as the business secretary six months ago, George and Donna told her about Frank's habit of "isolation." They also told her that he was not one of the friendliest members of the company. Although everyone in the company recognizes Frank's nature, they also recognize that he is a competent, hard-working man. He is generally working during lunch or keeping up on company activities by reading the house organ or incoming memoranda. During regular working hours, he is not prone to chatting around the coffee pot or "shooting the breeze" on the phone like other members of the office.

After her first two months with Carlton, Kay needed a morning off to go to the dentist. She asked George whether he thought Frank would let her take the time.

George responded dryly, "Put an ad in the *Carlton News*. Maybe he'll read it during lunch and put an answer in for you."

Kay decided to try to talk to Frank about it during lunch. She knocked hesitantly on his door while George and Donna watched curiously. Although Frank did not indicate for her to enter, Kay opened the door cautiously and ventured in.

"Mr. Caufield," she said quietly, "I need to ask you something." Frank did not look up from his work but she continued. "I have to go to the dentist next week for my wisdom teeth and I was wondering if I could have Wednesday morning off."

Frank took a sip of his coffee still without looking at Kay. "Two hours," he answered.

Kay thanked Frank and left. Donna and George were especially interested in what had happened. When she told them, Donna laughed and said, "At least he said something. When I first came here I had a question about my job. I asked him once when he was passing through the office and he just ignored me. Then I tried to talk to him about it as we were going to the parking lot. He just got in his car and drove off. Without saying a word! Then, about a week later, I got a memo in my "in" box from him. He answered my question in one sentence. Typewritten!"

George shook his head. "You know, I've worked here for eight years and I've never had a real conversation with that man. Dave's been here for fifteen years and he says when Frank first came here he was fairly nice. But then he got divorced and Dave claims he got turned down for a promotion. Dave thinks he resents that because this job is too easy for him. Not enough of a challenge. I guess he's got a degree and everything and he thinks he's too good to do the same thing for twelve years. Nobody asks him to lunch or dinner any more because he turns everyone down. Since I've been here I've never seen him at the picnic and he always leaves before the Christmas party begins. At first it was hard to work for him, but I've gotten used to his closed-mouth attitude. He's not really mean or anything. He's just . . . ."

Since that time, Kay has wondered how long she can work for someone who is unwilling to discuss anything — even business problems. She likes the job fairly well and the other employees but Frank's behavior clouds the office morale frequently. She feels uncomfortable just taking letters in for him to sign. She also dislikes the way the other employees talk about Frank when he is not around. No one makes any attempt at warming up to Frank and, of course, he never seeks out anyone to talk to. Except for an occasional smile, Frank does not reveal any feelings to his employees. Kay has asked other employees about Frank and she has heard several stories. Most of them confirm George's statements about the divorce and promotion. One coworker revealed that Frank frequently gets pressure "from upstairs" about office efficiency and overspending in his department. But none of these rumors resolve the dissatisfaction that George, Donna, and especially Kay feel.

Guidelines for Analysis

1. In terms of the organizational communication system presented in this part, what is wrong with the communication within the business department of Carlton? What solutions can you offer?

2. What problems are likely to result because of Frank's behavior? Of the problems you have suggested, which are directly attributable to Frank's communication "style"?

3. Do you think it is possible to improve communication within the business department? What steps might you suggest for doing so?

4. Generate a list of terms which describe the climate of the business department. Compare your list with a classmate's list.

5. Is there a difference between the "social" climate in an office and a "work" climate in the same office? How would you characterize the differences in terms of the situation above?

6. To what extent do you think Frank's communication behavior influenced his method of supervision? Can an individual be a poor communicator and still be an effective supervisor? Why?

7. Is it likely that one's personal problems could influence his or her job? Would you say that this was the case in the situation above?

8. Is it likely that a manager's lack of interpersonal skills may influence the climate in an organization? Do you think that this was happening in the situation above? How?

The Ecumenical Committee

The Committee for Ecumenical Brotherhood (CEB) is composed of clergypersons and laypersons in a large city in the Midwest. CEB was founded to promote social justice, fight poverty, and facilitate understanding among religious groups within the city. A board of directors, composed of thirty-two people, elected from religious and community groups, govern CEB. A paid, full-time professional staff of four and three clerical assistants are employed by CEB to do the "work" of the committee. Each of the professional staff is a minister and they represent different denominational backgrounds. Within the community, CEB enjoys an excellent reputation. The committee has been called upon to mediate a conflict between striking teachers and the local school board. When inmates at the state prison erupted recently in a demand for better treatment, CEB was called upon to restore order.

However, in the last few months, CEB seemed to be having trouble accomplishing its tasks. The committee's monthly luncheon meetings have gone hours past their two-hour limits. Meetings have turned into gripe sessions with everyone talking at once. One layman recently complained:

"I have a job to go to. I don't have four hours to give to listening to somebody else's complaints. If I ran my business the way we are running this committee, I'd be broke within a year."

The staff is responsible for setting up the agenda for the meeting but the agenda does not seem to satisfy anyone. The committee members tend to modify and change the agenda at will on meeting days.

A young rabbi, who is new to the committee, was heard saying:

"The staff seems to want to talk about what it wants to talk about at meetings. The staff has to recognize that we want the agenda to represent the committee's priorities instead of the staff's."

Only about fifteen of thirty CEB members have been coming to the last few meetings. Because of the limited participation, the staff has been hesitant to suggest any new programs for the committee. The executive director, the head of the professional staff, made a number of speeches to the committee last month about the lack of progress on such important issues as the reduction of unemployment among the young blacks in the community and the creation of a civilian review board for police actions. The speeches have met with little enthusiasm among committee members. Only ten regular CEB members attended this month's meeting and it had to be dismissed after lunch because of a lack of quorum.

After the disastrous meeting, the executive director called his staff together to talk with them. "We must find out what's on the committee members' minds. We have a real breakdown here. We have to reach the members some way."

Guidelines for Analysis

1. What recommendations do you have for the executive director of CEB?

2. Describe what you think the problem is with CEB. What solutions can you offer to help solve the problems? How would your solutions be implemented?

3. What content from this part would be helpful if you were to try to improve organizational communication within CEB?

4. Characterize the expectations the staff may have of the members of the CEB. Now, characterize the expectations that the CEB members might have of the staff. How are the expectations similar? How are they different? What might be done to bring the expectations together?

5. What procedures or methods would you recommend to help the CEB identify its apparent difficulty? How would you implement these procedures?

6. Assuming you were able to propose a solution to help CEB, to whom would you propose the solution? The committee? The staff? The executive director?

7. What techniques might be helpful in facilitating information transfer between members and staff? Among committee members?

8. Attempt to diagram what you perceive to be the organizational chart of CEB. What are some of the elements of its formal subsystem? What changes might you recommend?

Good Time Charlie

Charles (Charlie) Peterson is the manager of the State Department of Motor Vehicles (DMV) office in Skywae Junction, a city of 62,000 in a southwestern state. Charlie supervises an office of seventeen workers. In all, there are six driver-inspectors, who test license applicants, seven clerk-typists, a business manager, an administrative assistant, an executive secretary, and an assistant branch manager. The task of the branch office is to test and certify drivers and to register automobiles in an eight-county area surrounding Skywae Junction. Normally about 500 people visit the branch weekly. Charlie started in the DMV as a driver-inspector and worked his way up to his present position.

Many people in the community think that Charlie is a "great guy." He is a member of the Rotary Club, the Elks, served as a chairman of the Red Cross Blood Drive, is a member of the board of directors of the United Way, and was appointed by the city council to a vacant seat on the Skywae Junction Recreation Commission. Charlie is a humorous, out-going guy who is often called upon to act as master of ceremonies for community programs in Skywae Junction. He enjoys this very much and never seems to be able to say "no." He is married and has two children who are away at college. His wife is also quite active in community affairs.

With all of Charlie's activities in the community, there have been some problems which have come up recently at the DMV branch. The following conversation took place in the lunchroom one day:

"When I first came here, I really liked Charlie a lot," Dave Stone, a driver-inspector said. "He seemed to care about me and I thought I could talk to him. But I have changed my mind. Now I don't trust him at all. That 'nice guy' facade he wears is phony."

"I went to him about a problem I was having with one of the clerks in the head-quarters at the capital. He smiled and said, 'Janis, I'll look into this right away. Is there anything else wrong?' But I never heard anything about it," Janis Hill, a clerk typist complained. "I went to him again and it was the same old story, big smile and no response."

"He told me that he was going to recommend me for a branch manager's position in the Hamilton office," added Lynn Holstein, another driver-inspector. "I went in to see him about the opening one day. He put his arm around me and told me that I was very qualified. He said he'd call the state personnel director that very afternoon with a recommendation. I submitted my letter of application and my resume. I didn't hear anything from personnel, so I gave them a call about three weeks later. They told me that the opening had been filled and that they never received Charlie's recommendation."

"But Charlie always has that big grin on his face and he's always doing something for the community. It's really hard to be mad at him. Now, I just ignore him if I can," Dave sighed.

In recent weeks, the state headquarters had been putting pressure on the local office to provide detailed reports of local income and expenditures and about the number of citizens who use the branch. Charlie had been through a number of "crackdowns" before so he really did not take it too seriously. He delegated much of the responsibility for submitting the reports to Carolyn Davis, his assistant manager, and Tim Thompson, his administrative assistant.

"Don't worry about these things too much. Just submit a weekly report to the 'bosses.' No big deal," Charlie told Carolyn and Tim on his way out of the office to a committee meeting.

Carolyn and Tim followed Charlie's guidance and submitted the reports as requested. A couple of irregular matters came up in the reports, but when Carolyn tried to talk to Charlie about them, he just said, "Look, you guys are doing a great job. Just go ahead and follow through on this."

About four weeks later, members of the state auditor's office were waiting for Charlie as he came into the office on Monday morning.

"Mr. Peterson, the state auditor thinks he has evidence of criminal mismanagement of this office. Nearly $7,200 has been reported missing by your own report. The auditor is going to seek a complaint from the grand jury in Skywae Junction tomorrow. As of this day, you are suspended from your position, this office is closed and we advise you to find an attorney."

Charlie, visibly shaken, slumped in his chair, "I just don't understand how this could happen to me. All of my employees love me."

Guidelines for Analysis

1. Returning to those interpersonal communication skills considered in this part, which of those skills were lacking in Charlie's behavior?

2. Because of Charlie's communication behavior, what was the climate in the Skywae Junction office?

3. Early on, what could Charlie have done to have prevented the charge of mismanagement?

4. Do you think there is a difference between someone who appears to be sensitive to the needs of his or her employees and someone who actually is sensitive?

5. Make a list of what you consider to be the five things most wrong with the organizational communication system within the Skywae Junction DMV office. How could the things on your list have been prevented?

6. Had one of Charlie's subordinates attempted to warn him of the upcoming problems, what do you think his reaction would have been? Why?

7. Describe Charlie's communication style. What is wrong with that style?

8. Describe your own communication style. What are the strong points of your style? What are the weaknesses?

The Assistant Minister

Rev. Harvey Stockton, thirty-five, is the pastor of the Second Hillsdale Church, in Hillsdale, a city of about 65,000 in an eastern state. Second Hillsdale was founded in 1825 and about 300 families regularly attend Sunday services. Recently Rev. Stockton has been feeling overworked. He took the matter to his church council and they approved the hiring of an assistant minister. Rev. Stockton called some friends and he obtained the name of Rev. Steve Parker as an outstanding candidate for the position. Rev. Parker had finished first in his class at Eastern Theological Seminary and had two years experience as a youth director at a church in Philadelphia. After an initial interview with Rev. Stockton and the church council, he was hired. Both the church council and Rev. Stockton were very careful to indicate to Rev. Parker that his duties would include the church's youth program and parish visitation, along with a monthly assignment to preach in the Sunday morning worship service.

"Rev. Steve is a sincere young man and seems to get along really well with the young people," a parishioner was overheard to remark after Steve had been at the church a few weeks.

Since coming to Second Hillsdale, Rev. Parker has assumed his duties in the youth program and parish visitation with unusual vigor. He seems to be handling both responsibilities quite well. But, Rev. Parker has had some other ideas which he proposed to Rev. Stockton. He suggested that the church start a drug counseling center to combat drug abuse among young people in Hillsdale. Rev. Parker noticed that there was no interdenominational fellowship among ministers, rabbis, and priests in Hillsdale and wrote Rev. Stockton a memorandum requesting permission to organize an interdenominational study group on Monday nights in the church conference hall.

"We need the opportunity, as ministers, to meet and learn about our colleagues from other churches in town. I feel that Second Hillsdale should take the leadership in this program," Rev. Parker wrote in the memorandum.

Rev. Parker's community activities have also come to the attention of the congregation of his church, especially since a news item appeared in yesterday's Hillsdale *Tribune*. The article noted:

"Rev. Steve Parker, Assistant Pastor of Second Hillsdale Church, was elected Vice-President of the Local Women's Equality Caucus, a group founded to insure fair treatment of women in Hillsdale.

"The election of Rev. Parker, at last night's meeting, marked the first time in the group's three-year history that a man has been elected to a leadership position in the organization."

The article included a picture of Rev. Parker and appeared on the first page of the newspaper under the headline "Local Male Minister Elected Officer in Women's Group."

Since the article appeared, Rev. Stockton has received eight telephone calls from parishioners about the participation of Rev. Parker in the Caucus. Two of the members who called own industries which have received complaints from the Caucus about their treatment of their women employees.

"Steve is a terrific guy and we're lucky to have him. But he appears to have stepped out of his designated areas of responsibility at the church," Rev. Stockton told the president of the church council, one of the callers.

The president suggested to Rev. Stockton that he have a talk with Rev. Parker to find out why he felt it necessary to be so active in Hillsdale, after only a few weeks in town.

Rev. Stockton did not like limiting the activities of his assistant but he recognized that Rev. Parker's visibility in Hillsdale was causing some concern within the flock.

He suggested to Steve at a morning devotional that they go out to lunch the next day to talk about "some church reaction to the recent article in the *Tribune.*"

"Yes, wasn't that great coverage of our caucus meeting? I really feel good about my election. I bet the church is pretty excited about the publicity. Sure, I'm free around 12:30 tomorrow. Shall we go over to the Hillsdale cafe?"

"Okay," Rev. Stockton replied, not looking forward to the luncheon meeting the next day.

Guidelines for Analysis

1. What do you think transpired at the luncheon meeting the next day?

2. Discuss what you think Rev. Stockton might have said at the meeting. What was Rev. Parker's probable reaction?

3. Use the material presented in this part related to superior-subordinate communication to analyze the interaction between Rev. Stockton and Rev. Parker.

4. Characterize the supervision style of Rev. Stockton. Would you say that he placed narrow or wide parameters around Rev. Parker's behavior?

5. What terms might be used to describe the climate within the Second Hillsdale Church?

6. If you were in Rev. Parker's position, would you have felt challenged in your job? Why?

7. What role do you think the president of the church council played in bringing this situation to its present point? Did he have a legitimate right to intervene?

8. If you were called in as an "expert" in communication, what recommendations would you have for Rev. Stockton?

The New Course

Marilyn Garcia is a second-year history teacher at Williamstown High School, located in a suburb of a major western city. Marilyn completed her M.A. by writing a thesis in the area of Western United States History before accepting the teaching position at Williamstown High. Marilyn teaches U.S. history to juniors and government to seniors, but recently has been talking with her colleagues about a new history course, "The Role of Women in the Development of Western America." She would like to add the course to a list of ten semester electives which are available to juniors and seniors, after they have completed their history requirements.

Although she has impressed her colleagues with the thoroughness and relevance of the course reflected in early preparations, she has been having problems. Since coming to Williamstown, Marilyn has had trouble talking with her department chairman, George Tipton. Tipton, who teaches World History to freshmen, has been at Williamstown for fifteen years and has served as history department chairman for the last five.

To add a new elective to the curriculum the proposing teacher must first win the approval of the department chairman who in turn submits the proposal to Clifton Harding, the principal of Williamstown. Marilyn has been able to establish her credibility with Harding since she has been recognized a "Woman of Excellence" in the community by the local women's club and often has been asked to talk to community groups, such as the Rotary Club, the Kiwanis Club, and the local History Society, about her thesis research. Also, Harding has been receiving highly complimentary reports about Marilyn's teaching from students and her peers. During her appraisal interview, at the end of her first year at Williamstown, Harding was very complimentary of her performance.

"You are one of our best teachers, Marilyn. You have added to our program and you have brought a fresh perspective to our school. We hope that you will stay at Williamstown for a long time," Harding said, at the close of the interview.

But after the last history faculty meeting, however, Marilyn was seriously considering submitting her resignation. In that meeting, Tipton verbally assaulted Marilyn as well as the other two younger faculty members.

"We have a problem in our faculty with these new mini-courses from some of our younger colleagues. We have had a course proposal on the History of Communism and another on Women's Liberation. We'll never have courses like that in this department as long as I am chairman," Tipton shouted at the meeting.

With the exception of the younger faculty members, Tipton seemed to have the support of the other members within the history department. After the meeting, Marilyn asked for a conference with Tipton the next day to discuss her proposal for the mini-course, "The Role of Women in the Development of Western America."

Marilyn began the meeting by telling Mr. Tipton that she had really put a great deal of work into her proposal. Further, she indicated that she had talked about the course with a number of students and there appeared to be some interest among juniors and seniors. She said that she assumed, from his remarks at the recent faculty meeting, that he would not support the proposal.

"Couldn't you just forward the proposal on to Mr. Harding and let him make the final decision? I wouldn't even mind if you submitted a negative recommendation on the proposal. But at least let Mr. Harding see it," Marilyn argued during the conference.

"Oh, now Miss Garcia. I have given your proposal a fair hearing. I am very alarmed that you went ahead and talked to students about the course before it was approved. That's certainly going out of channels. I have made up my mind. I am rejecting the proposal and I want the matter to stay within our department. Do you understand, Miss Garcia?" Tipton said forcefully.

Marilyn responded, "Yes, I understand," and left the room.

Guidelines for Analysis

1. What do you think happened after Marilyn left the room? Ultimately, how do you think this matter was resolved?

2. Characterize the climate within the history department. Do you think that the climate in the department was different from the climate in the entire school? If so, how?

3. If you had been treated the way Marilyn had been treated by your supervisor on one of your jobs, how would you have reacted?

4. In terms of the four "Dimensions of Climate" presented in this part, what aspects are missing from the climate of the history department? What aspects are present?

5. Referring to the section in this part on "superior-subordinate communication," describe the communication between Marilyn and Tipton.

6. In light of the earlier chapters dealing with structure and leadership, do you think that this was a situation which called for Marilyn to go "out of channels"? Why?

7. Speculate about the behavior of Harding. Do you think that he would have supported Marilyn? Why?

8. If you were called in as an "expert in organizational communication," what suggestions would you have to improve this situation?

Part Five

Improving Organizational Communication

Chapter Fifteen

Organizational Change Model

Up to this point, the focus of this book has been on understanding the components of the organizational communication system and their relationships. Little has been said about planned or unplanned change. While it is trite to say that "change is inevitable," it is nevertheless true. In fact, based on what we have discussed about organizational communication systems, change is often desired to increase organizational effectiveness. This inevitable and/or desired change can be planned and managed, or left to chance. In this final part of the book (Part Five), we are attempting to bring together the materials which were presented in Part Three dealing with internal organizational elements and in Part Four which was concerned with the organizational communication system.

Planned, managed change has a much greater chance of producing positive results than unplanned change. This is not to say that all planned change produces good results, but rather that the chances are improved by a systematic approach to ongoing change.

Managers in organizational communication systems have the responsibility for managing change. This is becoming a more important responsibility as the economic and cultural environments accelerate in their rate of change. To fulfill this responsibility, managers need to understand the nature of change and be able to plan and implement changes that are necessary for long-run organizational effectiveness.

The remainder of this chapter is devoted to creating an understanding of planned change. The first part of the chapter looks at the nature of change, how it takes place, and the responsibility for change. The next part of the chapter describes a model for planned organizational change. A detailed discussion of the alternative approaches to change is given in chapters sixteen and seventeen.

Nature of Organizational Change

In order to fully understand and manage change, managers need to understand what change is, how it takes place, and their responsibility for it. This explanation of the nature of organizational change serves as a foundation for this and the following two chapters.

Definition of Change

When we speak of change, whether it is individual, group, or organization change, we mean essentially that there has been a planned or unplanned alteration in the way things get done (Spier 1973). There has been a modification in the status quo (Lippitt 1969).

The implications of this definition of change are that there has been movement from one set of conditions to another; there has been some force which causes change to take place; and finally there are some consequences or effects of the change (Sanford 1973). These implications can be demonstrated by the following example. In the early seventies a set of conditions provided American consumers cheap energy sources (status quo). The Far East imposed an oil embargo while per capita consumption of energy was increasing (forces). This led to significant increases in energy prices (effect).

In contrast to change in general, planned change is an intended, designed, and goal-oriented attempt to alter the status quo (Lippitt 1969). In the previous example of change, the change was unplanned. An example of planned change was demonstrated by the automobile manufacturers during the energy crisis of the seventies. Their sales dropped to an all-time low (status quo). To change the situation, the manufacturers offered cash refunds directly to the consumers (force) when they purchased a vehicle. The result was an increase in sales (effect).

Our interest in change focuses on planned changes in organizational variables to increase organizational effectiveness — planned alterations in the status quo that affect the way things get done in the organization and that lead to greater effectiveness in terms of goal attainment, satisfaction, and development. This refers to both changes in the internal organizational elements that ultimately affect the variables in the organizational communication system and to direct changes in the organizational communication system variables themselves. Thus, planned organizational changes refer to intended, designed, and goal-oriented altering of the organization structure, technology, leadership styles, and so on, and/or to directly altering the formal communication subsystem, communication climate, or interpersonal communication skills in order to improve decision making and production so as to increase goal attainment, satisfaction, and development, i.e. organizational effectiveness.

An example of planned organization change occurred in a national firm that was having difficulty in reaching its production goals (status quo). A study of the situation revealed that a significant cause of the low production was due to machine downtime. The high machine downtime was traced to a dysfunctional formal communication subsystem. The workers had to request a machine repair from the foreman who then completed a repair requisition and submitted it to a supervisor. The supervisor would send it to the plant maintenance supervisor, who would assign a maintenance person to the task. The maintenance person actually received the task assignment after coming to the maintenance office. This flow of information in the formal communication subsystem resulted in lengthy machine downtime and the consequent low production level.

A planned alteration in the formal communication subsystem was designed with the goal of reaching the desired production level. A microphone was installed in each work area so that the workers could call for a maintenance person directly and by name (force). The maintenance work was completed much sooner which resulted in a significant reduction in machine downtime and the company exceeding its production goal (effect).

How Change Takes Place

It is important for managers to understand how change takes place so that they can plan and implement desired changes. One useful and popular way of thinking about, analyzing, and understanding change is Kurt Lewin's "Force Field Analysis" (Lewin 1969).

Lewin's idea is that change represents a movement from the status quo, which can be looked at as the existing balance — quasi-stationary equilibrium — between two opposing sets of forces (Davis 1972). Figure 15–1 illustrates that the existing status quo is the result of the balance between a set of driving forces and a set of restraining forces. One set of forces — restraining forces — operates to maintain and preserve the status quo while the other set — driving forces — operates to change the status quo.

This group of forces is called a "force field." The length of the arrows represent the relative strength of the forces, that is, the longer the arrow the stronger the force. In the illustration, the sum of the restraining forces is equal to the sum of the driving forces which results in the current status quo.

Change results when there is an imbalance in the sum of the restraining forces and the sum of the driving forces. This imbalance causes an alteration from the status

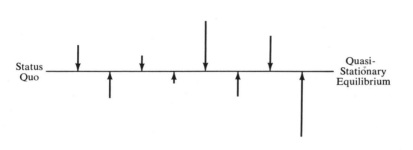

Figure 15-1   The Force Field

quo until the two sets of forces are again in balance and a new quasi-stationary equilibrium is reached.

An imbalance can be created by any one or a combination of the following three ways: (1) strengthening or adding forces in the direction of the changes, (2) reducing or removing forces, or (3) changing the direction of the forces. Managers can use one or a combination of these three ways of causing change to bring about changes in internal organization elements and in the organizational communication system.

An example of using Force Field Analysis should increase understanding of its use and application. We will refer to the previous example of a low production level due to how the formal communication subsystem influenced the delivery of maintenance services. Suppose the line in figure 15-1 representing the status quo refers to the low level of production.

The forces operating to raise the level of production (driving forces) might include (1) supervisory pressures to produce more; (2) the desire of some workers to be recognized by their supervisors for doing a good job; (3) the desire of the maintenance department to lower downtime; and (4) the desire of the workers to earn more due to an incentive plan. The forces operating to lower the level of production (restraining forces) might include (1) feelings of helplessness by the workers and supervisors; (2) the desire of the maintenance supervisor to retain control over all maintenance personnel; (3) some workers feeling that the incentive system is unfair due to their low influence over downtime; and (4) the slowness of maintenance orders flowing in the formal system.

The balance of these two sets of forces results in the low level of production. To bring about a change in the production level, managers must create an imbalance in the two sets of forces, for example, the driving forces could be increased by the supervisors putting more pressure on the workers; a restraining force could be decreased by adjusting the incentive rate for downtime; or management could change the direction of the restraining force by making the workers feel responsible for downtime by training them to fix their own machines. There are numerous additional alternatives or combinations of alternatives.

Management actually decided to change the formal communication subsystem in order to reduce the restraining forces (1, 3, and 4 in the example above). The reduction in restraining forces created an imbalance in the sum of restraining and driving forces; thus, an alteration in the status quo was required to get the forces back into balance. The result or effect of reducing the restraining forces created a new status quo which was a sustained increase in the production level.

Change can be brought about by increasing (or adding to) the driving forces or decreasing (or eliminating) the restraining forces. In general, however, change which is brought about by strengthening or adding driving forces creates a relatively high degree of tension. This tension may reduce effectiveness. That is, the increase in driving forces may be met by corresponding increases in resistances.

Attempts to implement change by decreasing (or eliminating) the restraining forces will generally lead to a lower level of tension and the change is more likely to be stable (Spier 1973). The important thing is that managers can bring about desired changes for increased organizational effectiveness by creating an imbalance in the two forces and they are charged with this responsibility.

Responsibility for Change

As has been stated, managers of organizations are responsible for organizational effectiveness and, thus, for changes in organizations. The change can be planned or unplanned, but in both cases managers are responsible for consequences, whatever they are. The chances are greater for improved organizational effectiveness when managers take a systematic approach to managing change in organizations. Only in this way can they be assured of maximizing the probability of the desired consequences of the inevitable change.

Model for Organizational Change

The model illustrated in figure 15-2 is useful for understanding and implementing organizational changes. It consists of four steps which are interrelated and tied together in a logical sequence. Managers need to understand and systematically go through each of the steps to maximize the probability of change that improves organizational effectiveness.

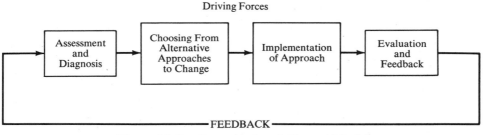

Figure 15-2   Organizational Change Model

The first step in the organization change model is to assess and diagnose the need for change. One of the assumptions of the model is that forces for change are ever present due to the dynamic nature of organizations and their external environmental influences. The manager's task is to constantly assess and diagnose the information available inside and outside the organization to determine when change is needed, or not needed. When change is not needed, and there are cases when stability is really important, the manager's energies should be spent on maintaining stability. The clear implication of the model, however, is that managers should constantly assess and diagnose the need for change and to plan and manage change when it is needed to improve goal attainment, satisfaction, and development.

When it is determined that change is needed to improve organizational effectiveness, the next step is to choose among the alternative approaches to change. The alternative chosen is determined by what needs to be changed in the organization. Two overall approaches to change are training and development, and organizational development.

After deciding which approach or combination of approaches seems most likely to bring about the desired change, the approach is implemented. The way the change is implemented can be as significant as the approach chosen since people often resist change. Thus, it is important to implement change in a way that minimizes resistance and maximizes people's commitment to the change.

The last step in the model is feedback to the change program and into the organization. This feedback serves as a basis for evaluation so that corrective action can be taken if the approach implemented is not producing the desired results. Feedback also serves as new information to be assessed and diagnosed to determine what further or future changes need to be made.

Another implication of feedback is that change is never ending. That is, the very fact that changes are made produces effects or conditions that require future changes to maintain or increase organizational effectiveness (Blau and Scott 1962).

Assessment and Diagnosis

Before managers engage in any change effort, it is necessary to know (1) what needs to be improved on or solved; (2) what has to be changed to make the improvement or solve the problem; and, (3) what outcomes (goals or objectives) are expected from the change and how will it be measured (Hellriegel and Slocum 1974). To answer these questions, it is necessary to assess and diagnose the internal organizational elements and organizational communication system.* Assessment is the act of gathering data from the organization that can serve as the basis of action. Diagnosis is making judgments about and evaluating the data once it is obtained.†

There are several useful techniques for assessing and diagnosing organizations which can be broadly classified into four categories — individual appraisal, surveys, sensing interviews, and group self-evaluations. The techniques are not mutually exclusive and it is not unusual to find all of the techniques or some combination being utilized at the same time in an organization. By having some understanding of each assessment and diagnosis technique, managers can decide what technique or combination of techniques to utilize.

Individual Appraisal. Assessing and diagnosing by individual appraisal focuses on the individual in order to determine personal problems and areas for personal improvement. As used here, we are referring to appraising the individual in order to correct problems or improve the individual's performance in order to improve organizational effectiveness, i.e., the focus is on the individual's performance in the organization. Appraisal systems were treated as part of the formal subsystem in chapter twelve.

Individual appraisal may involve employee performance reviews, counseling, psychological testing, career testing, life planning, or therapy. These activities are utilized to help the person diagnose and identify problems and areas for change and improvement. Examples of problems or areas for change and improvement include such things as (1) work skills, (2) interpersonal skills, (3) leadership skills, (4) improper job placement, (5) skills not utilized in current job, (6) intrapersonal issues hindering job performance, (7) personal life goals not aligned with job, (8) off the job issues hindering job performance, (9) interpersonal conflict, and so on.

Individual appraisal is useful where the target of assessment and diagnosis for change is the individual. The next technique, surveys, is useful when the target of change is the organization or a subunit in it.

---

*The focus here is on internal variables under the assumption that various members of the organization will provide data on external forces for change.

†We are indebted to John E. Jones of University Associates, Inc., for assistance with these definitions.

Surveys. A second method of assessing and diagnosing an organization is by surveys. The more popular survey is the attitude survey* which is administered to employees of the organization (managers included) in order to assess their feelings on such things as pay, benefits, supervisors, opportunity for growth and advancement, organization problems, management practices, working conditions, the work itself, and the like.

The survey is usually distributed to employees to complete anonymously but coded so that they can be grouped by department. The data are tabulated and then diagnosed by a consultant, manager, or the employees who filled out the survey instrument. But our preference is for the employees who completed the questionnaires to diagnose the data generated by the assessment and report the results of their diagnosis to management. This form of diagnosis is an organization development technique and is discussed in more detail in chapter seventeen.

Other forms of surveys used to assess organizations are standardized instruments designed to systematically measure certain dimensions of organizations. Some of the more popular instruments are CRUSK — Survey of Organizations (Center for Utilization of Scientific Knowledge 1969), Organization Climate Index (Stern 1974), Organizational Climate (Likert 1967), Organizational Climate Questionnaire (Litwin and Stringer, Jr. 1967), and Organization Health Survey (Kehoe and Reddin). A sample of dimensions measured by these instruments includes leadership, organization effectiveness, satisfaction, organization structure, creativity, conflict

---

*For a practical example of attitudinal surveys, see Aubrey C. Sanford and Hyler J. Bracey, "Attitude Survey: A Tool for Improving Managerial Effectiveness," *Magazine of Bank Administration* 48 (October 1972): 32-44.

management, productivity, communication, work, intellectual climate, responsibility, reward, identity, risk, warmth, and support.*

These standardized instruments are administered and diagnosed much like the attitude surveys mentioned above. Their primary advantages are that they generate organization-wide data for diagnosis and are standardized, theory based, and able to be summarized and validated. Their *potential* disadvantages are their expense, complexity, and length. Also, they generate false confidence in the diagnosis since they are quantifiable.

Attitude surveys and standardized surveys are primarily used where the target of change is the organization or subunits within it. They often supplement the other methods used for organizational assessment and diagnosis.

Sensing Interview.† Another method of assessment and diagnosis is the sensing interview which involves interviewing members of the organization. There are three objectives of the sensing interview: (1) to generate data that supplement and expand data from surveys, individual appraisal, and/or observations; (2) to be able to clarify information that is generated; and (3) to create greater sense of "ownership" of the data by directly involving members of the organization in generating the data for diagnosis.

The interview consists of the interviewer meeting with one or more members of the organization and conducting an in-depth interview around specific organizational issues—roles, goals, the job itself, the organization, interpersonal relations, interpersonal perceptions, the work teams, needed changes (Argyris 1970). The interviewee knows the goals of the interview and that it is anonymous, but not "confidential." This allows the data to be shared with others for diagnosis and action without disclosing "who said what." The interviewer usually takes notes unobtrusively or records the interview so that specific quotes can be recaptured for diagnosis.

After all the data are gathered, they can then be diagnosed by the interviewer or the interviewees. When the interviewer diagnoses the data, it usually results in a report of recommended changes and the approach to the change. When the interviewees diagnose the data, the interviewer usually summarizes the responses by "eye-balling" the data to discover trends and communications themes. Direct quotations are imbedded in the report in such a way as not to violate the expectations of anonymity. The interviewees then diagnose the data to determine changes or improvements needed.

The advantages of the sensing interview are that it provides the data gatherer with a communication device for gaining understanding, checking assumptions, discovering issues that questionnaires often miss, amplifying issues that come up, supplementing other data so that data become supportive, using the language of the interviewee in the report, and gaining credibility and rapport through direct contact with the interviewees. The disadvantages of the sensing interview are that it is expensive, it can get into counseling/therapy, the data gathered are difficult to compare

---

*For detailed information on dimensions of each instrument and where to order instruments, see J.W. Pfeiffer and L. Heslin, *Instrumentation in Human Relations Training* (La Jolla, Calif.: University Associates, 1973).

†This discussion draws heavily on an excellent article by John E. Jones, "The Sensing Interview," in John E. Jones and J. William Pfeiffer (Eds.), *The 1973 Annual Handbook for Group Facilitators*. La Jolla, Calif., University Associates, 1973, pp. 213-24. Used by permission.

with other data, it is hard to reduce the data to summaries, it threatens some people, and it requires that people be accessible for the interview.

The sensing interview has as the target of change the organization and work teams within it. It is especially useful in organization development efforts discussed in chapter seventeen.

Group Self-Evaluation.   The group self-evaluation, which is similar to the survey method, is another useful assessment and diagnosis method. This method involves a group in an organization developing an instrument to assess the group. The instrument is then administered to the group members to generate data to diagnose for changes needed in the group to make it more effective.

For example, we have been involved in organizations where groups decided to do a self-evaluation. The groups designed an instrument by writing statements of how an ideal team would operate, and scaled responses were then attached to each of the statements. The instrument was administered to the group to generate data for their diagnosis.

The distinct advantages of this technique are that the instrument is relevant and valid to the group members, the members have a sense of ownership, there is flexibility in the instrument, the technique is inexpensive, and users learn the process of assessment and diagnosis by doing it. Its primary disadvantages are that it is group dependent, time consuming and the data are not comparable to other methods.

This method is especially useful where the target of change is a group or team in the organization. Of course, it can be adopted for organization wide assessment and diagnosis.

Internal versus External Administration.   Any of the four methods of assessment and diagnosis discussed here may be performed by internal or external persons. It is important that the person have expertise and experience with the technique. The primary advantage of an internal person doing the assessment and diagnosis is his or her familiarity with the organization on a day-to-day basis. The advantage of an external person is that he or she may be more objective and have a willingness to do some things that an internal person may avoid. Also, people who work in the organization may be more open with an external person. Regardless of who does the assessment and diagnosis, managers are responsible for either doing assessment and diagnosis or having it done.

Once it is decided who will do the assessment and diagnosis, and it is performed, the managers should be able to determine what, if any, changes or improvements are needed. This information serves as input to the next step in the model for change — choosing from the alternative approaches for change.

Alternative Approaches to Change*

The diagnosis of the data gathered through sensing provides the basis for deciding on needed changes or improvements in the organization to increase organizational effectiveness. Once this is determined, managers need to select from the alternative approaches to change and implement the approach. The alternatives can be grouped into two broad categories — training and development, and organizational development. Included in each of the categories are several specific methods or techniques useful for change.

Training and Development. The training and development approach to change has the individual as its target for change. That is, the methods and techniques attempt to bring about behavioral change in the individual for improved organizational effectiveness. This change may be to make people more alike or it may be aimed at developing the individual's unique potential.

For example, people may be trained in certain jargon so that the meanings of certain words are more similar among organization members. The results hoped for are that their behavior and cognitive understanding is more alike. In contrast, there are development techniques that increase self-awareness and understanding under the assumption that this can lead to attitude and behavioral changes that increase personal and communication effectiveness and, thus, organizational effectiveness, i.e. individual differences are legitimized to encourage people to develop their unique potential for increased goal attainment, satisfaction, and development.

Methods and techniques included in training and development include on-the-job training, lecture, lecture-discussion, role playing and simulations, case analysis, programmed learning, instrumented team learning, experience-based learning, and growth groups. Internal organization elements are often changed through utilization of one or more of the training and development techniques. These techniques are also utilized to change or improve interpersonal skills directly in listening, responding, speaking, writing, perception, and so on. They can also be used to influence the formal communication subsystem and communication climate indirectly. That is, by changing the individuals' cognitive understanding, attitudes or behavior, we often hope to have some impact on who communicates what to whom and the communication climate in which they say it. Thus, when the focus of change is the individual's behavior, training and development techniques and methods are useful.

---

*This discussion draws from A.J. Reilly, "Three Approaches to Organizational Learning" in John E. Jones and J. William Pfeiffer (Eds.), *The 1973 Annual Handbook for Group Facilitators*. La Jolla, Calif., University Associates, 1973, pp. 130-31. Used by permission.

Organization Development. As the term implies, organization development has the organization as its target for change. As described by Beckhard, OD is a long-term planned effort of organizational culture change aimed at increasing the organization's health and effectiveness (Beckhard 1969).

The techniques and methods of OD, called interventions, are designed to bring about direct change in the formal communication subsystem and organization's communication climate. An indirect effect is that the individuals' interpersonal skills are impacted. This is not to imply that the individual is not important but rather that the focus is on " . . . how the individual relates to his own work group and how his group interfaces with other groups in the organization" (Reilly 1973, p. 131).

In an excellent summary of OD, John Sherwood says the general objective of OD is " . . . to develop self-renewing, self-correcting systems of people who learn to organize themselves in a variety of ways according to the nature of their task and who continue to expand the choices available to the organization as it copes with the changing demands of a changing environment" (Sherwood 1972, p. 153). This is accomplished through various interventions based on behavioral science knowledge. Some examples of interventions or building blocks of organization development are team building, intergroup problem solving, confrontation meetings, survey feedback, management by objectives, corporate strategy model building, job enrichment, third party consultation, process consultation, and role negotiations. OD in general and each of the interventions specifically will be covered in more detail in chapter seventeen.

While OD focuses on organizational change, it and training and development are not mutually exclusive. In fact, they are complementary. Often individuals need certain communication skills as prerequisites to an OD effort. In that case, the focus of change is the individual through training and development. In fact, in its strictest sense, when training and development is a subpart of a long-term planned organization culture change effort, it could be considered as an OD intervention. For our purpose, however, we will differentiate them by saying that training and development has the individual as its target for change and OD has the organization as its target for change.

The sensing and diagnosing steps should provide the basis for choosing which broad approach to change is appropriate and needed. The specific method, technique, or intervention (or some combination) can then be chosen for implementation.

Implementation

The implementation of the approach to change is just as significant as the sensing and diagnosis step and choosing from alternative approaches to change step. Three critical questions have to be answered and the answers put into effect before the actual change approach is taken. Will the approach be implemented inside or outside the organization? How much management support do we need before we start the change effort? What type of expertise do we need?

Inside Versus Outside. Determining whether to implement the change approach inside or outside the organization is influenced by the specific approach taken, organization size, available expertise, costs, and management support. In general, training and development can be done inside or outside the organization, while OD has to be performed inside the organization.

The specific approach taken to change influences whether it should be implemented inside or outside the organization. Certain training and development efforts, such as the leadership labs or growth groups discussed in the next chapter, seem to produce the best results where the participants are "strangers." Therefore, these approaches are best done outside the organization when the organization is not large enough for stranger groups to be formed inside.

Small organizations usually cannot justify an internal training department; therefore, training and development efforts are simply more economically done outside the organization.

Expertise is another influencing factor in determining whether to implement the change approach inside or outside the organization. Obviously, if the organization does not have the internal expertise, it must go outside or bring the expertise inside. It is often more economical to hire "part-time help" in the form of a consultant and bring that one person in rather than send several organization members to outside training and development events. An OD effort requires the expertise to be exercised inside the organization, so it must exist inside the organization or be brought in.

The amount of management support also influences the inside and outside issue. In an organization where planned change is supported and encouraged, there is more rationale for internal expertise since expertise will be utilized more often and more fully, thus making it more economical and valuable. In these situations, we would expect the approach to change to be implemented internally. Certainly all of these variables play a part in determining whether to implement the change approach inside or outside the organization.

Management Support.   Another important issue to be resolved prior to implementing the change effort is the amount of management support needed. Certainly we could all agree that any attempt to change has a higher probability for success if it receives full management support. However, the issue here is, how much is required as a minimum?

Generally, training and development efforts require much less support than OD. OD is a long-term organization culture change effort that at a minimum requires full support of top management. Training and development focuses on the individual and requires at least the support of the person's superior for the change effort to have high chance for the attitudinal, cognitive, or behavior change to be transferred to the work setting.

After the manager has resolved the inside/outside issue, and has obtained the necessary management support, he or she must locate the appropriate expertise and implement the program.

Expertise.   A certain level of expertise is needed to implement the approach. In general, the person should not only know the skill or knowledge to be taught but must also have the ability to teach others learning it. The specific skills needed vary from lecture skills to intense small group facilitating skills, depending on the specific change approach chosen.

If the expertise is inside the organization, the job of selecting someone is fairly simple. However, outside sources are difficult to find and assess. The expertise may reside in a supply organization, consulting firm, university, college, trade association, or another firm. Our recommendation is to check the references listed below, get several prospects and check them out through references provided by them.

1. "Applied Behavioral Science Consulting Organizations: A Directory," in *The 1975 Annual Handbook for Group Facilitators,* ed. John E. Jones and J. W. William Pfeiffer, La Jolla, Calif.: University Associates, 1975), pp. 249–63.

2. OD Network, NTL Institute, 1815 North Fort Myer Drive, Arlington, Virginia 22209.

3. Contact a local chapter of the American Society for Training and Development. Write ASTD, P. O. Box 5307, Madison, Wisconsin 53705, for the name and address of the local chapter.

4. Contact Regional Consulting Firms, Universities, Colleges, Trade Associations, and so on.

Once the expertise is located, the goals of the change approach need to be agreed on or checked against the goals of the outside training and development event to see that they coincide with the change or improvements needed. After preparing any needed syllabus, intervention plans and materials, course outline, lesson plan, or registrations, members can be scheduled and the change approach implemented. Evaluation and feedback provided through open communication should indicate if the desired change or improvements are resulting from the effort.

Evaluation and Feedback

Evaluation and feedback from the change effort implemented can take place at three levels (Byars and Crane 1969) — while the approach is in progress, just after the completion of the event or effort, and after sufficient time for the change effort to be reflected in organization effectiveness. All three levels are mutually reinforcing and serve as data to be diagnosed to determine changes in current efforts or to decide on further changes and improvements needed.

There are several informal and formal techniques for evaluation and feedback that are useful during a change effort. The change agent, whether a trainer, teacher, instructor, manager, worker, or consultant, can analyze the effort through observation, questioning, performance critiques, short quizzes, outside observers, and private discussions. The more formal methods include questionnaires, tests, pre- and post-tests, final performance evaluation by the change agent and fellow participants, and comparing people in the change effort to those not in it. Evaluations and feedback are especially useful in making corrections in the change effort as it is taking place.

Once the change effort is completed or after organization members have completed their participation in the event, the impact of the efforts can be further evaluated. The techniques for doing this are very similar to the ones in the previous paragraph. The members' performance or behavior can be evaluated to check for transfer of change to the job. This can be done by observation, records, or through ratings by the superior or subordinates. Other commonly used techniques for intermediate evaluation and feedback are tests and opinionnaires to check for retention and opinions over time.

The final level of evaluation and feedback is how the change effort affects organizational effectiveness — goal attainment, satisfaction, and development. In the long run, these things can be measured through accounting data, human resource inventories, assessment and diagnosis techniques, or organization survival. Admittedly, it is difficult to separate the effect of planned change efforts from other variables discussed in previous chapters. Some of the more short-run measures of increasing organizational effectiveness would include profit, costs, sales, employee turnover, productivity, quality, absenteeism, attitude surveys, and exit interviews.

In the final analysis, the change effort provides feedback to the organization whether it is intended, planned, formal or informal, or otherwise. This data can be uncovered in future sensing and diagnosis efforts that managers engage in and ultimately impacts or causes the need for further change or improvement in communication in order to increase organizational effectiveness. Knowing and using the planned change model is an important responsibility of managers in organizations, for it is through their efforts in planning and implementing change that organizational effectiveness is improved.

Summary

Change is inevitable and is often desired to increase organizational effectiveness. Managers are charged with the responsibility of planning and managing the change rather than leaving it to chance. An understanding of the nature of change and how to manage it is essential for improving goal attainment, satisfaction, and development in organizations.

Change is any alteration or modification in the status quo. This alteration can occur by altering the driving forces and restraining forces that initially led to the status quo. By altering the forces a new status quo will result in order to balance out the forces. Managers can bring about change by consciously planning and managing alterations in the driving and restraining forces.

A practical and useful model for organizational change involves systematically proceeding through the steps of assessment and diagnosis, choosing from alternative approaches to change, implementation of the approach, evaluation and feedback. Assessment and diagnosis involves gathering data for the organization that serves as a basis of action and making judgments about and evaluating the data to plan action steps. Four techniques of assessment and diagnosis are individual appraisal, surveys, sensing interviews, and group self-evaluation. One or more of these techniques are administered by internal or external people to gather data that serves as a basis for choosing from the alternative approaches for change.

Two alternative approaches to change are training and development, and organization development. Training and development focuses on changing the individual in order to increase organizational effectiveness. Organization development has the organization as its target for change. Through various interventions changes are brought about in the formal communication subsystem in the organization's communication climate. It is not uncommon in an OD effort to use various training and development techniques.

The next step in the organization change model involves implementing the specific approach or combination of approaches. Implementation requires determining whether it will be inside or outside the organization, obtaining the amount of management support needed, and acquiring the needed expertise. Once this is done, the specific change approach is put into action.

The final step in the organization change model is the evaluation of the change effort and feedback to the program itself and to the organization in general. Evaluation and feedback can occur while the approach is in progress, just after the completion of the event or effort, and after sufficient time for the change effort to be reflected in organizational effectiveness. Usually a combination of these is used and ultimately all efforts in organization change provide feedback to the organization which generates new data that will be assessed and diagnosed at a later time for needed change in order to further improve goal attainment, satisfaction, and development.

REVIEW AND DISCUSSION

1. Briefly explain the concept of "force field."

2. Diagram and explain the model for organizational change discussed in the chapter.

3. How do assessment and diagnosis differ? Give two examples of assessment techniques. What is done with the data generated through assessment and diagnosis?

4. How does training and development differ from organization development?

5. What are some of the more important issues in the implementation step of the organizational change model?

6. What are some ways that an organization may evaluate its change efforts in the short run?

7. Determine some status quo situation in your personal life that you would like to change. Specifically identify all of the driving forces for change and restraining forces against change. What can you do to alter the balance in the driving and restraining forces in order to bring about the desired change?

8. Analyze a specific situation in the class, university, local community, economic system, or the like; identify the current status quo balance and identify the driving and restraining forces that create the balance.

9. Assume this class is an organization. How would you go about assessing and diagnosing the organization for needed change? Be specific.

10. What is the relationship in the assessment and diagnosis technique used and the communication climate in the organization?

11. What is the relationship of the alternative approaches to change and interpersonal communication skills of members in the organization?

Chapter Sixteen

Changing
the
Individual

The previous chapter covered planned, managed organizational change for improving organizational effectiveness by exploring the organizational change model. The model was covered in detail with the exception of the step dealing with alternative approaches to change. Two broad categories of alternatives were discussed in general — training and development, and organization development. Training and development focuses on changing the individual and his or her skills while organization development focuses on changing the formal communication subsystem and communication climate. Both approaches to change in organizations strive to improve decision making and production so as to increase goal attainment, satisfaction, and development.

In this chapter we will explore the nature of individual change and alternative approaches to individual change through training and development. While change can take place in many dimensions, we will focus on changes in interpersonal communication skills as discussed in chapter fourteen to improve decision making and production and ultimately organizational effectiveness.

In the first part of the chapter we will explore the nature of individual change by discussing a model of individual development. This model is used to aid managers in understanding how people arrive at their current state of attitudes, knowledge and behavior and in understanding the process of how changes take place in the individual. The later part of the chapter will explore specific alternative approaches to change, including a description of the alternatives, their uses, advantages, disadvantages, and so on.

The Nature of Individual Change

A Model of Individual Development

At any particular point in time a person has a given set of beliefs, attitudes, knowledge, values, and ideas that ultimately determines his or her behavior. Figure 16-1 is a conceptual model of how all these affect behavior and the consequences of that behavior. The implications from the model are that there are forces operating on the individual that determine his or her conceptual system or, as Argyris calls it, the "self." The operation of a person's conceptual system determines his or her behavior. So, knowing how an individual's conceptual system is formed by the forces and how it operates and changes is important to understanding and changing behavior. An individual's behavior results in consequences — the degree of individual goal accomplishment, satisfaction, and development. These consequences are feedback to the conceptual system.

Forces. The forces which operate to form a person's conceptual system are biological, cultural, role, and situational.

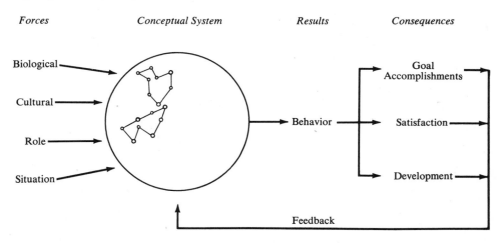

Figure 16-1   Model of Individual Development

Biological forces — These forces are hereditary in nature. There is substantial evidence that various genetic structures influence one's potential for learning, reaction time, energy level, frustration, tolerance, and the like. Our conceptual system is also influenced by such traits as stature, pigmentation, our similarity to others in our culture, strength, and so on. For example, the way people react to our color and sex influences our concept of people of a different color and/or sex.

Cultural forces — As a person experiences his or her environment he or she forms concepts about issues that ultimately influence his or her behavior. For example, all people get hungry (biological) but we do not inherit the same desire for steak, snake, snails, or chicken. This desire is learned and valued based on the culture we have experienced. Our cultural aspects of our conceptual system are factual knowledge, basic assumptions, values, tastes, skills, and the like.

Roles — The roles we have been in and the one we currently are in also influence our conceptual system and how it operates. The idea of the role force can be looked at as a special subgroup of culture. That is, the different ways we have experienced roles from others or directly ourselves in our cultural impact the concepts of how one "should" behave in certain roles ("Students should study hard to get a good grade.").

You probably can identify your own concepts about certain roles by reading the following list and identifying how you think such persons should behave: doctor, college professor, preacher, marine, con artist, banking executive, federal employee, college student, boss. Now, think back to when you have either experienced the role or experienced someone else in the role. Is your concept similar to your past experience? Do others behave in the way you conceptualize their role? Chances are that the answers are yes and that if you interact with someone in that role or play the role yourself in the future, your concept of the role will influence your behavior in a predictable way.

Situational forces — These are some events that "just happen" to people. These situational forces are differentiated from other aspects of our environment in that they are not standard for the whole group but are unique to a person. A person may be involved in a freak accident and lose an arm; his or her father runs off with another woman; he or she happens to sit next to a charismatic person on a long flight who persuades him or her to change jobs. These incidents may not immediately affect our conceptual system but they put into action a chain of events that mold our concepts. These concepts significantly influence our behavior.

Interaction of forces. The interaction of the four forces shape and mold our conceptual system, but not independently. Rather, the forces operate in a complex interdependent way that makes it difficult to say that behavior is associated with any one or combination of forces. For example, a woman does not strive for an executive position even when the opportunity clearly exists. Is this due to a hereditary force, or do role forces determine acceptable behavior? Or, could we attribute it to some situational force (her mother was an executive and killed herself over a bad business decision) or a cultural force where women executives are excluded from "in groups" of other women? It probably is some complex interdependent action of all the forces.

Conceptual system. In order to understand ourselves, others, things, relations with others, concepts, and relationships we organize the world we live in according to "concepts," or categories. The concepts and the connections between them make up our conceptual system.

Concepts — Part of our conceptual system is formed by concepts. We arrange things on all sorts of dimensions — good-bad; hot-cold; conservative-liberal; comfortable-uncomfortable; hard-easy; cheap-expensive; simple-complex. We take events, issues, people, things, relationships and all other states of affairs and place them on one or more of the dimensions. By doing this we are able to think and learn about the world around us. Thus, when we think of someone else, our job, our boss, it is essential for the very thought to occur that we have some concepts to use — love-hate; easy-hard; good-bad.

Connections — Another part of our conceptual system is formed by connections between the concepts which create a network of relationships. We use the concepts and the relationships among them to understand and operate in the world. For example, as a result of the forces on us in the past, we may say that "When managers are deceptive with their subordinates they will lose their ability to influence the subordinates." This is an example of the conceptual system linking the concepts of managers, deception, subordinates, lose, ability, and influence in order to understand the phenomenon, predict its consequences and act to react to it.

The above example deals with an intangible abstract issue. Our conceptual system also enables us to cope with physical attributes on the job. By having links between a fair day's work, safe behavior around machines, proper operating procedures, achievement, a good job, and other concepts we may or may not end up with a highly skilled machine operator, depending on what concepts he or she has and how they are related.

Value — Our conceptual system has great value to us in real life for two reasons. First, it enables us to be effective in the world. We are able to think, reason, perform, solve problems, build things, or be with people. Thus, if we need to know how to operate a piece of machinery and get along with the workers around us, we use our conceptual system to determine the actions to take to get the desired results.

The second value is that our conceptual system serves as the basis for evaluation. We are all familiar with people saying some state of affairs is better than others — love is better than hate; success is better than failure; or intelligence is better than stupidity.

Effect — As we use our conceptual system and get payoffs from it over and over, its parts and relationships become a more permanent part of us for understanding the world and deciding what to do in it. To the degree that we value, that is, think some concept is on the good end of the continuum, is the degree to which we will protect our conceptual system. For example, if we value success and loving to a high degree we will organize events so that we can see ourselves as successful and loving. Thus, the operations of our conceptual system ultimately determines how we behave.

Behavior — As we interact in the world we rely on our concepts and links among concepts to determine our behavior in order to cope with the world. For example, if we value hard work, see the boss as fair and equitable, and desire success in the form of promotion, we may do everything we can to be a terrific worker.

The extent to which our conceptual system helps us satisfy our needs and fulfill our self-concept is the extent to which we will rely on it and stick with it. So, our behavior results in some consequences which provide feedback to the conceptual system that creates change or rigidity.

Consequences. Our behavior has consequences that can be classified on three continuums: interrelated individual goal achievement, satisfaction, and development.

Goal achievement — This refers to the degree that our behavior accomplishes identifiable goals that we have set for ourselves. The goals may be things, personal, or interpersonally oriented. We may strive to buy a house, grow a beautiful head of hair, or have someone like us. You probably can think of some of your own goals and how your behavior has led to some degree of goal accomplishment.

Satisfaction — This is the degree to which our behavior leads to positive feelings. We often do things just to feel good or satisfied — exercise, party, see a show, vacation. However, what may create positive feelings for one person may not do so for another. If one person has a conceptual system that values "behaving like a Christian," which means to him or her no drinking, smoking, or dancing, and another has values of "eat and be merry," we can expect the first to have negative feelings (guilt, anger) about engaging in a wild party while the second would have positive feelings. Our conceptual system leads to behavior that to some degree gives us satisfaction or dissatisfaction.

Development — This refers to how we mature, gain more knowledge, increase skills, or become enlightened. Some behavior we exhibit is for the sake of developing as a person in some way. As Harrison (1965) has pointed out, we have a "need to know." We would like to expand this to a "need to know and do." Think of the things you have pursued because you wanted to know about them or be able to do them — learning about the Bible; learning how to work on a car; increasing your ability to dive, swim, iceskate, ski, and so on.

Certainly these three consequences are interrelated. People may learn to ski to accomplish a goal, and/or gain satisfaction and/or develop. It is not important to be able to identify the behavior with any one consequence. What is important is that behavior does have consequences and these consequences provide feedback to the conceptual system.

Feedback. Feedback to the conceptual system either reinforces or changes the system. When our behavior leads to positive consequences, our conceptual system is reinforced and becomes more permanent in nature. When some consequence does not meet our expectations, the feedback may be discounted or it may impact the system, depending on how reliable the system has been for us in the past.

In general, the more important the particular part of the system is to us in meeting our needs, the more strain and turmoil it is to change it. For example, if we think heavy objects fall faster than lighter ones it probably will not be too disconcerting to learn and change our concept to fit that all objects fall at the same rate. However, if we have a conceptual system that says masculine people do not express emotion and we know someone who we have experienced as masculine in the past and who now shows a clear expression of affection, we may just pass it off. Our response may be "He's just not himself today," "He's not really that affectionate," or even "He's not really as masculine as I thought."

To alter that one little part of our conceptual system is not so simple since all the concepts are closely and complexly linked. One change in the system would require many others and soon we might have a complete reorganization. So it is not uncommon that the last alternative we might choose in the above example would be "a person can be masculine and show deep affection." This phenomenon has serious implications for how individual behavioral change occurs.

Individual Change

The model of individual development is useful for understanding how someone changes. Now we must understand how change occurs and what conditions are necessary for change.

How Change Occurs. To change a person's behavior we must change attitudes, values, or knowledge. All of these things exist in our conceptual system. Therefore, to change individual behavior we have to add a concept, subtract a concept or change the relationships among concepts. This is no small order, for what we are asking a person to do is to give up his or her old concept which has helped him or her exist in the world, attain goals, gain satisfaction, and develop. Instead, he or she must now trust a new concept to do it better. While we are making the process of individual change bleak (and it is), there are some conditions that will greatly increase the probability of changing a person's behavior.

Conditions for Change. There are four conditions that have a significant influence on changing a person's behavior — the individual's motivation, the learning environment, feedback and reinforcement, and transfer of learning.

The individual's motivation — High individual motivation for change is necessary for a person to be receptive and open to change. There are several things that can lead to this condition. The person may recognize the need for more communication skills in dealing with people. The individual may see others get rewards by being different from each other and thus himself or herself desire to be different. Also, the person may be getting feedback (such as low goal attainment) from the consequences of his or her behavior that gives him or her the desire to change.

In order for a person to feel the need for change certain conditions are universal. First the person in some way must be aware of his or her behavior and its impact on consequences. That is, awareness precedes change. This awareness can come from the person's own thought processes or from communication with others. For example, an individual may hear a lecture on planning and realize what a poor planner he or she is and how this makes him or her ineffective. Or his or her boss may give him or her feedback on his or her poor planning and its consequences.

A second condition necessary for change is that the person must perceive that there is some alternative to his or her current behavior. For example, until the person is aware of alternative ways to plan, no opportunity for change is available to him or her (except no planning at all).

Third, the individual must perceive that the new behavior has some chance of leading to better consequences than his or her current behavior. Until we believe that some new behavior has a chance for success, it is unlikely that we will try it. The amount of chance required depends on how much we value our concept and how reliable it has been. For example, it may be no great problem to try a new way of planning our day, but it may be very risky to try to be more open and affectionate with people.

The learning environment — This condition can have a significant influence on changing people's behavior. The ideal environment is one in which it is safe to try old and new behaviors and not suffer, be penalized or punished. That is, it's acceptable to make a mistake and learn from it. Risk-taking is even encouraged. This point was made in our discussion of climate in chapter thirteen.

Ideally the climate is one in which people have trust and respect for each other and are mutually supporting. To the degree that it meets these criteria, the greater the chances of changing, because in that environment people will be more likely to try new behavior. In doing so the chances of changing the conceptual system are greater. Constructive feedback and reinforcement in this environment accelerate the change process.

Feedback and reinforcement — The concept of reinforcement was widely publicized by B. F. Skinner. The idea is that when people receive positive rewards, information, or feelings for desired behavior, the chances are greater that the behavior will be repeated. While we can decrease undesirable behavior through punishment, the research indicates that it is easier to get sustained behavioral change through positive reinforcement. One of the problems, however, is that it is difficult to determine what is a reinforcer for different people. For some it is money and praise and others it is self-satisfaction or promotion, and so on.

A similar concept to reinforcement is feedback. People learn and change faster when they get accurate, constructive feedback* on their behavior or performance. People in general desire to know the impact of their behavior, particularly when it is new behavior. The awareness of the results of their behavior provides reinforcement of new, desirable behavior and encourages people to continue their development. Feedback is more useful when it occurs soon after the event, is specific, is descriptive, and is requested by the person wanting the feedback.

To tell someone "you have a bad attitude" is not nearly as constructive as saying "When you come in ten minutes late to class, as you did today and yesterday, it makes me think you don't care about me or the class." This feedback, plus reinforcing behavior when the person does show up for class on time, can have a significant impact on an individual's behavior.

Transfer of learning — Learning must be transferred to the organization for improved performance to lead to improved organizational effectiveness. Behavior change is highly influenced by how related the training situation is to the work situation and by the climate in which a person works.

The change approach chosen and implemented will have greater transferability when the content and context of the approach is consistent with the work situation. For example, if we are trying to change and increase engineers' interpersonal skills in speaking to workers, it will be more useful if they have to design and give presentations in the workers' language rather than in highly technical terms, as was pointed out in chapter fourteen.

The change will have greater transferability where new behavior is supported by superior, subordinates, and peers in the work setting. If the superior, subordinates, and peers approve of the new behavior and encourage the person to use it, the person will be more inclined to continue using and improving on the behavior. Conversely, if the individual meets with disapproval, he or she will be discouraged from improving his or her new-found and improved self. This is the basis of the idea that superiors should be trained first.

While it is implied, it needs to be expressly stated that when the work environment meets the previously mentioned conditions for an effective learning environment, the chances of transfer of learning are improved. The ideal work environment for the transfer of learning and change itself is where improvements in behavior are

---

*For an excellent description of constructive feedback see Philip G. Hanson, "Giving Feedback: An Interpersonal Skill." In *The 1975 Annual Handbook for Group Facilitators,* ed. John E. Jones and J. William Pfeiffer (La Jolla, Calif.: University Associates, 1975), pp. 147-54.

desired and rewarded; where trying new behavior is low risk; where the environment is supportive; and where people have mutual trust and respect and receive positive reinforcement and constructive feedback.

Based on the assessment and diagnosis of data discussed in the previous chapter, an understanding of the model of individual development, and an understanding of how individual change takes place and the conditions that promote it, a manager should have the basis for choosing among the alternative training and development approaches to change. However, an understanding of these alternatives is necessary in order to make an effective choice.

Alternative Approaches to Individual Change

There are many alternative training and development approaches to changing and improving individuals. All of the approaches have as their objective changing individuals' behavior to increase decision making and production and ultimately organizational effectiveness.

This section of the chapter will describe the more popular and representative approaches. The approaches will also be evaluated to determine their advantages and disadvantages, limitations, and usefulness.

On-the-Job Training

On-the-job training (OJT) is one of the more popular and widespread techniques used today for changing employees' behavior.

Nature and Use. OJT basically involves a person actually learning how to do the job while on the job. Usually the person has fairly close supervision and instruction from an experienced worker, trainer, or supervisor while performing the job and receives communication on his or her performance frequently (Miner et al. 1973).

Most writers focus their discussion of OJT on the learning of technical skills because of its importance and usefulness in that area. OJT can be equally as useful in developing people's interpersonal communication skills when these skills are included in the training program. As we see it, OJT should include people formally getting constructive feedback on interpersonal issues through the performance review process and informally in an ongoing manner.

It is important to understand that we are not recommending that people be told how they "should" behave interpersonally. We are recommending, as part of receiving communication on job performance, that people get feedback on how their interpersonal communication behavior affects others. This would include helpful and hindering behaviors — what behaviors made people react positively and negatively, people's interpersonal communication strengths and weaknesses, and so on. The feedback would create a condition of awareness and give the person a choice about his or her future behavior.

An example should help clarify how OJT can be used to develop interpersonal communication skills. In the more traditional form of OJT a person's performance is reviewed and he or she is told what needs changing. In addition we recommend that he or she be told such things as "When we have meetings I find that I am often interrupted by you. For instance, this morning you interrupted me six times and that irritates me and I don't listen to what you say"; or "I notice that you rarely look me or your subordinates in the eye. The impact that has is that I think you are not hearing me or that what you are looking at is more important"; or "I really like how you summarize our conversation at the end. I've noticed you do this with others and I like that. I always feel good when you do that because I know you have listened and we have a common understanding." By giving the person feedback he or she knows how to have the impact again and has the option of changing it.

Advantages. The advantages of OJT are that it occurs in the work setting and no production time is "lost" while the person is away learning interpersonal communication skills. By receiving ongoing feedback, the communication climate provides a perpetual environment to make changes and get feedback since there is no lag between training sessions. In addition, since change is reinforced, rewarded, and supported internally, the person has the incentive to change.

Disadvantages. The disadvantages of OJT rest primarily in that few people have the competency to give constructive communication on interpersonal issues. Our experience is that information transfer usually occurs long after the event, is general and highly evaluative. This results in defensiveness and hard feelings. Also, many people are oblivious to how interpersonal issues are affecting them and others. But these are primarily shortcomings of the users, not of the technique.

Managers need to recognize that the level of skills held by the users of OJT is a limitation. This may require that users acquire a certain level of interpersonal communication skills through one of the other alternative approaches to training and development before OJT can be effective for changing and improving subordinates' interpersonal communication skills.

Lecture

The lecture technique or presentational communication, is familiar to anyone who has been to school. It is one of the more widespread techniques utilized in organizations to develop people.

Nature and Use. Its typical form is one of participants sitting at desks or tables while a person talks or reads to them. Interaction of participants is intrapersonal and their role is rather passive.

The lecture technique is useful where knowledge acquisition is the objective (Verner and Dickinson 1967). Where the objective is changing attitudes, beliefs, or improving interpersonal skills, the lecture technique by itself is of little value. However, lectures can be a very effective way of creating understanding of theories, techniques, ideas, and so on which can be useful for a person in understanding his or her and others' behavior. Important skills used in the presentational approach for message retention were considered in chapter fourteen.

Advantages. The advantages of the lecture technique are its simplicity and control. The lectures can be prepared in advance of presentation and the content of subject matter is controllable. In addition, the lecture can be used over and over.

Disadvantages. The disadvantage of the lecture technique is that it does not involve the learner and puts primary responsibility for the event on the lecturer. It seems to ignore the idea that participants have to be motivated to learn and mere attendance does not assure that this will happen. Readers probably have experienced a well-prepared and presented lecture that has had little, if any, personal impact on the interpersonal communication skills of the members of the audience.

Lecture/Discussion

Lecture/discussion has come into more widespread use in recent years. This is especially true in noneducational organizations.

Nature and Use. The lecture/discussion has the added dimension over the lecture of providing participants the opportunity to exchange ideas and experiences. Usually a person gives a short lecture and then leads a discussion among participants. Interaction of participants is interpersonal. However, it is usually between the lecturer and participants.

Lecture/discussion is more useful than straight lecture for participants gaining understanding of information. As Yoder (1962) indicates, through interaction in discussion the participants stimulate and broaden each other's thinking and outlook and improve their communication abilities.

Advantages. The advantages of lecture/discussion are that participants share in the responsibility for the event and that it provides the opportunity for the lecturer to give the participants feedback. In addition, it is more flexible than the lecture only.

Disadvantages. The disadvantages of lecture/discussion are that it takes time and requires a more skilled person. Interaction requires considerably more time than straight lecture. Also, the leader has to have skills in discussion leadership and be aware of and be able to give reinforcement and feedback.

Programmed Learning

Programmed learning increases in use as electronic components become less expensive. It has wide use where the same information needs to be transferred to large numbers.

Nature and Use. Programmed learning is a self-teaching method where participants learn at their own pace. The program is designed so that participants move step by step toward the desired objective.

The actual tools used in programmed learning vary a great deal. They range from simple flip cards to sophisticated computer terminals. These differences influence the costs and applicability of programmed learning.

During the last few years programmed learning has increased in practice. It is especially useful where knowledge acquisition is the objective and the knowledge is rather fixed and needs to be imparted to large numbers of participants. It has not been found useful for changing interpersonal communication skills. However, it has been used to impart theories that help people make sense out of their and others' behavior.

Advantages. The primary advantage of programmed learning is that participants can move at their own pace. The slow learners who may get further and further behind in a conventional setting are able to receive the extra instruction they need to grasp the subject. Also, the fast learners who often become bored and frustrated at an average pace are able to move at a more rapid rate and retain interest.

Disadvantages. The primary disadvantage of programmed learning is its cost. It takes special technical ability and equipment to prepare the programs. Therefore, to be feasible the programs have to be used over and over for large numbers of participants.

Case Analysis

Case analysis is another alternative approach to changing and improving individual behavior.

Nature and Use. The case analysis approach is one in which a problem or case is given to the participants, usually in written form, for solution. The participants are required to imagine the situation and arrive at a solution.

There is some evidence that the case approach is useful for developing analytical skills (Fox 1963). The managers have to identify and analyze complex problems and make their own decisions. In the process there is evidence that participants develop problem-solving skills where they have the background and ability to come up with meaningful case analysis (Gibson et al. 1973). The problem-solving skills are useful for solving actual on-the-job problems.

Advantages.   The advantages of the case approach are that participants have high involvement and are required to think. They have a "stake" in the learning.

Disadvantages.   The disadvantages of the case method are that the cases usually have no right or wrong answer and the approach requires considerable time. Also, the approach is dependent on the participants having knowledge of the roles involved and basic knowledge and ability to analyze the cases.

Role Playing and Simulations

Role playing and simulations grew out of the Harvard Business School and M.I.T. Today the approach has wide use in schools of business and in industry.

Nature and Use.   Role playing has an added dimension to case analysis in that the participant actually plays out one or more roles in the case. So, if a case concerns a situation involving a superior and several subordinates, people will be assigned certain roles to play. Since the participants actually behave in the roles rather than just think about them, a more realistic learning situation is created.

The basis of the roles takes several forms. The more traditional form is a written case or description of each role. More recently we have seen the introduction of computer games and simulations as a basis of role playing. The participants play a business game on the computer and each person has a certain role to play.

Role playing has been found to be useful in improving interpersonal communication skills. In a recent study, 117 training directors ranked several training methods on accomplishing certain objectives (Carroll et al. 1972). Table 5 shows how they ranked the lecture, case, and role-playing methods on the four objectives.

Table 5   Rank Order of Three Training Methods in Accomplishing Training Objectives

Method	Objectives			
	Knowledge Acquisition	Changing Attitudes	Improving Problem-Solving Skills	Improving Interpersonal Skills
Lecture	9	8	9	8
Case	2	4	1	4
Role playing	7	2	3	2

SOURCE: S. J. Carroll, F. T. Paine, and J. M. Ivancevich, "The Relative Effectiveness of Alternative Training Methods for Various Training Objectives," *Personnel Psychology* 25 (Fall 1972): 29. Used by permission.

As the table indicates, the training directors thought the role playing was effective in changing attitudes and improving interpersonal communication skills. One writer also found that role playing was especially effective where the participants played a role that was opposite their own (Mann 1965).

Advantages.   The advantages of role playing are that the participants have more of themselves in the learning and the learning is personally focused. Not only do they think, but they also feel the role. This increases sensitivity to the role and to their and others' motivation and behaviors. Role playing also provides the opportunity to "practice" communication skills under supervision for evaluation and feedback.

Disadvantages.   The disadvantages of role playing are similar to the case approach. Participants must know enough about the role to play it and it takes a more skilled trainer to facilitate the learning. Also, the learnings among participants vary in amount and in what they learn.

Instrumented Team Learning$_{T.M.}$

Instrumented Team Learning* was developed by Blake and Mouton. The more popular and widespread use of Instrumented Team Learning is the Grid® Seminar conducted by Scientific Methods, Inc.

Nature and Use.   In Instrumented Team Learning participants learn from each other and from their own personal investigations and reflections. The trainer is in more of the role of a learning manager.

Participants complete an instrument as a first step in the learning process. Usually some dilemma is presented and the participant is asked to determine how he or she would react to the situation. The form may be to rank certain ways of reacting, rate how well the participant responds, chooses between two choices, completes a sentence, and chooses the most correct and complete answer from a set of multiple choice responses.

The next step in the learning process is for the individual or a team to compare and critique answers. This usually takes the form of a team arriving at a team consensus. For example, the individuals may be asked to rank order some alternative responses on the ideal way to deal with interpersonal conflict. They then indicate how they actually deal with conflict. At that point they can compare what they believe is ideal with what they actually do.

Later, the individuals would operate as members of a team to come up with a team consensus on the ideal. At this point the participants test and compare their ideas and assumptions with others in the team.

Once the team has reached consensus the individual and team answers can be compared against a theory, against what the "experts" say, against how they react, and against how others see them react. This allows the participants to assess their own behavior and to investigate the validity of their assumptions. Out of this the learner can draw generalizations about his or her behavior in a broader sense. For example, he or she may be able to generalize how he or she reacts in certain situations and what leadership style he or she exhibits.

Another common step that follows the teamwork is for the team to critique how they operated. During this stage participants are encouraged to give each other personal communication. To continue our example, each person may receive feedback on how he or she has handled conflict in the team meetings. In this way each

---

*This discussion includes paraphrased material from Robert R. Blake and Jane S. Mouton, "What is Instrumented Learning?" *Training and Development Journal,* January 1972, pp. 12-20. Reproduced with permission. Instrumented Team Learning is copyrighted by Scientific Methods, Inc., Austin, Texas.

member can make a comparison of how he or she sees himself or herself and how others see him or her. This can serve as a basis for further generalizations.

Instrumented Team Learning is useful for both knowledge acquisition and behavioral change (Blake et al. 1964, Blake and Mouton 1964). Instrumented Team Learning has been utilized effectively to teach everything from organization policy to nursing practices. It has also been used as a basis to get to interpersonal issues by participants giving each other feedback on interpersonal communication style and skills.

Advantages. One of the primary advantages of Instrumented Team Learning is that it puts the total responsibility for learning on the participants. They derive their learning directly from written materials and team interaction.

A second advantage is that participants have the incentive to participate and involve their own ideas, beliefs, values, and the like. They are motivated to listen and respond to others' ideas and express their own.

Other advantages are that members get personal communication, the approach is not teacher dependent, and people learn interpersonal skills. Also, the approach almost always involves some form of critique and the interaction and learning is not so dependent on the teacher.

Disadvantages. There are several disadvantages of Instrumented Team Learning. Preparing the materials requires time and skills, and it is difficult to deal with subjective data. Also, learning varies among participants and teams since it is dependent on who is in the team.

In summary, Instrumented Team Learning has great value for *content* and *knowledge* issues and justifies the time and trouble. People get excited, learn and retain information. It is also particularly useful when integrated with some of the previously discussed approaches to change in order to create understanding of information.

However, experience with Instrumented Team Learning in general and the Grid seminars specifically reveals that it takes an inordinate amount of time and expense to get to interpersonal communication skills issues as compared to other types of experience based learning.

Experienced Based Learning

Experience based learning evolved from sensitivity training, growth groups, and encounter groups. These will be discussed fully in the growth groups section later in this chapter. While experience based learning evolved from these things and utilizes what has been learned from them, experience based learning is not the same thing as sensitivity training, or any of the others. The use of experience based learning in all sorts of organizations is increasing at a rapid rate.

Nature and Use. The marked distinction of experience based on learning from other approaches is that participants "learn by doing" through active involvement in small group problem solving, structural experiences, and pair and trio skill building sessions. The major element of experience based learning is that participants "learn by doing" through participating in exercises or experiences that are structured to accomplish specific learning goals. The experiences are reviewed by the participants to draw generalizations and new knowledge that have practical utility. In addition, by sharing their thoughts and feelings participants learn from others how they can become more effective in their roles. This cycle is repeated to build and reinforce skills and learning.

An example of using experience based learning should be helpful at this point. During a communications skill workshop it was evident that some participants were not listening to each other. We were suspicious that it was due to low listening skills. In a subsequent activity the participants were given a problem to solve as a team. Each member was given a data sheet that was to simulate information in their head. They could solve the problem only through oral communication.

Usually teams discover in about ten to fifteen minutes that their sheets contain different data, and one team did that in the workshop we are discussing. That one team went on to solve the problem in another thirty minutes for a total of forty minutes.

The other teams took thirty to forty-five minutes just to discover that they had different data. In one team a person had even done the exercise in a previous workshop. He kept telling the other team members that they were not listening, and obviously they were not. Finally after one hour and fifteen minutes all the teams had solved the problem, however two teams solved it incorrectly.

All the teams then reviewed the experience for learnings and generalizations. They had no trouble discovering that several participants in each team were not listening. As one participant pointed out, "We're just like a bunch of radio stations — a lot of sending out but no receiving."

Individuals either owned up to not listening or were given feedback that they did things (like interrupting, not responding, arguing) that made others think they were not listening. For most participants, it was the first time they "realized" the level of their listening skills and they were receptive and excited about building their skills in future listening exercises. This is a simple example of experience based learning but the results are markedly different from the more traditional approaches to individual change.

Other techniques utilized in experience based learning are pair and trio skill building sessions, discussion groups, helping pairs and small group problem-solving exercises. After each of the activities the participants review the experience for learnings and suggestions on how they may increase their skills in future experiences.

As one might guess, experience based learning has great applicability for changing and improving interpersonal communication skills. By participating in the experiences participants generate real life data about themselves that can be analyzed and that serves as the basis for constructive feedback from others.

Advantages. One advantage of experience based learning is that participants have high involvement and responsibility in the learning. When this is coupled with a low risk workshop environment the participants usually have the inclination to examine and change their behavior. Also, they get feedback and reinforcement on their behavior which increases the chance of transfer to the organization setting.

The results of experience based learning are not surprising when we consider that participants have a real stake in the learning experience. Also, we all know there is a distinct difference in "knowing about" something and "knowing" it through direct experience.

Disadvantages. The disadvantages of experience based learning are that the learning is difficult to focus and it varies from participant to participant. Also, the approach is dependent on the skills of the trainer in designing and facilitating the experiences.

While experience based learning has great applicability to behavioral issues, its development and use for content or subject issues is in the infant stage. As a result of this, the authors have found that supplementing experience based learning with Instrumented Team Learning, role playing and lecture/discussion can be a very effective approach to increasing behavioral and analytical skills (interpersonal, communication, leadership, problem solving, decision making, conflict resolution). We expect this approach to be utilized more and more in organizations to change and improve people's interpersonal communication skills for better decision making and producing and, ultimately, organizational effectiveness.

Growth Groups

Growth groups grew out of the study of group dynamics by Kurt Lewin. His idea was that changing values and behavior requires unfreezing the old value system, changing values and refreezing the new value system. Growth groups are an attempt to do that.

Nature and Use.   The primary objective of growth groups is to make participants more aware of themselves, their impact on others, their reaction to other people, how they impact others, how people relate, and how groups operate (Campbell and Dunnette 1968). This is usually accomplished in a "stranger group" meeting for a weekend, week or longer and interacting for learning. The significant difference in this and other training is that there is much less focus or structure.

The group experience itself provides the environment and opportunity for learning (Bradford et al. 1964). Members engage in communication but with certain "ground rules." These usually include limiting interaction to the "here and now," dealing only with people and issues in the room, speaking for one's self, "owning" one's own feelings, taking responsibility for oneself, and other rules, depending on the trainer. Participants are also encouraged to share and deal with feelings and to give each other constructive feedback on how their behavior is impacting others. The norms that are supported by the trainees are openness, honesty, personal confrontations, self-disclosure, and expression of feelings.

The interaction of participants in the growth group environment provides the opportunity for learning. Each participant is encouraged to pay attention to how they and others interact. Also, they explore their motives and reactions to others, and others reactions to them and how all this impacts their behavior. This is supported through giving and receiving feedback.

Growth groups are very useful for interpersonal communication skill building. Participants report that growth groups improve listening ability, increase empathetic understanding, increase perceptual skills, increase effectiveness in expressing and responding, improve skills in giving and receiving feedback, and increase understanding of group process.

Advantages and Disadvantages.   There is considerable evidence that growth groups meet the goals of increasing awareness and skills. However, the evidence is unclear as to how well it transfers back to the job and leads to more effective performance (Gibson et al. 1973). It varies depending on the trainer, the back home environment, the nature of the group member background, the length of the program, and several other variables. Argyris and Odiorne (1963) have openly debated the pros and cons on growth groups. The next section gives our own conclusions.*

Conclusions

Our conclusion, based on the research and experience, is that growth groups have a more positive and stronger impact on individuals' interpersonal behavior and self-concept than other forms of training and development under certain conditions. The trainer needs to be a skilled communicator, a warm and supportive person who offers some low and flexible, but not controlling or arbitrary, structure. The participants need to be volunteers and not have any formal reporting relationship (boss-subordinate, husband-wife). And the training needs to last a minimum of fifteen to thirty hours.

Another conclusion is that while the growth group can have significant personal value, we are unsure of its value to the organization in terms of performance. Thus, our preference is for experience based learning where interpersonal communication skills are learned in the context of organizational issues. The experiences are structured so that the learning outcomes are consistent with improved decision making and producing in order to increase organizational goal attainment, satisfaction, and development.

Summary

Individuals' behavior influences decision making and production which ultimately affects organizational effectiveness. Managers must understand the nature of individual change and alternative approaches to individual change through training and development in order to bring about changes in interpersonal communication skills so as to improve decision making and production for increased goal attainment, satisfaction, development.

At any point in time, biological, cultural, role, and situational forces operate on the individual to determine his or her conceptual system. The concepts in the conceptual system and the connection among the concepts determine our behavior and help us understand and cope with the world. The consequences of our behavior are the amount of individual goal achievement, satisfaction, and development. These consequences serve as feedback to the conceptual system either to reinforce or to change.

To change individual behavior we must add a concept, subtract a concept, or change the relationships among concepts. This is no small order and the chance of individual change is influenced by the individual's motivation, the learning environment, feedback and reinforcement, and transfer of learning.

Based on an understanding of individual development and how change takes place and the conditions that promote change, managers should have the basis for choosing among several alternative training and development approaches for im-

---

*For opposing views on sensitivity training see a debate between an outspoken critic, George Odiorne, and a major proponent, Chris Argyris, in *Training Directors Journal* 17, no. 10 (October 1963): 4-37. Also see J. P. Campbell and M. D. Dunnette, "Effectiveness of T-Group Experience in Managerial Training and Development," *Psychological Bulletin* 70, no. 2 (August 1968): 73-104.

proving interpersonal communication skills. On the job training usually focuses on technical skill building and can be expanded very beneficially to include improving interpersonal communication skills.

The lecture technique is another widely used training and development method that is simple and easy to control but has little value in improving interpersonal communication skills. Lecture discussion provides more interpersonal action and has a greater chance of improving communication skills but has many limitations.

Programmed learning has growing use and it is very good in transfer of knowledge to large numbers and to allow people to move at their own pace. It has severe limitations in terms of its costs and application to interpersonal communication skill building.

Case analysis is widely used and provides a situation where people have more of a stake in their learning. It has limited use in interpersonal communication skill building.

Role playing and simulation offer a lot of opportunity for improving skills and seem to have a better chance of changing attitudes and improving interpersonal skills.

Instrumented Team Learning, developed by Scientific Methods, Inc., is useful for both knowledge acquisition and behavioral change. However, using Instrumented Team Learning seems to take an inordinate amount of time and expense to get to interpersonal communication skill issues as compared to experience based learning.

Experience based learning is one of the newer training and development methods and is an outgrowth of sensitivity training. The technology primarily involves learning by doing, by participants becoming involved in experiences, and reviewing experiences to draw learnings and generalizations for themselves.

Growth groups are very useful for interpersonal communication skill building, however the evidence is unclear as to how well the results transfer back to the job and lead to more effective decision making and production.

Our own preference is to use experience based learning coupled with some of the other techniques so that the learning outcomes are consistent with improved decision making and producing in order to increase organization goal attainment, satisfaction, and development.

REVIEW AND DISCUSSION

1. Give some specific examples of biological, cultural, role, and situational forces that have formed your conceptual system.

2. Based on your answer to the previous question, identify how one item under each of the four forces interacts to cause you to behave in a specific way. For example, I am a male (biological) who has enjoyed partying in Houston several times (cultural). The role I have played has been a successful consultant. My friend just happened to know of a small, but really nice, place to go where rich people usually congregated and really enjoyed themselves (situational). The interaction of all these forces influenced my conceptual system such that now when I return to Houston I always frequent this particular place to impress my friends and look even more successful.

3. Explain how the consequences of our behavior influence our conceptual system. Briefly explain how change occurs in an individual. Use your explanation and give a personal example of how you have changed .

4. Analyze your academic environment in terms of the four conditions that influence changing a person's behavior.

5. What is the relationship between interpersonal communications skill building and the lecture technique of training and development?

6. Compare and contrast role playing and simulations with instrumented team learning.

7. Why does experience based learning seem to be valuable for increasing interpersonal communication skills?

8. Which training and development technique would you choose to reach goals of this class? Defend your position.

Chapter Seventeen

Organization Development

To increase organizational effectiveness, managers must be skilled at managing organizational change. For managers to be skilled at managing organizational change, they must understand how change occurs and be able to choose among and utilize alternatives to change. Chapter fifteen covered the concept of planned, managed organization change and indicated there were two alternative approaches to change, training, and development, and organization development (hereafter referred to as OD). The previous chapter focused on individual change through various training and development techniques. This chapter will cover the other alternative approach to planned, managed change, OD. The first part of this chapter will discuss the concept of planned organizational change through OD for increased organizational effectiveness. Specific OD techniques will be covered later in the chapter.

Organizational Change Through Organization Development

To understand how OD can be used for organizational change to increase organizational effectiveness, it is important to understand how organizational change occurs. First we will briefly review planned, managed organizational change and then discuss the nature of OD, its underlying assumptions and how it works.

In essence, the organizational communication system model used in this book is a model for organizational change. That is, organizations "are" what they are as a result of the variables interacting, and change is always taking place. This change can be planned and managed by influencing the variables in such a way as to improve the chance that the change will improve decision making and production and, thus, increase organizational effectiveness.

For a manager to have planned, managed change, it is necessary that he or she implement the organization change model covered in chapter fifteen. He or she must go through the steps of assessing and diagnosing the organization, choosing from alternative approaches to change, implementing the approach, and evaluating it, and so on. When the assessment and diagnostic step points toward the need for organizational change for increased organizational effectiveness, versus individual change, the manager has OD as the appropriate alternative approach.

The Nature of OD

In an excellent paper on OD, John T. Sherwood (1972, p. 153) says, "Organization development is an educational process by which human resources are continuously identified, allocated, and expanded in ways that make these resources more available to the organization, and, therefore, improve the organization's problem-solving capabilities."

(1) A long-range effort to introduce planned change based on a diagnosis which is shared by the members of an organization.

(2) An OD program involves an entire organization, or a coherent "system" or part thereof.

(3) Its goal is to increase organizational effectiveness and enhance organizational choice and self-renewal.

(4) The major strategy of OD is to intervene in the ongoing activities of the organization to facilitate learning and to make choices about alternative ways to proceed.*

Thus, the ultimate goal of OD is to increase organizational effectiveness, i.e., goal attainment, satisfaction, and development, by enhancing the problem-solving capabilities of the organization so as to improve decision making and production. It does this primarily by impacting the formal communication subsystem and the communication climate.

There are certain characteristics of OD† that make it different from other change approaches (French and Bell 1974). First, it is a long-range, ongoing planned change effort involving the total organization or some autonomous subpart of it. The change effort involves the whole organization and has as its goal increasing organizational effectiveness.

Second, OD is initiated and managed from the top of the organization (or independent subunit). While all things seem to work better when they are supported from the top, this is considered a necessary condition by most OD practitioners.

---

* John T. Sherwood, "An Introduction to Organization Development." Copyright © 1971 by the American Psychological Association, Inc., Washington, D.C. Issue No. 11 (April 1971), Ms. No. 396-1. Used by permission of the author. This article appears later in John E. Jones and J. William Pfeiffer (Eds.), *The 1972 Annual Handbook for Group Facilitators* (La Jolla, Calif.: University Associates, 1972), pp. 213-23.

†For a detailed discussion of the characteristics of OD, see Wendell L. French and Cecil H. Bell, Jr., *Organization Development* (Englewood Cliffs, N. J.: Prentice-Hall, 1974), pp. 45-64.

A third and critical difference between OD and other change approaches is the use of planned behavioral science "interventions" in the organization's processes. That is, the knowledge and technology we have of the behavioral sciences about such processes as motivation, communication, power, norms, perception, goal setting, problem solving, interpersonal relations, intergroup relations, and conflict management are utilized to make planned interventions to impact how things get done in the organization. Thus, OD pays attention to both process and content issues to change patterns of activities, norms, interactions, feelings, beliefs, values, and attitudes at the formal and informal level since the formal and informal communication subsystems merge.

Another major characteristic of OD is that it relies on experience based learning. The experiences members have with each other and the organization are shared and studied for learning and become the basis for planned change.

In summary, OD is a long-term, ongoing, planned change effort to influence the organizational communication system, particularly the formal subsystem and communication climate, to improve decision making and production for increased organizational effectiveness.

Assumptions of OD

The assumptions underlying OD are critical because if the beliefs, values, and asumptions of the managers in the organization are in conflict with the assumptions of OD, it is unlikely that OD will "work." However, OD can be used to change the beliefs, attitude values, and so on of organization members when top management can "buy" the underlying assumptions of OD.

The assumptions underlying OD are:

(1) The attitudes most members of organizations hold toward work and their resultant work habits are usually more reactions to their work environment and how they are treated by the organization, than they are intrinsic characteristics of an individual's personality.

(2) Work which is organized to meet people's needs as well as to achieve organizational requirements tends to produce the highest productivity and quality of production.

(3) Most individuals seek challenging work and desire responsibility for accomplishing organizational objectives to which they are committed; and they are capable of making a much higher level of contribution than the organization will permit.

(4) The basic building blocks of organizations are groups of people; therefore, the basic units of change are also groups, not simply individuals.

(5) The culture of most organizations tends to suppress the open expression of our feelings. The suppression of feelings adversely affects problem-solving, personal growth, and satisfaction with one's work.

(6) People who learn to work in a constructively open way by providing feedback for members become more able to profit from their own experience and become more able to fully utilize their resources on the task. Furthermore, the growth of individual members is facilitated by relationships which are open, supportive, and trusting.

(7) There is an important difference between agreement and commitment. People are committed to and care about that which they help create. Com-

mitment is more likely attained where there is active participation in the planning and conduct of the change. Agreement is simpler to achieve and results in a simpler outcome—people do what they are told, or something sufficient or similar.

(8) For improved performance resulting from an OD effort to be sustained, there must be appropriate changes in appraisal, compensation, training, staffing, etc.*

It should be obvious that these assumptions in large part are consistent with our understanding of the humanistic managerial philosophy. Out of these assumptions, specific goals evolve that are an attempt to create a system closely approximating the team style described in the Managerial Grid and System 4 as described by Likert.

The Goals of OD

The ultimate goal of OD is to increase organizational effectiveness. The specific goals of any OD program vary depending on what is discovered in the assessment and diagnosis step of the organizational change model presented in chapter fifteen. However, there are some more typical goals that seem to emerge in OD efforts. Since these goals usually emerge, they reflect the problems common in organizations that hinder full organizational effectiveness.

The typical goals of OD are:

(1) To increase the level of trust and support among organization members.

(2) To create an open, problem-solving climate throughout the organization— where problems are confronted and differences are clarified, both within groups and between groups in contrast to "sweeping problems under the rug" or "smoothing things over."

(3) To locate decision-making and problem-solving responsibilities as close to the information sources and the relevant resources as possible, rather than in a particular role or level of the hierarchy.

(4) To create an environment in which authority of assigned role is augmented by authority based on knowledge and skill.

(5) To increase the openness of communications laterally, vertically, and diagonally.

(6) To increase awareness of group "process" and it consequences for performance that is, to help persons become aware of what is happening between and to group members while the group is working on the task, e.g., communication, influence, feelings, leadership styles and struggles, relationships between groups, how conflict is managed, etc.

(7) To increase the level of personal enthusiasm and satisfaction of organization members by increasing their sense of "ownership" of organizational goals and objectives through involvement in planning and implementation.

---

*Sherwood, "Introduction to Organization Development." Used by permission.

(8) To find synergistic solutions to problems through collaboration between interdependent persons and groups.*

These goals are the ones commonly pursued in an OD effort to change the formal subsystem and communication climate in order to improve decision making and production for increased organizational effectiveness. A brief general description of OD in action will be described now and specific OD "interventions" described in detail later.

OD in Action

OD in action is very different from training and development with which most people are familiar. We will look at OD in action by discussing the OD strategy model in figure 17-1.

The beginning point of an OD effort usually involves the key executive becoming aware of organizational pains that get in the way of organizational effectiveness. When the pain becomes great enough, the executive usually seeks some assistance from an internal or external behavioral science consultant.

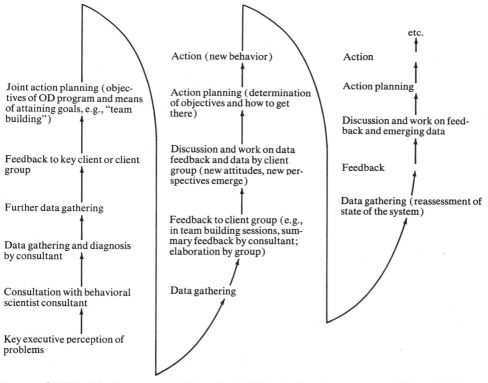

SOURCE: ©1969 by The Regents of the University of California. Reprinted from Wendell French, "Organization Development: Objectives, Assumptions and Strategies," *California Management Review*, Vol. XII, No. 2, p. 26 by permission of the Regents.

Figure 17-1   An Action Research Model for Organization Development

---

*© 1969 by The Regents of The University of California. Reprinted from Wendell French, "Organization Development: Objectives, Assumptions and Strategies," *California Management Review*, Vol. XII, No. 2, pp. 23-34 by permission of the Regents.

An alternative way for OD to get started involves the key executive becoming aware of the organization's style and alternatives to the current style. This can occur through visiting with other key executives or through workshops and conferences relative to OD.

Once the key executive initiates the contact with the behavioral science consultant, the next step usually involves the consultant gathering data through one of the sensing techniques discussed in chapter fifteen. The consultant then diagnoses the data and communicates them to the key executive or client group. At this point, the client* and the consultant do some joint action planning to determine the specific objectives of the OD program and the means for attaining the goals. The general outcome is for the board of directors or executives to commit themselves to a long-run OD effort and to agree to some initial steps toward attaining the goals. These initial steps usually involve one or more of the interventions discussed later.

Most of the interventions involve gathering or generating data that are fed back to the group on which the intervention is being made. The group may be all members of the organization or some subgroup within it. Based upon the data, the group has discussions and works on the data to determine some specific actions to take for improvement. Specific objectives are set and specific plans made for how to attain the objectives. Action is taken based on plans.

The action usually involves some new behavior, for example, the data gathered from an executive committee may support the idea that an agenda for meetings would really be helpful, and that their effectiveness would be increased by stopping every hour to determine how the committee is making decisions and to assess the effectiveness of the decision-making process. The new action then would involve coming up with an agenda and carrying through the idea of the group discussing how the team is operating and assessing its effectiveness. This cycle of gathering data and feeding it back is recycled over and over in the organization. The data then serves as a basis for determining specific plans which lead to specific actions which can be put into action.

This, then, is the general strategy for implementing OD in an organization. It may be general and vague at points, but it should come to life and be clear based upon a study and understanding the specific interventions covered next.

Organization Development Interventions

OD interventions are specific activities, methods, or techniques on which organization members and clients engage. They are, in essence, the building blocks of an OD effort that "make things happen" and are "what's happening." More specifically, they are structured activities that some identified group or groups engage in (French and Bell 1974) to change the formal subsystem and communication climate for improved decision making and production so as to increase organizational effectiveness, i.e., goal attainment, satisfaction, and development.

---

*The "client" is actually the organization. The consultant's commitment is to the organization, not an individual or subgroup of individuals. However, he or she must meet with individuals of subgroups for action planning and so forth that focuses on improving the organization's effectiveness.

The various interventions can be classified according to their primary focus, which may be on the individual, teams or groups, intergroup relations, or the total organization.

The Individual

It is not unusual during the initial stages of an OD effort to discover that individuals need specific interpersonal communication skills to bring about planned changes in the organizational communication system. Consequently, one of the first OD interventions may be specific training and development activities to build interpersonal communication skills necessary to increase organizational effectiveness. As mentioned in chapter fifteen, while it may seem conflicting, training and development is an OD intervention when it is part of a long-term planned change effort.

Most organizations that are involved in OD efforts have rather extensive training and development activities integrated into the other interventions discussed later. We refer you to chapter fifteen for a specific discussion of the various training and development techniques. The major point here is that training and development is an OD intervention when it focuses on changing the organization through changing the individual and is part of a long-term plan change effort to increase organizational effectiveness.

Teams or Groups

One of the basic building blocks of organizations are interdependent groups or teams. Consequently, one of the more important classes of interventions are team building interventions.* When we refer to a team in this section, we are referring to a group of people with a common responsibility which is interdependent. This usually is a boss and his or her immediate subordinates.

Team building interventions are based on the assumption that certain tasks and interpersonal issues get in the way of team effectiveness. The goal of team building is to work through these issues to improve the problem-solving ability of the team in order to improve decision making and production for increased goal attainment, satisfaction, and development. Some subgoals of team building are:

(1) A better understanding of each team member's role in the work group;

(2) A better understanding of the team's character—its purpose and role in the total functioning of the organization;

(3) Increased communication among team members about issues that affect the efficiency of the group;

(4) Greater support among group members;

(5) A clearer understanding of group process—the behavior and dynamics of any group that works closely together;

(6) More effective ways of working through problems inherent to the team—at both task and interpersonal levels;

(7) The ability to use conflict in a positive rather than a destructive way;

(8) Greater collaboration among team members and the reduction of competition that is costly to individual, group, and organization;

(9) A group's increased ability to work with other work groups in the organization;

(10) A sense of interdependence among group members.†

The hoped-for result of team building is a cohesive, supportive, trusting group with high task orientation and respect for individual preferences (Reilly and Jones 1974). Two of the more popular team building interventions are process consultation and team building through data feedback.

Process Consultation. Process consultation differs from most consulting in that the consultant does not give expert advice. Rather, the process consultant helps the organization members gain "insight" into how they are operating by helping them perceive, understand, and act upon their own process (Schein 1969).

There are several ways this can be done depending on the style of the consultant. The more popular way is for the consultant to attend meetings of the group or team and during the meeting have the members look at their own processes and for the consultant to make process observations. The processes usually focused on are communication, decision making, roles, interpersonal, and task functions.

An example of process consulting should be helpful in understanding how it

---

*For an excellent discussion of team building, see Anthony J. Reilly and John E. Jones, "Team Building," in John E. Jones and J. William Pfeiffer (Eds.), *The 1974 Annual Handbook for Group Facilitators.* La Jolla, Calif.,University Associates, 1974.

†Ibid., pp. 227-28. Used by permission.

works. An organization had an ongoing OD effort, and process consultation was one of many interventions. At the first meeting with the team, the process consultant clarified his role and his relationship with the group. The group agreed they needed help on how they functioned as a group. They said they always seemed to be "bogged down." They agreed to look at their own processes at any level — task, thoughts, feelings, interpersonal, boss/subordinate, and so on.

Each team member was instructed to pay attention to one of the following items during the meeting — participation, influence, task functions, maintenance functions, feelings, styles of influence, group atmosphere, and norms. Every fifteen minutes, the consultant stopped them and had them discuss as openly as possible what they were seeing. They switched items after each discussion.

In addition, the consultant made certain process observations during the meeting. Some examples were:

"The group gets into the task without defining its goal."

"Silence seems to be interpreted as agreement."

"Greg, you disagreed with every statement made by Bob and Sam."

"Drew, you changed the subject six times in the last ten minutes even though others kept trying to discuss the problem."

"Sue's ideas are not commented on or acknowledged."

In the middle of the one-day meeting, the group agreed to spend some time talking about how it wanted to operate the rest of the day. It operated with the consultant making process observations and, at the end of the day, critiqued the last half of the meetings. The members set specific change goals for the next meeting. The consultant met with them several times at future meetings. The group now reports handling its job much more efficiently and feeling much more committed to its task, and that the members now study their own processes without a consultant. Process consulting can be an effective team intervention to improve the group's performance.

Team Building Through Data Feedback. Team building through data feedback is usually initiated by the superior calling in an internal or external consultant to help a team improve its own effectiveness. Again, this is done by the team taking an inward look into its own processes to analyze how things get done in the team.

The difference between this approach and the previous one is that once the consultant has the commitment of the total team, he or she conducts sensing interviews with each of the team members to gather data about the team. Depending on the consultant, the interviews last from twenty minutes to one hour. The members usually are asked such questions as: "What is your role on the team?" "How does the team go about making decisions?" "Why do you keep showing up for work around here?" "What are the strengths/weaknesses of the team?" 'Who would you predict is going to say they have an interpersonal problem with you?" "If you were king, what data would you change about the team?"

Once the consultant has gathered the data, he or she categorizes them into themes and presents them to the group at a later meeting. The meeting usually lasts three or four days.

Here are some examples of data that might be presented to a team:

"Once members see that Joe (the boss) and Odell want a decision, other members give in and are not committed."

"Jim and Carol are great at brainstorming."

"It's tough to trust Jay's information."

"Virginia and Wyatt are always in a power struggle."

"Doc waits to see where others stand before he states his opinion."

"We all listen well when there is a crisis."

The data gathered may be presented in total, all at one time, or a little at a time. When they are presented in total, the group examines and discusses the issues, ranks them in terms of importance, and deals with them in rank order. When the data are presented in a piecemeal fashion, the consultant gives them a "bit" of data; when they think they have finished with that bit, he or she presents another. In either case, they discuss or "work through" as much data as possible.

"Working through" the data involves the team examining the dynamics of the problem to determine solutions to the problems and to establish some action steps to bring about desirable changes. In the course of doing this, additional data are generated by the group interacting. These data are studied also. That is, as in process consultation, the group studies its own processes as a basis of understanding and taking action for improvement. So the group is working on two sets of data, the sensing interview data and the data generated through group interaction.

As the data are analyzed for solutions, specific action steps for improvement are identified. Some of these may be implemented during the team building session. Here are some examples of action steps:

(a) The group will develop the meeting agenda at the start of the meeting.

(b) Jim and Ted will stop interrupting each other.

(c) Barb will run our brainstorming sessions.

(d) Each meeting will be critiqued for at least ten minutes.

(e) A draft of policies to be considered will be distributed a week before the meeting.

(f) Meetings will be called off if two or more members are unprepared.

(g) Joe (the boss) will attend the Leadership Skills Workshop by April 18.

The action steps are usually followed up on and new ones developed in subsequent meetings.

It is not unusual while using either of these team building interventions that time is devoted to some interpersonal communication skill building activities around such things as conflict resolution, consensus seeking, listening, problem solving, counseling, perception, and decision making. The data produced by the team serve as the basis for deciding on the need for the various skill building activities.

Intergroup Relations*

As groups rub against each other in organizations, it is not unusual for tension, conflict, and competition to build up between them. When this occurs, we usually find that groups see each other as enemies, have negative attitudes toward each other, communicate very little, and distort what communications exist. Each group believes that it is right and the other groups are wrong. This clearly hinders organizational effectiveness.

Technology has been developed to reduce intergroup conflict and increase the effectiveness of intergroup relations for improved organizational effectiveness. The primary OD interventions to improve intergroup relations are the intergroup image exchange and organization mirroring (French and Bell 1974). These interventions are very important ones since organizations are made up of interdependent groups.

The goal of the interventions is to improve decision making and production for increased organizational effectiveness by reducing dysfunctional competition, increasing collaboration between groups, reducing dysfunctional behavior between groups, and increasing communications and interactions between groups.

Intergroup Image Exchange.   As with most of the interventions, the intergroup image exchange begins by the leaders of two groups calling in a consultant to help improve intergroup relations. When the leaders commit themselves to the image exchange, the two groups are called together and asked to go to separate rooms and complete two lists. On one list they are to indicate how they see the other group, that is, what are their thoughts, feelings, and perceptions of the other group. On the second list, they predict how the other group sees them, that is, they predict what the other group thinks and feels about them.

---

*This section draws heavily on Wendell L. French and Cecil H. Bell, Jr., *Organization Development: Behavioral Science Interventions for Organization Improvement,* © 1973, pp. 121-26. Reprinted by permission of Prentice Hall, Inc., Englewood Cliffs, New Jersey.

Once both groups have built the two lists, they come together in a common room to share the lists. While the lists are being presented, the consultant allows the participants to ask only clarifying questions.

The sharing procedure is as follows. Group 1 reads its list of how it sees Group 2; Group 2 then reads its list of how it sees Group 1. Once each of the lists on how they see the other group is completed, then Group 1 reads what it expected Group 2 to say about it, and Group 2 reads the list of what it thought Group 1 would say about it.

The two groups then go back to separate rooms with two tasks. First, they are to react to and discuss what they learned about themselves from the other group. Second, they make a list of priority issues that need to be resolved between the two groups.

As the groups privately discuss their reaction to the other group and what they learned about themselves, they usually discover that a lot of the friction that exists between the groups is based on misperceptions and miscommunications. Sharing the lists often resolves a lot of the differences. Also, the differences are rarely seen to be as bad as imagined. The problems are fewer than imagined.

Based on their reaction to the other group and an analysis of what they learned about themselves, each group develops a list of priority issues that need to be resolved between the groups. The lists are generally much smaller than originally anticipated.

The two groups then come back together and share their reactions and learnings, and issues that need to be resolved between the groups. They then work together to come up with a common list containing the issues and problems which should be resolved. The items are ranked in order, and specific action steps are developed to be taken to resolve the issues. Members are assigned responsibilities for the various actions.

In subsequent meetings, the action steps are critiqued by the two groups and the critiques shared in a common meeting. It is not unusual that groups wish to go through the image exchange at specific future dates as a basis of comparing how their intergroup relations differ.

The image exchange has wide applicability in organizations and communities. The image exchange has been utilized to build relations between races, sexes, various community action agencies, law enforcement groups, and so on. Some work has been done simultaneously with three groups with some success.

Our experiences indicate that the image exchange can result in improved intergroup relations in all sorts of situations and relatively short periods of time.

Organization Mirroring. The organization mirror intervention has the same objectives as the previous intervention. The significant difference is that a specific group receives communication from representatives of several other groups (helping groups) about how it is perceived. Usually, three or more groups are involved in giving feedback to the host group. Consequently, representatives of the helping group, rather than a full membership, meet with all of the members of the host group.

The intervention usually starts with the leader of one of the organizational groups requesting help from a consultant to improve its relationships with other groups. Once commitment is gained, the host groups invite key people from other groups to attend the meeting to provide feedback on how they see the host group.

The consultant usually meets with the representatives of the helping group before the meeting to conduct sensing interviews to gather data that will be presented to the host group in the presence of the helping group. At that time, he or she prepares the participants for the meeting and answers any questions they might have.

The host group and the representatives of the helping group meet in a single room. The meeting usually starts with the manager of the host group establishing a communication climate of wanting the helping groups to "tell it like it is" in terms of how they perceive the host group. The consultant then feeds back to the total group the information he or she gained in the sensing interviews. The representatives of the helping group usually sit in a circle in the middle of the room and discuss the data presented by the consultant. This allows the representatives to talk about the host group in a natural way while the host group members overhear them.

Next, the host group sits in the middle of the room and talks about what they have heard, asks clarifying questions and basically makes sure they understand the information they have heard. Once the host group is sure that they understand the information that has been presented, they begin to work on the problems.

One common way of working on the problems for solution and action steps is for subgroups of the host group and representatives of the helping group to be formed. The subgroups then identify solutions and action steps that need to be taken to increase the host group's effectiveness.

The total group is pulled back together to develop a master list of specific action steps needed for improved effectiveness. Subgroups then discuss and react to the list, and the list is finalized and priorities outlined. Specific actions are assigned to various people and completion dates agreed upon. Follow-up meetings are utilized to assess the progress and review the action steps and to develop new action steps.

This intervention can be very powerful for improving intergroup communication and, thus, organizational effectiveness. In a very short period of time, the host group gets meaningful and significant feedback on what it needs to do to improve its effectiveness with other work-related groups. Again, both experience and research indicate that this intervention can be significant for improving intergroup effectiveness for improved organizational effectiveness.

The Total Organization

There are several OD interventions that can virtually involve all members of the organization. These interventions are discussed here and have as their objective increasing organizational effectiveness as we have discussed previously. The interventions are survey feedback, confrontation meeting, grid OD, management by objectives, and job enrichment.

Survey Feedback. A widely used OD intervention is the use of survey feedback* or attitude survey (Sanford 1973). The way the information generated by the survey is analyzed and utilized is significantly different and talked about in most traditional textbooks. In survey feedback, information is collected from the members of the system and fed back to the individuals who completed the questionnaire. From their own analysis and interpretation, they recommend specific action steps to be

---

*For a discussion of survey feedback, see Aubrey C. Sanford, *Human Relations Theory and Practice* (Columbus, Ohio: Charles E. Merrill, 1973), pp. 270-97.

taken to improve organization effectiveness. This difference is a significant one and makes survey feedback a potentially powerful intervention.

A discussion of how survey feedback operates should help in understanding how it differs from the classical attitude survey approach to organization change. The process usually begins with a consultant meeting with the top team to lay out the plans for the survey feedback and to be sure that all members are committed to go through all of the various steps, including making changes.

Once they are committed, a task group is set up to coordinate the effort. Its first job is generally to identify the goals of the survey feedback effort and develop a questionnaire to gather data. Standardized questionnaires are available for its use if it chooses.

The questionnaire is used to collect data from the organizational members anonymously, but in a way that the data can be tabulated by group, departments, subunits, and the like. The idea is to be able to identify the data with the smallest subunits, but be able to protect the anonymity of the data.

The data is then communicated to the persons who actually completed the questionnaires. Usually the boss calls the subordinates in and gives them the results of the survey. At this point, one approach is for the superior to work with the subordinates to help them interpret the data and to develop specific action plans to bring about changes.

The alternative approach that we generally choose is for the boss to turn the data over to the subordinates. Then the subordinates as a group, or some subgroup chosen by the subordinates, are asked to develop a list of specific problems and their recommended solutions to the problems.

The subordinates then meet with the boss and present their report to him or her. The boss merely accepts the reports and assures them that in a certain number of days he or she will give them an answer to their recommendations. Within the chosen number of days, the boss then responds to their recommendations by saying, "Yes, this change will be made," or "No, this change will not be made, and here's why," or "Yes, this change will be made, but it will not be done until _____."

Another alternative is to take the information generated by the attitude survey and use it as a basis for team building sessions. Our experience with this, however, has been that a consultant is needed to facilitate a meeting of this sort. The more economical and widely used approaches are the two previously mentioned ones. Survey feedback using the two approaches mentioned for handling the data generated have produced excellent results for us and others in terms of making changes for improved organizations.

Confrontation Meeting.*   The confrontation meeting was developed by Richard Beckhard (1967) as a quick, simple, and reliable way to gather data to serve as the basis for establishing action plans for improved organizational effectiveness. The confrontation meeting basically is a one-day meeting where all members of management assess their organization's health. The confrontation meeting is appropriate where total management groups need to look at themselves, time is limited, there is a desire to improve conditions quickly, the top team is committed to the

---

*This discussion draws heavily on Richard Beckhard, "The Confrontation Meeting," *Harvard Business Review* 45 (March-April 1967): 149-55. Used by permission.

program, and where there is or has been major organizational change. The meeting itself is fairly structured and involves several steps.

The first step is for management to commit itself to the confrontation meeting. Then all of the members of management meet at one location. During the first forty-five minutes to one hour, the top manager sets a climate for the meeting by stating the goals of the meeting, asking people to communicate freely and openly on organizational issues and problems, and by making it clear that the managers will not be penalized for what they say. In addition, a behavioral science consultant may make some comments about the importance of open communication within organizations, the necessity for collaborative problem solving, and the desirability of identifying and solving internal problems.

Small groups of seven to eight members are formed such that superiors and subordinates are not on the same team; also, members of the teams are made up of managers scattered around the organization. The top management team meets as a separate group. The groups are given the following instructions:

> Think of yourself as an individual with needs and goals. Also think as a person concerned about the total organization. What are the obstacles, "demotivators," poor procedures or policies, unclear goals, or poor attitudes that exist today? What different conditions, if any, would make the organization more effective and make life in the organization better? (Beckhard 1967, p. 154)

The groups spend an hour working on the task, and the recorder lists the results of their discussion.

During the next step, which lasts approximately one hour, the reporters from each group report the group's findings to the rest of the managers. These reports are written on large newsprint and posted for others to see. The meeting leader, who may be the manager or consultant, categorizes the total list into a few major categories such as communication problems, planning, top management problems, or accounting department. Once all of the lists are posted and categorized, there is usually a break.

During the break, the categorized lists are duplicated for distribution to everyone. The members are called back together, and the meeting leader goes through the list of items and distributes the duplicated lists to the other members. In this way, everybody is familiar with the problems and whether they are influenced by them. The participants then form into their natural work groups based on how they are grouped in the organization. Each group is headed by a top manager in that group. The groups have three tasks to perform. First, they identify and discuss the issues and problems that are related to their area, give their problems priorities, and determine immediate action steps that they are willing to commit themselves to that will help remedy the problem. Second, they are asked to identify problems to which they think top teams should give priority. Third, they are to determine how the results of the confrontation meeting will be communicated to their subordinates.

The top managers who are meeting with the various groups come back together to plan follow-up action steps and to determine what action should be taken based upon what they have learned that day. The action plans are communicated to the rest of the management group in several days. Four to six weeks after the confrontation meeting, a follow-up meeting is held to report progress and to review the action resulting from the confrontation meeting.

The confrontation meeting is an excellent way to get fast results for improving organizational effectiveness. It provides a quick and accurate means for diagnosing organizational health, encourages constructive problem identification and solving, stimulates open communication in the organization, and increases involvement and commitment on the part of the entire management team.

Grid Organization Development. One of the most widely used and systematic organization programs is the Grid Organization Development Program* designed by Robert R. Blake and Jane S. Mouton of Scientific Methods, Inc. (1968). It is a six-phase program lasting three to six years in which an organization moves systematically through six phases that culminate in the development and implementation of an ideal strategic corporate model. The program is highly instrumented such that internal members of the organization can be pre-trained to carry out organization development without requiring a skilled small-group facilitator or OD consultant.

Embarking on a Grid OD program usually requires that one or more members of the organization attend public Managerial Grid Seminars and subsequent advance seminars. One advanced seminar is the Organizational Development Seminar where participants are exposed to the materials and techniques utilized in the future OD phases. Another advanced course is the Instructors Preparation Seminar in which participants learn how to conduct a Grid seminar internally. Attending these seminars enables managers to evaluate the Grid approach to OD and be able to conduct Grid seminars internally. With some additional training internally in Grid OD, an organization can prepare to quickly develop its own internal resources for conducting Grid OD. After a company has decided to implement a Grid OD program based upon attending public seminars or after it has conducted a pilot Managerial Grid Seminar internally, it is ready to begin Phase 1 of the six-phase program.

Phase 1: The Managerial Grid. In this phase, a Managerial Grid Seminar is conducted for in-company managers. The seminar is a week-long workshop in which managers learn about Grid concepts, learn problem-solving and critiquing skills, develop team action skills, and become more aware of their own leadership style.

Managers work in small groups where they do various problem-solving activities utilizing various instruments. After each session, they critique their own individual and team performance to learn about themselves and group process.

Phase 2: Teamwork Development. This phase focuses on developing teams by having teams utilize various instruments to analyze their own culture and traditions. They do various activities to develop skills in planning, setting objectives, and problem solving.

Also, team members receive feedback from each other about their own and the team's behavior. This feedback allows each team member to understand how others see their strength and weaknesses in the team's workings. The teamwork activities are done in the actual context of the work setting so that the problem issues dealt with are real ones in the team.

---

*This discussion includes paraphrased material from Robert R. Blake and Jane S. Mouton, *Corporate Excellence Through Grid Organization Development* (Houston, Texas: Gulf Publishing, 1968). Copyright © 1968. Reproduced with permission.

Phase 3: Intergroup Development. This phase attempts to move groups from what is often an ineffective win/lose situation to a more ideal model of intergroup communication. Again, by utilizing various instruments, groups study the dynamics of intergroup cooperation and competition.

Groups separately define what the ideal relationship would be between their group and some other group. These are shared among groups. Specific action steps are assigned to individuals.

Phase 3 involves all teams that have important interfaces to meet together for intergroup development in pairs. This procedure helps to link managers who are at the same management level but who belong to different working units. It is not unusual for only selected members of the teams who are critical to the two teams' relationships to meet and take part in the exercises and activities.

Phase 4: Developing an Ideal Strategic Corporate Model. The fourth phase involves setting up a model for an effective organizational system for the future. The top management team may work for as long as a year in strategic planning activities to design an ideal strategic corporate model. Basically, the team defines what its organization would look like if it were truly excellent.

While the top team develops the model, its plans and ideas are evaluated and critiqued with other corporate members. Once they develop the ideal model, they are able to compare it with their current culture to decide what must be changed to achieve excellence. The necessary steps are taken in the next phase.

Phase 5: Implementing the Ideal Strategic Model. The goal of this phase is to implement the Ideal Model developed in the previous phase. To do this, the organization must be reorganized. Consequently, components of the organization are designated and each component appoints a planning team whose task is to investigate and examine the components' operation to determine how the organization can be more aligned with the Ideal Model. A coordinator is appointed to act as a resource to the planning teams and to coordinate their efforts.

After the planning teams have investigated their components' performance, specific steps for conversion to the ideal strategic model are designated and implemented.

Phase 6: Systematic Critique. This phase involves measuring the results of the Grid OD program from Phase 1 to after Phase 5. Systematic critiquing and evaluating is done to measure the progress that has been made, identify what problems still exist that must be overcome for excellence, and to identify what new opportunities are available to be exploited.

Through the process of internal organizational members establishing where the organization has been, how far it has come, and where it is now begins a new starting plane from which to strive for additional excellence.

There is empirical evidence that Grid OD works. The evidence shows that the results appear in the bottom line in terms of profit, lower costs, and less waste. Managers involved in the program also report that the program has led to better results.

Our opinion is that the Grid OD program is an effective program that will increase the organizational effectiveness. However, due to its rigid instrumentation, costs of materials, and the time that it consumes of the managers in the organization, we believe that where organizations have resources available to make the other interventions, they would be a more efficient and economical approach for increasing organizational effectiveness.

*Likert's Systems-Four Approach.** Likert has a program to move an organization from its current system toward Systems Four. He believes that an organization can be described in terms of eight operating characteristics: (1) leadership, (2) motivation, (3) communication, (4) interaction, (5) decision making, (6) goal setting, (7) control, and (8) performance. Each of these characteristics can be measured and located on a continuum through the use of a questionnaire completed by members of the organization. The results of the questionnaire can be tabulated and plotted on a continuum so that an organization can determine its present state of affairs.

The data generated through the questionnaire are utilized as a basis for future OD efforts. Various training programs are utilized to emphasize the concepts of Systems Four and how these concepts can be applied to the present organization. Likert believes that through the use of supportive, group-oriented leadership and equalization of authority to set goals, implement control, and make decisions, higher earnings and efficiency will usually result.

The main point is that through various interventions organizations can move from a Systems One to a Systems Four organization for improved organizational effectiveness. The technology and interventions are similar to those previously described.

Management by Objectives. Management by objectives † is a rather broadly based approach to the management of people. It is believed to increase managerial effectiveness through better leadership, motivation, and communication. It is based upon the assumption that people respond to specific short-term goals and objectives which they have set and the achievement of which is measurable. Odiorne describes the technique as follows:

> In brief, the system of management by objectives can be described as a process whereby superior and subordinate managers of an organization jointly identify its common goals, define each individual's major area of responsibility in terms of results expected of him, and use these measures as guides for operating the unit and assessing the contribution of each of its members. ‡

The process of management by objectives is not something revolutionary or new. In fact, it is a return to the systematic practice of some of the basics of management that makes use of our knowledge about behavior (Humble 1970). The difference between MBO and other approaches to the management of subordinates is one of degree of system rather than one of a kind system. It is considered a more systematic and effective approach than others. In concept, management by objectives is a relatively simple three-part process which involves the following steps (see fig. 17-2).

1. Superiors and subordinates meet and discuss jobs of subordinates and determine the important areas of performance in their jobs, in light of the objectives of the department and the overall organizational goals.

2. Superiors and subordinates then mutually agree and jointly set realistically attainable but challenging specific, short-term goals (quantifiable, if possible,

---

*For a more detailed explanation of this section, see Rensis Likert, *The Human Organization* (New York: McGraw Hill, 1967).

†This section draws heavily on a description of MBO in Sanford, *Human Relations Theory and Practice*, pp. 322-80.

‡George S. Odiorne, *Management by Objectives* (New York: Pitman Publishing, 1965), pp. 55-56. Used by permission.

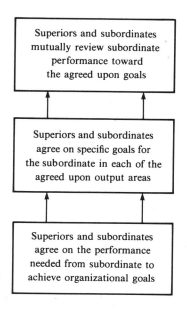

SOURCE: Aubrey C. Sanford, *Human Relations Theory and Practice* (Columbus, Ohio: Charles E. Merrill, 1973), p. 328.

Figure 17-2   The MBO Process

but always measurable by some systematic standard), in terms of the results to be achieved by subordinates.

3. Superior and subordinate meet again at a predetermined, specified future time and jointly review subordinate performance in terms of goal achievement. The two parties jointly analyze performance not only to determine what has been achieved, but also in what manner. At this stage, the MBO cycle is complete and the entire process begins anew (Donnelly et al. 1971, p. 145).

The simplicity of the MBO process should not be interpreted to mean that its effective application is easy. As with anything else that produces significant value, it is difficult to practice the three steps well. Our experience has been that the initial value of the benefits derived from MBO are almost in proportion to the difficulty encountered in establishing objectives and reviewing performance.

In organizations we are familiar with that use MBO, the process described takes place between all superiors and all subordinates, with the exception of line help. The process starts at the top of the organization and continues sequentially down with all superiors and all subordinates. So, the three-step process is performed many times.

When the MBO cycle has traveled the length and breadth of the organization, the result is that at any one time all managers have specific result objectives that have to be achieved. The operation of an organizational MBO system is illustrated in figure 17-3.

In essence, MBO is a systematic way to apply the behavioral concepts discussed in previous chapters. Where people operate in an open and trusting environment

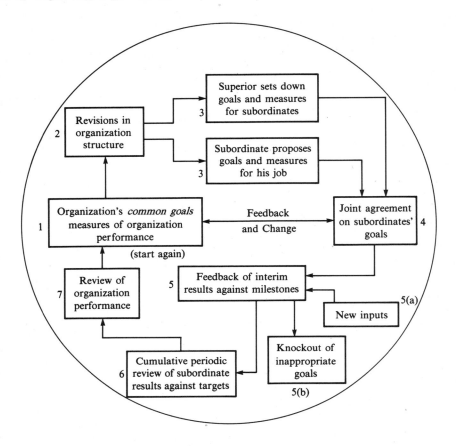

SOURCE: From the book, *Management By Objectives* by George S. Odiorne, p. 78. Copyright, ©, 1965 by Pitman Publishing Corporation. Reprinted by permission of Pitman Publishing Corp.

Figure 17-3   The Cycle of Management by Objectives

and have high interpersonal skills, MBO promotes communication and understanding by forcing better superior-subordinate interaction. It provides a systematic but flexible framework, which produces better leadership for subordinates. Subordinates are provided with specific result objectives to serve as guides in their day-to-day activities and with such objectives they can be delegated specific authority and freedom to act.

MBO tends to have a motivational effect on subordinates because its participatory nature leads to the involvement of subordinates in their own jobs. More specifically, the MBO process is a systematic method of applying Herzberg's Motivation-Hygiene Theory by providing the Motivators of responsibility, achievement, recognition, and growth and development. MBO motivates because it provides increased responsibility for subordinates.

MBO is also a systematic way to perform the operational functions of managers. An MBO system that is effective is a primary part of the planning process. Also, the operation of the MBO process identifies a goal that has to be accomplished and from this various activities can be identified and grouped for the accomplishment of goals. Thus, MBO is associated directly with traditionally managerial functions of organizing. Clearly, MBO is a method of appraisal. In fact, it is a more systematic and effective method of appraisal than most of the methods because it concentrates on results and outputs instead of inputs. In addition, the appraisal of results is generally tied to the compensation system such that MBO becomes the basis for wages and salary administration.

The major advantages of MBO are that it offers a systematic method of implementing communication, motivation, and leadership theory and a concrete method of integrating the various management subsystems into effective overall management systems. The major limitation and disadvantage of MBO is that it is difficult to initiate and its practice can be distorted so that it becomes merely another pressure device.

We believe that MBO can be a significant OD intervention which can increase organizational effectiveness significantly. However, as with any intervention, there are times when it is appropriate and inappropriate. Most MBO systems that fail do so because they are an inappropriate OD intervention at the time the intervention is made. That is, the members of the organization do not have the necessary interpersonal communication skills to operate the system in a way that gains the commitment of people toward goals. In addition, until the formal subsystem and communication climate are fairly open and trusting and have some of the characteristics of Likert's Systems Four or the Managerial Grid Style, MBO just becomes another mechanical system to be tolerated and one to which people often succumb.

MBO is potentially powerful for an organization, both positively and negatively. The appropriateness of the intervention needs to be critically tested and when it is implemented, it needs to be done with an amount of energy and expertise that correlates with the potential value that is anticipated.

Job Enrichment. Job enrichment* is another significant OD intervention that can impact the total organization and improve organizational effectiveness. It is a systematic attempt to apply the motivation theory presented in chapter six. Specifically, job enrichment techniques are primarily attempts to apply motivational theory in general and Herzberg's Motivational Hygiene Theory specifically. The techniques represent attempts to enrich the work or jobs that people do by creating conditions in which the things that motivate most people are inherent in the work and jobs. Job enrichment is a specific attempt to align organizational and individual objectives in order for them to be mutually reinforced.

Job enrichment should not be confused with job enlargement. Job enlargement is merely a process of adding to jobs more of the same type of activity being performed. In contrast, job enrichment, as it is used in this book, refers to changing the basic nature of the work done on the job by ". . . giving the worker more of a say about what he or she is doing, including more responsibility for deciding how to proceed, more responsibility for setting goals, and more responsibility for the excellence of the completed product" (Gooding 1970, pp. 69-71).

The ultimate objective of job enrichment is more effective and efficient organizations through increasing the performance and productivity of employees. Specifically, job enrichment seeks to create and change jobs so that the jobs themselves

---

*This discussion draws heavily on a concise description discussion in Sanford, *Human Relations Theory and Practice,* pp. 381-410. For a more detailed discussion, see M. Scott Myers, *Every Employee A Manager* (New York: McGraw-Hill, 1970); Frederick Herzberg et al., "One More Time: How Do You Motivate Employees?" *Harvard Business Review* 46 (January-February 1968): 56-57; and Fred K. Foulkes, *Creating More Meaningful Work* (New York: American Management Association, 1969).

result in more highly satisfied and motivated employees. In turn, the higher levels of satisfaction and motivation result in better performance and greater productivity. The objective of job enrichment, therefore, is a creation of jobs in which the work is meaningful enough to cause employees to become emotionally involved and motivated.

Most of the practical application of job enrichment has been done at lower organizational levels. There is nothing in the techniques themselves which inherently restrict or limit the use of job enrichment to particular levels in the organization. The restriction of the practical use of job enrichment techniques to the lower levels is not because they are not applicable elsewhere, but because other techniques, such as MBO, seem more appropriate at higher levels. Job enrichment has wide applicability at all levels in the organization and is appropriately used in conjunction with other OD interventions. For example, MBO, in essence, enriches management jobs; they can be more enriched through the application of job enrichment techniques.

There are two conceptually similar but operationally different approaches to job enrichment — job restructuring and problem-solving goal setting. Job restructuring, developed primarily by Herzberg, is a term used to refer to the process of enriching jobs. It is based upon the specific assumption that many jobs are simple, meaningless work; therefore, enriching them is a matter of restructuring the basic nature of the work being performed in order that it is loaded with the motivators of the Motivation Hygiene Theory.

Herzberg identifies seven principles useful as guides to restructuring jobs in order that loading may result. As each of the principles are implemented, certain specific motivators should be built into jobs. The seven principles are (1) remove controls; (2) increase personal accountability; (3) provide complete, natural units of work; (4) grant additional authority; (5) provide employees with information directly; (6) introduce more difficult tasks; and (7) allow individuals to become specialists.

The actual step-by-step procedure that has been followed in attempts at job restructuring is varied, but attempts generally have followed a basic pattern suggested by Herzberg (1968):

1. In the initial attempts at job restructuring set up a controlled experiment composed of two equivalent groups—one to be used as an experimental group in which job changes will be made, and one to be used as a control group to provide a basis for evaluating the effect of job restructuring in the experimental group.

2. Try to select jobs for restructuring where the investment in engineering and technology will not make job changes too expensive. In addition, attempts should be made to select jobs which present recognized problems, such as high absenteeism and turnover, poor attitude and performance, and jobs where motivation makes a difference in performance.

3. Use first and second level supervision to brainstorm a list of job changes in accordance with the restructuring principles. The list of changes should be developed initially with no regard for the practicality of the changes.

4. Screen the list of suggested changes to determine which ones actually should be made. Eliminate from the list any changes in hygiene factors and any change generalities which would be impossible to implement. Eliminate any changes which result in horizontal rather than vertical loading of the jobs;

then, decide which changes can be made to produce the greatest motivational effect with the least amount of difficulty. Finally, implement these
changes relatively slowly.*

Both research and experience indicate that job enrichment through job restructuring produces measurable benefits. As with most valuable things, the implementation of job enrichment is difficult, and it should not be entered into unless the
jobs are approached with the genuine belief that they can be changed to enrich them.

Another approach to job enrichment is through problem-solving goal setting
(Myers 1970). This approach was developed in Texas Instruments, Inc., by M.
Scott Myers and is conceptually similar to job restructuring. It has the same theo-
retical basis and objectives in that it is an attempt to create or restore motivational
meaning to work in jobs through application of Herzberg's Motivational Hygiene
Theory. However, the operational approach is entirely different.

In job restructuring, outside parties, generally supervisors or higher level managers,
change the basic nature of the work that employees do in order that the work becomes
more meaningful and satisfying. In contrast, problem-solving goal setting attempts
primarily not to change the nature of the basic work done but to involve employees
emotionally by the addition of management responsibility to jobs.

The basic assumption of problem-solving goal setting is that there are three broad
aspects to work. The first two are planning and controlling of work which involves
solving problems, setting goals, planning the use of resources, and evaluating performance against goals. They have been performed traditionally for employees by
supervisors and managers. The third aspect of the work is the actual doing of the
work while doing the implementation. It is this third aspect of work that traditionally
has been performed by workers or employees.

To be meaningful, employees' work should include the aspect of planning and
control as well as the aspect of doing the work. When one considers the motivators,
achievement recognition, work itself, responsibility, growth and development, they
are either inherent or more closely associated with the planning and control of the
work than the actual doing of the work. The planning of work is meaningful because
it aligns the doing aspect with the goals. The control of work is meaningful because
it produces a feedback meaningful for satisfaction. Thus, the most meaningful and
motivating work involves a complete cycle of planning, doing, and controlling. The
process of problem-solving goal setting allows employees to participate in the planning
and control of their work as well as the doing of their work. In this way, problem-
solving goal setting adds management duties and responsibility to the workers' jobs
and virtually makes all employees managers.

A prerequisite to getting started in the process is that supervisors must be thoroughly
familiar with the motivation theory and meaningful aspects of work. The process
starts when the supervisor of a work group has a problem that he or she has not
been able to solve adequately even with staff assistance. He or she calls a more
or less formal meeting of the work group concerned and presents it with the problem.
The supervisor then provides a complete and frank communication about the problem and adequate background information leading to the problem. He or she identi-

---

*F. Herzberg et al., "One More Time: How Do You Motivate Employees?" *Harvard Business
Review* 46 (January-February 1968): 61-62. Used by permission.

fies costs and the factors affecting them in terms of overhead, materials, and labor and then explains the quality and scheduling aspects of the problem.

The supervisor then asks for the group's help in solving the problem. The process at this stage simply is to attain or allow the group to produce ideas. Evaluation of ideas is a subsequent step in the process. The supervisor acts only as a conference leader and recorder of the ideas developed by the groups. He or she does not contribute to the production of ideas or evaluate any of the ideas brought forth. As conference leader, he or she may ask questions for purposes of clarification and may ask for opinions from members to stimulate them to contribute. Employee participation and the production of ideas, however, is entirely voluntary and no pressure is exerted on them to contribute. Again, the success of these meetings will depend upon the communication skill of the conference leader.

When it is evident that the employees have brought forth most of their ideas, the group is asked to classify and evaluate each of the suggestions developed. Ideas are grouped first into the operational categories, such as inspection, inventory, shortages, defective materials, maintenance, and work methods, with which they are associated. The group is next asked to evaluate all of the suggestions and select for implementation the ones which it feels are likely to produce the best results in the immediate future. The employee group, not the supervisor, evaluates the ideas and decides which ones will be implemented (Myers 1970).

Finally, the group is asked to set goals in the problem area, based upon the assumption that the recommended changes will be made. The group is provided with the technical help needed to implement the selected changes; it is asked to work according to the revised procedures and set realistic goals in terms of both quantity and time. With quantitative goals set by the group itself, employees return to make the changes and try to achieve the goals. No formal arrangement is made for another problem-solving goal setting conference, but the group is kept informed of its progress toward goal achievement. The entire procedure is repeated on an ad hoc basis as problems arise, instead of on a predetermined time schedule (Myers 1970).

Problem-solving goal setting produces results because it makes better use of the employees' abilities and specifically because it makes use of their detailed familiarity with their work and jobs. As with any valuable technique, it is also difficult to implement and has limitations.

There are several factors critical to the use of the technique. First of all, the approach should be based upon a sincere belief that it will work. Second, the approach should be centered on specific problems presented to the employees. And, third, the organization must be willing to buy employees' ideas.

Job enrichment can be a significant OD intervention to more fully utilize people's abilities in organizations for increased organizational effectiveness. It influences the communication within an organization and the problem-solving ability of the organization. When used in conjunction with other OD interventions, it can have added significance for changing the formal subsystem and communication climate to improve decision making and production for increased organizational effectiveness, i.e., goal attainment, satisfaction, and development.

Summary

Managing change is critical for increasing organizational effectiveness. To be skilled in managing change managers must understand organizational change and be able to choose among and utilize alternatives to change. One alternative approach to organizational change is OD.

OD is an educational process to increase the problem-solving capability of the organization so as to improve decision making and production for increased organizational effectiveness. It is a long-range effort involving the entire organization and makes use of behavioral science interventions.

The basic OD strategy involves a key executive calling in an OD consultant who gathers data and diagnoses the data. The data are then fed back to the client system. The client system then sets specific objectives and specific action plans for improving organizational effectiveness. The plans are implemented and critiqued in this cycle which is repeated over and over. There are several OD interventions utilized to increase organizational effectiveness. These interventions are classified according to their primary focus — individual, teams or groups, intergroup relations, and the total organization.

Interventions that focus on the individual are the training and development activities discussed in chapter sixteen. When these activities are part of a long-term change effort for change in the organization they are considered OD interventions.

Interventions focusing on teams or groups are process consultation and team building through data feedback. Both of these interventions are to build a cohesive, supportive, trusting group with a high task orientation and respect for individual differences. Process consultation involves a consultant observing groups interacting and helping members gain insight into how they are operating by helping them perceive, understand and act on their own processes. This usually involves the consultant making certain process observations and the team taking a look at its own communication process. Team building through data feedback involves a consultant conducting sensing interviews and feeding the information back to the team. The team then works through the data and plans action steps for improvement.

Interventions focusing on intergroup issues are the intergroup image exchange and organization mirroring. The intergroup image exchange involves two groups exchanging information on how they see each other and how they expect others to see them. Based on that information, they identify and resolve issues that need to be solved between the two groups. Organization mirroring involves one group getting feedback from representatives of several other groups based upon the feedback. Action steps are planned to increase the group's effectiveness, particularly in terms of how it interacts with the other representative groups.

There are several interventions that focus on the total membership. One of the more widely used is survey feedback. This basically involves gathering information from members of the organization and feeding the information back to those specific members. They then analyze and interpret the data and come up with specific action steps they will recommend be taken to improve organization effectiveness.

Another organization-wide intervention is the confrontation meeting which involves all members of the management team assessing the organization's health. They basically identify things that hinder an organization's effectiveness and identify action steps that they are willing to commit themselves to and that the top team should give priority to. The top team and others follow through on the action steps and the information is communicated back to all people involved in the organization. This technique is a way to get fast results for improving organizational effectiveness.

One of the more widely used and systematic OD programs is the Grid organization development approach. It involves systematically going through six instrumented phases. The phases involve conducting manager Grid seminars, doing team work development, conducting intergroup meetings, developing an ideal strategic corporate model, implementing the ideal strategic corporate model, and doing systematic critiquing.

Likert's Systems Four approach is a systematic way to move an organization from Systems One to Systems Four. This is done through various interventions that are similar to the one previously discussed.

Management by objectives is another OD intervention that can apply to the total organization. It basically is a systematic method of applying the behavioral concepts discussed in previous chapters. It involves superiors and subordinates meeting to discuss and set objectives and meeting at future times to jointly review performance and solve job-related problems. The major advantage of MBO is that it offers a systematic method of implementing communication, motivation, and leadership theory. It can be a significant intervention both positively and negatively.

Job enrichment is another significant OD intervention that can impact the total organization for improved organizational effectiveness. It is a systematic way to apply the motivation theory presented in previous chapters. It basically involves creating conditions in which the things that motivate most people are inherent in the work and jobs. One approach is job restructuring which involves restructuring the basic nature of the work being performed so that it is loaded with the motivators of the motivation hygiene theory. Another approach to job enrichment is problem-solving goal setting which involves including the workers in the planning and controlling of the work through solving problems, setting goals, planning the use of resources, and evaluating the performance against goals.

All of the above OD interventions involve changing the formal subsystem and communication climate to improve decision making and production for increased organizational effectiveness, i.e. goal attainment, satisfaction, and development.

REVIEW AND DISCUSSION

1. What is behavioral science intervention?
2. Why must managers buy the assumptions of OD?
3. Discuss the OD strategic model.
4. Differentiate between training and development and organization development. How are the two related?
5. How does process consultation differ from team building through data feedback?
6. How does process consulting differ from expert consulting?
7. Explain how the intergroup image exchange can be used where you are currently going to school. Be specific.
8. How does organization mirroring differ from the intergroup image exchange?
9. Explain how survey feedback differs from the classical approach to attitude surveys.
10. What impact on climate do OD interventions cause?
11. What is the relationship between interpersonal communication skills, formal subsystem, communication climate, and MBO?
12. How does job enrichment influence the communication climate?
13. What is the relationship between the communication climate and job enrichment?

PART FIVE: Improving Organizational Communication

Incidents

The Attitude Problem

The Baystate Rubber Company employs about 800 people in three small factories located in an eastern state. Baystate has a history of making a good profit on a moderate investment. In the highly competitive rubber industry, Baystate has held its own and has proven that a good small firm can succeed in a field dominated by giants. The management of Baystate has concentrated on producing rubber products which many other companies do not make. In their production, Baystate uses high-quality raw materials, sells its goods for a little higher price, but markets them as longer-wearing than their competitors' products. This approach has worked through the years but recently Baystate has fallen on hard times. For the first time in the company's history, Baystate reported a loss last year.

To management it appeared that Baystate was having problems in three areas: (1) resales to customers, (2) waste of raw materials, and (3) turnover of employees. In years past, Baystate could always count on repeat customers because of the high quality of its products. But salespersons have come back to the main offices and reported that customers are complaining about the high cost of Baystate goods not being justified because quality has deteriorated. The marketing department has determined that many long-time customers are going to larger companies for their rubber goods. Problems have also surrounded raw materials. In the past Baystate would allow 7 percent margin of waste but for the last two years that margin has eased up to 15 percent. This has caused alarm in the Baystate industrial engineering department. Since its founding, many of Baystate's workers have started and ended their careers in the organization. Always, within the communities where plants are located, Baystate has been considered a good place to work. The first generation workers who began at Baystate nearly forty years ago have been replaced by a younger group. About five years ago, the American Rubber Union (ARU) was successful in organizing the Baystate workers. The union has been effective in getting raises and increased fringe benefits for its members, although many members have complained about the formality between management and labor since the ARU was certified as the bargaining agent.

The Baystate management has decided that it must do something about the current situation. It has called Behavioral Consultants, an industrial consulting firm in Boston, to come in to help them find out what must be done to improve the situation.

"Help us find the source of our problems," said the Baystate president. "You have complete freedom and we want you to be very thorough."

A team of five consultants established an office in the largest Baystate factory. They made a decision to do some preliminary "sensing interviews" and they also administered a brief attitude survey. Almost immediately, the consultants seemed to uncover a trend.

"I heard a lot about 'Baystate quality' when I first came here three years ago. But I don't know what that means. This is just a job to me," Dave Buffing, twenty-five, said during one of the early interviews. "My superior wants me at my machine at 7:15 A.M., he rarely says anything to me unless I goof up. I just sit here all day long to operate this machine. I don't think the company even knows my name. I got a kid at home who is five years old. I call in sick every other Friday to take my kid fishing at the beach. He plays in the sand, I fish. I love it. No company can make me give that up."

Many of Dave's colleagues at Baystate seemed to express attitudes similar to his. Data from the attitude survey supported the trends uncovered in the interviews. It is now time for a preliminary report from the consultants to the Baystate management.

Guidelines for Analysis

1. If you were a member of the consulting team, what would you say to the Baystate management? What would you use to support your viewpoint?

2. What other data do you think should be collected by the consultants to determine if their preliminary trends carry through?

3. Assuming that further data gathering tends to support earlier trends, what recommendations would you offer the Baystate management?

4. Make a list of five possible causes which may have contributed to the attitudes which Dave expressed in the incident above. Tell how you think each of your causes may have contributed to the present difficulty within Baystate.

5. Do you think that Dave's attitudes are typical of people who have jobs similar to his? Why?

6. What type of training programs might be used by Baystate to help workers such as Dave improve their perceptions about their jobs and the company?

7. Is it management's responsibility to implement such a training program? Why?

8. Describe the kind of communication which exists between Dave and his supervisor. What recommendations can you offer to improve communication between the two?

The Junior High

The teachers of Marlin Junior High have been meeting throughout the current school year to examine the school's educational program. Bill Bates, twenty-six, chairman of the Social Studies Department, originated the idea of a year long self-study because of some criticism Marlin had received from the teachers of Westport and Emerson High Schools, where Marlin students attend after graduation. Much of the criticism from the high-school teachers centered on the content, course coverage, and teaching methods used in the social studies, language arts, and science programs at Marlin.

"You guys are teaching courses which are no longer relevant to students," Bill's old college roommate, Chuck Larson, who teaches at Westport, told him last summer. "Your students are way behind the rest of the tenth graders when we get them. They have no idea about certain social science concepts and they are unable to express themselves orally or in writing."

This bothered Bill because he had been aware that Marlin's eighth graders had done very poorly on recent statewide achievement tests. But Bill felt that this was a function of the environmental backgrounds of the students. His summer conversation with Chuck was the impetus for him to make some calls to his colleagues on the Marlin faculty. Many of his fellow teachers were concerned about the comments regarding Marlin students' readiness for high school. Some further checking determined that Chuck's feelings were shared by many other high-school teachers in the area. This information prompted the beginning of the self-study at Marlin. Every Wednesday each department, social studies, language arts, science and math, fine arts, and industrial arts, met for two hours during the fall semester to review and evaluate their respective programs. During the spring semester, the entire faculty met to review the findings of the fall deliberations. Sometimes subcommittees would be formed to examine particular aspects of the curriculum (quality of materials, availability of supplemental resources, audiovisual support). During the spring, the faculty gathered extensive data about the programs in other schools. These programs were compared with Marlin's. When the self-study was complete, nearly two file cabinets full of materials had been accumulated.

In the final report, which was submitted to the Marlin principal Dr. Arlene Dayton, five conclusions were presented. (1) The curriculum in every department at the school was significantly outdated when it was compared with other junior high schools in the area. (2) Many of the methods used by teachers at Marlin would be characterized as very traditional. There appeared to be very little innovation within the Marlin faculty. (3) Students were not being exposed to some of the more current academic subjects such as American studies, foreign language, radio and television, and astronomy. Most of the courses offered were required and students were not given the opportunity to select courses of their choice. (4) Marlin had done a poor job in providing students with information about possible careers. (5) The five Marlin department chairpersons had not been doing a thorough job in providing inspirational leadership to the faculty. The report pulled no punches and was supported unanimously by the faculty.

Bill and Grace Develen, the language arts chairperson, presented the report of the self-study to Dr. Dayton at the end of the school year.

"This is a very honest and thoughtful document," Dr. Dayton said to the five department chairpersons two weeks later. "I have reported the results of our self-study to the school board and they are very impressed by the initiative demonstrated by our faculty. They have appropriated an extra $5000 for us to use this year. They would like to see us use this year and the money to begin a program of planned change to improve the quality of our educational program. We can use the money in any way we wish. They have made Dr. Tracey Walters, the school district's organizational development specialist, available to us and she said that she will help us any way she can."

"That's good news. I think that our faculty is willing to grow and change. We just now have to spend some time thinking about our goals and how to attain them," Grace said.

Guidelines for Analysis

1. Develop a model budget for how you would spend the $5000 allotted to the Marlin faculty. Provide a rationale as to why you would spend the money as you have proposed.

2. Suggest five possible change programs which might be implemented by the Marlin faculty. Of the programs you have suggested, which one do you think will have the most impact?

3. Propose some ways in which Dr. Walters, the district's OD expert, might be used.

4. In presenting the results of their self-study, the Marlin faculty was remarkably honest and straightforward. Do you think that it is realistic to think that members of an organization would be this critical of themselves during data gathering? Is there a tendency to "downplay," or minimize, the severity of existing problems?

5. Design a method, starting with the first step, which might be used by the Marlin faculty to establish goals for next year's change program. Talk over your approach with a classmate.

6. What role will good organizational communication play in insuring the success of a change program? Can organizational development or training be accomplished without good communication?

7. Putting yourself in the position of one of the Marlin faculty members, do you think that the previous year's self-study was a good experience? What attitudes or emotions might have been manifested by the faculty during the process?

8. Does it make sense to consider a change program without first taking stock of "where we are"? Can an organization establish goals for a change effort without knowing its current status?

Trouble with the Consultants

Hal Chester, twenty-three, has worked for Data Analysis Associates Corporation (DAAC) for the past two years. Before joining DAAC, Hal completed his M.A. in Communication at Western State University. In his job, Hal is responsible for conducting surveys in organizations. He is a member of a team which enters a client's firm to gather data about company morale, production processes, and management practices. Beside surveys, Hal's team often is called upon to interview employees first-hand about their impressions of the client's organization. After the team has collected data in an organization, it returns to the DAAC headquarters in Ferndale, California, to put together its report. In the report, the DAAC team makes recommendations to the client about improving productivity and organizational operations.

But problems have been developing in Hal's team recently. Dr. Paul Stout, an industrial engineer, heads Hal's team. The other members are Kris Kastenmiller, an M.B.A. from an eastern university, Barry Imell, who was recently awarded his Ph.D. in sociology, and Sylvia Reynolds, a specialist in operations research. Until about three months ago, the team had been performing very well together. In fact, in last year's appraisal Hal's team had been rated "superior" which is the highest rating among the twelve working teams within DAAC. But trouble began developing during the team's visit to the Whittier Manufacturing Company in Texas. Originally, Whittier had called in a DAAC team to investigate problems in the manufacturing process.

Bill Darcey, the general foreman of the largest Whittier plant, told the DAAC team, "We have been having some trouble with turnover and absenteeism. The main line has been out of commission about 20 percent of the time the last two months. Before that we were averaging a 7 percent downtime. We aren't sure what the problem is, but we hope that you can give us some new perspectives."

After nearly three weeks of investigation, the team uncovered some rather startling facts. During an attitude survey, workers in one plant reported that they did not trust their superiors, they did not feel that they were important at Whittier and that they did not feel challenged in their jobs. In-depth interviews tended to support the findings of the survey.

During the full-scale analysis of the Whittier production processes the team determined that many of the methods used by the Whittier firm were outmoded. The team also found that many first-line foremen were unfamiliar with some of the important production methods. It also seemed that the company had not been successful in teaching their workers the components of the production methods.

As the team returned to Ferndale to compile its final report, trouble developed among members of the team.

"It seems to me that we have a communication problem at Whittier. The management has done a poor job of communicating with employees," Hal said during one of the team's work sessions. "What we need to do is develop a program to help improve communication within Whittier."

"You're wrong Hal, I think that we have a problem with production process. We must take time to go through all of the methods and revamp those which are no longer productive," responded Sylvia, the operations expert.

"I don't know if I agree with either of you. Basically, it's a management problem. I don't think that the managers within Whittier have really any idea about management concepts," Barry Imell added.

After nearly three hours of increasingly heated discussion, Hal's team had to break up with still no progress made to resolve their impasse. The next morning the team got together for another meeting. By lunch time, the team was shouting and screaming at each other. In the past, Hal's team had always been able to resolve differences, but such was not the case this time. It seems that the team was unable to work together on the Whittier problem.

Guidelines for Analysis

1. If you were a member of the DAAC team, what recommendation would you offer to help? How would you implement the recommendation?

2. What changes would be necessary for the group to work together? Would it be likely that the team would be able to generate these changes themselves?

3. Do you think that enough data is reported in the situation to draw any conclusions about which member of the team is "right" in the Whittier case?

4. How would you characterize the communication within Hal's team? Why?

5. Nothing is mentioned in the situation about the behavior of Dr. Stout, the team leader. Suggest some ways which Dr. Stout might have been able to resolve the conflict. Should Dr. Stout have exercised greater authority over his team?

6. In light of the previous chapters in this book, do you think that the conflict demonstrated in the DAAC was productive or destructive? Why? Describe destructive conflict. How does it differ from productive conflict?

7. Suggest some possible explanations to account for the possibility that Hal, Sylvia, and Barry were all "right" about the problems occurring at Whittier. Do you think that such an occurrence is likely? Why?

8. Would you say that this is a situation which calls for training? Organizational development? Both?

Bibliography

Ackoff, R. S. 1971. Towards a system of systems concepts. *Management Science* 17: 661-71.

Alderfer, C. P. 1969. A new theory of human needs. *Organizational Behavior and Performance* 4: 142-75.

Andersen, K., and Clevenger, T. 1963. A summary of experimental research on ethos. *Speech Monographs* 30: 59-78.

Anthanassiades, J. C. 1973. The distortion of upward communication in hierarchical organizations. *Academy of Management Journal* 16: 207-26.

Applied behavioral science consulting organizations: a directory. In *The 1975 Annual Handbook for Group Facilitators*, pp. 249-63. Edited by John E. Jones and J. William Pfeiffer. La Jolla, Calif.: University Associates.

Ardrey, R. 1966. *The territorial imperialism*. New York: Atheneum.

Argyris, C. 1957. The individual and organization: Some problems of mutual adjustment. *Administrative Science Quarterly* 2: 1-24.

————. 1970. *Intervention theory and methods*. Reading, Mass.: Addison-Wesley.

Argyris, C., and Odiorne, G. *Training Directors Journal* 17, no. 10: 4-37.

Athos, A. G., and Coffey, R. 1968. *Behavior in organizations: a multidimensional view*. Englewood Cliffs, N.J.: Prentice-Hall.

Atkinson, J. W. 1957. Motivational determinants of risk taking behavior. *Psychological Review* 904 (November): 359-72.

Atkinson, J. W., ed. 1958. *Motives in fantasy, action, and society.* Princeton, N.J.: D. Van Nostrand.

Atkinson, J. W. et al. 1966. *A theory of achievement motivation.* New York: Wiley.

Bales, R. F. 1970. *Personality and interpersonal behavior.* New York: Holt, Rinehart and Winston.

Bales, R. F., and Strodtbeck, R. 1950. *Interaction process analysis: a method for the study of small groups.* Reading, Mass.: Addison-Wesley.

Barnard, C. I. 1938. *The functions of the executive.* New York: McGraw-Hill.

Barnlund, D. C., and Harland, C. 1963. Propinquity and prestige as determinants of communication networks. *Sociometry* 26: 467-79.

Beckhard, R. 1967. The confrontation meeting. *Harvard Business Review* 45 (March-April): 149-55.

_____. 1969. *Organization development: strategies and models.* Reading, Mass.: Addison-Wesley.

Behling, O. et al. 1968. The Herzberg controversy. *Academy of Management Journal* 11 (March): 99-104.

Benne, K. D., and Sheats, P. 1948. Functional roles of group members. *Journal of Social Issues* 4: 41-49.

Berelson, B., and Steiner, G. 1964. *Human behavior: An inventory of scientific findings.* New York: Harcourt Brace Jovanovich.

Berlo, D. K. 1960. *The process of communication.* New York: Holt, Rinehart and Winston.

Blake, R. R. et al. 1964. Breakthrough in organization development. *Harvard Business Review* 42: 133-35.

_____. 1968. *Corporate excellence through grid organization development.* Houston: Gulf Publishing.

_____. 1972. What is instrumented learning? *Training and Development Journal* 26 (January): 12-20.

Blake, R. R., and Mouton, J. S. 1964. *The managerial grid.* Houston: Gulf Publishing.

Blau, P., and Scott, W. 1962. *Formal organization: a comparative approach.* San Francisco: Chandler.

Borgatta, E. F. 1954. Analysis of social interaction and sociometric perception. *Sociometry* 17: 7-31.

Bradford, L. P. et al. 1964. *T-group theory and laboratory method.* New York: Wiley.

Brayfield, A., and Crockett, W. H. 1955. Employee attitudes and employee performance. *Psychological Bulletin* 52: 396-428.

Brilhart, J. D. 1974. *Effective group discussion.* 2d ed. Dubuque, Iowa: William C. Brown.

Brunswik, E. 1938. The conceptual focus of some psychological systems. *Journal of Unified Science* 8: 36-49.

Burack, E. H. 1975. *Organization analysis.* Hinsdale, Ill.: Dryden Press.

Byars, L., and Crane, B. 1969. Training by objectives. *Training and Development Journal* 23 (June): 38.

Campbell, J. P., and Dunnette, M. D. 1968. Effectiveness of T-group experience in managerial training and development. *Psychological Bulletin* 70, no. 2 (August): 73-104.

Campbell, J. P. et al. 1970. *Managerial behavior, performance and effectiveness.* New York: McGraw-Hill.

_____. 1971. Organizational climate: its measurement and relationship to work group performance. Paper presented at American Psychological Association Annual Meeting, Washington, D.C.

Carroll, S. J. et al. 1972. The relative effectiveness of alternative training methods for various training objectives. *Personnel Psychology* 25 (Fall): 495-99.

Carzo, R., and Yanouzas, J. 1969. Effects of flat and tall organization structure. *Administrative Science Quarterly* 14: 178-91.

Center for Utilization of Scientific Knowledge. 1969. Survey of organizations. Ann Arbor: Institute for Social Research, University of Michigan.

Clark, J. V. 1961. Motivation in work groups: a tentative view. *Human Organization* 19: 199-208.

Coser, L. 1956. *The functions of social conflict.* New York: Free Press.

Dahle, T. L. 1954. Transmitting information to employees: a study of five methods. *Personnel* 31: 243-46.

Davis, K. 1972. *Human behavior at work.* 4th ed. New York: McGraw-Hill.

Dennis, H. S., Jr. 1975. The construction of a managerial "communication climate" inventory for use in complex organizations. Paper presented at International Communication Association Annual Meeting, Chicago.

Deutsch, M. 1969. Productive and destructive conflict. *Journal of Social Issues.* 25: 7-42.

Dewey, J. 1910. *How we think.* New York: Heath.

Donnelly, J. H., Jr. et al. 1971. *Fundamentals of management.* Dallas, Tex.: Business Publications.

Dunlevy, M. D. 1974. The relationship of the first-line supervisor and the subordinate as it relates to communication and job satisfaction. Master's thesis, Department of Communication, Ohio State University, Columbus.

Dunn, J. D., and Rachel, F. 1971. *Wage and salary administration: total compensation systems.* New York: McGraw-Hill.

Etzioni, A. 1965. Organization control and structure. In *Handbook of Organizations.* Edited J. March. Chicago: Rand McNally.

Ewing, D. W. 1971. Who wants corporate democracy. *Harvard Business Review* 49 (November-December): 148-49.

Farace, R. V., and MacDonald, D. 1974. New directions in the study of organizational communication. *Personnel Psychology* 27: 1-15.

Farmer, R. N., and Richman, B. 1965. *Comparative management and economic progress.* Homewood, Ill.: Irwin.

Fayol, H. 1949. *General and industrial administration.* London: Sir Isaac Pitman and Sons.

Ferguson, J. M. 1938. *Landmarks of economic thought.* New York: Longmans, Green.

Festinger, L. 1957. *A theory of cognitive dissonance.* Evanston, Ill.: Row, Peterson.

Fiedler, F. E. 1967. *A theory of leadership effectiveness.* New York: McGraw-Hill.

Foulkes, F. K. 1969. *Creating more meaningful work.* New York: American Management Association.

Fox, W. M. 1963. A measure of the effectiveness of the case method in teaching human relations. *Personnel Administration* 26 (July-August): 53-57.

Frederiksen, N. 1966. Administrative performance in relation to organizational climate. Paper presented at American Psychological Association Annual Meeting, San Francisco.

French, W. L. 1969. Organization development: objectives, assumptions, and strategies. *California Management Review* 12, no. 2: 23-34.

French, W. L., and Bell, C. 1974. *Organizational development.* Englewood Cliffs, N.J.: Prentice-Hall.

Friedlander, F., and Pickle, H. 1968. Components of effectiveness in small organizations. *Administrative Science Quarterly* 13 (September): 289-304.

Galbraith, J., and Cummings, L. 1967. An empirical investigation of the motivational determinants of task behavior: interactive effects between instrumentality-valance and motivation-ability. *Organizational Behavior and Human Performance* 2: 237-57.

Geogopoulos, B. S. et al. 1957. A study of organizational effectiveness. *American Sociological Review* 22 (October): 534-40.

Gibb, J. 1961. Defensive communication. *Journal of Communication* 11: 141-48.

_____. 1974. The message from research. In *The 1974 Annual Handbook for Group Facilitators.* Edited by J. William Pfeiffer and John E. Jones. La Jolla, Calif.: University Associates.

Gibson, J., et al. 1973. *Organizations: structure, processes, behavior.* Dallas: Business Publications.

Giffin, K. 1967a. The contribution of studies of source credibility to a theory of interpersonal trust in communication. *Psychological Bulletin* 68: 104-20.

_____. 1967b. Interpersonal trust in small group communication. *Quarterly Journal of Speech* 53: 224-34.

Goldhaber, G. M. 1974. *Organizational communication.* Dubuque, Iowa: Wm. C. Brown.

Gooding, J. 1970. Blue collar blues on the assembly lines. *Fortune* 82 (June): 69-71ff.

Gouldner, A. 1960. The noun of reciprocity in social stabilization. *American Sociological Review* 25 (April): 161-78.

Goyer, R. S. et al. 1963. *Interviewing principles and techniques: a project text.* Lafayette, Ind.: Purdue University.

Guetzkow, H. 1965. Communication in organizations. In *Handbook of Organization,* Chapter 12. Edited by J. March. Chicago: Rand McNally.

Guion, R. M. 1973. A note on organizational climate. *Organizational Behavior and Human Performance* 9: 120-25.

Hackman, R. J., and Lawler, E. 1971. Employee reactions to job characteristics. *Journal of Applied Psychology,* Monograph 55 (June): 259-86.

Halm, G. N. 1968. *Economic Systems.* 3rd ed. New York: Holt, Rinehart and Winston.

Haney, W. V. 1973. *Communication and organizational behavior.* Homewood, Ill.: Irwin.

Hanson, P. G. 1975. Giving feedback: an interpersonal skill. In *The 1975 Annual Handbook for Group Facilitators,* pp. 147-54. Edited by John E. Jones and J. William Pfeiffer. La Jolla, Calif.: University Associates.

Harrison, R. 1965. Defenses and the need to know. In *Organizational Behavior and Administration*, pp. 266-72. Edited by P. Lawrence et al. Homewood, Ill.: Irwin.

Heckhausen, H. 1963. *The analogy of achievement motivation*. New York: Academic Press.

Hellriegel, D., and Slocum, J. 1974. *Management: a contingency approach*. Reading, Mass.: Addison-Wesley.

Herzberg, F. et al. 1957. Job attitudes: review of research and opinion. Pittsburgh: Psychological Services of Pittsburgh.

————. 1959. *The motivation to work*. New York: Wiley.

————. 1968. One more time: how do you motivate employees? *Harvard Business Review* 46 (January-February): 53-62.

Hicks, H. G. 1972. *The management of organizations: a systems and human approach*. 2d ed. New York: McGraw-Hill.

Hormans, G. C. 1950. *The human group*. New York: Harcourt Brace Jovanovich.

Hovland, C. I. et al. 1953. *Communication and persuasion*. New Haven: Yale University Press.

Hulin, C. L., and Blood, M.R. 1968. Job enlargement, individual differences, and worker responses. *Psychological Bulletin* 69: 41-55.

Humble, J. W., ed. 1970. *Management by objectives and action*. London: McGraw-Hill.

Hunt, G. et al. 1974. Communication attitudes of corporate presidents. Department of Communication, Ohio State University, Columbus.

Indik, B. P. et al. 1961. Superior-subordinate relationships and performance. *Personnel Psychology* 14: 357-74.

James, L. R. et al. 1974. Organizational climate: a review of theory and research. *Psychological Bulletin* 81, no. 12: 1096-1112.

Janis, I. L. 1972. *Victims of group think*. Boston: Houghton Mifflin.

Johannesson, R. E. 1973. Some problems in the measurement of organizational climate. *Organizational Behavior and Human Performance* 10: 118-44.

Johnson, R. A. et al. 1973. *The theory and management of systems*. 3rd ed. New York: McGraw-Hill.

Jones, J. E. 1973. The sensing interview. In *The 1973 Annual Handbook for Group Facilitators*. Edited by John E. Jones and J. William Pfeiffer. La Jolla, Calif.: University Associates.

Katz, D., and Kahn, R. 1966. *The social psychology of organizations*. New York: McGraw-Hill.

Kehoe, P. T., and Reddin, R. n.d. Organizational health survey. Organizational Tests Limited. Fredericton, N. B., Canada.

Kelly, C. M. 1974. Empathic listening. In *Small Group Communication: A Reader*, pp. 340-48. Edited by R. S. Cathcart et al. Dubuque, Iowa: Wm. C. Brown.

Kelly, J. 1974. *Organizational behavior*. Homewood, Ill.: Irwin.

Kolb, D. A. et al. 1974. *Organizational psychology*. Englewood Cliffs, N.J.: Prentice-Hall.

La Follette, W. R., and Sims, H. P. 1975. Is satisfaction redundant with climate? *Organizational Behavior and Human Performance* 13: 252-78.

Lassey, W. R. 1971. Dimensions of leadership. In *Leadership and Social Change*. La Jolla, Calif.: University Associates.

Lawler, E. E. et al. 1967. The effects of performance on job satisfaction. *Industrial Relations* 7(October): 5ff.

————. 1973. A casual correlational test of the need hierarchy concept. *Organizational Behavior and Human Performance* 7: 265-87.

————. 1974. Organizational climate: relationship to organizational structure, process, and performance. *Organizational Behavior and Human Performance* 11: 139-55.

Lawler, E. E., and Porter, L. W. 1967. Antecedent job attitudes of effective managerial performance. *Organizational Behavior and Human Performance* 2: 122-42.

Lawrence, P. R. et al. 1961. *Organizational behavior and administration.* Homewood, Ill.: Irwin.

————. 1965. *Organizational behavior and administration.* 2d ed. Homewood, Ill.: Irwin.

————. 1969. *Developing organizations: diagnosis and action.* Reading, Mass.: Addison-Wesley.

Lawrence, P. R., and Lorsch, J. 1967. *Organization and environment: managing and integration.* Boston: Harvard Business School.

Leavitt, H. J. 1972. *Managerial psychology.* 3rd ed. Chicago: University of Chicago Press.

Leavitt, H. J. et al. 1973. *The organizational world.* New York: Harcourt Brace Jovanovich.

Lee, C. 1975. Organizational climate: a laboratory approach. Master's thesis, Department of Communication, Ohio State University, Columbus.

Lesikar, R. V. 1968. *Business communication theory and practice.* Homewood, Ill.: Irwin.

Levinson, H. 1964. What work means to a man. *Think* 30 (January-February): 7-11.

————. 1965. Reciprocation: the relationship between man and organization. *Administrative Science Quarterly* 9: 370-90.

Lewin, K. 1938. *The conceptual representation and the measurement of psychological forces.* Durham, N.C.: Duke University Press.

————. 1951. *Field theory in social science.* New York: Harper and Bros.

————. 1969. Quasi-stationary social equilibria and the problems of permanent change. In *The Planning of Change.* Edited by W. G. Bennis et al. New York: Holt, Rinehart and Winston.

Likert, R. 1961. *New patterns of management.* New York: McGraw-Hill.

————. 1967. *The human organization.* New York: McGraw-Hill.

Lippitt, G. L. 1969. *Organization renewal.* New York: Appleton-Century-Crofts.

Litwin, G., and Stringer, R. 1967. *Motivation and organizational climate.* Boston: Harvard University Press.

Lorsch, J., and Lawrence, P. 1972. The diagnosis of organizational problems. In *The Management of Conflict and Change,* pp. 271-83. Edited by J. M. Thomas and W. G. Bennis. London: Penguin Books.

Lull, P. E. et al. 1955. What communication means to the corporation president. *Advanced Management* 20 (March): 17-20.

McClelland, D. C. et al. 1953. *The achievement motive.* New York: Appleton-Century-Crofts.

McClelland, D. C., ed. 1955. *Studies in motivation.* New York: Appleton-Century-Crofts.

McConnell, C. R. 1975. *Economics.* 6th ed. New York: McGraw-Hill.

McGregor, D. 1960. *The human side of enterprise.* New York: McGraw-Hill.

Maier, N. R. F. 1963. *Problem-solving discussions and conferences — leadership methods and skills.* New York: McGraw-Hill.

Mann, J. 1965. Effectiveness of emotional role-playing in modifying smoking habits and attitudes. *Journal of Experimental Research in Personality* 1: 84-90.

Maslow, A. H. 1954. *Motivation and personality.* New York: Harper & Row.

————. 1965. *Eupsychian management.* Homewood, Ill.: Irwin.

————. 1969. A theory of human motivation. In *People and Productivity,* pp. 83-103. Edited by R. W. Sutermeister. 2d ed. New York: McGraw-Hill.

Mellinger, G. D. 1956. Interpersonal trust as a factor in communication. *Journal of Abnormal and Social Psychology* 52: 304-9.

Miles, R. E. 1965. Human relations or human resources. *Harvard Business Review* 43 (July-August): 148-63.

————. 1975. *Theories of management.* New York: McGraw-Hill.

Miner, J. B. et al. 1973. *Personnel and industrial relations.* 2d ed. New York: Macmillan.

Mitchell, P., and Bigland, A. 1971. Instrumentality theories: current uses in psychology. *Psychological Bulletin* 76: 432-54.

Mott, P. E. 1972. *The characteristics of effective organizations.* New York: Harper & Row.

Myers, M. S. 1964. Who are your motivated workers? *Harvard Business Review* 42 (January-February): 73-88.

————. 1966. Conditions of manager motivation. *Harvard Business Review* 44: 58-71.

————. 1970. *Every employee a manager.* New York: McGraw-Hill.

Negandhi, A. R., and Estafen, B. 1965. A research model to determine the applicability of management know how in differing cultures and/or environments. *Academy of Management Journal* 8 (December): 309-18.

Nichols, R. G. 1961. Do we know how to listen? Practical helps in a modern age. *Speech Teacher* 10, no. 2: 118-24.

Odiorne, G. S. 1965. *Management by objectives.* New York: Pitman Publishing.

Oser, J. 1963. *The evolution of economic thought.* New York: Harcourt Brace Jovanovich.

Patton, B. R., and Giffin, K. 1974. *Interpersonal communication.* New York: Harper & Row.

Paul, W. J., Jr. et al. 1969. Job enrichment pays off. *Harvard Business Review* 46 (January-February): 61-78.

Pelz, D. 1951. Influence: a key to effective leadership in the first-line supervisor. *Personnel* 29: 209-17.

Perrow, C. 1965. Hospitals: technology, structure, and goals. In *Handbook of Organizations,* chapter 8. Edited by J. March. Chicago: Rand McNally.

Peter, J. L. 1970. *The peter principle.* New York: Morrow.

Pfeiffer, J. W. et al. *Instrumentation in human relations training.* La Jolla, Calif.: University Associates.

Phillips, G. M. 1973. *Communication and the small group.* Indianapolis: Bobbs-Merrill.

Porter, L. W. 1961. A study of perceived need satisfaction in bottom and middle management jobs. *Journal of Applied Psychology* 45 (February): 1-10.

————. 1963. Job attitudes in management: perceived deficiencies in need fulfillment as a function of job level. *Journal of Applied Psychology* 46 (December): 375-84.

Porter, L. W., and Lawler, E. 1965. Properties of organization structure in relation to job attitudes in job behavior. *Psychological Bulletin* 64: 23-51.

Pritchard, R. D., and Karasick, B. 1973. The effect of organizational climate on managerial job attitudes and job satisfaction. *Organizational Behavior and Human Performance* 9: 126-46.

Read, W. H. 1962. Upward communication in industrial hierarchies. *Human Relations* 15: 3-15.

————. 1967. Communicating across the power structure. *Cost and Management,* June.

Redding, W. C. 1972. *Communication within organizations.* New York: I.C.C.

Redding, W. C. et al. 1964. *Business and industrial communication: a source book.* New York: Harper & Row.

Reilly, A. J. 1973. Three approaches to organizational learning. In *The 1973 Annual Handbook for Group Facilitators.* Edited by John E. Jones and J. William Pfeiffer. La Jolla, Calif.: University Associates.

Reilly, A. J., and Jones, J. 1974. Team building. In *The 1974 Annual Handbook for Group Facilitators.* Edited by J. William Pfeiffer and John E. Jones. La Jolla, Calif.: University Associates.

Rice, A. K. 1958. *Productivity and social organization: the ahmedabad experiment.* London: Tavistock Publishers.

Roberts, K. H., and O'Reilly, C. 1974a. Failures in upward communications: three possible culprits. *Academy of Management Journal* 17: 205-15.

————. 1974b. Measuring organizational communication. *Journal of Applied Psychology* 69: 321-26.

————. 1974c. Organizational theory and organizational communication: a communication failure? *Human Relations* 27: 501-24.

Rogers, C. R. 1959. A theory of therapy, personality, and interpersonal relationships as developed in client-centered framework. *Psychology: The Study of a Science, Vol. 3, Formulations of the Person and the Social Context.* New York: McGraw-Hill.

Samuelson, P. A. 1973. *Economics.* 9th ed. New York: McGraw-Hill.

Sanford, A. C. 1973. *Human relations theory and practice.* Columbus, Ohio: Charles E. Merrill.

Sanford, A. C., and Bracey, H. 1972. Attitude survey: a tool for improving managerial effectiveness. *Magazine of Bank Administration* 48 (October): 32-44.

Schein, E. H. 1969. *Process consultation: its role in organization development.* Reading, Mass.: Addison-Wesley.

————. 1970. *Organization psychology.* 2d ed. Englewood Cliffs, N. J.: Prentice-Hall.

Schneider, A. E. et al. 1975. *Organizational communication.* New York: McGraw-Hill.

Scott, W. G. 1965. *Organization theory: A behavioral analysis for management.* Homewood, Ill.: Irwin.

Seiler, J. A. 1961. A conceptual scheme for describing work group behavior. In *Organizational Behavior and Administration,* P. R. Lawrence. Homewood, Ill.: Irwin, pp. 213-23.

————. 1967. *Systems analysis in organizational behavior.* Homewood, Ill.: Irwin.

Shannon, C., and Weaver, N. 1949. *The mathematical theory of communication.* Champaign: University of Illinois Press.

Sherwood, J. T. 1972. An introduction to organization development. In *The 1972 Annual Handbook for Group Facilitators.* Edited by J. William Pfeiffer and John E. Jones. La Jolla, Calif.: University Associates.

Sirota, D. 1973. Job enrichment: Is it for real? *SAM Advanced Management Journal* 38 (April): 22-27.

Smith, A. 1937. *An inquiry into the nature and causes of the wealth of nations.* Edited by Edwin Cannan. New York: Modern Library.

Spier, M. S. 1973. Kurt Lewin's force field analysis. In *The 1973 Annual Handbook for Group Facilitators.* Edited by John E. Jones and J. William Pfeiffer. La Jolla, Calif.: University Associates.

Steinmetz, L. L., and Todd, F. 1975. *First-line management.* Dallas: Business Publications.

Stern, G. G. 1974. Organization climate index. Psychological Research Center, Syracuse University, Syracuse, N. Y.

Stewart, C. J., and Cash, W. 1974. *Interviewing principles and practices.* Dubuque, Iowa: W. C. Brown.

Stogdill, R. M., and Coons, A. 1957. *Leader behavior: its description and measurement.* Monograph 88. Columbus: Bureau of Educational Research, Ohio State University.

Tannenbaum, R., and Schmidt, W. 1958. How to choose a leadership pattern. *Harvard Business Review* 36 (March-April): 95-101.

Tannenbaum, R., and Massarik, F. 1968. Leadership: a frame of reference. In *Organizational behavior and management,* pp. 301-22. Edited by D. E. Porter et al. Scranton, Pa.: International Textbook Company.

Thompson, J. D., and Van Houten, D. R. 1970. *The behavioral sciences: an interpretation.* Reading, Mass.: Addison-Wesley.

Tiffin, J. et al. 1973. *Industrial psychology.* Englewood Cliffs, N. J.: Prentice-Hall.

Tosi, H. L., and Hamner, C. 1974. *Organizational behavior and management: a contingency approach.* Chicago: St. Clair Press.

Townsend, R. 1970. *Up the organization.* New York: Knopf.

Trent, J. D., and Redding, W. C. 1964. A survey of communication opinions in large corporations. Report No. 8. Lafayette, Ind.: Communication Research Center, Purdue University.

Trist, E. L., and Bamforth, K. 1951. Some social and psychological consequences of the long-wall method of goal-setting. *Human Relations* 4 (February): 3-38.

Turner, A. N. 1961. A conceptual scheme for describing work group behavior. In *Organizational Behavior and Administration,* pp. 150-94. Edited by P. H. Lawrence et al. Homewood, Ill.: Irwin.

Van Beck, H. G. 1964. The influence of assembly line organization on output, quality, and morale. *Occupational Psychology* 38: 161-72.

Verner, C., and Dickinson, G. 1967. The lecture, an analysis and review of research. *Adult Education* 17 (Winter): 85-100.

Viteles, M. S. 1957. *Motivation and morale in industry.* New York: W. W. Norton.

Vroom, V. H. 1964. *Work and motivation.* New York: Wiley.

————. 1968. Industrial social psychology. In *Handbook of Social Psychology,* chapter 39. Edited by G. Lindzey et al. 2d ed. Reading, Mass.: Addison-Wesley.

Weber, M. 1946. *Essays in sociology.* Trans. H. H. Gerth et al. London: Oxford University Press.

Weick, K. 1969. *The social psychology of organizing.* Reading, Mass.: Addison-Wesley.

Westley, B. H., and McLean, M. 1957. A conceptual model for communication research. *Journalism Quarterly* 34: 31-38.

Woodward, J. 1965. *Industrial organizations.* London: Oxford University Press.

Worthy, J. C. 1950. Organization structure and employee morale. *American Sociological Review* 15: 169-79.

Yoder, D. 1962. *Personnel management and industrial relations.* Englewood Cliffs, N. J.: Prentice-Hall.

Subject Index

Author
Index